The History of the Conquest of New Spain

by Bernal Díaz del Castillo

essay
I quote Diaz
I qute outside source
mostly cover 2 events
read "with" And "against"
each
agency problem of reddity "with
why read "against"

3 examples
for 3rd.

The HISTORY of the CONQUEST of NEW SPAIN
by
BERNAL DÍAZ del CASTILLO

Edited and with an Introduction by

DAVÍD CARRASCO

with additional essays by

ROLENA ADORNO, DAVÍD CARRASCO,

SANDRA CYPESS, AND KAREN VIEIRA POWERS

University of New Mexico Press

Albuquerque

Library of Congress Cataloging-in-Publication Data

Díaz del Castillo, Bernal, 1496–1584.
[Historia verdadera de la conquista de la Nueva España. English. Selections]
The history of the conquest of New Spain / by Bernal Díaz del Castillo ;
edited and with an introduction by Davíd Carrasco with additional essays
by Rolena Adorno, Davíd Carrasco, Sandra Cypess, and Karen Vieira Powers.
p. cm.
ISBN 978-0-8263-4287-4 (pbk. : alk. paper)
1. Mexico—History—Conquest, 1519–1540.
2. Cortés, Hernán, 1485–1547.
I. Carrasco, Davíd. II. Title.
F1230.D56513 2008
972'.02—dc22
2008038713

Designed and typeset by Mina Yamashita
Composed in Adobe Garamond Pro, bringing together elements
of Claude Garamond's Garamond and Robert Granjon's Granjon
in a contemporary typeface by Robert Slimbach.
Printed by Thomson-Shore, Inc. on 55# Natures Natural.

I dedicate this book on the "conquest" of the New World
to two great teachers, Carlos Fuentes and William Tribby.

Carlos Fuentes taught me through his writings and
friendship that Tenochtitlan was built in the
true image of gigantic heaven.

William Tribby taught me through his classes the
deep meaning of the Theater of the Absurd.

CONTENTS

ESSAYS

Acknowledgments

I thank Rolena Adorno for assisting me throughout the work to prepare this abridgment. Rolena started out as coeditor of the project and continued to serve as a constant and generous resource of advice, bibliography, and encouragement when she needed to turn her attention to her other publications. Sarah Lefebvre, program coordinator of the Moses Mesoamerican Archive at Harvard, worked diligently in all areas of manuscript preparation. I especially want to thank the members of the 2008 Harvard Freshmen Seminar "Aztec and Maya" who joined me in finding ways to make this abridgment more useful for readers. Their names are Spencer Dylan Burke, Charles James Hernandez, Akshata Kadagathur, Lorena Lama, Diego Rentería, Tiziana Smith, Tobias Stein, Alexandra Torres, and Jessica Villegas. William B. Taylor, Scott Sessions, and Luther Wilson gave me very helpful feedback about how to frame and contextualize this abridgment through the use of scholarly essays and illustrations. I thank Luther and Judy Wilson especially for lending me their home in Albuquerque, New Mexico, during the Christmas holidays of 2006 while I read through the five volumes of Maudslay's 1908 English translation of *La verdadera historia de la conquista de Nueva España* in search of the specific passages that make up this version. I thank Octavio Carrasco for his research and reading of the other English language abridgments that helped evaluate the problem of "literary and political alliances" between other translations/abridgments and Bernal Díaz's polemics. I also thank the staff of the Tozzer Library at Harvard University for their assistance in locating earlier publications of Bernal Díaz del Castillo's great work. My research and writing, which included a research trip to Bernal Díaz's birthplace of Medina del Campo, Spain, was generously supported by Harvard Divinity School and the Peabody Museum at Harvard University. Thanks to Dylan Clark who assisted me in the final editing of the manuscript.

Introduction
The Dream of the Conquistador
and a Book of Desire and Destruction

Davíd Carrasco

The dream of the conquistador—his astonishment—was quickly converted into the indigenous world's nightmare. Of the enchantment that was Tenochtitlan no stone upon stone remained. The dreamer was converted into the destroyer. But in between we should not forget he was also the man of desire; complex desire for fame and gold, for space and energy, for imagination and faith.

—Carlos Fuentes, *This I Believe: An A to Z of a Life*

This abridgment provides a new understanding of some of the political and religious forces that gave life and direction to the great cultural encounter between Spain and the Americas known as the "conquest of Mexico." It does so in three ways. First, this abridgment includes important passages, events, and scenes from Bernal Díaz del Castillo's original *La verdadera historia de la conquista de la Nueva España* (*True History of the Conquest of New Spain*) never before included in other abridgments.* These inclusions reveal some of the travels, battles, failures, and achievements of the Spaniards before and after they took control of the Aztec

---

*Extended italic passages are summaries by the editor of sections of the original manuscript not included in this version. Notes within brackets (unless italicized) were incorporated into the text from footnotes in the original English translation by Maudslay.

capital of Tenochtitlan in August of 1521. They help give us access to the conquistadores' dreams for land and fame and aid us in reading more clearly this book of desire and destruction. The passages also deepen our knowledge about some of the ways indigenous peoples struggled to maintain their sense of identity and place in the oppressive and tumultuous early months and years of colonial society in Mexico. Secondly, in order to help the reader get below the polemical surface of Bernal Díaz's narrative, this volume includes eight short, focused interpretive essays designed to help understand (a) the role of indigenous women and colonial sexuality in the conquest, (b) the political and economic purposes behind Díaz del Castillo's narrative, (c) the religious cosmology of the ceremonial capital of Tenochtitlan, (d) ritual sacrifice and cannibalism, and (e) the identification of Spaniards as returning gods. One purpose of these essays is to alert readers to the complexity and diversity of several indigenous societies *before* the Spaniards arrived as well as the interlocking cultures and histories that went into motion beginning in 1492 and especially during the encounters between Europeans and indigenous peoples in Mesoamerica. Thirdly, this abridgment contains a series of maps designed to help the reader visualize the routes of the conquistadores, the variegated terrain of central and southern Mexico, the organization of indigenous settlements, the war for the Mexica lake capital of Tenochtitlan, as well as the disastrous Spanish expedition to Guatemala. Let me explain how my readings of other abridgments led to this publication and why I believe it makes important and innovative contributions to our understanding of the wars and cultural encounters in New Spain as narrated by the Spanish soldier.

Díaz del Castillo's Book as Initiatory Reading

When I began to teach the Mesoamerican Civilizations course at Harvard University in 2002, I discovered that two English language abridgments of Bernal Díaz del Castillo's *True History* were the most widely read accounts about the European encounter with the peoples of the Americas on college campuses. The Spanish conquistador's long, though truncated, narrative was serving as a kind of "initiatory reading," a beginning point of comprehension for thousands of students who wanted to learn about the Spanish conquest as well as the indigenous New World civilizations and the transformations and disasters that befell them with the coming of the Spaniards. Its significance as a literary tour de force extended far beyond the student reader. For instance, Francisco Rico, scholarly editor of numerous medieval classics, included Bernal Díaz's *True History* in a list of the greatest works of Spanish literature along with *The Song of the Cid, Don Quixote, Amadís of Gaul,* and *Celestina.* When I asked students what they took away from the book, they said they now had an initial understanding of "where and how the 'Americas' began," and "how the Spaniards managed through cunning and viciousness, in two years, the conquest of the greatest empire of the New World,"[1] or "what a shrewd and effective leader Hernán Cortés really was" and that "the Aztecs were both civilized and barbaric in their cultural and religious practices." But these students also asked for guidance in reading more deeply into Bernal Díaz's story to gain a fuller understanding of the nature of Aztec and Maya cities, the role of women and sexuality in the conquest, the scope of the role of indigenous warriors in the Spanish success, the life of Malintzin (better known as Doña Marina or Malinche) who became the translator and mistress of Cortés, the theology of both the Spaniards and the Aztecs, the practices of sacrifice and cannibalism in Mesoamerica, the techno-logical differences in European and Mesoamerican cultures, the narrator's justification of Spanish cruelty, the indigenous points of view about the encounter with the Europeans, and most importantly, "what happened to the city, the Aztecs, and the Spaniards after Cuauhtemoc surrendered to Cortés on August 14, 1521."

As my students and I worked through the most widely read abridg-ments, namely Alfred Maudslay's 1927 *The Discovery and Conquest of Mexico* (reprinted several times) and J. M. Cohen's 1963 Penguin Classic *The Conquest of New Spain,* two serious problems arose. The first is the lack of any interpretive aids that enable the reader to understand the cultural complexities and historical setting of the book or the author's narrative purposes in writing it.[2] Instead, readers were fed a series of distorted "blurbs" on the cover and one-dimensional introductions that made Díaz del Castillo not only the author of the story but its hero as well. There is a literary and political alliance between these blurbs, introductions, and editors that encourages the readers to swallow lock, stock, and barrel Díaz del Castillo's views of Spanish overall cultural superiority and his religious and political justifications for the transformative and destructive human events of 1517–38. These previous abridgments continued to celebrate the *veracity* of Bernal Díaz without alerting the reader to valuable critical scholarship that discussed his craft *and* craftiness in composing his narrative.[3] The second problem is that the editors chose to end their abridgments nearly two hundred pages before Bernal Díaz ended his story, that is, at the moment of the fall of the Aztec capital to the Spaniards.[4] This ending strategy gives the false impression of a final, sweeping, dramatic "mission accomplished" victory by the Spaniards over the indigenous peoples of Mesoamerica. Díaz del Castillo did not stop his story with this event and neither should we, regardless of what other subtractions from the longer original we make. Let me address both of these problems in sequence.

The Literary Alliance between Abridgments and Bernal Diaz's *True History*

The introductions and blurbs present the author and the work not as a complex, paradoxical, and often contradictory man and book, but more as an old righteous soldier looking back over the years with a slightly flawed memory, who told it, for the most part, like it really was. Bernal Díaz appears, even before you read him, almost in the spirit of Miguel de Cervantes (minus the humor and satire), recording the high adventures of how he and his Spanish comrades courageously righted the wrongs of indigenous cruelty and idolatry in the service of their sovereign ruler Charles V.[5] One influential commentator, J. M. Cohen, who produced an otherwise compelling abridged translation, goes so far as to write, "For Bernal Diaz was singularly free from the temptation to pervert his story in the interests of affections or feuds or personal vanity. To have marched with Cortés was for him sufficient glory. He did not need to increase his reputation or self-esteem by tricks of the pen."[6] Nothing could be further from the truth, but this naive and idealized attitude is what prepares the reader to read the text. The famous British historian Hugh Thomas continues the illusion when, in the most recent publication of an English language abridgment, he takes a large side step away from Díaz del Castillo's political and economic motives and narrative complications by stating, in his most critical moment, that "on occasion Bernal Díaz's memory is at fault."[7] The *New York Times* announced that Bernal Díaz had given us "the most complete and trustworthy of the chronicles of the Conquest" while the *Chicago Sunday Tribune* claimed it was "the most reliable narrative that exists . . . of the actors in that golden age." The reputable *Library Journal* swooned that it was "one of the most thrilling adventure stories of all time" and "a joy to read," while another review said it was an "artless depiction of the atrocities."[8]

The problem for students was that as they read through the stirring, repetitious, and sensational text they became suspicious of this triumphant, single-minded framing of the book and its celebrated "reliability," "completeness," and artless presentation of the "true history." Students could see that the author, while in fact writing one of the few books of the sixteenth century that is still readable in the twentieth,[9] had artfully distorted scenes of meetings and speeches between Spaniards and indigenous leaders, invented the numbers of the wounded and the dead always favoring Spanish valor and success, and not understood what indigenous people were saying or doing on many occasions even while claiming he knew what local elites were actually thinking about the Spaniards. These inventions and distortions are interwoven with invaluable eyewitness descriptions and detailed discussions of people, clothes, temples, gestures, landscapes, battles, ceremonies, and settlements, which make the work rich and compelling, but also complex and problematic.

We should not be surprised that Bernal Díaz used polemics and passions to inform his writing, but the most widely read abridgments fail to alert the readers to these narrative complications. For example, neither

editors nor introductions acknowledge that Bernal Díaz purposely down-
played the powerful and indispensable role of native warriors in Spanish
victories even while he acknowledged the heroism of both native enemies
and allies. Readers are then shocked when they learn what Ross Hassig
points out so well in his excellent study of the conquest, namely that after
Cortés was beaten by the Tlaxcalans, who then made peace with him,
"he was always accompanied by far larger allied forces, such that his own
Spaniards constituted no more than 10 percent of the army's force."[10] This
fact, that up to 90 percent of the army that attacked the Aztec capital of
Tenochtitlan was made up of indigenous warriors, indicates that the so-
called conquest of Mexico was as much a rebellion of rival city-states against
Moctezuma's capital. The readers of other abridgments are given little
indication of this powerful political ambiguity. Even a casual reading of
the abridgments shows that Díaz del Castillo was carrying on polemical arguments with at least two other books (the *Letters of Cortés* and
The History of the Conquest of México by Francisco López de Gómara)
and also energetically pushing a certain theological justification for the
vicious destruction of towns and people. Students were taken aback by
the detailed and callous descriptions of violence committed by the Maya
and the Mexica, but they also were troubled by Díaz del Castillo's justifications of Spanish brandings, sexual abuse, exemplary punishments,
and massacres. These violent practices and theological attitudes, which
make up significant elements of the narrative, call out for contextual
information and interpretive aid. Furthermore, none of the previous
abridgments seriously alerts the readers to Bernal Díaz's economic agenda
for writing the book; that is, he wrote it largely to protect his right to
keep his *encomienda* in Guatemala, when the Spanish Crown was moving to eliminate the practice. Also, students can finish these abridgments
without knowing anything meaningful about the debate within Spanish
society concerning whether the "conquest" was a just war or carried out
in ways that violated Christian values. Yet this debate greatly influenced
Bernal Díaz's thinking and writing of the book and appears in camou-
flaged references throughout.[11]

Obviously, some aids were needed for the general reader to enter into a more informed, balanced, and critical understanding of this document, its author, and the tumultuous events of the early sixteenth century in Mesoamerica.[12] The purpose of these new excerpts, essays, and maps is, in part, to illuminate some of the paradoxes of the conquest (referred to but disguised in Bernal Díaz's narrative) and invite the readers to work with contradictory ideas in mind rather than drift toward simplistic conclusions about the wars of conquest and rebellion in Mexico and Guatemala.

The Problem of the Triumphant Ending

The second problem arose when I compared the Maudslay and Cohen abridgments with the much, much longer Spanish original (known as the Guatemala manuscript) and the complete 1908 Maudslay English translation. Maudslay's 1927 abridgment ends right at the moment of Cuauhtemoc's surrender to Cortés at Tlatelolco in 1521, while Cohen goes just one chapter further into the original narrative. Both abridgments leave the reader with a sense of Spanish triumph and Aztec collapse. This ending strategy by Maudslay, who had translated the entire Spanish manuscript and who knew that the story went on for another book and a half, also gives emphasis to the notion that the Aztecs were to blame for the destruction of their city. A passage on the last page of his abridgment tells us that Cortés "wished that Guatemoc [Cuauhtemoc] had made peace of his own free will before the city had been so far destroyed and so many of his Mexicans had died." The Maudslay version then ends in the rain with the defeated ruler and his entourage given "the best that at that time there was in the camp to eat," followed by a grand thanks to "Our Lord Jesus Christ and Our Lady the Virgin Santa Maria, His Blessed Mother. Amen." This final scene of Spanish generosity and devotion to Jesus and the Virgin Mary serves to seal, in the reader's mind, the perception of a divinely ordained triumph of the Europeans.

As the additional passages included in this abridgment show, Díaz del Castillo's subsequent narrative of over 150 pages depicts not so much moments of divine grace or Spanish generosity and triumph, but disorientation and chaos, infighting among the Spaniards (sometimes humorous), the murder by hanging of Cuauhtemoc and Cortés's subsequent depression, Spanish defeats and brandings of natives in Oaxaca, extreme brutality in Chiapas, catastrophe in Santiago Atitlan, the death of Pedro de Alvarado, the ceremonial arrival of twelve Franciscans to officially initiate Christianity, and the theatrical transformation of the center of Mexico-Tenochtitlan into a public stage-play designed on the Spanish fantasy of Roman conquests! The present abridgment includes a modest but revealing series of new excerpts that give the reader a fuller picture of the fate of Spaniards, Aztecs, Maya, and other indigenous peoples following Cuauhtemoc's surrender at Tlatelolco in August of 1521. The inclusion of these sections of the original, plus the interpretive essays to be discussed later in this introduction, enables the reader to finish the text not with a sense of triumph or defeat but knowing that a colonial process of domination, resistance, asymmetrical negotiation, and change was under way.

Readers of Bernal Díaz will be greatly impressed with the descriptions of landscape and geography as well as the territories organized by Tlaxcalan, Maya, and Aztec city-states. Díaz's memories are intimately tied to the coastlines, valleys, lakes, mountain passes, and diverse ecologies that Cortés's forces crossed and in which their dramatic encounters with indigenous peoples and other Spaniards continued to take place after the fall of Tenochtitlan in 1521. In a profound way, the story of the conquest of Mexico is a story of the crossing, invasion, battles for, and the political reorganization of huge and valued territories and borderlands. Therefore, this volume includes attractive and instructive maps that complement the narrative pathways of the various landfalls, marches, visits to towns, battles and alliances, retreats, sieges, conquests, and defeats. These maps, artistically presented by the University of New Mexico Press, illuminate further the territorial organizations of these parts of Mesoamerica as well as the geopolitical achievements of the Spaniards.

Bernal Díaz's Two Wars: Soldier and Writer

Bernal Díaz thus understood that, regarding the conquest of Mexico,

there was a second war to be fought and won; it would take place at

court and it had to be engaged on the battlefield of the documentary

record and especially written history.

—ROLENA ADORNO, "Bernal Díaz del Castillo:
Soldier, Eyewitness, Polemicist"

As Rolena Adorno writes elsewhere in this volume, Bernal Díaz actually fought in two wars in Mesoamerica: one as a foot soldier in Cortés's troops and the second in the writing of his *True History*. A basic outline of Díaz del Castillo's life and the life of his grand narrative will help the reader understand some of the cultural and political complexities of both wars and this abridgment.

He was born around 1495 in the great market town of Medina del Campo in Castile into a middle-class family. The visitor to Medina del Campo today will discover that just off the huge main square there is a short street named for him at the end of which is a corner building with a plaque that states it was the birthplace of Bernal Díaz del Castillo, the conquistador. As of this writing, the building houses a public Internet café. While we know little about his life before he left Spain in 1514, he states in the first sentence of his narrative that his father, Francisco Díaz del Castillo, known as "the Graceful," was a *regidor* or councilor of the town. We know that Medina del Campo was a political and cultural crossroads in this part of Spain. Queen Isabel the Catholic had a special affection for this town, and, during one of the royal tours of the kingdom, she died in an apartment on the main square in 1504 when the future conquistador was about ten years old.

This huge square served as a magnet for traders and goods that were linked to trade routes beyond Spain and its neighbors. When Bernal saw the huge Aztec market at Tlatelolco, it reminded him, with its bustle, noises, and endless collections and exchanges of goods, of what he had witnessed growing up in Medina del Campo. Remarkably, Bernal's father, Francisco, worked with the famous author Garci Rodríguez de Montalvo who rewrote for publication the most widely read book in sixteenth-century Spain, the famous romance, read by a number of the conquistadores, *Amadís de Gaula*. As readers of this book will discover, Bernal referred to the romantic spirit and descriptions of this book when recounting his first astonishing view of the Aztec capital. He writes, "We were amazed and said that it was like the enchantments they tell of in the legend of Amadis, on account of the great towers and cues and buildings rising from the water, and all built of masonry" (156).

Bernal Díaz first arrived in the New World in 1514 on an expedition led by a Pedrarias Dávila to Tierra Firme or Nombre de Dios in Panama. He claims to have participated in three expeditions to Mexico including the ones led by Francisco Hernández de Córdoba of 1517, Juan de Grijalva of 1518, and Hernán Cortés of 1519. That he actually participated in the Grijalva expedition is highly doubtful, but what is most important is his full involvement in Cortés's overland march to Tenochtitlan, the Noche Triste that led to the Spanish retreat to Tlaxcala and their subsequent return to the Valley of Mexico, and the siege and destruction of the capital. Following the Spanish victory in the capital, he was given an encomienda in the area of Coatzacoalcos, and he formed a domestic alliance with an indigenous woman (whom he renamed Doña Francisca) who had been given to him by Moctezuma. He had two daughters with her. Soon, however, he went on the disastrous expedition with Cortés to Hibueras (Honduras) in 1524–26.

Bernal Díaz spent the rest of his life in New Spain, except for two trips back to Spain to seek rewards of encomienda and recognition for himself and other conquistadores. That he was motivated by dreams of wealth in the form of land and laborers to fight both of these wars referred to previously shows up on the first page of his narrative. He writes that upon landing in Cuba, "we went at once to pay our respects to the Governor, who was pleased at our coming, and promised to give us Indians as soon as there were any to spare. I was then twenty-four years old" (2). The "promises to give us Indians" referred to titles of trusteeship or encomienda, which meant plantations or mines worked by natives. Bernal Díaz was amply rewarded when he received (but later lost) encomiendas in both Tabasco and Chiapas after the conquest. He settled in his third encomienda in Guatemala in the 1540s where he took up with another Indian woman, Angelina, with whom he had a son, Diego Luis del Castillo. He found a more fruitful opportunity in marrying a Castilian widow named Teresa Becerra with whom he had nine sons. He eventually became, like his father had been in Medina del Campo, a regidor or councilor in the town of Santiago. After his second trip to Spain in 1549, he realized that his future control of his lands was seriously threatened. When he thought he might lose his settlement in a new land, he began to write his narrative. The long, repetitious, and often stirring narrative covers his life in New Spain and Guatemala from 1514 to 1568, but "the heart and soul of the work," as Adorno makes clear, are the campaigns led by Cortés in and around the Valley of Mexico to capture the Aztec capital. Throughout he writes repeatedly about the political intrigues and infighting among various groups of Spaniards all seeking legitimate access to the lands, labor, and goods of New Spain.

Bernal Díaz drew on a variety of sources to write his *True History*, including his own memory; Cortés's *Letters*; histories by Francisco López de Gómara, Gonzalo de Illescas, Paolo Giovio, and González Fernández de Oviedo, as well as memories of other conquistadores who lived in Guatemala; and Bartolomé de Las Casas, against whom he polemicized. He also utilized indigenous drawings of Spanish-indigenous encounters, and he relied on the memories of some native peoples who participated in the wars of conquest. What is crucial for readers to know is that he framed, in part, his historical writings with the theological and legal arguments developed by the Spanish philosopher and theologian Juan Ginés de Sepúlveda who had argued forcefully at the Council of the Indies that the conquistadores were completely justified in their violent treatment of native peoples to carry out the conquest and Christianization of the "natural slaves" of Mexico. In some ways his "true history" is a theological polemic.

He composed and corrected his manuscript from the 1550s until he died in 1584. A copy of his manuscript (the original remained in Guatemala) went to Madrid in 1575 where the Mercedarian friar Alonso Remón added fabricated passages while deleting others. This version, with its extensive corruption, was published in 1632, and it became the model for various editions and translations. This distorted version was translated into English in 1800 and in 1844. It appeared in German in 1838 and again in 1844, in French in 1876 and 1877, and it was also translated into Hungarian in 1877, 1878, and 1899. Fortunately, in 1904, the Mexican scholar Género García went to Guatemala and was given permission to publish a copy of the Guatemala manuscript that excluded Remón's fabrications as well as some additions that Bernal's son had made to the Guatemala manuscript. Soon afterward, Alfred Percival Maudslay began to translate García's Spanish language version into English, and, beginning in 1908, the Hakluyt Society published, with maps and notes in five volumes, *The True Story of the Conquest of New Spain*. This present abridgment, published on the one hundredth anniversary of Maudslay's full translation, is taken from his 1908 publication.

Aids for Readers: Pursuing the Author's Words and Repetitions
My decision to include a collection of short essays as aids to the reader took clues and signs from Díaz del Castillo's own words and repetitions as well as student requests. For instance, throughout the other abridgments and even more so in the longer manuscript, he constantly refers to the other authors he read and disputed, thus signaling the political and polemical nature of his narrative and indicating that he was doing much more than giving us his "plain speech" and "unvarnished truth." He has a running argument with López de Gómara's account of the conquest as well as with Cortés's repeated self-importance expressed in his letters. Bernal Díaz repeatedly reminds us that López de Gómara never visited New Spain while his own writings are thoroughly based on what he saw with his own eyes and heard with his own ears. Against Cortés's authority

as a writer, he reminds the reader that his own views are those of the foot soldier and reflect what the majority of the conquistadores did and thought. To aid the reader in understanding these political and narrative tensions in Bernal Díaz's writings, I have included Rolena Adorno's new and revealing essay, "Bernal Díaz del Castillo: Soldier, Eyewitness, Polemicist," which locates the narrative within the legal and political context of Spanish interpretive frameworks of the sixteenth century.

Other repetitions in the text that cry out for contextualization and explanation are the references to the many women given to the Spaniards by indigenous rulers. The sexual story of the "conquest" deserves attention because, as is clear to any reader, Spaniards consistently sought out, kidnapped, abused, and sometimes fell in love with and set up domestic settings with indigenous women. Other abridgments provide no assistance in understanding either the indigenous attitudes and social practices toward women or the struggles, abuse, and survival strategies these women underwent and developed. For this reason I have included an excerpt from Karen Powers's insightful chapter "Colonial Sexuality: Of Women, Men, and *Mestizaje*," which describes the social pressures and sexual abuses that indigenous women underwent.

Related to this theme of women, sexuality, and cultural negotiation is the fascinating story of the most prominent indigenous woman of this colonial encounter, Doña Marina or Malinche. She has become one of the most powerful cultural symbols of gender relations in Mexico and among Latinos in the United States, as evidenced by the scores of studies, recent novels, paintings, and debates about her actions and historical significance. Díaz del Castillo makes ample references to her life and contribution, writing at one point, "Without the help of Doña Marina we could not have understood the language of New Spain and Mexico" (51). For these reasons, I have included the essay by Sandra Messinger Cypess, "La Malinche as Palimpsest II," which summarizes her profile in Bernal Díaz's narrative but also traces her layers of significance in literary culture since the conquest.

No previous abridgments have aided the reader in understanding indigenous cultural practices or religious beliefs and symbols even though they are constantly described and condemned. This avoidance has the accumulative effect of making indigenous culture and religion, apart from admirable scenes of monumental Tenochtitlan and richly arrayed elites, appear crude, superstitious, and culturally inferior. Yet Díaz del Castillo often made important observations and descriptions that, when opened to even basic explanations, reveal important aspects of indigenous ritual and cosmology. A single example will illustrate the value of helping the reader get deeper into the old conquistador's report of indigenous rites: a number of times in his account, Díaz del Castillo reports that indigenous hosts or visitors would suddenly rub their fingers in the dirt and then put their fingers to their lips. Readers are left completely in the dark about the significance of this unusual gesture. One passage tells about the old caciques from Tlaxcala arriving at the Spanish camp who "with every sign of respect made three obeisances to Cortes and to all of us, and they burnt copal and touched the ground with their hands and kissed it" (115). Indigenous worldview and ritual practices concealed in this reference become interesting to us when we learn that Mesoamerican people had a rite named *tlalcualiztli* in Nahuatl, which translates as "action to eat earth." The meaning of this rite, especially important when people were meeting and negotiating with allies and enemies, was to demonstrate, through making contact with the Earth Mother Goddess, that what they were saying was the truth. A parallel practice among Christians is when they put their hand on the Bible to swear a truth.

That indigenous actions, like the ones described in this passage, were often filled with religious significance is also shown in the reference to burning copal that is repeated throughout the text. This action was called *copaltemaliztli*, meaning "action of burning copal," a resin extracted from various species of small trees. The rite was performed to honor gods or notable people and to help in carrying out important actions such as making a speech, singing, or pronouncing a judicial sentence. Copal was thought to be especially appetizing to the Mesoamerican gods.

One of Díaz's loudest narrative repetitions comes in his nearly endless reports of Cortés's sermons (reenactments of the infamous *requerimiento* that offered the natives the choice of voluntary submission to the Spaniards or war to the death), which seem to take place every time a native town or group comes into view. These speeches almost always focus on three terrible indigenous sins that, according to Cortés, the Spanish king has sent them across the sea for the sole purpose of changing. They are *idol worship* ("even if the cost is our lives, leave no idol standing" [80]), *sacrifice*, and *sodomy*. Another repeated reference is to the apparent indigenous belief that the Spaniards were related to Aztec ancestors and gods. To aid the reader in seeing *through* these many references into the thought and practices of indigenous peoples, I have written five short essays on ritual sacrifice, cannibalism, Maya cosmology, the sacred city of Tenochtitlan, and the vague identification of Cortés and the Spaniards with Quetzalcoatl, the Toltec culture hero and deity.

In sum, this abridgment with its new passages, interpretive essays, and maps invites the reader into a richer learning experience about the political and religious forces that animated the writing of the *True History of the Conquest of New Spain* and the cultural encounter between Spain and the Americas. Bernal Díaz del Castillo referred to the scale of these forces in the very first paragraph when, after assuring the reader of his own fine pedigree originating in Medina del Campo, Spain, and now manifest in his role as regidor in Santiago, Guatemala, he gives us the four key purposes of his adventures *and* his writings. He will "speak about that which concerns myself and all the true conquerors my companions who served His Majesty by *discovering, conquering, pacifying, and settling* most of the provinces of New Spain" (1). There, in rapid succession, are the major themes of the book, weaving together adventure, violence, possession, and domestication. I hope this abridgment represents Bernal Díaz's telling of them as powerful and paradoxical, comprehensive and extravagant, invaluable, and polemical. This volume strives to give us increased accessibility to the original text as well as to the dreams, desires, and political intentions of the author, placing it and him in a wider social and narrative context, and encouraging the readers toward their further learning, research, and understanding.

Notes

1. Students noted that the earliest Spanish voyages into Mesoamerica were for the purpose of getting Indian slaves. On page (2) Bernal Díaz del Castillo writes that their first voyage from Cuba was to "make war on the natives and load the vessels with Indians, as slaves." He goes on to say that he and others protested this cruel intention, but in part it was one of their main goals—to use Indians as free labor on their plantations.

2. One notable attempt to introduce readers of an abridgment to some of the social and literary contexts impinging on Bernal Díaz can be found in Irving Leonard's stirring "Introduction to the American Edition" found in the 1956 Farrar, Straus, and Giroux edition of Maudslay's abridged translation.

3. A valuable short summary of the history of scholarship on Bernal Díaz's *True History* up to 2005 can be found in the *prólogo* to *Historia verdadera de la conquista de la Nueva España (Manuscrito Guatemala)*, ed. José Antonio Barbón Rodríguez (Mexico City: Colegio de México, Universidad Nacional Autónoma de México, Servicio Alemán de Intercambio Académico, Agencia Española de Cooperación Internacional, 2005). As the Barbón Rodríguez book shows, Bernal Díaz del Castillo's manuscript is a much larger text than appears in any abridgment. It consists of 214 chapters on 296 folios, handwritten on both sides, and covers 863 single-spaced pages. I worked with both the Spanish version of the "Guatemala Manuscript" and A. P. Maudslay's five-volume English translation of 1908 (one volume consists of maps). My abridgment contains significant portions of the full text that have never appeared in other abridgments and that introduce the reader to the narrative after the fall of Tenochtitlan, including the encounters between the Spaniards and the Zapotecs in Oaxaca as well as indigenous peoples in Chiapas and Guatemala.

4. Maudslay's decision to end the more popular version, that is, the abridgment, at this triumphal-looking moment may have been influenced by a potent narrative decision made by William Prescott in his 1843 *Conquest of Mexico*, which was tremendously popular among English-speaking Americans. Prescott said he made a conscious literary decision to end the book soon after the climax of the fall of Tenochtitlan because he did not want to make the same mistake he thought Washington Irving had made with his 1828 book on Columbus. Prescott was convinced that Irving had carried the narrative way too far beyond the climax of the story, which was the initial discovery of the New World. Unfortunately this triumphal way of ending the story has concealed the more dynamic and complex story of indigenous-European interactions, which I have attempted to include in this book.

5. Consider Díaz del Castillo's claims in his one-paragraph preface where he writes, anticipating Cervantes, of his purpose to "properly extol the adventures which we met with and the heroic deeds we accomplished . . . as a fair eyewitness without twisting events one way or another."

6. J. M. Cohen, introduction to *The Conquest of New Spain*, by Bernal Díaz del Castillo (London: Penguin, 1963), 11.

7. Hugh Thomas, introduction to *The Discovery and Conquest of Mexico, 1517–1521*, by Bernal Díaz del Castillo (Cambridge, MA: Da Capo Press, 2003), xi.

8. See the hyperboles on the opening pages and covers of the Da Capo edition.

9. This is a slight paraphrase from Hugh Thomas's introduction to *The Discovery and Conquest of Mexico*, xi.

10. Ross Hassig, *Mexico and the Spanish Conquest* (Norman: University of Oklahoma Press, 2006), 93.

11. In forming this literary and political alliance with the triumphant cultural agenda of the Spanish story of the conquest, these translators and commentators ignored what is so well-known about narratives of wars, namely, that the first casualty is truth. As Jean Giroudoux once wrote, "Everyone, when there's war in the air learns to live in a new element: falsehood."

12. This is especially so due to the many critical essays and interpretations, especially since the 1940s, that have uncovered important historical and social facts about the author's life in Guatemala and the polemical purposes of his writing. See especially Rolena Adorno, *The Polemics of Possession in Spanish American Narrative* (New Haven, CT: Yale University Press, 2007), for both a summary of some of this scholarship and an innovative reading of Bernal Díaz and numerous other writers on the early colonial period.

Preface by Bernal Díaz del Castillo

I have observed that the most celebrated chroniclers, before they begin to write their histories, first set forth a Prologue and Preface with the argument expressed in lofty rhetoric in order to give lustre and repute to their statements, so that the studious readers who peruse them may partake of their melody and flavour. But I, being no Latin scholar, dare not venture on such a preamble or prologue, for in order properly to extol the adventures which we met with and the heroic deeds we accomplished during the Conquest of New Spain and its provinces in the company of that valiant and doughty Captain, Don Hernando Cortés (who later on, on account of his heroic deeds, was made Marqués del Valle) there would be needed an eloquence and rhetoric far beyond my powers. That which I have myself seen and the fighting I have gone through, with the help of God, I will describe quite simply, as a fair eyewitness without twisting events one way or another. I am now an old man, over eighty-four years of age, and I have lost my sight and hearing, and, as luck would have it, I have gained nothing of value to leave my children and descendants but this my true story, and they will presently find out what a wonderful story it is.

The HISTORY of the
CONQUEST of NEW SPAIN
by
BERNAL DÍAZ del CASTILLO

THE EXPEDITION UNDER CÓRDOVA

I, Bernal Díaz del Castillo, citizen and Regidor of the most loyal city of Santiago de Guatemala, one of the first discoverers and conquerors of New Spain and its provinces, and the Cape of Honduras and all that lies within that land, a Native of the very noble and distinguished town of Medina del Campo, and the son of its former Regidor, Francisco Díaz del Castillo, who was also called "The graceful" (may his soul rest in glory), speak about that which concerns myself and all the true conquerors my companions who served His Majesty by discovering, conquering, pacifying, and settling most of the provinces of New Spain, and that it is one of the best countries yet discovered in the New World, we found out by our own efforts without His Majesty knowing anything about it.

In the year 1514, there went out as Governor of Tierra-firme [Tierra Firme = the Spanish Main], a gentleman named Pedrárias Dávila. I agreed to go with him to his Government and the country conquered by him, and we arrived at Nombre de Dios, for so it was named.

Some three or four months after the settlement was formed, there came a pestilence from which many soldiers died, and in addition to this, all the rest of us fell ill and suffered from bad ulcers on the legs. Then disputes arose between the Governor and a nobleman named Vasco Nuñez de Balboa, the captain, who had conquered that province, to whom Pedrárias Dávila had given his daughter in marriage. But it seems that after marriage, he grew suspicious of his son-in-law, believing that he would rise in rebellion and lead a body of soldiers towards the South Sea, so he gave orders that Balboa should have his throat cut and certain of the soldiers should be punished.

As we were witnesses of what I have related, and of other revolts among the captains, and as the news reached us that the Island of Cuba had lately been conquered and settled, and that a gentleman named Diego

Velásquez, who was my kinsman, had been made Governor of the Island, some of us gentlemen and persons of quality, who had come out with Pedrárias Dávila, made up our minds to ask him to give us permission to go to Cuba, and he willingly did so.

As soon as leave was granted we embarked in a good ship and with fair weather reached the Island of Cuba. On landing we went at once to pay our respects to the Governor, who was pleased at our coming, and promised to give us Indians as soon as there were any to spare. I was then twenty-four years old.

When three years had gone by, counting both the time we were in Tierra-firme and that which we had passed in the Island of Cuba, and it became evident that we were merely wasting our time, one hundred and ten of us got together, most of us comrades who had come from Tierra-firme, and the other Spaniards of Cuba who had had no Indians assigned to them, and we made an agreement with a gentleman named Francisco Hernández de Córdova, that he should be our leader, for he was well fitted for the post, and that we should try our fortune in seeking and exploring new lands where we might find employment.

With this object in view, we purchased three ships, two of them of good capacity, and the third, a bark, bought on credit from the Governor, Diego Velásquez, on the condition that all of us soldiers should go in the three vessels to some islands lying between Cuba and Honduras, which are now called the Islands of the Guanajes [Roatan, Bonacca, etc., islands near the coast of Honduras], and make war on the natives and load the vessels with Indians, as slaves, with which to pay him for his bark. However, as we soldiers knew that what Diego Velásquez asked of us was not just, we answered that it was neither in accordance with the law of God nor of the king, that we should make free men slaves. When he saw that we had made up our minds, he said that our plan to go and discover new countries was better than his, and he helped us in providing food for our voyage.

To return to my story, we now found ourselves with three ships stored with Cassava bread, which is made from a root, and we bought some pigs which cost three dollars apiece, for in those days there were neither sheep nor cattle in the Island of Cuba, for it was only beginning to be settled, and we added a supply of oil, and bought beads and other things of small value to be used for barter. We then sought out three pilots, of whom the chief, who took charge of the fleet, was called Anton de Alaminos, a native of Palos. We also engaged the necessary number of sailors and procured the best supply that we could afford of ropes, cordage, cables, and anchors, and casks for water and other things needed for the voyage, and this all to our own cost.

When all the soldiers were mustered, we set out for a port on the North Coast. In order that our voyage should proceed on right principles we wished to take with us a priest named Alonso Gonzalez, and he agreed to come with us. We also chose for the office of *Veedor* [veedor = overseer] (in His Majesty's name) a soldier named Bernaldino Yñiguez, so that if God willed that we should come on rich lands, or people who possessed gold or silver or pearls or any other kind of treasure, there should be a responsible person to guard the Royal Fifth.

After all was arranged we set out on our voyage in the way I will now relate.

On the eighth day of the month of February in the year fifteen hundred and seventeen, we left the port on the North coast, and in twelve days we doubled Cape San Antonio. When we had passed this Cape we were in the open sea, and trusting to luck we steered towards the setting sun, knowing nothing of the depth of water, nor of the currents, nor of the winds which usually prevail in that latitude, so we ran great risk of our lives, when a storm struck us which lasted two days and two nights, and raged with such strength that we were nearly lost. When the weather moderated, we kept on our course, and twenty-one days after leaving port, we sighted land, at which we rejoiced greatly and gave thanks to God. This land had never been discovered before, and no report of it had reached us. From the ships we could see a large town standing back about two leagues from the coast, and as we had never seen such a large town in the Island of Cuba nor in Hispaniola, we named it the Great Cairo.

We arranged that the two vessels which drew the least water should go in as near as possible to the Coast, to examine the land and see if there was any anchorage near the shore. On the morning of the 4th March, we saw ten large canoes, called *piraguas*, full of Indians from the town, approaching us with oars and sails. The canoes were large ones made like hollow troughs cleverly cut out from huge single logs, and many of them would hold forty Indians.

They came close to our ships, and we made signs of peace to them, beckoning with our hands and waving our cloaks to induce them to come and speak to us, although at the time we had no interpreters who could speak the languages of Yucatan and Mexico. They approached quite fearlessly and more than thirty of them came on board the flagship, and we gave them each a present of a string of green beads, and they passed some time examining the ships. The chief man among them, who was a Cacique, made signs to us that they wished to embark in their canoes and return to their town, and that they would come back again another day with more canoes in which we could go ashore.

These Indians were clothed in cotton shirts made like jackets, and covered their persons with a narrow cloth, and they seemed to us a people superior to the Cubans, for the Cuban Indians go about naked, only the women wearing a cloth reaching to the thighs.

The next morning the same Cacique returned to the ships and brought twelve large canoes, with Indian rowers, and with a cheerful face and every appearance of friendliness, made signs that we should go to his town.

He kept on saying in his language, "cones catoche," "cones catoche," which means "come to my houses," and for that reason we called the land Cape Catoche, and it is still so named on the charts.

When our captain and the soldiers saw the friendly overtures the chief was making to us, we agreed to lower the boats from our ships, and in the vessel of least draught, and in the twelve canoes, to go ashore all together, and because we saw that the shore was crowded with Indians from the town, we arranged to land all of us at the same moment. When the Cacique saw us all on shore, but showing no intention of going to his town, he again made signs to our captain that we should go with him to his houses, and he showed such evidence of peace and goodwill, that we decided to go on, and we took with us fifteen crossbows and ten muskets, so with the Cacique as our guide, we began our march along the road, accompanied by many Indians.

We moved on in this way until we approached some brush-covered hillocks, when the Cacique began to shout and call out to some squadrons of warriors who were lying in ambush ready to fall upon us and kill us. On hearing the Cacique's shouts, the warriors attacked us in great haste and fury, and began to shoot with such skill that the first flight of arrows wounded fifteen soldiers.

These warriors wore armour made of cotton reaching to the knees and carried lances and shields, bows and arrows, slings and many stones.

After the flight of arrows, the warriors, with their feathered crests waving, attacked us hand to hand, and hurling their lances with all their might, they did us much damage. However, thank God, we soon put them to flight when they felt the sharp edge of our swords, and the effect of our guns and crossbows, and fifteen of them fell dead.

A short distance ahead of the place where they attacked us, was a small plaza with three houses built of masonry, which served as *cues* [*Díaz del Castillo uses the term as a synonym for "temple"*] and oratories. These houses contained many pottery Idols, some with the faces of demons and others with women's faces.

Within the houses were some small wooden chests, and in them were some other Idols, and some little discs made partly of gold but more than half of copper, and some necklaces and three diadems, and other small objects in the form of fish and others like the ducks of the country, all made of inferior gold.

When we had seen the gold and the houses of masonry, we felt well content at having discovered such a country.

In these skirmishes we took two Indians prisoners, and later on, when they were baptized, one was named Julian and the other Melchior, both of them were cross-eyed. When the fight was over we returned to our ships, and as soon as the wounded were cared for, we set sail.

We travelled with the greatest caution, sailing along the coast by day only, and anchoring by night. After voyaging in this manner for fifteen days, we descried from the ship, what appeared to be a large town, and we thought that there might be a river or stream there, where we could provide ourselves with water of which we had great need, because the casks and other vessels which we had brought with us, were not watertight.

We agreed to approach the shore in the smallest of the vessels, and in the three boats, with all our arms ready, so as not to be caught as we had been at Cape Catoche.

In these roadsteads and bays the water shallows vary considerably at low tide, so that we had to leave our ships anchored more than a league from the shore.

We went ashore near the town which is called Campeche, where there was a pool of good water, for as far as we had seen there were no rivers in this country. We landed the casks, intending to fill them with water, and return to our ships. When the casks were full, and we were ready to embark, a company of about fifty Indians, clad in good cotton mantles, came out in a peaceful manner from the town, and asked us by signs what it was we were looking for, and we gave them to understand that we had come for water, and wished to return at once to our ships. They then made signs with their hands to find out whether we came from the direction of the sunrise, repeating the word "Castilan" "Castilan" and we did not understand what they meant by Castilan. They then asked us by signs to go with them to their town, and we decided to go with them, keeping well on the alert and in good formation.

They led us to some large houses very well built of masonry, which were the Temples of their Idols, and on the walls were figured the bodies of many great serpents and other pictures of evil-looking Idols. These walls surrounded a sort of Altar covered with clotted blood. On the other side of the Idols were symbols like crosses, and all were coloured. At all this we stood wondering, as they were things never seen or heard of before.

It seemed as though certain Indians had just offered sacrifices to their Idols so as to ensure victory over us. However, many Indian women moved about us, laughing, and with every appearance of goodwill, but the Indians gathered in such numbers that we began to fear that there might be some trap set for us, as at Catoche. While this was happening, many other Indians approached us, wearing very ragged mantles and carrying dry reeds, which they deposited on the plain, and behind them came two squadrons of Indian archers in cotton armour, carrying lances and shields, slings and stones, and each captain drew up his squadron at a short distance from where we stood. At that moment, there sallied from another house, which was an oratory of their Idols, ten Indians clad in long white cotton cloaks, reaching to their feet, and with their long hair reeking with blood, and so matted together, that it could never be parted or even combed out again, unless it were cut. These were the priests of the Idols, and they brought us incense of a sort of resin which they call copal, and with pottery braziers full of live coals, they began to fumigate us, and by signs they made us understand that we should quit their land before the firewood which they had piled up there should burn out, otherwise they would attack us and kill us. After ordering fire to be put to the reeds, the priests withdrew without further speech. Then the warriors who were drawn up in battle array began to whistle and sound their trumpets and drums. When we perceived their menacing appearance and saw great squadrons of Indians bearing down on us we remembered that we had not yet recovered from the wounds received at Cape Catoche, and had been obliged to throw overboard the bodies of two soldiers who had died, and fear fell on us, so we determined to retreat to the coast in good order, and began to march along the shore towards a large rock which rose out of the sea, while the boats and the small bark laden with the water casks coasted along close in shore. We had not dared to embark near the town where we had landed, on account of the great press of Indians, for we felt sure they would attack us as we tried to get in the boats. As soon as we had embarked and got the casks on board the ships, we sailed on for six days and nights in good weather, then we were struck by a norther which is a foul wind on that coast and it lasted four days and nights, and so strong was the storm that it nearly drove us ashore, so that we had to drop anchor, but we broke two cables, and one ship began to drag her anchor. Ah! the danger was terrible, for if our last cable had given way we should have been driven ashore to destruction, but thank God we were able to ease the strain on the cable by lashing it with pieces of rope and hawsers, and at last the weather moderated. Then we kept on our course along the coast, going ashore whenever we were able to do so to get water, for, as I have already said, the casks we carried were leaky, and we hoped that by keeping near the coast we should be able to find water, whenever we landed, either in pools or by digging for it.

As we were sailing along on our course, we came in sight of a town, and about a league on the near side of it, there was a bay which looked as though it had a river running into it; so we determined to anchor. On this coast the tide runs out so far that there is a danger of ships being stranded, so for fear of this we dropped anchor at the distance of a league from the shore, and we landed from the vessel of least draught and from the boats, well armed and carrying all our casks along with us. This landing place was about a league from the town, near to some pools of water, and maize plantations, and a few small houses built of masonry. The town is called Champoton.

As we were filling our casks with water there came along the coast towards us many squadrons of Indians clad in cotton armour reaching to the knees, and armed with bows and arrows, lances and shields, and swords like two-handed broadswords, and slings and stones and carrying the feathered crests, which they are accustomed to wear. Their faces were painted black and white, and ruddled and they came in silence straight towards us, as though they came in peace, and by signs they asked whether we came from where the sun rose, and we replied that we did come from the direction of the sunrise. We were at our wit's end considering the matter, and wondering what the words were which the Indians called out to us for they were the same as those used by the people of Campeche, but we never made out what it was that they said.

All this happened about the time of the Ave Maria, and the Indians then went off to some villages in the neighbourhood, and we posted watchmen and sentinels for security.

While we were keeping watch during the night we heard a great squadron of Indian warriors approaching from the town and from the farms, and we knew well, that their assembly boded us no good, and we took counsel together as to what should be done. However, some said one thing and some said another. While we were still taking counsel and the dawn broke, and we could see that there were about two hundred Indians to every one of us, and we said one to the other "let us strengthen our hearts for the fight, and after commending ourselves to God let us do our best to save our lives."

As soon as it was daylight we could see, coming along the coast, many more Indian warriors with their banners raised. When their squadrons were formed up they surrounded us on all sides and poured in such showers of arrows and darts, and stones thrown from their slings that over eighty of us soldiers were wounded, and they attacked us hand to hand, some with lances and the others shooting arrows, and others with two-handed knife-edged swords [*macana* (or *macuahuitl*), a wooden sword edged with sharp flint or obsidian], and they brought us to a bad pass. At last feeling the effects of our swordplay they drew back a little, but it was not far, and only enabled them to shoot their stones and darts at us with greater safety to themselves.

While the battle was raging the Indians called to one another in their language "al Calachuni, Calachuni" which means "let us attack the Captain and kill him," and ten times they wounded him with their arrows; and me they struck thrice, one arrow wounding me dangerously in the left side, piercing through the ribs. All the other soldiers were wounded by spear thrusts and two of them were carried off alive.

Our captain then saw that our good fighting availed us nothing; other squadrons of warriors were approaching us fresh from the town, bringing food and drink with them and a large supply of arrows. All our soldiers were wounded with two or three arrow wounds, three of them had their throats pierced by lance thrusts, our captain was bleeding from many wounds and already fifty of the soldiers were lying dead.

Feeling that our strength was exhausted we determined with stout hearts to break through the battalions surrounding us and seek shelter in the boats which awaited us near the shore; so we formed in close array and broke through the enemy.

Ah! then to hear the yells, hisses and cries, as the enemy showered arrows on us and hurled lances with all their might, wounding us sorely.

Then another danger befell us; as we all sought shelter in the boats at the same time they began to sink, so in the best way we could manage hanging on to the waterlogged boats and half swimming, we reached the vessel of lightest draught which came in haste to our assistance.

Many of us were wounded while we embarked, especially those who were sitting in the stern of the boats, for the Indians shot at them as targets, and even waded into the sea with their lances and attacked us with all their strength. Thank God! by a great effort we escaped with our lives from the clutches of those people.

Within a few days we had to cast into the sea five others who died of their wounds and of the great thirst which we suffered. The whole of the fighting occupied only one hour.

After we had attended to the wounded (and there was not a man among us who had not two, three or four wounds, and the Captain was wounded in ten places and only one soldier escaped without hurt) we decided to return to Cuba.

As almost all the sailors also were wounded we were short-handed for tending the sails, so we abandoned the smallest vessel and set fire to her after removing the sails, cables and anchors, and we divided the sailors who were unwounded between the two larger vessels. However, our greatest trouble arose from the want of freshwater, for owing to the attack made on us and the haste with which we had to take to the boats, all the casks and barrels which we had filled with water were left behind.

So great was our thirst that our mouths and tongues were cracked with the dryness, and there was nothing to give us relief. Oh! what hardships one endures, when discovering new lands, in the way we set out to do it; no one can appreciate the excessive hardships who has not passed through them as we did.

We kept our course close to the land in hope of finding some stream or bay where we could get freshwater, and at the end of three days we found a bay where there appeared to be a creek which we thought might hold freshwater. Fifteen of the sailors who had remained on board and were unwounded and three soldiers who were out of danger from their wounds went ashore, and they took hoes with them, and some barrels; but the water of the creek was salt, so they dug holes on the beach, but there also the water was as salt and bitter as that in the creek. However, bad as the water was, they filled the casks with it and brought it on board, but no one could drink such water and it did harm to the mouths and bodies of the few soldiers who attempted to drink it.

There were so many large alligators in that creek that it has always been known as the *éstero de los Lagartos*.

While the boats went ashore for water there arose such a violent gale from the Northeast that the ships began to drag their anchors and drift towards the shore. The sailors who had gone on shore returned with the boats in hot haste and arrived in time to put out other anchors and cables, so that the ships rode in safety for two days and nights. Then we got up anchor and set sail continuing our voyage back to the island of Cuba.

The pilot Alaminos then took counsel with the other two pilots, and it was settled that from the place we then were we should cross over to Florida, for he judged that it was about seventy leagues distant, and that it would be a shorter course to reach Havana than the course by which we had come.

We did as the pilot advised, for it seems that he had accompanied Juan Ponce de Leon on his voyage of discovery to Florida fourteen or fifteen years earlier. After four days' sail we came in sight of the land of Florida.

When we reached land, it was arranged that twenty of the soldiers, those whose wounds were best healed, should go ashore. I went with them, and also the Pilot, Anton de Alaminos, and we carried with us such vessels as we still possessed, and hoes, and our crossbows and guns. As the Captain was very badly wounded, and much weakened by the great thirst he had endured, he prayed us on no account to fail in bringing back freshwater, as he was parching and dying of thirst, for the water we had on board was salt and not fit to drink.

We landed near a creek, the Pilot Alaminos carefully examined the coast and said that it was at this very spot when he came with Juan Ponce de Leon that the Indians of the country had attacked them and had killed many soldiers, and that it behooved us to keep a very sharp lookout. We at once posted two soldiers as sentinels while we dug holes on a broad beach where we thought we should find freshwater, for at that hour the tide had ebbed. It pleased God that we come on very good water, and so overjoyed were we that what with satiating our thirst, and washing out cloths with which to bind up wounds, we must have stayed there an hour. When, at last, very well satisfied, we wished to go on board with the water, we saw one of the soldiers whom we had placed on guard coming towards us crying out, "to arms, to arms! many Indian warriors are coming on foot and others down the creek in canoes." The soldier who came shouting and the Indians reached us nearly at the same time.

These Indians carried very long bows and good arrows and lances, and some weapons like swords, and they were clad in deerskins and were very big men. They came straight on and let fly their arrows and at once wounded six of us, and to me they dealt a slight arrow wound. However, we fell on them with such rapidity of cut and thrust of sword and so plied the crossbows and guns that they left us to ourselves and set off to the sea and the creek to help their companions who had come in the canoes and were fighting hand to hand with the sailors, whose boat was already captured and was being towed by the canoes up the creek, four of the sailors being wounded, and the Pilot Alaminos badly hurt in the throat. Then we fell upon them, with the water above our waists, and at the point of the sword, we made them abandon the boat. Twenty of the Indians lay dead on the shore or in the water, and three who were slightly wounded we took prisoners, but they died on board ship.

As soon as the skirmish was over we asked the soldier who had been placed on guard what had become of his companion. He replied that he had seen him go off with an axe in his hand to cut down a small palm tree, and that he then heard cries in Spanish, and on that account he had hurried towards us to give us warning, and it was then that his companion must have been killed.

The soldier who had disappeared was the only man who had escaped unwounded from the fight at Champoton, and we at once set to work to search for him. We found a palm tree partly cut through, and nearby the ground was much trampled by footsteps, and as there was no trace of blood we took it for certain that they had carried him off alive. We searched and shouted for more than an hour, but finding no trace of him we got into the boats and carried the freshwater to the ship, at which the soldiers were as overjoyed as though we had given them their lives. One soldier jumped from the ship into the boat, so great was his thirst, and clasping a jar of water to his chest drank so much water that he swelled up and died within two days.

As soon as we had got the water on board and had hauled up the boats, we set sail for Havana, and during the next day and night the weather was fair and we were near some Islands called Los Martires, when the flagship struck the ground and made water fast, and with all of us soldiers working at the pumps we were not able to check it, and we were in fear of foundering.

Ill and wounded as we were, we managed to trim the sails and work the pump until our Lord carried us into the port, where now stands the city of Havana, and we gave thanks to God.

We wrote in great haste to the Governor of the Island, Diego Velásquez, telling him that we had discovered thickly peopled countries, with masonry houses, and people who covered their persons and went about clothed in cotton garments, and who possessed gold and who cultivated maize fields, and other matters which I have forgotten.

From Havana our Captain Francisco Hernández went by land to the town of Santispíritus; but he was so badly wounded that he died within ten days.

The Expedition under Grijalva

Bernal Díaz's manuscript includes an account of the 1518 Juan de Grijalva–led expedition to the mainland of Mesoamerica. Many scholars doubt that he actually participated in this journey, but rather inserted into his book what he read and heard elsewhere. I simply summarize the salient points of his account so this abridgment can move directly to the crucial expedition led by Hernán Cortés.

On April 8, 1518, 240 Spaniards set off from Cuba for Yucatan having been motivated ("were greedily eager") by the accounts from the Córdova expedition of gold, houses of masonry, and heavily populated lands. They first land at the island of Cozumel and meet an indigenous woman from Jamaica who had been shipwrecked two years earlier. She speaks the local language and initially serves as their messenger to local people. The expedition sails on to Champoton where fifty-six Spaniards had been killed in battle under Córdova the year before. Another battle takes place, resulting in seven more Spanish dead, plus sixty wounded, including Grijalva. The Spaniards enter a deserted town and fail, even with the help of Julianillo and Melchorejo, two baptized Indians captured the year before, to communicate with local leaders who refuse Spanish efforts to meet face-to-face. Successful in hunting for food on shore, the Spaniards sail on and stop at the Río Tabasco, which they rename Río Grijalva. A fleet of fifty canoes prepares to attack the Spaniards, but the battle is averted when Julianillo and Melchorejo, "who spoke their language very well," convey the Spanish invitation for talk and barter aboard the Spanish ships. Realizing they are greatly outnumbered, the Spaniards seek information about Indian wealth, barter for food with beads, and ask to talk with the caciques on shore. The next day the caciques invite the Spaniards to trade and exchange gifts and give a tantalizing piece of information: "that further on, in the direction of the sunset, there was plenty of gold, and they said, 'Colua, Colua, Méjico, Méjico.'" This comment serves as a pointer for the

Spaniards, turning their attention toward what they soon learn is the distant city ruled by Moctezuma in the central highlands. The Spaniards sail along the coast passing the Tonolá, Coatzacoalcos, Papaloapan, and Banderas rivers. At one point they are taunted on shore by native warriors "with shields made of the shells of turtle, which sparkled as the sun shone on them, and some of our soldiers contended that they were made of low grade gold."

Addressing the "studious readers in Spain" and summarizing what he learns much later in his adventure about the Aztec ruler and his communication system, Bernal Díaz discloses that "Mexico was a very great city built in the water like Venice." Further, that Moctezuma had been shown native paintings, on cloth, of details of the Spanish expeditions and was controlling, through his widespread political network, native responses to the invaders. Bernal Díaz mentions, for the first time, that Spaniards have heard from the natives "their Indian ancestors had foretold that men with beards would come from the direction of the sunrise and would rule over them." (See the essay on this belief later in this abridgment.) Responding to Indians waving poles with white cloths on the shore, a group of Spaniards lands and meets with three caciques, one a representative of Moctezuma who offers them a feast and gifts of gold. These Indians, however, speak a different language, "which is Mexican" and not Maya. After six days of trading and getting "more than sixteen thousand dollars worth of jewelry of low grade gold, worked into various forms," the Spaniards "took possession of the land in the name of His Majesty" and sailed onward.

Arriving at an island, the Spaniards come upon a ceremonial center with altars, stone idols, and the remains of five Indians who had been sacrificed the night before and dismembered. "Greatly amazed," the Spaniards name the place "Isla de Sacrificios." Fatigued, depressed by the death of thirteen soldiers in various battles, and harassed by mosquitoes, they return on a forty-five-day journey to Cuba. When the six hundred axes they had bartered for during the journey turn out to be copper instead of gold, "there was a good laugh at us, and they made great fun of our trading."

The Expedition under Cortés Begins
Intrigues in Cuba

After the return of the Captain Juan de Grijalva to Cuba, when the Governor Diego Velásquez understood how rich were these newly discovered lands, he ordered another fleet, much larger than the former one to be sent off, and he had already collected in the Port of Santiago, where he resided, ten ships, four of them were those in which he had returned with Juan de Grijalva, which had at once been careened, and the other six had been got together from other ports in the Island. He had them furnished with provisions, consisting of Cassava bread and salt pork. These provisions were only to last until we arrived at Havana, for it was at that port that we were to take in our stores, as was afterwards done.

I must cease talking of this and tell about the disputes which arose over the choice of a captain for the expedition. There were many debates and much opposition.

Most of us soldiers who were there said that we should prefer to go again under Juan de Grijalva, for he was a good captain, and there was no fault to be found either with his person or his capacity for command.

While things were going on in the way I have related, two great favourites of Diego Velásquez named Andrés de Duero, the Governor's Secretary, and Amador de Lares, His Majesty's accountant, secretly formed a partnership with a gentleman named Hernando Cortés, a native of Medellin, who held a grant of Indians in the Island. A short while before, Cortés had married a lady named Catalina Juarez la Marcayda. As far as I know, and from what others say, it was a love match.

I will go on to tell about this partnership, it came about in this manner:—These two great favourites of Velásquez agreed that they would get him to appoint Cortés Captain General of the whole fleet, and that they would divide between the three of them, the spoil of gold, silver and jewels which might fall to Cortés' share. For secretly Diego Velásquez was sending to trade and not to form a settlement, as was apparent afterwards from the instructions given about it, although it was announced and published that the expedition was for the purpose of founding a settlement.

Andrés de Duero drew up the documents in very good ink, as the proverb says, in the way Cortés wished with very ample powers.

One Sunday when Diego Velásquez went to Mass,—and as he was Governor he was accompanied by the most distinguished persons in the town,—he placed Hernando Cortés on his right hand so as to pay him honour. A buffoon, called the mad Cervantes, ran in front of Diego Velásquez, making grimaces and cracking jokes and he cried out—

> The parade of my friend Diego, Diego,
> Who then is this captain of your choice?
> He comes from Medellin in Estramadura
> A very valiant captain indeed
> Have a care lest he run off with the fleet
> For all judge him a man to take care of his own.

And he cried out other nonsense, all of it somewhat malicious. And as he would go on shouting in this way, Andrés de Duero who was walking near Diego Velásquez, gave the buffoon a cuff and said "Silence thou crazy drunkard, and don't be such a rogue, for we are well aware that these malicious sayings, passed off as wit, are not made up by thee," and still the madman ran on, notwithstanding the cuffs, saying, "Viva, Viva, the parade of my friend Diego and his daring Captain Cortés, I swear friend Diego that so as not to see thee weeping over the bad bargain thou hast made this day, I wish to go with Cortés to these rich lands." There is no doubt that some kinsman of the Governor had given gold pieces to the buffoon to utter these malicious sayings, passing them off as witty. However, this all came true, and it is said that madmen do sometimes hit the mark in their speeches.

Truly Hernando Cortés was chosen to exalt our holy faith and to serve his Majesty, as I will tell later on.

Before going any further I wish to say that the valiant and energetic Hernando Cortés was a gentleman by birth (*hijo-d'algo*) by four lines of descent. The first through the Cortéses, for so his father Martin Cortés was named, the second through the Pizarros, the third through the Monroys and the fourth through the Altamiranos. Although he was such a valiant, energetic and daring captain, I will not from now on, call him by any of these epithets of valiant, or energetic, nor will I speak of him as Marqués del Valle, but simply as Hernando Cortés. For the name Cortés alone was held in as high respect throughout the Indies as well as in Spain, as was the name of Alexander in Macedonia, and those of Julius Caesar and Pompey and Scipio among the Romans, and Hannibal among the Carthaginians, or in our own Castille the name of Gonzalo Hernández, the Great Captain. And the valiant Cortés himself was better pleased not to be called by lofty titles but simply by his name, and so I will call him for the future. And now I must cease talking of this, and relate in the next chapter what he undertook and accomplished about the preparation of his fleet.

As soon as Hernando Cortés had been appointed General he began to search for all sorts of arms, guns, powder and crossbows, and every kind of warlike stores which he could get together, and all sorts of articles to be used for barter, and other things necessary for the expedition.

Moreover he began to adorn himself and be more careful of his appearance than before, and he wore a plume of feathers with a medal, and a gold chain, and a velvet cloak trimmed with knots of gold, in fact he looked like a gallant and courageous Captain. However, he had no money to defray the expenses I have spoken about, for at that time he was very poor and much in debt, although he had a good *encomienda* of Indians who were getting him a return from his gold mines, but he spent all of it on his person and on finery for his wife, whom he had recently married, and on entertaining some guests who had come to visit him. For he was affable in his manner and a good talker, and he had twice been chosen Alcalde [Alcalde = Mayor] of the town of Santiago Baracoa where he had settled, and in that country it is esteemed a great honour to be chosen as Alcalde.

When some merchant friends of his saw that he had obtained this command as Captain General, they lent him four thousand gold dollars in coin and gave him merchandise worth another four thousand dollars secured on his Indians and estates. Then he ordered two standards and banners to be made, worked in gold with the royal arms and a cross on each side with a legend which said, "Comrades, let us follow the sign of the holy Cross with true faith, and through it we shall conquer." And he ordered a proclamation to be made with the sound of drums and trumpets in the name of His Majesty and by Diego Velásquez in the King's name, and in his own as Captain General, to the effect that whatsoever person might wish to go in his company to the newly discovered lands to conquer them and to settle there, should receive his share of the gold, silver and riches which might be gained, and an encomienda of Indians after the country had been pacified, and that to do these things Diego Velásquez held authority from His Majesty.

When this news was known throughout Cuba, and Cortés had written to all his friends in the different towns begging them to get ready to come with him on this expedition, some of them sold their farms so as to buy arms and horses, others began to prepare cassava bread and to salt pork for stores, and to make quilted cotton armour, and they got ready what was necessary as well as they could.

We assembled at Santiago de Cuba, whence we set out with the fleet more than three hundred and fifty soldiers in number. From the house of Velásquez there came Diego de Ordás, the chief Mayordomo, whom Velásquez himself sent with orders to keep his eyes open and see that no plots were hatched in the fleet, for he was always distrustful of Cortés, although he concealed his fears. There came also Francisco de Morla and an Escobar, whom we called The Page, and a Heredia, and Juan Ruano and Pedro Escudero, and Martin Ramos de Lares, and many others who were friends and followers of Diego Velásquez; and I place myself last on the list for I also came from the house of Diego Velásquez, for he was my kinsman.

Cortés worked hard to get his fleet under way and hastened on his preparations, for already envy and malice had taken possession of the relations of Diego Velásquez who were affronted because their kinsman neither trusted them nor took any notice of them, and because he had given charge and command to Cortés, knowing that he had looked upon him as a great enemy only a short time before, on account of his marriage, so they went about grumbling at their kinsman Diego Velásquez and at Cortés, and by every means in their power they worked on Diego Velásquez to induce him to revoke the commission.

Now Cortés was advised of all this, and for that reason never left the Governor's side, and always showed himself to be his zealous servant, and kept on telling him that, God willing, he was going to make him a very illustrious and wealthy gentleman in a very short time. Moreover Andrés de Duero was always advising Cortés to hasten the embarkation of himself and his soldiers, for Diego Velásquez was already changing his mind owing to the importunity of his family.

When Cortés knew this he sent orders to his wife that all provisions of food which he wished to take and any other gifts (such as women usually give to their husbands when starting on such an expedition) should be sent at once and placed on board ship.

He had already had a proclamation made that on that day by nightfall all ships, Captains, pilots and soldiers should be on board and no one should remain on shore. When Cortés had seen all his company embarked he went to take leave of Diego Velásquez, accompanied by his great friends and many other gentlemen, and all the most distinguished citizens of that town.

After many demonstrations and embraces of Cortés by the Governor, and of the Governor by Cortés, he took his leave. The next day very early after having heard Mass we went to our ships, and Diego Velásquez himself accompanied us, and again they embraced with many fair speeches one to the other until we set sail.

A few days later, in fine weather, we reached the Port of Trinidad, where we brought up in the harbour and went ashore, and nearly all the citizens of that town came out to meet us; and entertained us well.

From that town there came to join us five brothers, namely Pedro de Alvarado and Jorge de Alvarado, and Gonzalo and Gómez, and Juan de Alvarado, the elder, who was a bastard. There also joined us from this town Alonzo de Ávila, who went as a Captain in Grijalva's expedition, and Juan de Escalante and Pedro Sanchez Farfan, and Gonzalo Mejía who later on became treasurer in Mexico, and a certain Baena and Juanes of Fuenterrabia, and Lares, the good horseman, and Cristóbal de Olid, the Valiant, and Ortis the Musician, and Gaspar Sanchez, nephew of the treasurer of Cuba, and Diego de Pineda, and Alonzo Rodriguez, and Bartolomé Garcia and other gentlemen whose names I do not remember, all persons of quality.

From Trinidad Cortés wrote to the town of Santispíritus which was eighteen leagues distant, informing all the inhabitants that he was setting out on this expedition in His Majesty's service, adding fair words and inducements to attract many persons of quality who had settled in that town, among them Alonzo Hernándes Puertocarrero cousin of the Count of Medellin, and Gonzalo de Sandoval and Juan Velásquez de Leon came, a kinsman of Diego Velásquez, and Rodrigo Reogel, and Gonzalo Lópes de Jimena, and his brother, and Juan Sedeño also came. All these distinguished persons whom I have named came from the town of Santispíritus to Trinidad, and Cortés went out to meet them with all the soldiers of his company and received them with great cordiality and they treated him with the highest respect.

We continued to enlist soldiers and to buy horses, which at that time were both scarce and costly, and as Alonzo Hernándes Puertocarrero neither possessed a horse nor the wherewithal to buy one, Hernando Cortés bought him a gray mare, and paid for it with some of the golden knots off the velvet cloak which as I have said he had had made at Santiago de Cuba.

At that very time a ship arrived in port from Havana, which a certain Juan Sedeño, a settler at Havana, was taking, freighted with Cassava bread and salt pork to sell at some gold mines near Santiago de Cuba.

Juan Sedeño landed and went to pay his respects to Cortés, and after a long conversation Cortés bought the ship and the pork and bread on credit, and it all came with us. So we already had eleven ships and thank God all was going well with us.

I must go back a little from our story to say that after we had set out from Santiago de Cuba with all the ships, so many things were said to Diego Velásquez against Cortés that he was forced to change his mind, for they told him that Cortés was already in rebellion, and that he left the port by stealth, and that he had been heard to say that although Diego Velásquez and his relations might regret it, he intended to be Captain and that was the reason why he had embarked all his soldiers by night, so that if any attempt were made to detain him by force he might set sail. Those who took the leading part in persuading Diego Velásquez to revoke the authority he had given to Cortés were some members of the Velásquez family and an old man named Juan Millan whom some called the astrologer, but others said he had a touch of madness because he acted without reflection, and this old man kept repeating to Diego Velásquez: "Take care, Sir, for Cortés will take vengeance on you for putting him in prison [this refers to an earlier incident in the relations between Cortés and Diego Velásquez], and as he is sly and determined he will ruin you if you do not prevent it at once."

And Velásquez listened to these speeches and was always haunted by suspicions, so without delay he sent two messengers whom he trusted, with orders and instructions to Francisco Verdugo, the Chief Alcalde of Trinidad, who was his brother-in-law, to the effect that on no account should the fleet be allowed to sail, and he said in his orders that Cortés should be detained or taken prisoner as he was no longer its captain, for he had revoked his commission and given it to Vasco Porcallo. The messengers also carried letters to Diego de Ordás and Francisco de Mona and other dependents of his begging them not to allow the fleet to sail.

When Cortés heard of this, he spoke to Ordás and Francisco Verdugo, and to all the soldiers and settlers at Trinidad, whom he thought would be against him and in favour of the instructions, and he made such speeches and promises to them that he brought them over to his side. Diego Ordás himself spoke at once to Francisco Verdugo, the Alcalde Mayor advising him to have nothing to do with the affair but to hush it up, and bade him note that up to that time they had seen no change in Cortés, on the contrary that he showed himself to be a faithful servant of the Governor, and that if Velásquez wished to impute any evil to him in order to deprive him of the command of the fleet, it was as well to remember that Cortés had many men of quality among his friends, who were unfriendly to Velásquez, because he had not given them good grants of Indians. In addition to this, that Cortés had a large body of soldiers with him and was very powerful and might sow strife in the town, and perhaps the soldiers might sack the town and plunder it, and do even worse damage.

So the matter was quietly dropped and one of the messengers who brought the letters and instructions, joined our company and by the other messenger, Cortés sent a letter to Diego Velásquez written in a very friendly manner, saying that he was amazed at His Honour having come to such a decision that his desire was to serve God and His Majesty, and to obey him as His Majesty's representative, and that he prayed him not to pay any more attention to what was said by the gentlemen of his family, nor to change his mind on account of the speeches of such an old lunatic as Juan Millan. He also wrote to all his friends and especially to his partners Duero and the Treasurer.

When these letters had been written, Cortés ordered all the soldiers to polish up their arms, and he ordered the blacksmiths in the town to make headpieces, and the crossbowmen to overhaul their stores and make arrows, and he also sent for the two blacksmiths and persuaded them to accompany us, which they did. We were ten days in that town.

When Cortés saw that there was nothing more to be done at the town of Trinidad he sent Pedro de Alvarado by land to Havana [this is the old Havana on the south coast, not the present port] to pick up some soldiers who lived on farms along the road, and I went in his company, and he sent all the horses by land. Cortés then went on board the flagship to set sail with all the fleet for Havana.

It appears that the ships of the Convoy lost sight of the flagship in the nighttime, and we all arrived at the town of Havana, but Cortés did not appear, and no one knew where he was delayed. Five days passed without news of his ship, and we began to wonder whether he had been lost. We all agreed that three of the smaller vessels should go in search of Cortés, and in preparing the vessels and in debates whether this or the other man— Pedro or Sancho—should go, two more days went by and Cortés did not appear. Then parties began to be formed, and we all played the game of "Who shall be Captain until Cortés comes?"

Let us leave this subject and return to Cortés. In the neighbourhood of the Isle of Pines, or near the *Jardines*, where there are many shallows, his ship ran aground and remained there hard and fast and could not be floated.

Cortés ordered all the cargo which could be removed to be taken ashore in the boat, for there was land nearby where it could be stored, and when it was seen that the ship was floating and could be moved, she was taken into deeper water and was laden again with the cargo, sail was then set and the voyage continued to the port of Havana.

When Cortés arrived nearly all of us gentlemen and soldiers who were awaiting him were delighted at his coming, all except some who had hoped to be Captains, for the game of choosing captains came to an end.

Cortés now ordered all the artillery, which consisted of ten brass guns and some falconets, to be brought out of the ships, and gave them in charge of an artilleryman named Mesa, and of a Levantine named Arbenga, and a certain Juan Catalan, with orders to have them thoroughly cleaned and tested, and to see that the balls and powder were in readiness, and he gave them wine and vinegar with which to clean them. He gave the gunners as a companion a certain Bartolomé de Usagre. He also ordered that the crossbows with their cords, nuts and other necessaries should be overhauled, and that they should be tested at a target, so as to see how far each of them would carry.

As in the country round Havana there is much cotton, we made well-padded armour for ourselves, which is most necessary when fighting

Indians, on account of the great use they make of darts, arrows and lances, and stones which fall on one like hail.

It was here in Havana that Cortés began to organize a household and to be treated as a Lord. The first Marshal of the household whom he appointed was a certain Guzman who soon afterwards died or was killed by the Indians, and he had as *camarero* [camarero = chamberlain] Rodrigo Ranguel, and for Mayordomo, Juan de Cáceres.

When all this was settled we got ready to embark and the horses were divided among all the ships, and mangers were made for them and a store of maize and hay put on board. I will now call to mind all the mares and horses that were shipped:

The Captain Cortés: a vicious dark chestnut horse, which died as soon as we arrived at San Juan de Ulúa.

Pedro de Alvarado and Hernando López de Ávila: a very good sorrel mare, good both for sport and as a charger. When we arrived at New Spain Pedro de Alvarado bought the other half share in the mare or took it by force.

Alonzo Hernández Puertocarrero: a gray mare, a very good charger which Cortés bought for him with his gold buttons.

Juan Velásquez de Leon: a very powerful gray mare which we called "La Rabona" [La Rabona = The Bobtailed], very handy and a good charger.

Cristóbal de Olid: a dark chestnut horse, fairly good.

Francisco de Montejo and Alonzo de Ávila : a parched sorrel horse, no use for warfare.

Francisco de Morla: a dark chestnut horse, very fast and very easily handled.

Juan de Escalante: a light chestnut horse with three white stockings, not much good.

Diego de Ordás: a gray mare, barren, tolerably good, but not fast.

Gonzalo Domínguez: a wonderfully good horseman; a very good dark chestnut horse, a grand galloper.

Pedro Gonzalez de Trujillo: a good chestnut horse, all chestnut, a very good goer.

Moron, a settler at Bayamo: a dappled horse with stockings on the forefeet, very handy.

Baena, a settler at Trinidad: a dappled horse almost black, no good for anything.

Lanes, a very good horseman: an excellent horse of rather light chestnut colour, a very good goer.

Ortiz the musician and Bartolomé García, who once owned gold mines: a very good dark horse called "El Arriero" [El Arriero = The Muleteer, Carrier], this was one of the best horses carried in the fleet.

Juan Sedeño, a settler at Havana: a chestnut mare which foaled on board ship.

This Juan Sedeño passed for the richest soldier in the fleet, for he came in his own ship with the mare, and a negro and a store of cassava bread and salt pork, and at that the horses and negroes were worth their weight in gold, and that is the reason why more horses were not taken, for there were none to be bought.

To make my story clear, I must go back and relate that when Diego Velásquez knew for certain that Francisco Verdugo not only refused to compel Cortés to leave the fleet, but, together with Diego de Ordás, had helped him to get away, they say that he was so angry that he roared with rage, and said that Cortés was mutinous. He made up his mind to send orders to Pedro Barba, his lieutenant at Havana, and to Diego de Ordás and to Juan Velásquez de Leon who were his kinsmen praying them neither for good nor ill to let the fleet get away, and to seize Cortés at once and send him under a strong guard to Santiago de Cuba.

On the arrival of the messenger, it was known at once what he had brought with him, for by the same messenger Cortés was advised of what Velásquez was doing. It appears that a friar of the Order of Mercy wrote a letter to another friar of his order named Bartolomé del Olmedo, who was with us, and in that letter Cortés was informed of all that had happened.

Not one of those to whom Diego Velásquez had written favoured his proposal, indeed one and all declared for Cortés, and lieutenant Pedro

Barba above all, and all of us would have given our lives for Cortés. So that if in the Town of Trinidad the orders of Velásquez were slighted, in the town of Havana they were absolutely ignored.

Cortés wrote to Velásquez in the agreeable and complimentary terms which he knew so well how to use, and told him that he should set sail next day and that he remained his humble servant.

Cortés Finds an Interpreter

There was to be no parade of the forces until we arrived at Cozumel. Cortés ordered the horses to be taken on board ship, and he directed Pedro de Alvarado to go along the North coast in a good ship named the *San Sebastian*, and he told the pilot who was in charge to wait for him at Cape San Antonio as all the ships would meet there and go in company to Cozumel. He also sent a messenger to Diego de Ordás, who had gone along the North Coast to collect supplies of food with orders to do the same and await his coming.

On the 10th February, 1519, after hearing Mass, they set sail along the south coast with nine ships and the company of gentlemen and soldiers whom I have mentioned, so that with the two ships absent from the north coast there were eleven ships in all, including that which carried Pedro de Alvarado with seventy soldiers and I travelled in his company.

The Pilot named Camacho who was in charge of our ship paid no attention to the orders of Cortés and went his own way and we arrived at Cozumel two days before Cortés and anchored in the port which I have often mentioned when telling about Grijalva's expedition.

Cortés had not yet arrived, being delayed by the ship commanded by Francisco de Morla having lost her rudder in bad weather, however she was supplied with another rudder by one of the ships of the fleet, and all then came on in company.

To go back to Pedro de Alvarado. As soon as we arrived in port we went on shore with all the soldiers to the town of Cozumel, but we found no Indians there as they had all fled. So we were ordered to go on to another town about a league distant, and there also the natives had fled and taken to the bush, but they could not carry off their property and left behind their poultry and other things and Pedro de Alvarado ordered forty of the fowls to be taken. In an Idol house there were some altar ornaments made of old cloths and some little chests containing diadems, Idols, beads and pendants of gold of poor quality, and here we captured two Indians and an Indian woman, and we returned to the town where we had disembarked.

While we were there Cortés arrived with all the fleet, and after taking up his lodging the first thing he did was to order the pilot Camacho to be put in irons for not having waited for him at sea as he had been ordered to do. When he saw the town without any people in it, and heard that Pedro de Alvarado had gone to the other town and had taken fowls and cloths and other things of small value from the Idols, and some gold which was half copper, he showed that he was very angry both at that and at the pilot not having waited for him, and he reprimanded Pedro de Alvarado severely, and told him that we should never pacify the country in that way by robbing the natives of their property, and he sent for the two Indians and the woman whom we had captured, and through Melchorejo (Julianillo his companion was dead), the man we had brought from Cape Catoche who understood the language well, he spoke to them telling them to go and summon the Caciques and Indians of their town, and he told them not to be afraid, and he ordered the gold and the cloths and all the rest to be given back to them, and for the fowls (which had already been eaten) he ordered them to be given beads and little bells, and in addition he gave to each Indian a Spanish shirt. So they went off to summon the lord of the town, and the next day the Cacique and all his people arrived, women and children and all the inhabitants of the town, and they went about among us as though they had been used to us all their lives, and Cortés ordered us not to annoy them in any way. Here in this Island Cortés began to rule energetically, and Our Lord so favoured him that whatever be put his hand to it turned out well for him, especially in pacifying the people and towns of these lands, as we shall see further on.

When we had been in Cozumel three days, Cortés ordered a muster of his forces so as to see how many of us there were, and he found that we numbered five hundred and eight, not counting the shipmasters, pilots and sailors, who numbered about one hundred. There were sixteen horses and mares all fit to be used for sport or as chargers.

There were eleven ships both great and small, and one a sort of launch which a certain Gines Nortes brought laden with supplies.

There were thirty-two crossbowmen and thirteen musketeers, and some brass guns, and four falconets, and much powder and ball.

After the review Cortés ordered Mesa surnamed "The Gunner" and Bartolomé de Usagre and Arbenga and a certain Catalan who were all artillerymen, to keep their guns clean and in good order, and the ammunition ready for use. He appointed Francisco de Orozco, who had been a soldier in Italy to be captain of the Artillery. He likewise ordered two crossbowmen named Juan Benítez and Pedro del Guzman who were masters of the art of repairing crossbows, to see that every crossbow had two or three [spare] nuts and cords and fore cords and to be careful to keep them stored and to have smoothing tools and to see that the men should practise at a target. He also ordered all the horses to be kept in good condition.

Cortés sent for me and a Biscayan named Martin Ramos, and asked us what we thought about those words which the Indians of Campeche had used when we went there with Francisco Hernández de Córdova, when they cried out "Castilan, Castilan." We again related to Cortés all that we had seen and heard about the matter, and he said that he also had often thought about it, and that perhaps there might be some Spaniards living in the country, and added "It seems to me that it would be well to ask these Caciques of Cozumel if they know anything about them." So through Melchorejo, who already understood a little Spanish and knew the language of Cozumel very well, all the chiefs were questioned, and every one of them said that they had known of certain Spaniards and gave descriptions of them, and said that some Caciques, who lived about two days' journey inland, kept them as slaves. We were all delighted at this news, and Cortés told the Caciques that they must go at once and summon the Spaniards, taking with them letters. The Cacique advised Cortés to send a ransom to ·the owners who held these men as slaves, so that they should be allowed to come, and Cortés did so, and gave to the messengers all manner of beads. Then he ordered the two smallest vessels to be got ready, under the command of Diego de Ordás, and he sent them off to the coast near Cape Catoche where the larger vessel was to wait for eight days while the smaller vessel should go backwards and forwards and bring news of what was being done, for the land of Cape Catoche was only four leagues distant.

In the letter Cortés said:—"Gentlemen and brothers, here in Cozumel I have learnt that you are captives in the hands of a Cacique, and I pray you that you come here to Cozumel at once, and for this purpose I have sent a ship with soldiers, in case you have need of them, and a ransom to be paid to those Indians with whom you are living. The ship will wait eight days for you. Come in all haste, and you will be welcomed and protected. I am here at this Island with five hundred soldiers and eleven ships, in which I go on, please God, to a town called Tabasco or Potonchan."

The two vessels were soon despatched with the two Indian traders from Cozumel who carried the letters, and they crossed the strait in three hours and the messengers with the letters and ransom were landed.

In two days the letters were delivered to a Spaniard named Jerónimo de Aguilar, for that we found to be his name. When he had read the letter and received the ransom of beads which we had sent to him he was delighted, and carried the ransom to the Cacique his master, and begged leave to depart, and the Cacique at once gave him leave to go wherever he pleased. Aguilar set out for the place, five leagues distant, where his companion Gonzalo Guerrero was living, but when he read the letter to him he answered: "Brother Aguilar, I am married and have three children and the Indians look on me as a Cacique and captain in wartime—You go, and God be with you, but I have my face tattooed and my ears pierced what would the Spaniards say should they see me in this guise? and look how handsome these boys of mine are, for God's sake give me those green beads you have brought, and I will give the beads to them and say that my brothers have sent them from my own country." And the Indian wife of Gonzalo spoke to Aguilar in her own tongue very angrily and said to him: "What is this slave coming here for talking to my husband—go off with you, and don't trouble us with any more words."

Then Aguilar reminded Gonzalo that he was a Christian and said that he should not imperil his soul for the sake of an Indian woman, and as for his wife and children he could take them with him if he did not wish to desert them. But by no words or admonishments could he be persuaded to come. It appears that Gonzalo Guerrero was a sailor and a native of Palos.

When Jerónimo de Aguilar saw that Gonzalo would not accompany him he went at once, with the two Indian messengers, to the place where the ship had been awaiting his coming, but when he arrived he saw no ship for she had already departed. The eight days during which Ordás had been ordered to await and one day more had already expired, and seeing that Aguilar had not arrived Ordás returned to Cozumel without bringing any news about that for which he had come.

When Aguilar saw that there was no ship there he became very sad, and returned to his master and to the town where he usually lived.

When Cortés saw Ordás return without success or any news of the Spaniards or Indian messengers he was very angry, and said haughtily to Ordás that he thought that he would have done better than to return without the Spaniards or any news of them, for it was quite clear that they were prisoners in that country.

One morning the courtyard of the oratory where the Idols were kept was crowded with Indians, and many of them both men and women were burning a resin like our incense. As this was a new sight to us we stood round watching it with attention, and presently an old Indian with a long cloak, who was the priest of the Idols (and I have already said that the priests in New Spain are called *Papas*) went up on the top of the oratory and began to preach to the people. Cortés and all of us were wondering what would be the result of that black sermon. Cortés asked Melchorejo, who understood the language well, what the old Indian was saying, for he was informed that he was preaching evil things, and he sent for the Cacique and all the principal chiefs and the priest himself, and, as well as he could through the aid of our interpreter, he told them that if we were to be brothers they must cast those most evil Idols out of their temple, for they were not gods at all but very evil things which led them astray and could lead their souls to hell. Then he spoke to them about good and holy things, and told them to set up in the place of their Idols an image of Our Lady which he gave them, and a cross, which would always aid them and bring good harvests and would save their souls, and he told them in a very excellent way other things about our holy faith.

The Priest and the Caciques answered that their forefathers had worshipped those Idols because they were good, and that they did not dare to do otherwise, and that if we cast out their Idols we would see how much harm it would do us, for we should be lost at sea. Then Cortés ordered us to break the Idols to pieces and roll them down the steps [in the "Itinerary of Grijalva" a temple or oratory of the idols is thus described: "It was eighteen steps (of a stairway) in height and the base was solid, and the measurement round it was one hundred and eighty feet. On the top of this was a small tower the height of two men one above the other and inside were certain figures and bones and *Cenis* which are the Idols which they worship"], and this we did; then he ordered lime to be brought, of which there was a good store in the town, and Indian masons, and he set up a very fair altar on which we placed the figure of Our Lady; and he ordered two of our party named Alonzo Yáñez and Álvaro López who were carpenters and joiners to make a cross of some rough timber which was there, and it was placed in a small chapel near the altar and the priest named Juan Diaz said Mass there, and the Cacique and the heathen priest and all the Indians stood watching us with attention.

Cortés took leave of the Caciques and priests and confided to their care the Image of Our Lady and told them to reverence the cross and keep it clean and wreathed with flowers and they would see what advantage they would gain by so doing, and the Indians replied that they would do so, and they brought four fowls and two jars of honey and they embraced him.

We embarked again, and set sail on a day in the month of March, 1519, and went on our way in fair weather. At ten o'clock that same morning loud shouts were given from one of the ships, which tried to lay to, and fired a shot so that all the vessels of the fleet might hear it, and when Cortés heard this he at once checked the flagship and seeing the ship commanded by Juan de Escalante bearing away and returning towards Cozumel, he cried out to the other ships which were near him: "What is the matter? What is the matter?" And a soldier named Luis de Zaragoza answered that Juan de Escalante's ship with all the Cassava bread on board was sinking, and Cortés cried, "Pray God that we suffer no such disaster," and he ordered the Pilot Alaminos to make signal to all the other ships to return to Cozumel.

When the Spaniard who was a prisoner among the Indians, knew for certain that we had returned to Cozumel with the ships, he was very joyful and gave thanks to God, and he came in all haste with the two Indians who had carried the letters and ransom, and as he was able to pay well with the green beads we had sent him, he soon hired a canoe and six Indian rowers.

When they arrived on the coast of Cozumel and were disembarking, some soldiers who had gone out hunting (for there were wild pigs on the island) told Cortés that a large canoe, which had come from the direction of Cape Catoche, had arrived near the town. Cortés sent Andrés de Tápia and two other soldiers to go and see, for it was a new thing for Indians to come fearlessly in large canoes into our neighbourhood. When Andrés de Tápia saw that they were only Indians, he at once sent word to Cortés by a Spaniard that they were Cozumel Indians who had come in the canoe. As soon as the men had landed, one of them in words badly articulated and worse pronounced, cried *Dios y Santa Maria de Sevilla*, and Tápia went at once to embrace him.

Tápia soon brought the Spaniard to Cortés but before he arrived where Cortés was standing, several Spaniards asked Tápia where the Spaniard was? although he was walking by his side, for they could not distinguish him from an Indian as he was naturally brown and he had his hair shorn like an Indian slave, and carried a paddle on his shoulder, he was shod with one old sandal and the other was tied to his belt, he had on a ragged old cloak, and a worse loincloth, with which he covered his nakedness, and he had tied up, in a bundle in his cloak, a Book of Hours, old and worn. When Cortés saw him in this state, he too was deceived like the other soldiers, and asked Tápia: "Where is the Spaniard?" On hearing this, the Spaniard squatted down on his haunches as the Indians do and said "I am he." Cortés at once ordered him to be given a shirt and doublet and drawers and a cape and sandals, for he had no other clothes, and asked him about himself and what his name was and when he came to this country. The man replied, pronouncing with difficulty, that he was called Jerónimo de Aguilar, a native of Ecija, and that he had taken holy orders, that eight years had passed since he and fifteen other men and two women left Darien for the Island of Santo Domingo, and that the ship in which they sailed, struck on the *Alacranes* so that she could not be floated, and that he and his companions and the two women got into the ship's boat, thinking to reach the Island of Cuba or Jamaica, but that the currents were very strong and carried them to this land, and that the Calachiones of that district had divided them among themselves, and that many of his companions had been sacrificed to the Idols, and that others had died of disease, and the women had died of overwork only a short time before, for they had been made to grind corn; that the Indians had intended him for a sacrifice, but that one night he escaped and fled to the Cacique with whom since then he had been living, and that none were left of all his party except himself and a certain Gonzalo Guerrero, whom he had gone to summon, but he would not come.

Cortés questioned Aguilar about the country and the towns, but Aguilar replied that having been a slave, he knew only about hewing wood and drawing water and digging in the fields, that he had only once travelled as far as four leagues from home when he was sent with a load, but, as it was heavier than he could carry, he fell ill, but that he understood that there were very many towns. When questioned about Gonzalo Guerrero, he said that he was married and had three sons, and that his face was tattooed and his ears and lower lip were pierced, that he was a seaman and a native of Palos, and that the Indians considered him to be very valiant; that when a little more than a year ago a captain and three vessels arrived at Cape Catoche, it was at the suggestion of Guerrero that the Indians attacked them, and that he was there himself in the company of the Cacique of the large town. When Cortés heard this he exclaimed "I wish I had him in my hands for it will never do to leave him here."

When the Caciques of Cozumel found out that Aguilar could speak their language, they gave him to eat of their best, and Aguilar advised them always to respect and revere the holy image of Our Lady and the Cross, for they would find that it would benefit them greatly.

On the advice of Aguilar the Caciques asked Cortés to give them a letter of recommendation, so that if any other Spaniards came to that port they would treat the Indians well and do them no harm, and this letter was given to them.

On the 4th March, 1519, with the good fortune to carry such a useful and faithful interpreter along with us, Cortés gave orders for us to embark in the same order as before, and with the same lantern signals by night.

We sailed along in good weather, until at nightfall a headwind struck us so fiercely that the ships were dispersed and there was great danger of being driven ashore. Thank God, by midnight the weather moderated, and the ships got together again, excepting the vessel under the command of Juan Velásquez de Leon. However, when she still failed to appear, it was agreed that the whole fleet should go back and search for the missing ship, and we found her at anchor in a bay which was a great relief to us all. We stayed in that bay for a day and we lowered two boats and went on shore and found farms and maize plantations, and there were four Cues which are the houses of their Idols, and there were many Idols in them, nearly all of them figures of tall women so that we called that place the Punta de las Mugeres [Punta de las Mugeres = Cape of the Women].

On the 12th March, 1519, we arrived with all the fleet at the Rio de Grijalva, which is also called Tabasco, and as we already knew from our experience with Grijalva that vessels of large size could not enter into the river, the larger vessels were anchored out at sea, and from the smaller vessels and boats all the soldiers were landed at the Cape of the Palms (as they were in Grijalva's time) which was about half a league distant from the town of Tabasco. The river, the riverbanks and the mangrove thickets were swarming with Indians, at which those of us who had not been here in Grijalva's time were much astonished.

In addition to this there were assembled in the town more than twelve thousand warriors all prepared to make war on us, for at this time the town was of considerable importance and other large towns were subject to it and they had all made preparation for war and were well supplied with arms.

The reason for this was that the people of Champoton and Lázaro and the other towns in that neighbourhood had looked upon the people of Tabasco as cowards, and had told them so to their faces, because they had given Grijalva the gold jewels and they said that they were too faint-hearted to attack us although they had more towns and more warriors than the people of Champoton and Lázaro. This they said to annoy them and added that they in their towns had attacked us and killed fifty-six of us. So on account of these taunts, which had been uttered, the people of Tabasco had determined to take up arms.

When Cortés saw them drawn up ready for war he told Aguilar the interpreter to ask the Indians who passed near us, in a large canoe and who looked like chiefs, what they were so much disturbed about, and to tell them that we had not come to do them any harm, but were willing to give them some of the things we had brought with us and to treat them like brothers, and we prayed them not to begin a war as they would regret it, and much else was said to them about keeping the peace. However, the more Aguilar talked to them the more violent they became, and they said that they would kill us all if we entered their town, and that it was fortified all round with fences and barricades of large trunks of trees.

Aguilar spoke to them again and asked them to keep the peace, and allow us to take water and barter our goods with them for food, and permit us to tell the Calachones [calachiones (?) = leaders] things which would be to their advantage and to the service of God our Lord, but they still persisted in saying that if we advanced beyond the palm trees they would kill us.

When Cortés saw the state of affairs he ordered the boats and small vessels to be got ready and ordered three cannon to be placed in each boat and divided the crossbowmen and musketeers among the boats. We remembered that when we were here with Grijalva we had found a narrow path which ran across some streams from the palm grove to the town, and Cortés ordered three soldiers to find out in the night if that path ran right up to the houses, and not to delay in bringing the news, and these men found out that it did lead there. After making a thorough examination of our surroundings the rest of the day was spent in arranging how and in what order we were to go in the boats.

The next morning we had our arms in readiness and after hearing Mass Cortés ordered the Captain Alonzo de Ávila and a hundred soldiers among whom were ten crossbowmen, to go by the little path which led to the town, and, as soon as he heard the guns fired, to attack the town on one side while he attacked it on the other. Cortés himself and all the other Captains and soldiers went in the boats and light draft vessels up the river. When the Indian warriors who were on the banks and among the mangroves saw that we were really on the move, they came after us with a great many canoes with intent to prevent our going ashore at the landing place, and the whole riverbank appeared to be covered with Indian warriors carrying all the different arms which they use, and blowing trumpets and shells and sounding drums. When Cortés saw how matters stood he ordered us to wait a little and not to fire any shots from guns or crossbows or cannon, for as he wished to be justified in all that he might do he made another appeal to the Indians through the Interpreter Aguilar, in the presence of the King's Notary, Diego de Godoy, asking the Indians to allow us to land and take water and speak to them about God and about His Majesty, and adding that should they make war on us, that if in defending ourselves some should be killed and others hurt, theirs would be the fault and the burden and it would not be with us, but they went on threatening that if we landed they would kill us.

Then they boldly began to let fly arrows at us, and made signals with their drums, and like valiant men they surrounded us with their canoes, and they all attacked us with such a shower of arrows that they kept us in the water in some parts up to our waists. As there was much mud and swamp at that place we could not easily get clear of it, and so many Indians fell on us, that what with some hurling their lances with all their might and others shooting arrows at us, we could not reach the land as soon as we wished.

While Cortés was fighting he lost a shoe in the mud and could not find it again, and he got on shore with one foot bare. Presently someone picked the shoe out of the mud and he put it on again.

While this was happening to Cortés, all of us Captains as well as soldiers, with the cry of "Santiago!" fell upon the Indians and forced them to retreat, but they did not fall back far, as they sheltered themselves behind great barriers and stockades formed of thick logs until we pulled them apart and got to one of the small gateways of the town. There we attacked them again, and we pushed them along through a street to where other defences had been erected, and there they turned on us and met us face-to-face and fought most valiantly, making the greatest efforts, shouting and whistling and crying out "al calacheoni," "al calacheoni," which in their language meant an order to kill or capture our Captain. While we were thus surrounded by them Alonzo de Ávila and his soldiers came up.

As I have already said they came from the Palm grove by land and could not arrive sooner on account of the swamps and creeks. Their delay was really unavoidable, just as we also had been delayed over the summons of the Indians to surrender, and in breaking openings in the barricades, so as to enable us to attack them. Now we all joined together to drive the enemy out of their strongholds, and we compelled them to retreat, but like brave warriors they kept on shooting showers of arrows and fire-hardened darts, and never turned their backs on us until [we gained] a great court with chambers and large halls, and three Idol houses, where they had already carried all the goods they possessed. Cortés then ordered us to halt, and not to follow on and overtake the enemy in their flight.

Cortés Attacks the Ceiba Tree

There and then Cortés took possession of that land for His Majesty, performing the act in His Majesty's name. It was done in this way; he drew his sword and as a sign of possession he made three cuts in a huge tree called a Ceiba, which stood in the court of that great square, and cried that if any person should raise objection, that he would defend the right with the sword and shield which he held in his hands. [*See short essay "Cortés and the Sacred Ceiba" on page* (399).]

All of us soldiers who were present when this happened cried out that he did right in taking possession of the land in His Majesty's name, and that we would aid him should any person say otherwise. This act was done in the presence of the Royal Notary. The partizans of Diego Velásquez chose to grumble at this act of taking possession.

I call to mind that in that hard fought attack which the Indians made on us, they wounded fourteen soldiers, and they gave me an arrow wound in the thigh, but it was only a slight wound; and we found eighteen Indians dead in the water where we disembarked.

We slept there [in the great square] that night with guards and sentinels on the alert.

I have already said how we were marching along when we met all the forces of the enemy which were moving in search of us, and all the men wore great feather crests and they carried drums and trumpets, and their faces were coloured black and white, and they were armed with large bows and arrows, lances and shields and swords shaped like our two-handed swords, and many slings and stones and fire-hardened javelins, and all wore quilted cotton armour.

Immediately following the ceiba tree incident Cortés sends out two reconnaissance missions—Francisco de Lugo's in one direction and Pedro de Alvarado's in another. The two forces soon reunite to defend de Lugo's group from a ferocious attack. Cortés had sent "the Indian Melchorejo" as interpreter with Alvarado, but Melchorejo deserts and reports to native caciques the numbers and disposition of the Spanish forces. When Cortés learns of native plans for a massive attack, he recalls Alvarado and de Lugo and brings the horses, crossbowmen, and musketeers ashore from the ships to form a cavalry and prepare for the ensuing attack. On an open plain near the town of Cintla the Spaniards fight the indigenous warriors.

As they approached us their squadrons were so numerous that they covered the whole plain, and they rushed on us like mad dogs completely surrounding us, and they let fly such a cloud of arrows, javelins and stones that on the first assault they wounded over seventy of us, and fighting hand-to-hand they did us great damage with their lances, and one soldier fell dead at once from an arrow wound in the ear, and they kept on shooting and wounding us. With our muskets and crossbows and with good swordplay we did not fail as stout fighters, and when they came to feel the edge of our swords little by little they fell back, but it was only so as to shoot at us in greater safety. Mesa, our artilleryman, killed many of them with his cannon, for they were formed in great squadrons and they did not open out so that he could fire at them as he pleased, but with all the hurts and wounds which we gave them, we could not drive them off. I said to Diego de Ordás: "It seems to me that we ought to close up and charge them," for in truth they suffered greatly from the strokes and thrusts of our swords, and that was why they fell away from us, both from fear of these swords, and the better to shoot their arrows and hurl their javelins and the hail of stones. Ordás replied that it was not good advice, for there were three hundred Indians to every one of us, and that we could not hold out against such a multitude—so there we stood enduring their attack. However, we did agree to get as near as we could to them, as I had advised Ordás, so as to give them a bad time with our swordsmanship, and they suffered so much from it that they retreated towards a swamp.

During all this time Cortés and his horsemen failed to appear, although we greatly longed for him, and we feared that by chance some disaster had befallen him.

I remember that when we fired shots the Indians gave great shouts and whistles and threw dust and rubbish into the air so that we should not see the damage done to them, and they sounded their trumpets and drums and shouted and whistled and cried "Alala! Alala!"

Just at this time we caught sight of our horsemen, and as the great Indian host was crazed with its attack on us, it did not at once perceive them coming up behind their backs, and as the plain was level ground and the horsemen were good riders, and many of the horses were very handy and fine gallopers, they came quickly on the enemy and speared them as they chose. As soon as we saw the horsemen we fell on the Indians with such energy that with us attacking on one side and the horsemen on the other, they soon turned tail. The Indians thought that the horse and its rider was all one animal, for they had never seen horses up to this time.

The savannas and fields were crowded with Indians running to take refuge in the thick woods nearby.

After we had defeated the enemy, Cortés told us that he had not been able to come to us sooner as there was a swamp in the way, and he had to fight his way through another force of warriors before he could reach us, and three horsemen and five horses had been wounded.

As it was Lady-day we gave to the town which was afterwards founded here the name of Santa Maria de la Victoria, on account of this great victory being won on Our Lady's day. This was the first battle that we fought under Cortés in New Spain.

After this we bound up the hurts of the wounded with cloths, for we had nothing else, and we doctored the horses by searing their wounds with the fat from the body of a dead Indian which we cut up to get out the fat, and we went to look at the dead lying on the plain and there were more than eight hundred of them, the greater number killed by thrusts, the others by the cannon, muskets and crossbows, and many were stretched on the ground half dead. Where the horsemen had passed, numbers of them lay dead or groaning from their wounds. The battle lasted over an hour, and the Indians fought all the time like brave warriors, until the horsemen came up.

We took five prisoners, two of them Captains. As it was late and we had had enough of fighting, and we had not eaten anything, we returned to our camp. Then we buried the two soldiers who had been killed, one by a wound in the ear, and the other by a wound in the throat, and we seared the wounds of the others and of the horses with the fat of the Indian, and after posting sentinels and guards, we had supper and rested.

When Aguilar spoke to the prisoners he found out from what they said that they were fit persons to be sent as messengers, and he advised Cortés to free them, so that they might go and talk to the Caciques of the town. These two messengers were given green and blue beads, and Aguilar spoke many pleasant and flattering words to them, telling them that they had nothing to fear as we wished to treat them like brothers, that it was their own fault that they had made war on us, and that now they had better collect together all the Caciques of the different towns as we wished to talk to them, and he gave them much other advice in a gentle way so as to gain their goodwill. The messengers went off willingly and spoke to the Caciques and chief men, and told them all we wished them to know about our desire for peace.

When our envoys had been listened to, it was settled among them that fifteen Indian slaves, all with stained faces and ragged cloaks and loincloths, should at once be sent to us with fowls and baked fish and maize cakes. When these men came before Cortés he received them graciously, but Aguilar the Interpreter asked them rather angrily why they had come with their faces in that state, that it looked more as though they came to fight than to treat for peace; and he told them to go back to the Caciques and inform them, that if they wished for peace in the way we offered it, chieftains should come and treat for it, as was always the custom, and that they should not send slaves. But even these painted-faced slaves were treated with consideration by us and blue beads were sent by them in sign of peace, and to soothe their feelings.

The next day thirty Indian Chieftains, clad in good cloaks, came to visit us, and brought fowls, fish, fruit and maize cakes, and asked leave from Cortés to burn and bury the bodies of the dead who had fallen in the recent battles, so that they should not smell badly or be eaten by lions and tigers. Permission was at once given them and they hastened to bring many people to bury and burn the bodies according to their customs.

Cortés learnt from the Caciques that over eight hundred men were missing, not counting those who had been carried off wounded.

They said that they could not tarry with us either to discuss the matter or make peace, for on the morrow the chieftains and leaders of all the towns would have assembled, and that then they would agree about a peace.

As Cortés was very sagacious about everything, he said, laughing, to us soldiers who happened to be in his company, "Do you know, gentlemen, that it seems to me that the Indians are terrified at the horses and may think that they and the cannon alone make war on them. I have thought of something which will confirm this belief, and that is to bring the mare belonging to Juan Sedeño, which foaled the other day on board ship, and tie her up where I am now standing and also to bring the stallion of Ortiz the musician, which is very excitable, near enough to scent the mare, and when he has scented her to lead each of them off separately so that the Caciques who are coming shall not hear the horse neighing as they approach, not until they are standing before me and are talking to me." We did just as Cortés ordered and brought the horse and mare, and the horse soon detected the scent of her in Cortés' quarters. In addition to this Cortés ordered the largest cannon that we possessed to be loaded with a large ball and a good charge of powder.

About midday forty Indians arrived, all of them Caciques of good bearing, wearing rich mantles. They saluted Cortés and all of us, and brought incense and fumigated all of us who were present, and they asked pardon for their past behaviour and said that henceforth they would be friendly.

Cortés, through Aguilar the Interpreter, answered them in a rather grave manner, as though he were angry, that they well knew how many times he had asked them to maintain peace, that the fault was theirs, and that now they deserved to be put to death, they and all the people of their towns, but that as we were the vassals of a great King and Lord named the Emperor Don Carlos, who had sent us to these countries, and ordered us to help and favour those who would enter his royal service, that if they were now as well disposed as they said they were, that we would take this course, but that if they were not, some of those *Tepustles* would jump out and kill them (they call iron Tepustle in their language) for some of the Tepustles were still angry because they had made war on us. At this moment the order was secretly given to put a match to the cannon which had been loaded, and it went off with such a thunderclap as was wanted, and the ball went buzzing over the hills, and as it was midday and very still it made a great noise, and the Caciques were terrified on hearing it. As they had never seen anything like it they believed what Cortés had told them was true. Then Cortés told them, through Aguilar, not to be afraid for he had given orders that no harm should be done to them.

Just then the horse that had scented the mare was brought and tied up not far distant from where Cortés was talking to the Caciques, and the horse began to paw the ground and neigh and become wild with excitement, looking all the time towards the Indians and the place whence the scent of the mare had reached him, and the Caciques thought that he was roaring at them and they were terrified. When Cortés observed their state of mind, he rose from his seat and went to the horse and told two orderlies to lead it far away, and said to the Indians that he had told the horse not to be angry as they were friendly and wished to make peace.

While this was going on there arrived more than thirty Indian carriers, who brought a meal of fowls and fish and fruits and other food.

Cortés had a long conversation with these chieftains and Caciques and they told him that they would all come on the next day and would bring a present and would discuss other matters, and then they went away quite contented.

Early the next morning many Caciques and chiefs of Tabasco and the neighbouring towns arrived and paid great respect to us all, and they brought a present of gold, consisting of four diadems and some gold lizards, and two [ornaments] like little dogs, and earrings and five ducks, and two masks with Indian faces and two gold soles for sandals, and some other things of little value. I do not remember how much the things were worth; and they brought cloth, such as they make and wear, which was quilted stuff.

This present, however, was worth nothing in comparison with the twenty women that were given us, among them one very excellent woman called Doña Marina, for so she was named when she became a Christian. Cortés received this present with pleasure and went aside with all the Caciques, and with Aguilar, the interpreter, to hold converse, and he told them that he gave them thanks for what they had brought with them, but there was one thing that he must ask of them, namely, that they should reoccupy the town with all their people, women and children, and he wished to see it repeopled within two days, for he would recognize that as a sign of true peace. The Caciques sent at once to summon all the inhabitants with their women and children and within two days they were again settled in the town.

One other thing Cortés asked of the chiefs and that was to give up their idols and sacrifices, and this they said they would do, and, through Aguilar, Cortés told them as well as he was able about matters concerning our holy faith, how we were Christians and worshipped one true and only God, and he showed them an image of Our Lady with her precious Son in her arms and explained to them that we paid the greatest reverence to it as it was the image of the Mother of our Lord God who was in heaven. The Caciques replied that they liked the look of the great *Teleciguata* (for in their language great ladies are called Teleciguatas) and [begged] that she might be given them to keep in their town, and Cortés said that the image should be given to them, and ordered them to make a well-constructed altar, and this they did at once.

The next morning, Cortés ordered two of our carpenters, named Alonzo Yañez and Álvaro López, to make a very tall cross.

When all this had been settled Cortés asked the Caciques what was their reason for attacking us three times when we had asked them to the peace; the chief replied that he had already asked pardon for their acts and had been forgiven, that the Cacique of Champoton, his brother, had advised it, and that he feared to be accused of cowardice, for he had already been reproached and dishonoured for not having attacked the other captain who had come with four ships (he must have meant Juan de Grijalva) and he also said that the Indian whom we had brought as an Interpreter, who escaped in the night, had advised them to attack us both by day and night.

Cortés then ordered this man to be brought before him without fail, but they replied that when he saw that the battle was going against them, he had taken to flight, and they knew not where he was although search had been made for him; but we came to know that they had offered him as a sacrifice because his counsel had cost them so dear.

Cortés also asked them where they procured their gold and jewels, and they replied, from the direction of the setting sun, and said "Culua" and "Mexico," and as we did not know what Mexico and Culua meant we paid little attention to it.

Then we brought another interpreter named Francisco, whom we had captured during Grijalva's expedition, who has already been mentioned by me but he understood nothing of the Tabasco language only that of Culua which is the Mexican tongue. By means of signs he told Cortés that Culua was far ahead, and he repeated "Mexico" which we did not understand.

Enter Doña Marina

So the talk ceased until the next day when the sacred image of Our Lady and the Cross were set up on the altar and we all paid reverence to them, and Padre Fray Bartolomé de Olmedo said Mass and all the Caciques and chiefs were present and we gave the name of Santa Maria de la Victoria to the town, and by this name the town of Tabasco is now called. The same friar, with Aguilar as interpreter, preached many good things about our holy faith to the twenty Indian women who had been given us, and immediately afterwards they were baptized. One Indian lady, who was given to us here was christened Doña Marina*, and she was truly a great chieftainess and the daughter of great Caciques and the mistress of vassals, and this her appearance clearly showed. Later on I will relate why it was and in what manner she was brought here.

Cortés allotted one of the women to each of his captains and Doña Marina, as she was good-looking and intelligent and without embarrassment, he gave to Alonzo Hernández Puertocarrero. When Puertocarrero went to Spain, Doña Marina lived with Cortés, and bore him a son named Don Martin Cortés.

We remained five days in this town, to look after the wounded and those who were suffering from pain in the loins, from which they all recovered. Furthermore, Cortés drew the Caciques to him by kindly converse, and told them how our master the Emperor, whose vassals we were, had under his orders many great lords, and that it would be well for them also to render him obedience, and that then, whatever they might be in need of, whether it was our protection or any other necessity, if they would make it known to him, no matter where he might be, he would come to their assistance.

---

*To see how Doña Marina's name was changed to Malinche, see p. 116 in this volume.

The Caciques all thanked him for this, and thereupon all decl themselves the vassals of our great Emperor. These were the first vassals to render submission to His Majesty in New Spain.

Cortés then ordered the Caciques to come with their women and children early the next day, which was Palm Sunday, to the altar, to pay homage to the holy image of Our Lady and to the Cross, and at the same time Cortés ordered them to send six Indian carpenters to accompany our carpenters to the town of Cintla, there to cut a cross on a great tree called a Ceiba, which grew there, and they did it so that it might last a long time, *ceba* for as the bark is renewed the cross will show there forever. When this was done he ordered the Indians to get ready all the canoes that they owned to help us to embark, for we wished to set sail on that holy day because the pilots had come to tell Cortés that the ships ran a great risk from a Norther which is a dangerous gale.

The next day, early in the morning, all the Caciques and chiefs came in their canoes with all their women and children and stood in the court where we had placed the church and cross, and many branches of trees had already been cut ready to be carried in the procession. Then the Caciques beheld us all, Cortés, as well as the captains, and every one of us marching together with the greatest reverence in a devout procession, and the Padre de la Merced and the priest Juan Diaz, clad in their vestments, said Mass, and we paid reverence to and kissed the Holy Cross, while the Caciques and Indians stood looking on at us.

When our solemn festival was over the chiefs approached and offered Cortés ten fowls and baked fish and vegetables, and we took leave of them, and Cortés again commended to their care the Holy image and the sacred crosses and told them always to keep the place clean and well swept, and to deck the cross with garlands and to reverence it and then they would enjoy good health and bountiful harvests.

It was growing late when we got on board ship and the next day, Monday, we set sail in the morning and with a fair wind laid our course for San Juan de Ulda, keeping close in shore all the time.

Before telling about the great Montezuma and his famous City of

Mexico and the Mexicans, I wish to give some account of Doña Marina, who from her childhood had been the mistress and Cacica of towns and vassals. It happened in this way:

Her father and mother were chiefs and Caciques of a town called Paynala, which had other towns subject to it, and stood about eight leagues from the town of Coatzacoalcos. Her father died while she was still a little child, and her mother married another Cacique, a young man, and bore him a son. It seems that the father and mother had a great affection for this son and it was agreed between them that he should succeed to their honours when their days were done. So that there should be no impediment to this, they gave the little girl, Doña Marina, to some Indians from Xicalango, and this they did by night so as to escape observation, and they then spread the report that she had died, and as it happened at this time that a child of one of their Indian slaves died they gave out that it was their daughter and the heiress who was dead.

The Indians of Xicalango gave the child to the people of Tabasco and the Tabasco people gave her to Cortés. I myself knew her mother, and the old woman's son and her half brother, when he was already grown up and ruled the town jointly with his mother, for the second husband of the old lady was dead. When they became Christians, the old lady was called Marta and the son Lázaro. I knew all this very well because in the year 1523 after the conquest of Mexico and the other provinces, when Cristóbal de Olid revolted in Honduras, and Cortés was on his way there, he passed through Coatzacoalcos and I and the greater number of the settlers of that town accompanied him on that expedition as I shall relate in the proper time and place. As Doña Marina proved herself such an excellent woman and good interpreter throughout the wars in New Spain, Tlaxcala and Mexico (as I shall show later on) Cortés always took her with him, and during that expedition she was married to a gentleman named Juan Jaramillo at the town of Orizaba.

Doña Marina was a person of the greatest importance and was obeyed without question by the Indians throughout New Spain.

When Cortés was in the town of Coatzacoalcos he sent to summon to his presence all the Caciques of that province in order to make them a speech about our holy religion, and about their good treatment, and among the Caciques who assembled was the mother of Doña Marina and her half brother, Lázaro.

Some time before this Doña Marina had told me that she belonged to that province and that she was the mistress of vassals, and Cortés also knew it well, as did Aguilar, the interpreter. In such a manner it was that mother, daughter and son came together, and it was easy enough to see that she was the daughter from the strong likeness she bore to her mother.

These relations were in great fear of Doña Marina, for they thought that she had sent for them to put them to death, and they were weeping.

When Doña Marina saw them in tears, she consoled them and told them to have no fear, that when they had given her over to the men from Xicalango, they knew not what they were doing, and she forgave them for doing it, and she gave them many jewels of gold and raiment, and told them to return to their town, and said that God had been very gracious to her in freeing her from the worship of idols and making her a Christian, and letting her bear a son to her lord and master Cortés and in marrying her to such a gentleman as Juan Jaramillo, who was now her husband. That she would rather serve her husband and Cortés than anything else in the world, and would not exchange her place to be Cacica of all the provinces in New Spain.

Doña Marina knew the language of Coatzacoalcos, which is that common to Mexico, and she knew the language of Tabasco, as did also Jerónimo de Aguilar, who spoke the language of Yucatan and Tabasco, which is one and the same. So that these two could understand one another clearly, and Aguilar translated into Castilian for Cortés.

This was the great beginning of our conquests and thus, thanks be to God, things prospered with us. I have made a point of explaining this matter, because without the help of Doña Marina we could not have understood the language of New Spain and Mexico.

Signs of Empire

On Holy Thursday, in the year 1519, we arrived with all the fleet at the Port of San Juan de Ulúa, and as the Pilot Alaminos knew the place well from having come there with Juan de Grijalva he at once ordered the vessels to drop anchor where they would be safe from the northerly gales. The flagship hoisted her royal standards and pennants, and within half an hour of anchoring, two large canoes came out to us, full of Mexican Indians. Seeing the big ship with the standards flying they knew that it was there they must go to speak with the captain; so they went direct to the flagship and going on board asked who was the *Tatuan* [*Tlatoan*] which in their language means the chief. Doña Marina, who understood the language well, pointed him out. Then the Indians paid many marks of respect to Cortés, according to their usage, and bade him welcome, and said that their lord, a servant of the great Montezuma, had sent them to ask what kind of men we were, and of what we were in search, and added that if we were in need of anything for ourselves or the ships, that we should tell them and they would supply it. Our Cortés thanked them through the two interpreters, Aguilar and Doña Marina, and ordered food and wine to be given them and some blue beads, and after they had drunk he told them that we came to see them and to trade with them and that our arrival in their country should cause them no uneasiness but be looked on by them as fortunate. The messengers returned on shore well content, and the next day, which was Good Friday, we disembarked with the horses and guns, on some sand hills which rise to a considerable height, for there was no level land, nothing but sand dunes; and the artilleryman Mesa placed the guns in position to the best of his judgment. Then we set up an altar where Mass was said and we made huts and shelters for Cortés and the captains, and three hundred of the soldiers brought wood and made huts for themselves and we placed the horses where they would be safe and in this way was Good Friday passed.

The next day, Saturday, Easter Eve, many Indians arrived sent by a chief who was a governor under Montezuma, named Pitalpitoque [Pitalpitoque = Cuitalpitoc] (whom we afterwards called Ovandillo), and they brought axes and dressed wood for the huts of the Captain Cortés and the other ranchos near to it, and covered them with large cloths on account of the strength of the sun, for the heat was very great—and they brought fowls, and maize cakes and plums, which were then in season, and I think that they brought some gold jewels, and they presented all these things to Cortés; and said that the next day a governor would come and would bring more food. Cortés thanked them heartily and ordered them to be given certain articles in exchange with which they went away well content. The next day, Easter Sunday, the governor whom they spoke of arrived. His name was Tendile [Teuhtlilli], a man of affairs, and he brought with him Pitalpitoque who was also a man of importance amongst the natives and there followed them many Indians with presents of fowls and vegetables. Tendile ordered these people to stand aside on a hillock and with much humility he made three obeisances to Cortés according to their customs, and then to all the soldiers who were standing around. Cortés bade them welcome through our interpreters and embraced them and asked them to wait, as he wished presently to speak to them. Meanwhile he ordered an altar to be made as well as it could be done in the time, and Fray Bartolomé de Olmedo, who was a fine singer, chanted Mass, and Padre Juan Díaz assisted, and the two governors and the other chiefs who were with them looked on. When Mass was over, Cortés and some of our captains and the two Indian Officers of the great Montezuma dined together. When the tables had been cleared away— Cortés went aside with the two Caciques and our two interpreters and explained to them that we were Christians and vassals of the greatest lord on earth who had many great princes as his vassals and servants, and that it was at his orders that we had come to this country, because for many years he had heard rumours about the country and the great prince who ruled it. That he wished to be friends with this prince and to tell him many things in the name of the Emperor which things, when he knew and understood them, would please him greatly. Moreover, he wished to trade with their prince and his Indians in good friendship, and he wanted to know where this prince would wish that they should meet so that they might confer together. Tendile replied somewhat proudly, and said:—"You have only just now arrived and you already ask to speak with our prince; accept now this present which we give you in his name, and afterwards you will tell me what you think fitting." With that he took out a *petaca*—which is a sort of chest, many articles of gold beautifully and richly worked and ordered ten loads of white cloth made of cotton and feathers to be brought, wonderful things to see, besides quantities of food. Cortés received it all with smiles in a gracious manner and gave in return, beads of twisted glass and other small beads from Spain, and he begged them to send to their towns to ask the people to come and trade with us as he had brought many beads to exchange for gold, and they replied that they would do as he asked. Cortés then ordered his servants to bring an armchair, richly carved and inlaid and some *margaritas*, stones with many [intricate] designs in them, and a string of twisted glass beads packed in cotton scented with musk and a crimson cap with a golden medal engraved with a figure of St. George on horseback, lance in hand, slaying the dragon, and he told Tendile that he should send the chair to his prince Montezuma, so that he could be seated in it when he, Cortés, came to see and speak with him, and that he should place the cap on his head, and that the stones and all the other things were presents from our lord the King, as a sign of his friendship, for he was aware that Montezuma was a great prince, and Cortés asked that a day and a place might be named where he could go to see Montezuma. Tendile received the present and said that his lord Montezuma was such a great prince that it would please him to know our great King, and that he would carry the present to him at once and bring back a reply.

It appears that Tendile brought with him some clever painters such as they had in Mexico and ordered them to make pictures true to nature of the face and body of Cortés and all his captains, and of the soldiers, ships, sails and horses, and of Doña Marina and Aguilar, even of the two greyhounds, and the cannon and cannonballs, and all of the army we had brought with us, and he carried the pictures to his master. Cortés ordered our gunners to load the lombards with a great charge of powder so that they should make a great noise when they were fired off, and he told Pedro de Alvarado that he and all the horsemen should get ready so that these servants of Montezuma might see them gallop and told them to attach little bells to the horses' breastplates. Cortés also mounted his horse and said: "It would be well if we could gallop on these sand dunes but they will observe that even when on foot we get stuck in the sand—let us go out to the beach when the tide is low and gallop two and two"—and to Pedro de Alvarado whose sorrel-coloured mare was a great galloper, and very handy, he gave charge of all the horsemen.

All this was carried out in the presence of the two ambassadors, and so that they should see the cannon fired, Cortés made as though he wished again to speak to them and a number of other chieftains, and the lombards were fired off, and as it was quite still at that moment, the stones went flying through the forest resounding with a great din, and the two governors and all the other Indians were frightened by things so new to them, and ordered the painters to record them so that Montezuma might see. It happened that one of the soldiers had a helmet half gilt but somewhat rusty, and this Tendile noticed, for he was the more forward of the two ambassadors, and said that he wished to see it as it was like one that they possessed which had been left to them by their ancestors of the race from which they had sprung, and that it had been placed on the head of their God—Huichilobos [Huitzilopochtli, Aztec God of War], and that their prince Montezuma would like to see this helmet. So it was given to him, and Cortés said to them that as he wished to know whether the gold of this country was the same as that we find in our rivers, they could return the helmet filled with grains of gold so that he could send it to our great Emperor. After this, Tendile bade farewell to Cortés and to all of us and after many expressions of regard from Cortés he took leave of him and said he would return with a reply without delay. After Tendile had departed we found out that besides being an Indian employed in matters of great importance, Tendile was the most active of the servants whom his master, Montezuma, had in his employ, and he went with all haste and narrated everything to his prince, and showed him the pictures which had been painted and the present which Cortés had sent. When the great Montezuma gazed on it he was struck with admiration and received it on his part with satisfaction. When he examined the helmet and that which was on his Huichilobos, he felt convinced that we belonged to the race which, as his forefathers had foretold would come to rule over that land.

When Tendile departed the other governor, Pitalpitoque, stayed in our camp and occupied some huts a little distance from ours, and they brought Indian women there to make maize bread, and brought fowls and fruit and fish, and supplied Cortés and the captains who fed with him. As for us soldiers, if we did not hunt for shellfish on the beach, or go out fishing, we did not get anything.

About that time, many Indians came from the towns and some of them brought gold and jewels of little value, and fowls to exchange with us for our goods, which consisted of green beads and clear glass beads and other articles, and with this we managed to supply ourselves with food. Almost all the soldiers had brought things for barter, as we learnt in Grijalva's time that it was a good thing to bring beads—and in this manner six or seven days passed by.

Then one morning, Tendile arrived with more than one hundred laden Indians, accompanied by a great Mexican Cacique, who in his face, features and appearance bore a strong likeness to our Captain Cortés and the great Montezuma had sent him purposely, for it is said that when Tendile brought the portrait of Cortés all the chiefs who were in Montezuma's company said that a great chief named Quintalbor looked exactly like Cortés and that was the name of the Cacique, who now arrived with Tendile; and as he was so like Cortés, we called them in camp "our Cortés" and "the other Cortés." To go back to my story, when these people arrived and came before our Captain they first of all kissed the earth and then fumigated him and all the soldiers who were standing around him, with incense which they brought in braziers of pottery. Cortés received them affectionately and seated them near himself, and that chief who came with the present had been appointed spokesman together with Tendile. After welcoming us to the country and after many courteous speeches had passed he ordered the presents which he had brought to be displayed, and they were placed on mats over which were spread cotton cloths. The first article presented was a wheel like a sun, as big as a cartwheel, with many sorts of pictures on it, the whole of fine gold, and a wonderful thing to behold, which those who afterwards weighed it said was worth more than ten thousand dollars. Then another wheel was presented of greater size made of silver of great brilliancy in imitation of the moon with other figures shown on it, and this was of great value as it was very heavy—and the chief brought back the helmet full of fine grains of gold, just as they are got out of the mines, and this was worth three thousand dollars. This gold in the helmet was worth more to us than if it had contained twenty thousand dollars, because it showed us that there were good mines there. Then were brought twenty golden ducks, beautifully worked and very natural looking, and some [ornaments] like dogs, and many articles of gold worked in the shape of tigers and lions and monkeys, and ten collars beautifully worked and other necklaces; and twelve arrows and a bow with its string, and two rods like staffs of justice, five palms long, all in beautiful hollow work of fine gold. Then there were presented crests of gold and plumes of rich green feathers, and others of silver, and fans of the same materials, and deer copied in hollow gold and many other things that I cannot remember for it all happened so many years ago. And then over thirty loads of beautiful cotton cloth were brought worked with many patterns and decorated with many coloured feathers, and so many other things were there that it is useless my trying to describe them for I know not how to do it. When all these things had been presented, this great Cacique Quintalbor and Tendile asked Cortés to accept this present with the same willingness with which his prince had sent it, and divide it among the *teules* and men who accompanied him. Cortés received the present with delight and then the ambassadors told Cortés that they wished to repeat what their prince, Montezuma, had sent them to say. First of all they told him that he was pleased that such valiant men, as he had heard that we were, should come to his country, for he knew all about what we had done at Tabasco, and that he would much like to see our great emperor who was such a mighty prince and whose fame was spread over so many lands, and that he would send him a present of precious stones; and that meanwhile we should stay in that port; that if he could assist us in any way he would do so with the greatest pleasure; but as to the interview, they should not worry about it; that there was no need for it and they (the ambassadors) urged many objections. Cortés kept a good countenance, and returned his thanks to them, and with many flattering expressions gave each of the ambassadors two holland shirts and some blue glass beads and other things, and begged them to go back as his ambassadors to Mexico and to tell their prince, the great Montezuma, that as we had come across so many seas and had journeyed from such distant lands solely to see and speak with him in person, that if we should return thus, that our great king and lord would not receive us well, and that wherever their prince Montezuma might be we wished to go and see him and do what he might order us to do. The ambassadors replied that they would go back and give this message to their prince, but as to the question of the desired interview—they considered it superfluous. By these ambassadors Cortés sent what our poverty could afford as a gift to Montezuma; a glass cup of Florentine ware, engraved with trees and hunting scenes and gilt, and three holland shirts and other things, and he charged the messengers to bring a reply. The two governors set out and Pitalpitoque remained in camp; for it seems that the other servants of Montezuma had given him orders to see that food was brought to us from the neighbouring towns.

As soon as the messengers had been sent off to Mexico, Cortés despatched two ships to explore the coast further along, and to seek out a safe harbour, and search for lands where we could settle, for it was clear that we could not settle on those sand dunes, both on account of the mosquitoes and the distance from other towns. They did as they were told and arrived at the Rio Grande, which is close to Panuco. They were not able to proceed any further on account of the strong currents. Seeing how difficult the navigation had become, they turned round and made for San Juan de Ulúa, without having made any further progress.

I must now go back to say that the Indian Pitalpitoque, who remained behind to look after the food, slackened his efforts to such an extent that no provisions reached the camp and we were greatly in need of food, for the cassava turned sour from the damp and rotted and became foul with weevils and if we had not gone hunting for shellfish we should have had nothing to eat. The Indians who used to come bringing gold and fowls for barter, did not come in such numbers as on our first arrival, and those who did come were very shy and cautious and we began to count the hours that must elapse before the return of the messengers who had gone to Mexico. We were thus waiting when Tendile returned accompanied by many Indians, and after having paid their respects in the usual manner by fumigating Cortés and the rest of us with incense, he presented ten loads of fine rich feather cloth, and four *chalchihuites*, which are green stones of very great value, and held in the greatest esteem among the Indians, more than emeralds are by us, and certain other gold articles. Not counting the chalchihuites, the gold alone was said to be worth three thousand dollars. Then Tendile and Pitalpitoque went aside with Cortés and Doña Marina and Aguilar, and reported that their prince Montezuma had accepted the present and was greatly pleased with it, but as to an interview, that no more should be said about it; that these rich stones of chalchihuite should be sent to the great Emperor as they were of the highest value, each one being worth more and being esteemed more highly than a great load of gold, and that it was not worthwhile to send any more messengers to Mexico. Cortés thanked the messengers and gave them presents, but it was certainly a disappointment to him to be told so distinctly that we could not see Montezuma, and he said to some soldiers who happened to be standing near: "Surely this must be a great and rich prince, and some-day, please God, we must go and see him"—and the soldiers answered: "We wish that we were already living with him!"

Let us now leave this question of visits and relate that it was now the time of the Ave Maria, and at the sound of a bell which we had in the camp we all fell on our knees before a cross placed on a sand hill and said our prayers of the Ave Maria before the cross. When Tendile and Pitalpitoque saw us thus kneeling as they were very intelligent, they asked what was the reason that we humbled ourselves before a tree cut in that particular way. As Cortés heard this remark he said to the Padre de la Merced who was present: "It is a good opportunity, father, as we have good material at hand, to explain through our interpreters matters touching our holy faith." And then he delivered a discourse to the Caciques so fitting to the occasion that no good theologian could have bettered it. Cortés said many things very well expressed, which they thoroughly understood, and they replied that they would report them to their prince Montezuma. Cortés also told them that one of the objects for which our great Emperor had sent us to their countries was to abolish human sacrifices, and the other evil rites which they practised and to see that they did not rob one another, or worship those cursed images. And Cortés prayed them to set up in their city, in the temples where they kept the idols which they believed to be gods, a cross like the one they saw before them, and to set up in the same place an image of Our Lady, which he would give them, with her precious son in her arms, and they would see how well it would go with them, and what our God would do for them. I recall to mind that on this latest visit many Indians came with Tendile who were wishing to barter articles of gold, which, however, were of no great value. So all the soldiers set about bartering, and the gold which we gained by this barter we gave to the sailors who were out fishing in exchange for their fish so as to get something to eat, for otherwise we often underwent great privations through hunger. Cortés was pleased at this, although he pretended not to see what was going on.

When the friends of Diego Velásquez saw that some of us soldiers were bartering for gold, they asked Cortés why he permitted it, and said that Diego Velásquez did not send out the expedition in order that the soldiers should carry off most of the gold, and that it would be as well to issue an order that for the future no gold should be bartered for by anyone but Cortés himself and that all the gold already obtained should be displayed so that the royal fifth might be taken from it, and that some suitable person should be placed in charge of the treasury.

To all this Cortés replied that all they said was good, and that they themselves should name that person, and they chose Gonzalo Mejia. When this had been done, Cortés turned to them with angry mien and said: "Observe, gentlemen, that our companions are suffering great hardships from want of food, and it is for this reason that we ought to overlook things, so that they may all find something to eat; all the more so as the amount of gold they bargain for is but a trifle—and God willing, we are going to obtain a large amount of it. However, there are two sides to everything; the order has been issued that bartering for gold shall cease, as you desired; we shall see next what we will get to eat."

I will go on to relate how, one morning, we woke up to find not a single Indian in any of their huts, neither those who used to bring the food, nor those who came to trade, nor Pitalpitoque himself; they had all fled without saying a word. The cause of this, as we afterwards learned, was that Montezuma had sent orders to avoid further conversation with Cortés and those in his company; for it appears that Montezuma was very much devoted to his Idols, named Tezcatepuca, and Huichilobos, the latter the god of war, and Tezcatepuca the god of hell; and daily he sacrificed youths to them so as to get an answer from the gods as to what he should do about us; for Montezuma had already formed a plan, if we did not go off in the ships, to get us all into his power, and to raise a breed of us and also to keep us for sacrifice. As we afterwards found out, the reply given by the gods was that he should not listen to Cortés, nor to the message which he sent about setting up a cross and an image of Our Lady, and that such things should not be brought to the city. This was the reason why the Indians left our camp without warning. When we heard the news we thought that they meant to make war on us, and we were very much on the alert. One day, as I and another soldier were stationed on some sand dunes keeping a lookout, we saw five Indians coming along the beach, and so as not to raise a scare in camp over so small a matter, we permitted them to approach. When they came up to us with smiling countenances they paid us homage according to their custom, and made signs that we should take them into camp. I told my companion to remain where he was and I would accompany the Indians, for at that time my feet were not as heavy as they are now that I am old, and when we came before Cortés the Indians paid him every mark of respect and said: *Lope luzio, lope luzio*—which in the Totonac language means: "prince and great lord." These men had large holes in their lower lips, some with stone disks in them spotted with blue, and others with thin leaves of gold. They also had their ears pierced with large holes in which were placed disks of stone or gold, and in their dress and speech they differed greatly from the Mexicans who had been staying with us. When Doña Marina and Aguilar, the interpreters, heard the words *Lope luzio* they did not understand it, and Doña Marina asked in Mexican if there were not among them *Nahuatatos*, that is, interpreters of the Mexican language, and two of the five answered yes, that they understood and spoke it, and they bade us welcome and said that their chief had sent them to ask who we might be, and that it would please him to be of service to such valiant men, for it appeared that they knew about our doings at Tabasco and Champoton, and they added that they would have come to see us before but for fear of the people of Culua who had been with us (by Culua they meant Mexicans) and that they knew that three days ago they had fled back to their own country, and in the course of their talk Cortés found out that Montezuma had opponents and enemies, which he was delighted to hear, and after flattering these five messengers and giving them presents he bade them farewell, asking them to tell their chief that he would very soon come and pay them a visit. From this time on we called those Indians the *Lope luzios*.

Fearing more native attacks and irritated with Cortés's decision to move inland, supporters of Governor Velásquez argue for a return to Cuba. Others including Bernal Díaz del Castillo successfully plot to make Cortés "Captain and Chief Justice" and found the town of "Villa Rica de la Vera Cruz," thereby justifying the strategy to march toward Tenochtitlan and "settle" the land. Bernal Díaz explains the name choice: "we . . . landed on 'Holy Friday of the Cross' and 'rich' because of what that gentleman said, who approached Cortés and said to him: 'Behold rich lands! May you know how to govern them well!'" Once this "founding" is accomplished, including a promise that Cortés will receive one-fifth of the riches taken in Mexico, angry Velásquez supporters prepare to leave the group for Cuba. Cortés puts them in chains and eventually wins them over with rewards of gold and other promises.

Cortés sends Pedro de Alvarado on a reconnaissance mission for food and information. His group finds maize and further evidence of human sacrifice and bodily dismemberment. The entire Spanish force marches westward toward a fortified town called Quiahuitztlan and enters a territory ruled by the city of Cempoala. Drawing nearer they come to a ceremonial center where they see "many paper books doubled together in folds like Spanish cloth." Messengers from the caciques of Cempoala bring food and invite them to visit.

Spaniards Viewed as Gods

We slept at the little town where the twelve Indians I have mentioned had prepared quarters for us, and after being well informed about the road which we had to take to reach the town on the hill, very early in the morning we sent word to the Caciques of Cempoala that we were coming to their town and that we hoped they would approve. Cortés sent six of the Indians with this message and kept the other six as guides. He also ordered the guns, muskets, and crossbows to be kept ready for use, and sent scouts on ahead on the lookout, and the horsemen and all the rest of us were kept on the alert, and in this way we marched to within a league of the town. As we approached, twenty Indian chieftains came out to receive us in the name of the Cacique, and brought some cones made of the roses of the country with a delicious scent, which they gave to Cortés and those on horseback with every sign of friendliness, and they told Cortés that their Lord was awaiting us at our apartments, for, as he was a very stout and heavy man, he could not come out to receive us himself. Cortés thanked them and we continued our march, and as we got among the houses and saw what a large town it was, larger than any we had yet seen, we were struck with admiration. It looked like a garden with luxuriant vegetation, and the streets were so full of men and women who had come to see us, that we gave thanks to God at having discovered such a country.

Our scouts, who were on horseback, reached a great plaza with courts, where they had prepared our quarters, and it seems that during the last few days they had been whitewashed and burnished, a thing they knew well how to do, and it seemed to one of the scouts that this white surface which shone so brightly must be silver and he came back at full speed to tell Cortés that the walls of the houses were made of silver! Doña Marina and Aguilar said that it must be plaster or lime and we had a good laugh over the man's silver and excitement and always afterwards we told him that everything white looked to him like silver. I will leave our jokes and say that we reached the buildings, and the fat Cacique came out to receive us in the court. He was so fat that I shall call him by this name; and he made deep obeisance to Cortés and fumigated him, as is their custom, and Cortés embraced him and we were lodged in fine and large apartments that held us all, and they gave us food and brought some baskets of plums which were very plentiful at that season, and maize cakes, and as we arrived ravenous and had not seen so much food for a long time, we called the town Villa Viciosa.

Cortés gave orders that none of the soldiers should leave the plaza and that on no account should they give any offence to the Indians. When the fat Cacique heard that we had finished eating he sent to tell Cortés that he wished to come and visit him; and he came in company with a great number of Indian chieftains, all wearing large gold labrets and rich mantles. Cortés left his quarters to go out and meet them, and embraced the Cacique with great show of caressing and flattery, and the fat Cacique ordered a present to be brought which he had prepared, consisting of gold, jewels and cloths; but although it did not amount to much and was of little value he said to Cortés: "*Lope luzio, Lope luzio,* accept this in good part; if I had more I would give it to you!"

Cortés replied through Doña Marina and Aguilar that he would pay for the gift in good works, and that if the Cacique would tell him what he wanted to be done that he would do it for them for we were the vassals of a great prince, the Emperor Don Carlos, who had sent us to redress grievances and punish evildoers, and to put an end to human sacrifices. And he explained to them many things touching our holy religion. When the fat Cacique heard this, he sighed, and complained bitterly of the great Montezuma and his governors saying that he had recently been brought under his yoke; that all his golden jewels had been carried off, and he and his people were so grievously oppressed, that they dared do nothing without Montezuma's orders, for he was the Lord over many cities and countries and ruled over countless vassals and armies of warriors.

As Cortés knew that he could not attend at that time to the complaints which they made, he replied that he would see to it that they were relieved of their burdens, that he was now on the way to visit his *Acales* (for so they call the ships in the Indian language) and take up his residence and make his headquarters in the town of Quiahuitztlan, and that as soon as he was settled there he would consider the matter more thoroughly. To this the fat Cacique replied that he was quite satisfied that it should be so.

The next morning we left Cempoala, and there were awaiting our orders over four hundred Indian carriers, who carry fifty pounds' weight on their backs and march five leagues with it. When we saw so many Indians to carry burdens we rejoiced, as before this, those of us who had not brought Indians with us from Cuba had to carry knapsacks on our own backs. And only six or seven Cubans had been brought in the fleet. Doña Marina and Aguilar told us that in these parts in times of peace the Caciques are bound to furnish *tamenes* to carry burdens, as a matter of course, and from this time forward wherever we went we asked for Indians to carry loads.

Cortés took leave of the fat Cacique, and on the following day we set out on our march and slept at a little town which had been deserted near to Quiahuitztlan, and the people of Cempoala brought us food.

The next day about ten o'clock we reached the fortified town called Quiahuitztlan, which stands amid great rocks and lofty cliffs and if there had been any resistance it would have been very difficult to capture it. Expecting that there would be fighting we kept a good formation with the artillery in front and marched up to the fortress in such a manner that if anything had happened we could have done our duty.

We went halfway through the town without meeting a single Indian to speak to, at which we were very much surprised, for they had fled in fear that very day when they had seen us climbing up to their houses. When we had reached the top of the fortress in the plaza nearby where they had their cues and great idol houses, we saw fifteen Indians awaiting us all clad in good mantles, and each one with a brazier in his hand containing incense, and they came to where Cortés was standing and fumigated him and all the soldiers who were standing near and with deep obeisances they asked pardon for not coming out to meet us, and assured us that we were welcome and asked us to rest. And they said that they had fled and kept out of the way until they could see what sort of things we were, for they were afraid of us and of our horses, but that night they would order all the people to come back to the town.

Cortés displayed much friendship toward them, and he gave them some green beads and other trifles from Spain; and they brought fowls and maize cakes. While we were talking, someone came to tell Cortés that the fat Cacique from Cempoala was coming in a litter carried on the shoulders of many Indian chieftains. When the fat Cacique arrived he, together with the Cacique and chiefs of the town, addressed Cortés, relating their many causes of complaint against Montezuma and telling him of his great power, and this they did with such signs and tears that Cortés and those who were standing with him were moved to pity. Besides relating the way that they had been brought into subjection, they told us that every year many of their sons and daughters were demanded of them for sacrifice, and others for service in the houses and plantations of their conquerors; and they made other complaints which were so numerous that I do not remember them all; but they said that Montezuma's tax-gatherers carried off their wives and daughters if they were handsome, and ravished them, and this they did throughout the land where the Totonac language was spoken, which contained over thirty towns.

Cortés consoled them as well as he was able through our interpreters and said he would help them all he could, and would prevent these robberies and offences, as it was for that our lord the Emperor had sent us to these parts, and that they should have no anxiety, for they would soon see what we would do in the matter; and they seemed to gather some satisfaction from this assurance but their hearts were not eased on account of the great fear they had of the Mexicans.

While this conversation was going on, some Indians from the town came in great haste to tell the Caciques who were talking to Cortés, that five Mexicans, who were Montezuma's tax-gatherers, had just arrived. When they heard the news they turned pale and trembled with fear, and leaving Cortés alone they went off to receive the Mexicans, and in the shortest possible time they had decked a room with flowers, and had food cooked for the Mexicans to eat, and prepared plenty of cacao, which is the best thing they have to drink.

When these five Indians entered the town, they came to the place where we were assembled, where were the houses of the Cacique and our quarters, and approaching us with the utmost assurance and arrogance without speaking to Cortés, or to any of us, they passed us by. Their cloaks and loincloths were richly embroidered, and their shining hair was gathered up as though tied on their heads, and each one was smelling the roses that he carried, and each had a crooked staff in his hand. Their Indian servants carried fly whisks and they were accompanied by many of the chief men of the other Totonac towns, who until they had shown them to their lodgings and brought them food of the best, never left them.

As soon as they had dined they sent to summon the fat Cacique and the other chiefs, and scolded them for entertaining us in their houses, for now they would have to speak and deal with us which would not please their lord Montezuma; for without his permission and orders they should not have sheltered us, nor given us presents of golden jewels, and on this subject they uttered many threats against the fat Cacique and the other chiefs and ordered them at once to provide twenty Indians, men and women, to appease their gods for the wrong that had been done.

When he saw what was going on, Cortés asked our interpreters, Doña Marina and Jerónimo de Aguilar why the Caciques were so agitated since the arrival of those Indians, and who they were. Doña Marina who understood full well what had happened, told him what was going on; and then Cortés summoned the fat Cacique and the other chiefs, and asked them who these Indians were, and why they made such a fuss about them. They replied that they were the tax-gatherers of the great Montezuma and that they had come to inquire why they had received us in their town without the permission of their lord, and that they now demanded twenty men and women to sacrifice to their god, Huichilobos, so that he would give them victory over us, for they [the tax-gatherers] said that Montezuma had declared that he intended to capture and make slaves of us.

Cortés reassured them and bade them have no fear for he was here with all of us in his company and that he would chastise the tax-gatherers.

As soon as Cortés understood what the chiefs were telling him, he said that he had already explained to them that our lord the King had sent him to chastise evildoers and that he would not permit either sacrifice or robbery, and that as these tax-gatherers had made this demand, he ordered them to make prisoners of them at once and to hold them in custody until their lord Montezuma should be told the reason, namely, how they had come to rob them and carry off their wives and children as slaves and commit other violence. When the Caciques heard this they were thunderstruck at such daring. What!—to order the messengers of the great Montezuma to be maltreated? They said that they were too much afraid, and did not dare to do it. But Cortés went on impressing on them that the messengers should be thrown into prison at once, and so it was done, and in such a way that with some long poles and collars (such as are in use among them) they secured them so that they could not escape, and they flogged one of them who would not allow himself to be bound. Then Cortés ordered all the Caciques to pay no more tribute or obedience to Montezuma, and to make proclamation to that effect in all their friendly and allied towns, and if any tax-gatherers came to their other towns, to inform him of it, and he would send for them. So the news was known throughout that province, for the fat Cacique promptly sent messengers to spread the tidings, and the chiefs who had come in company with the tax-gatherers as soon as they had seen them taken prisoners, noised it abroad, for each one returned to his own town to deliver the order and relate what had happened.

When they witnessed deeds so marvellous and of such importance to themselves they said that no human beings would dare to do such things, and that it was the work of Teules, for so they call the idols which they worship, and for this reason from that time forth, they called us Teules, which, is as much as to say that we were either gods or demons.

I must go back and tell about the prisoners. It was the advice of all the Caciques that they should be sacrificed so that none of them could return to Mexico to tell the story; but when Cortés heard this he said that they should not be killed, and that he would take charge of them, and he set some of our soldiers to guard them. At midnight, Cortés sent for these soldiers who were in charge and said to them: "See to it that two of the prisoners are loosened, the two that appear to you the most intelligent, in such a way that the Indians of this town shall know nothing about it." And he told them to bring the prisoners to his lodging. When the prisoners came before him, he asked them through our interpreters, why they were prisoners and what country they came from, as though he knew nothing about them. They replied that the Caciques of Cempoala and of this town, with the aid of their followers and ours, had imprisoned them, and Cortés answered that he knew nothing about it, and was sorry for it, and he ordered food to be brought them and talked in a very friendly manner to them, and told them to return at once to their lord Montezuma, and tell him that we were all his good friends and entirely at his service, and that lest any harm should happen to them he had taken them from their prison, and had quarrelled with the Caciques who had seized them and that anything he could do to serve them he would do with the greatest goodwill, and that he would order the three Indians their companions who were still held prisoners to be freed and protected. That they two should go away at once and not turn back to be captured and killed.

The two prisoners replied that they valued his mercy and said they still had fear of falling into the hands of their enemies, as they were obliged to pass through their territory. So Cortés ordered six sailors to take them in a boat during the night a distance of four leagues and set them on friendly ground beyond the frontier of Cempoala. When the morning came and the Caciques of the town and the fat Cacique found that the two prisoners were missing they were all the more intent on sacrificing those that remained, if Cortés had not put it out of their power and pretended to be enraged at the loss of the two who had escaped. He ordered a chain to be brought from the ships and bound the prisoners to it, and then ordered them to be taken on board ship, saying that he himself would guard them, as such bad watch had been kept over the others. When they were once on board he ordered them to be freed from their chains and with friendly words he told them that he would soon send them back to Mexico.

Then all the Caciques of this town and of Cempoala, and all the other Totonac chiefs who had assembled, asked Cortés what was to be done, for all the force of the great Montezuma and of Mexico would descend upon them and they could not escape death and destruction.

Cortés replied with the most cheerful countenance that he and his brothers who were here with him would defend them and would kill anyone who wished to molest them. Then the Caciques and other townsmen vowed one and all that they would stand by us in everything we ordered them to do and would join their forces with ours against Montezuma and all his allies. Then, in the presence of Diego de Godoy, the scribe, they pledged obedience to His Majesty and messengers were sent to relate all that had happened to the other towns in that province. And as they no longer paid any tribute and no more tax-gatherers appeared there was no end to the rejoicing at being rid of that tyranny.

As soon as we had made this federation and friendship with more than twenty of the hill towns, known as the towns of the Totonacs, which at this time rebelled against the great Montezuma, and gave their allegiance to His Majesty, and offered to serve us—we determined with their ready help at once to found the Villa Rica de la Vera Cruz on a plain half a league from this fortresslike town, called Quiahuitztlan, and we laid out plans of a church, marketplace and arsenals, and all those things that are needed for a town, and we built a fort, and from the laying of the foundations until the walls were high enough to receive the woodwork, loopholes, watchtowers and barbicans, we worked with the greatest haste.

Cortés himself was the first to set to work to carry out the earth and stone on his back, and to dig foundations, and all his captains and soldiers followed his example; and we kept on labouring without pause so as to finish the work quickly, some of us digging foundations and others building walls, carrying water, working in the lime kilns, making bricks and tiles or seeking for food. Others worked at the timber, and the blacksmiths, for we had two blacksmiths with us, made nails. In this way we all laboured without ceasing, from the highest to the lowest; the Indians helping us, so that the church and some of the houses were soon built and the fort almost finished.

While we were thus at work it seems that the great Montezuma heard the news in Mexico about the capture of his tax-gatherers and the rebellion against his rule, and how the Totonac towns had withdrawn their allegiance and risen in revolt. He showed much anger against Cortés and all of us, and had already ordered a great army of warriors to make war on the people who had rebelled against him, and not to leave a single one of them alive. He was also getting ready to come against us with a great army with many companies.

Just at this moment there arrived two Indian prisoners whom Cortés had ordered to be set free, and when Montezuma knew that it was Cortés who had taken them out of prison, and had sent them to Mexico—and when he heard the words and promises which he had sent them to report, it pleased our Lord God that his anger was appeased, and he resolved to send and gather news of us. For this purpose he despatched his two young nephews under the charge of four old men who were Caciques of high rank, and sent with them a present of gold and cloth, and told his messengers to give thanks to Cortés for freeing his servants.

On the other hand, he sent many complaints saying that it was owing to our protection that those towns had dared to commit such a great treason as to refuse to pay him tribute and to renounce their allegiance to him, and that now, having respect for what he knew to be true—that we were those whom his ancestors had foretold were to come to their country, and must therefore be of his own lineage, how was it that we were living in the houses of these traitors? He did not at once send to destroy them, but the time would come when they would not brag of such acts of treason.

Cortés accepted the gold and the cloth, which was worth more than two thousand dollars, and he embraced the envoys and gave as an excuse that he and all of us were very good friends of the Lord Montezuma, and that it was as his servant that he still kept guard over the three tax-gatherers, and he sent at once to have them brought from the ships—where they had been well treated and well clothed, and he delivered them up to the messengers.

Then Cortés, on his part, complained greatly of Montezuma, and told the envoys how the Governor, Pitalpitoque, had left the camp one night without giving him notice, which was not well done and that he believed and felt certain that the Lord Montezuma had not authorized any such meanness, and that it was on account of this that we had come to these towns where we were now residing and where we had been well treated by the inhabitants. And he prayed him to pardon the disrespect of which the people had been guilty. As to what he said about the people no longer paying tribute, they could not serve two masters and during the time we had been there they had rendered service to us in the name of our Lord and King; but as he, Cortés, and all his brethren were on their way to visit him, and place themselves at his service, that when we were once there, then his commands would be attended to.

When this conversation and more of the same nature was over, Cortés ordered blue and green glass beads to be given to the two youths, who were Caciques of high rank, and to the four old men who had come in charge of them, who were also chieftains of importance, and paid them every sign of honour. And as there were some good meadows in the neighbourhood, Cortés ordered Pedro de Alvarado who had a good and very handy sorrel mare, and some of the other horsemen, to gallop and skirmish before the Caciques, who were delighted at the sight of their galloping, and they then took leave of Cortés and of all of us well contented, and returned to Mexico.

About this time Cortés' horse died, and he bought or was given another called "El Arriero," a dark chestnut which belonged to Ortiz, the musician, and Bartolomé García, the miner; it was one of the best of the horses that came in the fleet.

I must stop talking about this, and relate that as these towns of the sierra, our allies, and the town of Cempoala had hitherto been very much afraid of the Mexicans, believing that the great Montezuma would send his great army of warriors to destroy them, when they saw the kinsmen of the great Montezuma arriving with the presents I have mentioned, and paying such marked respect to Cortés and to all of us, they were fairly astounded and the Caciques said to one another that we must be Teules for Montezuma had fear of us, and had sent us presents of gold. If we already had reputation for valour, from this time forth it was greatly increased.

As soon as the Mexican messengers had departed, the fat Cacique with many other friendly chieftains came to beg Cortés to go at once to a town named Cingapacinga [not marked on the modern maps], two days' journey from Cempoala (that is about eight or nine leagues)—as there were many warriors of the Mexicans, assembled there, who were destroying their crops and plantations and were waylaying and ill-treating their vassals, and doing other injuries. Cortés believed the story as they told it so earnestly. He had promised that he would help them, and would destroy the Culuas and other Indians who might annoy them, and noting with what importunity they pressed their complaints, he did not know what to answer them, unless it were to say that he would willingly go, or send some soldiers under one of us, to turn these Mexicans out. As we stood there thinking the matter over he said laughingly to some of us companions who were with him: "Do you know, gentlemen, that it seems to me that we have already gained a great reputation for valour throughout this country, and that from what they saw us do in the matter of Montezuma's tax-gatherers, the people here take us for gods or beings like their idols. I am thinking that so as to make them believe that one of us is enough to defeat those Indian warriors, their enemies, who they say are occupying the town with the fortress, that we will send Heredia against them." Now, this old man was a Biscayan musketeer who had a bad twitch in his face, a big beard, a face covered with scars, and was blind of one eye and lame of one leg.

Cortés sent for him and said: "Go with these Caciques to the river which is a quarter of a league distant, and when you get there, stop to drink and wash your hands, and fire a shot from your musket, and then I will send to call you back. I want this to be done because the people here think that we are gods, or at least they have given us that name and reputation, and as you are ugly enough, they will believe that you are an idol." Heredia did what he was told, for he was an intelligent and clever man who had been a soldier in Italy, and Cortés sent for the fat Cacique and the other chieftains who were waiting for his help and assistance, and said to them: "I am sending this brother of mine with you to kill or expel all the Culuas from this town you speak of, and to bring me here as prisoners all who refuse to leave." The Caciques were surprised when they heard this and did not know whether to believe it or not, but seeing that Cortés never changed his face, they believed that what he told them was true. So old Heredia shouldered his musket and set out with them, and he fired shots into the air as he went through the forest so that the Indians might see and hear him. And the Caciques sent word to the other towns that they were bringing along a Teule to kill all the Mexicans who were in Cingapacinga. I tell this story here merely as a laughable incident, and to show the wiles of Cortés. When Cortés knew that Heredia had reached the river that he had been told about, he sent in haste to call him back, and when old Heredia and the Caciques had returned, he told them that on account of the goodwill he bore them that he, Cortés himself, would go in person with some of his brethren to afford them the help they needed and visit the country and fortress; and he ordered them at once to bring one hundred Indian carriers to transport the *tepusques*, that is, the cannon, and they came early the next morning, and we set out that same day with four hundred men and fourteen horsemen, and crossbowmen and musketeers who were all ready.

When the officers went to warn certain soldiers of the party of Diego

Velásquez to go with us, and those who had them to bring their horses, they answered haughtily that they did not want to go on any expedition but back to their farms and estates in Cuba; that they had already lost enough through Cortés having enticed them from their homes, and that he had promised them on the sand dunes that whosoever might wish to leave, that he would give them permission to do so and a ship and stores for the voyage; and for that reason there were now seven soldiers all ready to return to Cuba. When Cortés heard this he sent to summon these men before him, and when he asked them why they were doing such a mean thing they replied somewhat indignantly and said that they wondered at his honour, with so few soldiers under his command, wishing to settle in a place where there were reported to be such thousands of Indians and such great towns; that as for themselves, they were invalids and could hardly crawl from one place to another, and that they wished to return to their homes and estates in Cuba, and they asked him to grant them leave to depart as he had promised that he would do. Cortés answered them gently that it was true that he had promised it, but that they were not doing their duty in deserting from their captain's flag. And then he ordered them to embark at once without delay and assigned a ship to them and ordered them to be furnished with cassava bread and a jar of oil and such other supplies as we possessed.

When these people were ready to set sail, all of us comrades, and the Alcaldes and Regidores of our town of Villa Rica, went and begged Cortés on no account to allow anyone to leave the country, for, in the interest of the service of our Lord God and His Majesty any person asking for such permission should be considered as deserving the punishment of death in accordance with military law, as a deserter from his captain and his flag in time of war and peril, especially in this case, when, as they had stated, we were surrounded by such a great number of towns peopled by Indian warriors.

Cortés acted as though he wished to give them leave to depart, but in the end he revoked the permission and they remained baffled, and even ashamed of themselves.

We set out on our expedition to Cingapacinga and slept that night at the town of Cempoala. Two thousand Indian warriors divided into four commands, were all ready to accompany us, and on the first day we marched five leagues in good order. The next day, a little after dusk we arrived at some farms near the town of Cingapacinga, and the natives of the town heard the news of our coming. When we had already begun the ascent to the fortress and houses which stood amid great cliffs and crags, eight Indian chieftains and priests came out to meet us peacefully and asked Cortés with tears, why he wished to kill and destroy them when they had done nothing to deserve it; that we had the reputation of doing good to all and of relieving those who had been robbed and we had imprisoned the tax-gatherers of Montezuma; that these Cempoala Indians who accompanied us were hostile to them on account of old enmities over the land claims and boundaries, and under our protection they had come to kill and rob them. It was true, they said, that there was formerly a Mexican garrison in the town, but that they had left for their own country a few days earlier when they heard that we had taken the other tax-gatherers prisoner, and they prayed us not to let the matter go any further, but to grant them protection. When Cortés thoroughly understood what they had said through Doña Marina and Aguilar, without delay he ordered Captain Pedro de Alvarado, and the quartermaster Cristóbal de Olid, and all of us comrades who were with him, to restrain the Indians of Cempoala and prevent them from advancing; and this we did. But although we made haste to stop them, they had already begun to loot the farms. This made Cortés very angry and he sent for the captains who had command of the Cempoala warriors, and with angry words and serious threats, he ordered them to bring the Indian men and women and cloths and poultry that they had stolen from the farms, and forbade any Cempoala Indian to enter the town, and said that for having lied and for having come under our protection merely to rob and sacrifice their neighbours, they were deserving of death, they should keep their eyes wide open in order that such a thing did not happen again, otherwise he would not leave one of them alive. Then the caciques and captains of the Cempoalans brought to Cortés everything they had seized, both Indian men and women and poultry, and he gave them all back to their owners and with a face full of wrath he turned to the Cempoalans and ordered them to retire and sleep in the fields—and this they did.

When the caciques and priests [Papas] of that town saw how just we were in our dealings and heard the affectionate words that Cortés spoke to them through our interpreters, including matters concerning our holy religion, which it was always our custom to explain, and his advice to them to give up human sacrifices and robbing one another, and the worship of their cursed Idols, and much other good counsel which he gave them, they showed such goodwill towards us that they at once sent to call together the people of the neighbouring towns, and all gave their fealty to His Majesty.

They soon began to utter many complaints against Montezuma just as the people of Cempoala had done. On the next morning Cortés sent to summon the captains and caciques of Cempoala, who were waiting in the fields to know what we should order them to do, and still in terror of Cortés on account of the lies they had told him. When they came before him he made them make friends with the people of the town, a pact which was never broken by any of them.

Then we set out for Cempoala by another road and passed through two towns friendly to Cingapacinga, where we rested, for the sun was very hot and we were wearied with carrying our arms on our backs. A soldier took two chickens from an Indian house in one of the towns, and Cortés who happened to see it, was so enraged at that soldier for stealing chickens in a friendly town before his very eyes that he immediately ordered a halter to be put around his neck, and he would have been hanged there if Pedro de Alvarado, who chanced to be near Cortés, had not cut the halter with his sword when the poor soldier was half dead.

When we had left those towns in peace and continued our march towards Cempoala, we met the fat cacique and other chiefs waiting for us in some huts with food, for although they were Indians, they saw and understood that justice is good and sacred, and that the words Cortés had spoken to them, that we had come to right wrongs and abolish tyranny, were in conformity with what had happened on that expedition, and they were better affected towards us than ever before.

We slept the night in those huts, and all the caciques bore us company all the way to our quarters in their town. They were really anxious that we should not leave their country, as they were fearful that Montezuma would send his warriors against them, and they said to Cortés that as we were already their friends, they would like to have us for brothers, and that it would be well that we should take from their daughters, so as to have children by them; and to cement our friendship, they brought eight damsels, all of them daughters of caciques, and gave one of these cacicas, who was the niece of the fat cacique, to Cortés; and one who was the daughter of another great cacique was given to Alonzo Hernández Puertocarrero. All eight of them were clothed in the rich garments of the country, beautifully ornamented as is their custom. Each one of them had a golden collar around her neck and golden earrings in her ears, and they came accompanied by other Indian girls who were to serve as their maids. When the fat cacique presented them, he said to Cortés: "*Tecle* (which in their language means Lord)—these seven women are for your captains, and this one, who is my niece, is for you, and she is the señora of towns and vassals." Cortés received them with a cheerful countenance, and thanked the caciques for the gifts, but he said that before we could accept them and become brothers, they must get rid of those idols which they believed in and worshipped, and which kept them in darkness, and must no longer offer sacrifices to them, and that when he could see those cursed things thrown to the ground and an end put to sacrifices that then our bonds of brotherhood would be most firmly tied. He added that these damsels must become Christians before we could receive them. Every day we saw sacrificed before us three, four or five Indians whose hearts were offered to the idols and their blood plastered on the walls, and the feet, arms and legs of the victims were cut off and eaten, just as in our country we eat beef brought from the butchers. I even believe that they sell it by retail in the *tianguez* as they call their markets. Cortés told them that if they gave up these evil deeds and no longer practised them, not only would we be their friends, but we would make them lords over other provinces. All the caciques, priests and chiefs replied that it did not seem to them good to give up their idols and sacrifices and that these gods of theirs gave them health and good harvests and everything of which they had need.

When Cortés and all of us who had seen so many cruelties and infamies which I have mentioned heard that disrespectful answer, we could not stand it, and Cortés spoke to us about it and reminded us of certain good and holy doctrines and said: "How can we ever accomplish anything worth doing if for the honour of God we do not first abolish these sacrifices made to idols?" and he told us to be all ready to fight should the Indians try to prevent us; but even if it cost us our lives the idols must come to the ground that very day. We were all armed ready for a fight as it was ever our custom to be so, and Cortés told the caciques that the idols must be overthrown. When they saw that we were in earnest, the fat cacique and his captains told all the warriors to get ready to defend their idols, and when they saw that we intended to ascend a lofty cue— which stood high and was approached by many steps—the fat cacique and the other chieftains were beside themselves with fury and called out to Cortés to know why he wanted to destroy their idols, for if we dishonoured them and overthrew them, that they would all perish and we along with them. Cortés answered them in an angry tone, that he had already told them that they should offer no more sacrifices to those evil images; that our reason for removing them was that they should no longer be deluded, and that either they, themselves, must remove the idols at once, or we should throw them out and roll them down the steps, and he added that we were no longer their friends, but their mortal enemies, for he had given them good advice which they would not believe; besides he had seen their companies come armed for battle and he was angry with them and would make them pay for it by taking their lives.

When the Indians saw Cortés uttering these threats, and our interpreter Doña Marina knew well how to make them understood, and even threatened them with the power of Montezuma which might fall on them any day, out of fear of all this they replied that they were not worthy to approach their gods and that if we wished to overthrow them it was not with their consent, but that we could overthrow them and do what we chose.

The words were hardly out of their mouths before more than fifty of us soldiers had clambered up [to the temple] and had thrown down their idols which came rolling down the steps shattered to pieces. The idols looked like fearsome dragons, as big as calves, and there were other figures half men and half great dogs of hideous appearance. When they saw their idols broken to pieces the caciques and priests who were with them wept and covered their eyes, and in the Totonac tongue they prayed their gods to pardon them, saying that the matter was no longer in their hands and they were not to blame, but these Teules who had overthrown them, and that they did not attack us on account of the fear of the Mexicans.

When this was over the captains of the Indian warriors who, as I have said, had come ready to attack us, began to prepare to shoot arrows at us, and when we saw this, we laid our hands on the fat cacique and the six priests and some other chiefs, and Cortés cried out that on the least sign of hostility they would all be killed. Then the fat cacique commanded his men to retire from our front and not attempt to fight.

When the Caciques, priests, and chieftains were silenced, Cortés ordered all the idols which we had overthrown and broken to pieces to be taken out of sight and burned. Then eight priests who had charge of the idols came out of a chamber and carried them back to the house whence they had come, and burned them. These priests wore black cloaks like cassocks and long gowns reaching to their feet, and some had hoods like those worn by canons, and others had smaller hoods like those worn by Dominicans, and they wore their hair very long, down to the waist, with some even reaching down to the feet, covered with blood and so matted together that it could not be separated, and their ears were cut to pieces by way of sacrifice, and they stank like sulphur, and they had another bad smell like carrion, and as they said, and we learnt that it was true, these priests were the sons of chiefs and they abstained from women, and they fasted on certain days, and what I saw them eat was the pith of seeds of cotton when the cotton was being cleaned, but they may have eaten other things which I did not see.

Cortés made them a good speech through our interpreters, and told them that now we would treat them as brothers and would help them all we could against Montezuma and his Mexicans, and we had already sent to tell him not to make war on them or levy tribute, and that as now they were not to have any more idols in their lofty temples, he wished to leave with them a great lady who was the Mother of our Lord Jesus Christ whom we believe in and worship. He told them many things about our holy religion as well stated as only a priest could do it nowadays, so that it was listened to with goodwill. Then he ordered all the Indian masons in the town to bring plenty of lime so as to clean the place and clear away the blood which encrusted the cues and to clean them thoroughly. The next day when they were whitewashed, an altar was set up, and he told the people to adorn the altar with garlands and always keep the place swept and clean. He then ordered four of the priests to have their hair shorn, and to change their garments and clothe themselves in white, and always keep themselves clean, and he placed them in charge of the altar and of that sacred image of Our Lady. So that it should be well looked after, he left there as hermit one of our soldiers named Juan de Torres de Córdoba, who was old and lame. He ordered our carpenters to make a cross and place it on a stone support which we had already built and plastered over.

The next morning, Mass was celebrated at the altar by Padre Fray Bartolomé de Olmedo, and then an order was given to fumigate the holy image of Our Lady and the sacred cross with the incense of the country, and we showed them how to make candles of the native wax and ordered these candles always to be kept burning on the altar, for up to that time they did not know how to use the wax. The most important chieftains of that town and of others who had come together, were present at the Mass.

At the same time the eight Indian damsels were brought to be made Christians, for they were still in the charge of their parents and uncles.

And they were admonished about many things touching our holy religion and were then baptized. The niece of the fat Cacique was named Doña Catalina, and she was very ugly; she was led by the hand and given to Cortés who received her and tried to look pleased. The daughter of the great Cacique, Cuesco, was named Doña Francisca, she was very beautiful for an Indian, and Cortés gave her to Alonzo Hernández Puertocarrero. I cannot now recall to mind the names of the other six, but I know that Cortés gave them to different soldiers. When this had been done, we took leave of all the Caciques and chieftains, who from that time forward always showed us goodwill, especially when they saw that Cortés received their daughters and that we took them away with us, and after Cortés had repeated his promises of assistance against their enemies we set out for our town of Villa Rica.

The Diego Velásquez–Hernán Cortés rivalry intensifies when news arrives that the former had been granted greater powers to trade and found settlements on the mainland. Cortés's group counters by deciding to proceed inland in search of Montezuma's kingdom and in sending "all the gold that we had received" from the natives to His Majesty the Emperor. Cortés persuades all the soldiers to give up their shares for the king "so that he may bestow favours on us." This gift along with letters written by Cortés and many others is dispatched to Spain begging the king "to grant the government to Hernando Cortés."

Cortés Destroys the Ships

Within four days of the departure of our proctors to present themselves before our Lord the Emperor, some of the friends and dependents of Diego Velásquez, named Pedro Escudero, Juan Cermeño, and Gonzalo de Umbria a pilot, and a priest named Juan Diaz, and certain sailors who called themselves Peñates [*peñates* = rock men], who bore Cortés ill will, determined to seize a small ship and sail her to Cuba to give notice to Diego Velásquez and advise him how he might have an opportunity of capturing our proctors with all the gold and the messages. These men had already got their stores in the ship, and made other preparations, and the time being past midnight, were ready to embark, when one of them seems to have repented of his wish to return to Cuba, and went to report the matter to Cortés. When Cortés heard of it and learned how many there were and why they wished to get away, and who had given counsel and held the threads of the plot, he ordered the sails, compass and rudder to be removed at once from the ship, and had the men arrested, and their confessions taken down. They all told the truth, and their confessions involved in their guilt others who were remaining with us, but Cortés kept this quiet at the time as there was no other course open to him. The sentence which Cortés delivered was that Pedro Escudero and Juan Cermeño should be hanged; that the pilot Gonzalo de Umbria, should have his feet cut off, and the sailors, Peñates, should receive two hundred lashes each, and Father Juan Diaz, but for the honour of the church, would have been punished as well; as it was he gave him a great fright. I remember that when Cortés signed that sentence, he said with great grief and sighs: "Would that I did not know how to write, so as not to have to sign away men's lives!"

As soon as the sentence was carried out [as the signature of Juan Cermeño is attached to the letter written by the army in 1520, it looks as though the sentence was not executed], Cortés rode off at breakneck speed for Cempoala which was five leagues distant, and ordered two hundred of us soldiers, and all the horsemen to follow him.

Being in Cempoala, as I have stated, and discussing with Cortés questions of warfare, and our advance into the country, and going on from one thing to another, we, who were his friends, counselled him, although others opposed it, not to leave a single ship in the port, but to destroy them all at once, so as to leave no source of trouble behind, lest, when we were inland, others of our people should rebel like the last; besides, we should gain much additional strength from the masters, pilots and sailors who numbered nearly one hundred men, and they would be better employed helping us to watch and fight than remaining in port.

As far as I can make out, this matter of destroying the ships which we suggested to Cortés during our conversation, had already been decided on by him, but he wished it to appear as though it came from us, so that if anyone should ask him to pay for the ships, he could say that he had acted on our advice and we would all be concerned in their payment. Then he sent Juan de Escalante to Villa Rica with orders to bring on shore all the anchors, cables, sails, and everything else on board which might prove useful, and then to destroy the ships and preserve nothing but the boats, and that the pilots, sailing masters and sailors, who were old and no use for war, should stay at the town, and with the two nets they possessed should undertake the fishing, for there was always fish in that harbour, although they were not very plentiful. Juan de Escalante did all that he was told to do, and soon after arrived at Cempoala with a company of sailors, whom he had brought from the ships, and some of them turned out to be very good soldiers.

When this was done, Cortés sent to summon all the Caciques of the hill towns who were allied to us and in rebellion against Montezuma, and told them how they must give their service to the Spaniards who remained in Villa Rica, to finish building the church, fortress and houses, and Cortés took Juan de Escalante by the hand before them all, and said to them: "This is my brother," and told them to do whatever he should order them, and that should they need protection or assistance against the Mexicans, they should go to him and he would come in person to their assistance.

All the Caciques willingly promised to do what might be asked of them, and I remember that they at once fumigated Juan de Escalante with incense, although he did not wish it done. Escalante was a man well qualified for any post and a great friend of Cortés, so he could place him in command of the town and harbour with confidence, so that if Diego Velásquez should send an expedition there, it would meet with resistance.

When the ships had been destroyed, with our full knowledge, one morning after we had heard Mass, when all the captains and soldiers were assembled and were talking to Cortés about military matters, he begged us to listen to him, and argued with us as follows:

"We all understood what was the work that lay before us, and that with the help of our Lord Jesus Christ we must conquer in all battles and encounters [that fell to our lot], and must be as ready for them as was befitting, for if we were anywhere defeated, which pray God would not happen, we could not raise our heads again, as we were so few in numbers, and we could look for no help or assistance, but that which came from God, for we no longer possessed ships in which to return to Cuba, but must rely on our own good swords and stout hearts"—and he went on to draw many comparisons and relate the heroic deeds of the Romans. One and all we answered him that we would obey his orders, that the die was cast for good fortune, as Caesar said when he crossed the Rubicon, and that we were all of us ready to serve God and the King. After this excellent speech, which was delivered with more honied words and greater eloquence than I can express here, Cortés at once sent for the fat Cacique and reminded him that he should treat the church and cross with great reverence and keep them clean; and he also told him that he meant to depart at once for Mexico to order Montezuma not to rob or offer human sacrifices, and that he now had need of two hundred Indian carriers to transport his artillery. He also asked fifty of the leading warriors to go with us. Just as we were ready to set out, a soldier, whom Cortés had sent to Villa Rica with orders for some of the men remaining there to join him, returned from the town bearing a letter from Juan de Escalante, saying that there was a ship sailing along the coast, and that he had made smoke signals and others, and he believed that they had seen his signals, but that they did not wish to come into the harbour, and that he had sent some Spaniards to watch to what place the ships should go, and they had reported that the ship had dropped anchor near the mouth of a river distant about three leagues, and that he wished to know what he should do.

When Cortés had read the letter he at once ordered Pedro de Alvarado to take charge of all his army at Cempoala and with him Gonzalo de Sandoval. This was the first time that Sandoval was given a command.

Then Cortés rode off at once in company with four horsemen, leaving orders for fifty of the most active soldiers to follow him, and he named those of us who were to form this company and that same night we arrived at Villa Rica.

When we reached Villa Rica, Juan de Escalante came to speak to Cortés, and said that it would be as well to go to the ship that night, lest she should set sail and depart, and that he would go and do this with twenty soldiers while Cortés rested himself. Cortés replied that he could not rest, that "a lame goat must not nap," that he would go in person with the soldiers he had brought with him. So before we could get a mouthful of food we started to march along the coast and on the road we came on four Spaniards who had come to take possession of the land in the name of Francisco de Garay, the governor of Jamaica.

When Cortés heard this and knew that de Garay was staying behind in Jamaica and sending captains to do the work, he asked by what right and title those captains came. The four men replied that in the year 1518 as the fame of the lands we had discovered had spread throughout the Islands, that then Garay had information that he could beg from his Majesty the right to all the country he could discover from the Rio San Pedro and San Pablo towards the north.

As Garay had friends at Court who could support his petition, he hoped to obtain their assistance, and he sent his Mayordomo to negotiate the matter, and this man brought back a commission for him as *Adelantado* and Governor of all the land he could discover north of the Rio San Pedro and San Pablo. Under this commission he at once despatched three ships with about two hundred and seventy soldiers and supplies and horses under the captain Alonzo Álvarez Pinedo, who was settling on the Rio Panuco, about seventy leagues away; and these Spaniards said that they were merely doing what their captain told them to do, and were in no way to blame.

When Cortés had learned their business he cajoled them with many flattering speeches and asked them whether we could capture the ship. Guillen de la Loa, who was the leader of the four men, answered that they could wave to the ship and do what they could, but although they shouted and waved their cloaks and made signals, they would not come near, for, as those men said, their captain knew that the soldiers of Cortés were in the neighbourhood and had warned them to keep clear of us.

When we saw that they would not send a boat, we understood that they must have seen us from the ship as we came along the coast, and that unless we could trick them they would not send the boat ashore again. Cortés asked the four men to take off their clothes so that the four of our men could put them on, and when this was done we returned along the coast the way we had come so that our return could be seen from the ship and those on board might think that we had really gone away. Four of our soldiers remained behind wearing the other men's clothes, and we remained hidden in the wood with Cortés until past midnight, and then when the moon set it was dark enough to return to the mouth of the creek but we kept well hidden so that only the four soldiers could be seen. When the dawn broke the four soldiers began to wave their cloaks to the ship, and six sailors put off from her in a boat. Two of the sailors jumped ashore to fill two jugs with water, and we who were with Cortés kept in hiding waiting for the other sailors to land; but they stayed where they were and our four soldiers who were wearing the clothes of Garay's people pretended that they were washing their hands and kept their faces hidden. The men in the boat cried out: "Come on board, what are you doing? Why don't you come?" One of our men answered: "Come on shore for a minute and you will see." As they did not know his voice, they pushed off with their boat, and although we shouted to them they would answer nothing. We wanted to shoot at them with muskets and crossbows, but Cortés would not allow it, and said: "Let them go in peace and report to their captain."

So six soldiers from that ship remained in our company, the four we had first captured, and the two sailors who had come ashore. And we returned to Villa Rica without having had anything to eat since we first started.

War in Tlaxcala

From the little town belonging to Xalacingo, where they gave us a golden necklace and some cloth and two Indian women, we sent two Cempoalan chieftains as messengers to Tlaxcala, with a letter, and a fluffy red Flemish hat, such as was then worn. We well knew that the Tlaxcalans could not read the letter, but we thought that when they saw paper different from their own, they would understand that it contained a message; and what we sent to them was that we were coming to their town, and hoped they would receive us well, as we came, not to do them harm, but to make them our friends. We did this because in this little town they assured us that the whole of Tlaxcala was up in arms against us, for it appears that they had already received news of our approach and that we were accompanied by many friends, both from Cempoala and Xocotlan, and other towns through which we had passed. As all these towns usually paid tribute to Montezuma, the Tlaxcalans took it for granted that we were coming to attack Tlaxcala, as their country had often been entered by craft and cunning and then laid waste, and they thought that this was another attempt to do so. So as soon as our two messengers arrived with the letter and the hat and began to deliver their message, they were seized as prisoners before their story was finished, and we waited all that day and the next for an answer and none arrived.

Then Cortés addressed the chiefs of the town where we had halted, and repeated all he was accustomed to tell the Indians about our holy religion, and many other things which we usually repeated in most of the towns we passed through, and after making them many promises of assistance, he asked for twenty Indian warriors of quality to accompany us on our march, and they were given us most willingly.

After commending ourselves to God, with a happy confidence we set out on the following day for Tlaxcala, and as we were marching along, we met our two messengers who had been taken prisoner. It seems that the Indians who guarded them were perplexed by the warlike preparations and had been careless of their charge, and in fact, had let them out of prison. They arrived in such a state of terror at what they had seen and heard that they could hardly succeed in expressing themselves.

According to their account, when they were prisoners the Tlaxcalans had threatened them, saying: "Now we are going to kill those whom you call Teules, and eat their flesh, and we will see whether they are as valiant as you announce; and we shall eat your flesh too, you who come here with treasons and lies from that traitor Montezuma!"—and for all that the messengers could say, that we were against the Mexicans, and wished to be brothers to the Tlaxcalans, they could not persuade them of its truth.

When Cortés and all of us heard those haughty words, and learned how they were prepared for war, although it gave us matter for serious thought, we all cried: "If this is so, forward—and good luck to us!" We commended ourselves to God and marched on, the Alferez, Corral, unfurling our banner and carrying it before us, for the people of the little town where we had slept, as well as the Cempoalans assured us that the Tlaxcalans would come out to meet us and resist our entry into their country.

In this way we marched about two leagues, when we came upon a fortress strongly built of stone and lime and some other cement, so strong that with iron pickaxes it was difficult to demolish it and it was constructed in such a way both for offence and defence, that it would be very difficult to capture. We halted to examine it, and Cortés asked the Indians from Xocotlan for what purpose the fortress had been built in such a way. They replied that, as war was always going on between the people of Tlaxcala and their lord Montezuma, the Tlaxcalans had built this fort so strong the better to defend their towns, for we were already in their territory. We rested awhile and this, our entry into the land of Tlaxcala and the fortress, gave us plenty to think about. Cortés said: "Sirs, let us follow our banner which bears the sign of the holy cross, and through it we shall conquer!" Then one and all we answered him: "May good fortune attend our advance, for in God lies the true strength." So we began our march again in the order I have already noted.

We had not gone far when our scouts observed about thirty Indians who were spying. These spies wore devices and feather headdresses, and when our scouts observed them they came back to give us notice. Cortés then ordered the same scouts to follow the spies, and to try and capture one of them without hurting them; and then he sent five more mounted men as a support, in case there should be an ambush. Then all our army hastened on, for our Indian friends who were with us said that there was sure to be a large body of warriors waiting in ambush.

When the thirty Indian spies saw the horsemen coming towards them, and beckoning to them with their hands, they would not wait for them to come up and capture one of them; furthermore, they defended themselves so well, that with their swords and lances they wounded some of the horses.

When our men saw how fiercely the Indians fought and that their horses were wounded, they were obliged to kill five of the Indians. As soon as this happened, a squadron of Tlaxcalans, more than three thousand strong, which was lying in ambush, fell on them all of a sudden, with great fury and began to shower arrows on our horsemen who were now all together; and they made a good fight with their arrows and fire-hardened darts, and did wonders with their two-banded swords. At this moment we came up with our artillery, muskets and crossbows, and little by little the Indians gave way, but they had kept their ranks and fought well for a considerable time.

In this encounter, they wounded four of our men and I think that one of them died of his wounds a few days later.

As it was now late the Tlaxcalans beat a retreat and we did not pursue them; they left about seventeen dead on the field, and many wounded. Where these skirmishes took place the ground was level and there were many houses and plantations of maize and magueys, which is the plant from which they make their wine.

We slept near a stream, and with the grease from a fat Indian whom we had killed and cut open, we dressed our wounds, for we had no oil, and we supped very well on some dogs which the Indians breed [for food] for all the houses were abandoned and the provisions carried off, and they had even taken the dogs with them, but these came back to their homes in the night, and there we captured them, and they proved good enough food.

All night we were on the alert with watches and patrols and scouts, and the horses bitted and saddled, in fear lest the Indians would attack us.

The next day, as we marched on, two armies of warriors approached to give us battle. They numbered six thousand men and they came on us with loud shouts and the din of drums and trumpets, as they shot their arrows and hurled their darts and acted like brave warriors. Cortés ordered us to halt, and sent forward the three prisoners whom we had captured the day before, to tell them not to make war on us as we wished to treat them as brothers. He also told one of our soldiers, named Diego de Godoy, who was a royal notary, to watch what took place so that he could bear witness if it should be necessary, so that at some future time we should not have to answer for the deaths and damages which were likely to take place, for we begged them to keep the peace.

When the three prisoners whom we had sent forward began to speak to the Indians, it only increased their fury and they made such an attack on us that we could not endure it. Then Cortés shouted:—"Santiago— and at them!" and we attacked them with such impetuosity that we killed and wounded many of them with our fire and among them three captains. They then began to retire towards some ravines, where over forty thousand warriors and their captain general, named Xicotenga, were lying in ambush, all wearing a red and white device for that was the badge and livery of Xicotenga.

As there was broken ground there we could make no use of the horses, but by careful maneuvering we got past it, but the passage was very perilous for they made play with their good archery, and with their lances and broadswords did us much hurt, and the hail of stones from their slings was even more damaging. When we reached the level ground with our horsemen and artillery, we paid them back and slew many of them, but we did not dare to break our formation, for any soldier who left the ranks to follow some of the Indian captains and swordsmen was at once wounded and ran great danger. As the battle went on they surrounded us on all sides and we could do little or nothing. We dared not charge them, unless we charged all together, lest they should break up our formation; and if we did charge them, as I have said, there were twenty squadrons ready to resist us, and our lives were in great danger for they were so numerous they could have blinded us with handfuls of earth, if God in his great mercy had not succoured us.

While we found ourselves in this conflict among these great warriors and their fearful broadswords, we noticed that many of the strongest among them crowded together to lay hands on a horse. They set to work with a furious attack, laying hands on a good mare known to be very handy either for sport or for charging. The rider, Pedro de Moron, was a very good horseman, and as he charged with three other horsemen into the ranks of the enemy the Indians seized hold of his lance and he was not able to drag it away, and others gave him cuts with their broadswords, and wounded him badly, and then they slashed at the mare, and cut her head off at the neck so that it hung by the skin, and she fell dead. If his mounted companions had not come at once to his rescue they would also have finished killing Pedro de Moron. We might possibly have helped him with our whole battalion, but I repeat again that we hardly dared to move from one place to another for fear that they would finally rout us, and we could not move one way or another; it was all we could do to hold our own and prevent ourselves from being defeated. However, we rushed to the conflict around the mare and managed to save Moron from the hands of the enemy who were already dragging him off half dead, and we cut the mare's girths, so as not to leave the saddle behind. In that act of rescue, ten of our men were wounded and I remember that at the same time we killed four of the (Indian) captains, for we were advancing in close order and we did great execution with our swords. When this had happened, the enemy began to retire, carrying the mare with them, and they cut her in pieces to exhibit in all the towns of Tlaxcala, and we learnt afterwards that they made an offering to their idols of the horseshoes, of the Flemish felt hat and the two letters which we had sent them offering peace.

We were a full hour fighting in the fray and our shots must have done the enemy much damage for they were so numerous and in such close formation, that each shot must have hit many of them. Horsemen, musketeers, crossbowmen, swordsmen and those who used lance and shield, one and all, we fought like men to save our lives and to do our duty, for we were certainly in the greatest danger in which we had ever found ourselves. Later on they told us that we killed many Indians in this battle, and among them eight of their leading captains, sons of the old Caciques who lived in their principal towns, and for this reason they drew off in good order. We did not attempt to follow them, and we were not sorry for it as we were so tired out we could hardly stand, and we stayed where we were in that little town. All the country round was thickly peopled, and they even have some houses underground like caves in which many of the Indians live.

The place where this battle took place is called Tehuacingo, and it was fought on the 2nd day of the month of September in the year 1519. When we saw that victory was ours, we gave thanks to God who had delivered us from such great danger.

From the field of battle we withdrew the whole force to some Cues which were strong and lofty like a fortress. We dressed the wounded men, who numbered fifteen, with the fat of an Indian. One man died of his wounds. We also doctored four or five horses which had received wounds, and we rested and supped very well that night, for we found a good supply of poultry and little dogs in the houses. And taking every precaution by posting spies, patrols and scouts, we rested until the next morning.

In that battle we captured fifteen Indians, two of them chieftains. There was one peculiarity that the Tlaxcalans showed in this and all the other battles—that was to carry off any Indian as soon as he was wounded so that we should not be able to see their dead.

As we felt weary after the battles we had fought, and many of the soldiers and horses were wounded and some died there, and it was necessary to repair the crossbows and replenish our stock of darts, we passed one day without doing anything worthy of mention. The following morning Cortés said that it would be as well for all the horsemen who were fit for work to scour the country, so that the Tlaxcalans should not think that we had given up fighting on account of the last battle, and that they should see that we meant to follow them up; and it was better for us to go out and attack them than for them to come and attack us and thus find out our weakness. As the country was level and thickly populated, we set out with seven horsemen and a few musketeers and crossbowmen and about two hundred soldiers and our Indian allies, leaving the camp as well guarded as was possible. In the houses and towns through which we passed, we captured about twenty Indian men and women without doing them any hurt, but our allies, who are a cruel people, burnt many of the houses and carried off much poultry and many dogs for food. When we returned to the camp which was not far off, Cortés set the prisoners free, after giving them something to eat, and Doña Marina and Aguilar spoke kindly to them and gave them beads and told them not to be so mad any longer, but to make peace with us, as we wished to help them and treat them as brothers. Then we also released the two prisoners who were chieftains and they were given another letter, and were to tell the high Caciques who lived in the town—which was the capital of all the towns of the province—that we had not come to do them any harm or to annoy them, but to pass through their country on our way to Mexico to speak to Montezuma. The two messengers went to Xicotenga's camp which was distant about two leagues, and when they gave him the letter and our message the reply that their captain Xicotenga gave them was, that we might go to his town where his father was living; that there peace would be made by satiating themselves on our flesh, and honour paid to his gods with our hearts and blood, and that we should see his answer the very next day.

When Cortés and all of us heard that haughty message, as we were already tired out with the battles and encounters we had passed through, we certainly did not think that things looked well. So Cortés flattered the messengers with soft words for it seemed that they had lost all fear, and ordered them to be given some strings of beads, as he wished to send them back as messengers of peace.

Cortés then learned from them more fully all about the Captain Xicotenga, and what forces he had with him. They told him that Xicotenga had many more men with him now than he had when he attacked us before, for he had five captains with him and each captain had brought ten thousand warriors. This was the way in which the count was made: Of the followers of Xicotenga who was blind from age—the father of the captain of the same name—ten thousand; of the followers of another great chief named Mase Escasi, another ten thousand; of the followers of another great chief named Chichimecatecle the same number; of another great Cacique, lord of Topeyanco, named Tecapacaneca, another ten thousand; and of another great chief named Guaxoban, another ten thousand; so that there were in all fifty thousand. That their banner and standard had been brought out, which was a white bird with the appearance of an ostrich, with wings outstretched, as though it wished to fly, and that each company had its device and uniform, for each Cacique had a different one, as do our dukes and counts in our own Castile.

All that I have here said we accepted as perfectly true, for certain Indians among those whom we had captured and who were released that day, related it very clearly, although they were not then believed. When we knew this, as we were but human and feared death, many of us, indeed the majority of us, confessed to the Padre de la Merced and to the priest, Juan Diaz, who were occupied all night in hearing our repentance and commending us to God and praying that He would pardon us and save us from defeat.

The Spaniards' Plea for Peace and Alliance

The next morning, the 5th September, 1519, we mustered the horses. There was not one of the wounded men who did not come forward to join the ranks and give as much help as he could. The crossbowmen were warned to use the store of darts very cautiously, some of them loading while the others were shooting, and the musketeers were to act in the same way, and the men with sword and shield were instructed to aim their cuts and thrusts at the bowels [of their enemies] so that they would not dare to come as close to us as they did before. With our banner unfurled, and four of our comrades guarding the standard-bearer, Corral, we set out from our camp. We had not marched half a quarter of a league before we began to see the fields crowded with warriors with great feather crests and distinguishing devices, and to hear the blare of horns and trumpets.

All the plain was swarming with warriors and we stood four hundred men in number, and of those many sick and wounded. And we knew for certain that this time our foe came with the determination to leave none of us alive excepting those who would be sacrificed to their idols.

How they began to charge on us! What a hail of stones sped from their slings! As for their bowmen, the javelins lay like corn on the threshing floor; all of them barbed and fire-hardened, which would pierce any armour and would reach the vitals where there is no protection; the men with swords and shields and other arms larger than swords, such as broadswords, and lances, how they pressed on us and with what valour and what mighty shouts and yells they charged upon us! The steady bearing of our artillery, musketeers and crossbowmen, was indeed a help to us, and we did the enemy much damage, and those of them who came close to us with their swords and broadswords met with such swordplay from us that they were forced back and they did not close in on us so often as in the last battle. The horsemen were so skillful and bore themselves so valiantly that, after God who protected us, they were our bulwark. However, I saw that our troops were in considerable confusion, so that neither the shouts of Cortés nor the other captains availed to make them close up their ranks, and so many Indians charged down on us that it was only by a miracle of swordplay that we could make them give way so that our ranks could be reformed. One thing only saved our lives, and that was that the enemy were so numerous and so crowded one on another that the shots wrought havoc among them, and in addition to this they were not well commanded for all the captains with their forces could not come into action and from what we knew, since the last battle had been fought there had been disputes and quarrels between the Captain Xicotenga and another captain the son of Chichimecatecle over what the one had said to the other, that he had not fought well in the previous battle; to this the son of Chichimecatecle replied that he had fought better than Xicotenga, and was ready to prove it by personal combat. So in this battle Chichimecatecle and his men would not help Xicotenga and we knew for a certainty that he had also called on the company of Huexotzinco to abstain from fighting. Besides this, ever since the last battle they were afraid of the horses and the musketry, and the swords and crossbows, and our hard fighting; above all was the mercy of God which gave us strength to endure. So Xicotenga was not obeyed by two of the commanders, and we were doing great damage to his men, for we were killing many of them, and this they tried to conceal for as they were so numerous, whenever one of their men was wounded, they immediately bound him up and carried him off on their shoulders, so that in this battle, as in the last, we never saw a dead man.

The enemy were already losing heart, and knowing that the followers of the other two captains whom I have already named, would not come to their assistance, they began to give way. It seems that in that battle we had killed one very important captain, and the enemy began to retreat in good order our horsemen following them at a hard gallop for a short distance, for they could not sit their horses for fatigue, and when we found ourselves free from that multitude of warriors, we gave thanks to God.

In this engagement, one soldier was killed, and sixty were wounded, and all the horses were wounded as well. They gave me two wounds, one in the head with a stone, and one in the thigh with an arrow; but this did not prevent me from fighting, and keeping watch, and helping our soldiers, and all the soldiers who were wounded did the same; for if the wounds were not very dangerous, we had to fight and keep guard, wounded as we were, for few of us remained unwounded.

Then we returned to our camp, well contented, and giving thanks to God. We buried the dead in one of those houses which the Indians had built underground, so that the enemy should not see that we were mortals, but should believe that, as they said, we were Teules. We threw much earth over the top of the house, so that they should not smell the bodies, then we doctored all the wounded with the fat of an Indian. It was cold comfort to be even without salt or oil with which to cure the wounded. There was another want from which we suffered, and it was a severe one—and that was clothes with which to cover ourselves, for such a cold wind came from the snow mountains, that it made us shiver, for our lances and muskets and crossbows made a poor covering. That night we slept with more tranquillity than on the night before, when we had so much duty to do, with scouting, spies, watchmen and patrols.

After the battle which I have described was over, in which we had captured three Indian chieftains, our Captain Cortés sent them at once in company with the two others who were in our camp and who had already been sent as messengers and ordered them to go to the Caciques of Tlaxcala and tell them that we begged them to make peace and to grant us a passage through their country on our way to Mexico, and to say that if they did not now come to terms, we would slay all their people, but that as we were well disposed towards them we had no desire to annoy them, unless they gave us reason to do so; and he said many flattering things to them so as to make friends of them, and the messengers then set out eagerly for the capital of Tlaxcala and gave their message to all the Caciques already mentioned by me whom they found gathered in council with many other elders and priests. They were very sorrowful both over the want of success in the war and at the death of those captains, their sons and relations, who had fallen in battle. As they were not very willing to listen to the message, they decided to summon all the soothsayers, priests and those others called *Tacal naguas*, and they told them to find out from their witchcraft, charms and lots what people we were, and if by giving us battle day and night without ceasing we could be conquered, and to say if we were Teules, as the people of Cempoala asserted, and to tell them what things we ate, and ordered them to look into all these matters with the greatest care.

When the soothsayers and wizards and many priests had got together and made their prophecies and forecasts, and performed all the other rites according to their use, it seems that they said that by their divinations they had found out we were men of flesh and blood and ate poultry and dogs and bread and fruit, when we had them, and that we did not eat the flesh nor the hearts of the Indians whom we killed. It seems that our Indian friends whom we had brought from Cempoala had made them believe that we were Teules, and that we ate the hearts of Indians, and that the cannon shot forth lightning, such as falls from heaven and that the Lurcher, which was a sort of lion or tiger, and the horses, were used to catch Indians when we wanted to kill them, and much more nonsense of the same sort.

The worst of all that the priests and wizards told the Caciques was, that it was not during the day, but only at night that we could be defeated, for as night fell, all our strength left us. When the Caciques heard this, and they were quite convinced of it, they sent to tell their captain general Xicotenga that as soon as it was possible he should come and attack using great force by night. On receiving this order Xicotenga assembled ten thousand of the bravest of his Indians and came to our camp, and from three sides they began alternately to shoot arrows and throw single pointed javelins from their spear throwers, and from the fourth side the swordsmen and those armed with macanas and broadswords approached so suddenly that they felt sure that they would carry some of us off to be sacrificed. Our Lord God provided otherwise, for secretly as they approached, they found us well on the alert, and as soon as our outposts and spies perceived the great noise of their movement, they ran at breakneck speed to give the alarm, and as we were all accustomed to sleep ready shod, with our arms on us and our horses bitted and saddled, and with all our arms ready for use, we defended ourselves with guns, crossbows and swordplay so that they soon turned their backs. As the ground was level and there was a moon the horsemen followed them a little way, and in the morning we found lying on the plain about twenty of them dead and wounded. So they went back with great loss and sorely repenting this night expedition, and I have it said, that as what the priests and wizards had advised did not turn out well they sacrificed two of them.

That night, one of our Indian friends from Cempoala was killed and two of our soldiers were wounded and one horse, and we captured four of the enemy. When we found that we had escaped from that impetuous attack we gave thanks to God, and we buried our Cempoala friend and tended the wounded and the horse, and slept the rest of the night after taking every precaution to protect the camp as was our custom.

When we awoke and saw how all of us were wounded, even with two or three wounds, and how weary we were and how others were sick and clothed in rags, and knew that Xicotenga was always after us, and already over forty-five of our soldiers had been killed in battle, or succumbed to disease and chills, and another dozen of them were ill, and our Captain Cortés himself was suffering from fever as well as the Padre de la Merced, and what with our labours and the weight of our arms which we always carried on our backs, and other hardships from chills and the want of salt, for we could never find any to eat, we began to wonder what would be the outcome of all this fighting, and what we should do and where we should go when it was finished. To march into Mexico we thought too arduous an undertaking because of its great armies, and we said to one another that if those Tlaxcalans, which our Cempoalan friends had led us to believe were peacefully disposed, could reduce us to these straits, what would happen when we found ourselves at war with the great forces of Montezuma? In addition to this we had heard nothing from the Spaniards whom we had left settled in Villa Rica, nor they of us. As there were among us very excellent gentlemen and soldiers, steady and valiant men of good counsel, Cortés never said or did anything [important] without first asking advice, and acting in concert with us.

One and all we put heart into Cortés, and told him that he must get well again and reckon upon us, and that as with the help of God we had escaped from such perilous battles, our Lord Jesus Christ must have preserved us for some good end; that he [Cortés] should at once set our prisoners free and send them to the head Caciques, so as to bring them to peace, when all that had taken place would be pardoned, including the death of the mare.

Let us leave this and say how Doña Marina who, although a native woman, possessed such manly valour that, although she had heard every day how the Indians were going to kill us and eat our flesh with chili, and had seen us surrounded in the late battles, and knew that all of us were wounded and sick, yet never allowed us to see any sign of fear in her, only a courage passing that of woman. So Doña Marina and Jerónimo de Aguilar spoke to the messengers whom we were now sending and told them that they must come and make peace at once, and that if it was not concluded within two days we should go and kill them all and destroy their country and would come to seek them in their city, and with these brave words they were despatched to the capital where Xicotenga the elder and Mase Escasi were residing.

When the messengers arrived at Tlaxcala, they found the two principal Caciques in consultation, namely: Mase Escasi and Xicotenga, the elder (the father of the Captain General Xicotenga). When they had heard the embassy, they were undecided and kept silence for a few moments, and it pleased God to guide their thoughts towards making peace with us; and they sent at once to summon all the other Caciques and captains who were in their towns, and those of a neighbouring province called Huexotzingo who were their friends and allies, and when all had come together Mase Escasi and Xicotenga, the elder, who were very wise men, made them a speech, as we afterwards learned, to the following effect, if not exactly in these words:

"Brothers and friends, you have already seen how many times these Teules who are in this country expecting to be attacked, have sent us messengers asking us to make peace, saying that they come to assist us and adopt us as brothers; and you have also seen how many times they have taken prisoners numbers of our vassals to whom they do no harm, and whom they quickly set free. You well know how we have three times attacked them with all our forces, both by day and by night, and have failed to conquer them, and that they have killed during the attacks we made on them, many of our people, and of our sons, relations and captains. Now, again, they have sent to ask us to make peace and the people of Cempoala whom they are bringing in their company say that they are the enemies of Montezuma and his Mexicans, and have ordered the towns of the Totonac sierra and those of Cempoala no longer to pay tribute to Montezuma. You will remember well enough that the Mexicans make war on us every year, and have done so for more than a hundred years, and you can readily see that we are hemmed in in our own lands, so that we do not dare to go outside even to seek for salt, so that we have none to eat, and we have no cotton, and bring in very little cotton cloth, and if some of our people go out or have gone out to seek for it, few of them return alive, for those traitorous Mexicans and their allies kill them or make slaves of them. Our wizards [tacal naguas] and soothsayers and priests have told us what they think about the persons of these Teules, and that they are very valiant. It seems to me that we should seek to be friends with them, and in either case, whether they be men or Teules, that we should make them welcome, and that four of our chieftains should set out at once and take them plenty to eat, and should offer them friendship and peace, so that they should assist us and defend us against our enemies, and let us bring them here to us, and give them women, so that we may have relationship with their offspring, for the ambassadors whom they have sent to treat for peace, tell us that they have some women with them."

When they had listened to this discourse, all the Caciques and chiefs approved of it and said that it was a wise decision and that peace should be made at once, and that notice should be sent to the Captain Xicotenga and the other captains who were with him to return at once and not to attack again, and that they should be told that peace was already made, and messengers were immediately sent off to announce it. However, the Captain Xicotenga the younger would not listen to the four chiefs, and got very angry and used abusive language against them, and said he was not for peace, for he had already killed many of the Teules and a mare, and that he wished to attack us again by night and completely conquer us and slay us.

When his father, Xicotenga the elder, and Mase Escasi and the other Caciques heard this reply they were very angry and sent orders at once to the captains and to all the army that they should not join Xicotenga in attacking us again, and should not obey him in anything that he ordered unless it was in making peace. And even so he would not obey, and when they [the caciques] saw the disobedience of their captain, they at once sent the same four chieftains whom they had sent before, to bring food to our camp and treat for peace in the name of all Tlaxcala and Huexotzingo, but, from fear of Xicotenga the younger, the four old men did not come at that time.

When Mase Escasi and Xicotenga the elder, and the greater number of the Caciques of the capital of Tlaxcala sent four times to tell their captain not to attack us but to go and treat for peace, he was very close to our camp, and they sent to the other captains who were with him and told them not to follow him unless it was to accompany him when he went to see us peacefully.

As Xicotenga was bad tempered and obstinate and proud, he decided to send forty Indians with food, poultry, bread and fruit and four miserable looking old Indian women, and much copal and many parrots' feathers. From their appearance we thought that the Indians who brought this present came with peaceful intentions, and when they reached our camp they fumigated Cortés with incense without doing him reverence, as was usually their custom. They said: "The Captain Xicotenga sends you all this so that you can eat. If you are savage Teules, as the Cempoalans say you are, and if you wish for a sacrifice, take these four women and sacrifice them and you can eat their flesh and hearts, but as we do not know your manner of doing it, we have not sacrificed them now before you; but if you are men, eat the poultry and the bread and fruit, and if you are tame Teules we have brought you copal and parrots' feathers; make your sacrifice with that."

Cortés answered through our interpreters that he had already sent to them to say that he desired peace and had not come to make war, but had come to entreat them and make clear to them that they should not kill or sacrifice anyone as was their custom to do. That we were all men of bone and flesh just as they were, and not Teules but Christians, and that it was not the custom to kill anyone; that had we wished to kill people, many opportunities of perpetrating cruelties had occurred during the frequent attacks they had made on us, both by day and night. That for the food they had brought he gave them thanks, and that they were not to be as foolish as they had been, but should now make peace.

It seems that these Indians whom Xicotenga had sent with the food were spies. They remained with us that day and the following night, and some of them went with messages to Xicotenga and others arrived. Our friends from Cempoala were sure that they were spies, and were the more suspicious of them in that they had been told that Xicotenga was all ready with a large number of warriors to attack our camp by night, and the Cempoalans at that time took it for a joke or bravado, and not believing it they had said nothing to Cortés; but Doña Marina heard of it at once and she repeated it to Cortés.

So as to learn the truth, Cortés had two of the most honest looking of the Tlaxcalans taken apart from the others, and they confessed that they were spies; then two others were taken and they also confessed and added that their Captain Xicotenga was awaiting their report to attack us that night with all his companies. When Cortés heard this he let it be known throughout the camp that we were to keep on the alert. Then he had seventeen of those spies captured and cut off the hands of some and the thumbs of others and sent them to the Captain Xicotenga to tell him that he had had them thus punished for daring to come in such a way, and to tell him that he might come when he chose by day or by night, for we should await him here two days, and that if he did not come within those two days that we would go and look for him in his camp, and that we would already have gone to attack them and kill them, were it not for the liking we had for them, and that now they should quit their foolishness and make peace.

They say that it was at the very moment that those Indians set out with their hands and thumbs cut off, that Xicotenga wished to set out from his camp with all his forces to attack us by night as had been arranged; but when he saw his spies returning in this manner he wondered greatly and asked the reason of it, and they told him all that had happened, and from this time forward he lost his courage and pride, and in addition to this one of his commanders with whom he had wrangles and disagreements during the battles which had been fought, had left the camp with all his men.

While we were in camp and were busy polishing our arms and making arrows, each one of us doing what was necessary to prepare for battle, at that moment one of our scouts came hurrying in to say that many Indian men and women with loads were coming along the high road from Tlaxcala, and were making for our camp. Cortés and all of us were delighted at this news, for we believed that it meant peace, as in fact it did, and Cortés ordered us to make no display of alarm and not to show any concern, but to stay hidden in our huts. Then, from out of all those people who came bearing loads, the four chieftains advanced who were charged to treat for peace, according to the instructions given by the old Caciques. Making signs of peace by bowing the head, they came straight to the hut where Cortés was lodging and placed one hand on the ground and kissed the earth and three times made obeisance and burnt copal, and said that all the Caciques of Tlaxcala and their allies and vassals, friends and confederates, were come to place themselves under the friendship and peace of Cortés and of his brethren the Teules who accompanied him. They asked his pardon for not having met us peacefully, and for the war which they had waged on us, for they had believed and held for certain that we were friends of Montezuma and his Mexicans, who have been their mortal enemies from times long past, for they saw that many of his vassals who paid him tribute had come in our company, and they believed that they were endeavouring to gain an entry into their country by guile and treachery, as was their custom to do, so as to rob them of their women and children; and this was the reason why they did not believe the messengers whom we had sent to them; that now they came to beg pardon for their audacity, and had brought us food, and that every day they would bring more and trusted that we would receive it with the friendly feeling with which it was sent; that within two days the captain Xicotenga would come with other Caciques and give a further account of the sincere wish of all Tlaxcala to enjoy our friendship.

As soon as they had finished their discourse they bowed their heads and placed their hands on the ground and kissed the earth. Then Cortés spoke to them through our interpreters very seriously, pretending he was angry, and said that there were reasons why we should not listen to them and should reject their friendship, for as soon as we had entered their country we sent to them offering peace and had told them that we wished to assist them against their enemies, the Mexicans, and they would not believe it and wished to kill our ambassadors; and not content with that, they had attacked us three times both by day and by night, and had spied on us and held us under observation; and in the attacks which they made on us we might have killed many of their vassals, but he would not, and he grieved for those who were killed; but it was their own fault and he had made up his mind to go to the place where the old chiefs were living and to attack them; but as they had now sought peace in the name of that province, he would receive them in the name of our lord the King and thank them for the food they had brought. He told them to go at once to their chieftains and tell them to come or send to treat for peace with fuller powers, and that if they did not come we would go to their town and attack them.

He ordered them to be given some blue beads to be handed to their Caciques as a sign of peace, and he warned them that when they came to our camp it should be by day and not by night, lest we should kill them.

Then those four messengers departed, and left in some Indian houses a little apart from our camp, the Indian women whom they had brought to make bread, some poultry, and all the necessaries for service, and twenty Indians to bring wood and water. From now on they brought us plenty to eat, and when we saw this and believed that peace was a reality, we gave great thanks to God for it. It had come in the nick of time, for we were already lean and worn out and discontented with the war, not knowing or being able to forecast what would be the end of it.

Ambassadors from Montezuma Arrive

As our Lord God, through his great loving kindness, was pleased to give us victory in those battles in Tlaxcala, our fame spread throughout the surrounding country, and reached the ears of the great Montezuma in the great City of Mexico; and if hitherto they took us for Teules, from now on they held us in even greater respect as valiant warriors, and terror fell on the whole country at learning how, being so few in number and the Tlaxcalans in such great force, we had conquered them and that they had sued us for peace. So that now Montezuma, the great Prince of Mexico, powerful as he was, was in fear of our going to his city, and sent five chieftains, men of much importance, to our camp at Tlaxcala to bid us welcome, and say that he was rejoiced at our great victory against so many squadrons of warriors, and he sent a present, a matter of a thousand dollars' worth of gold, in very rich jewelled ornaments, worked in various shapes, and twenty loads of fine cotton cloth, and he sent word that he wished to become the vassal of our great Emperor, and that he was pleased that we were already near his city, on account of the goodwill that he bore Cortés and all his brothers, the Teules, who were with him and that he [Cortés] should decide how much tribute he wished for every year for our great Emperor, and that he [Montezuma] would give it in gold and silver, cloth and chalchihuites, provided we would not come to Mexico. This was not because he would not receive us with the greatest willingness, but because the land was rough and sterile, and he would regret to see us undergo such hardships which perchance he might not be able to alleviate as well as he could wish. Cortés answered by saying that he highly appreciated the goodwill shown us, and the present which had been sent, and the offer to pay tribute to His Majesty, and he begged the messengers not to depart until he went to the capital of Tlaxcala, as he would despatch them from that place, for they could then see how that war ended.

While Cortés was talking to the ambassadors of Montezuma, and he wanted to take some rest, for he was ill with fever, they came to tell him that the Captain Xicotenga was arriving with many other Caciques and Captains, all clothed in white and red cloaks, half of the cloak was white and the other half red, for this was the device and livery of Xicotenga [who was approaching] in a very peaceful manner, and was bringing with him in his company about fifty chieftains.

When Xicotenga reached Cortés' quarters he paid him the greatest respect by his obeisance, and ordered much copal to be burned. Cortés, with the greatest show of affection, seated him by his side and Xicotenga said that he came on behalf of his father and of Mase Escasi and all the Caciques, and Commonwealth of Tlaxcala to pray Cortés to admit them to our friendship, and that he came to render obedience to our King and Lord, and to ask pardon for having taken up arms and made war upon us. That this had been done because they did not know who we were, and they had taken it for certain that we had come on behalf of their enemy Montezuma, and for that reason had endeavoured to defend themselves and their country, and were obliged to show fight. He said that they were a very poor people who possessed neither gold, nor silver, nor precious stones, nor cotton cloth, nor even salt to eat, because Montezuma gave them no opportunity to go out and search for it, and that although their ancestors possessed some gold and precious stones, they had been given to Montezuma on former occasions when, to save themselves from destruction, they had made peace or a truce, and this had been in times long past; so that if they had nothing to give now, we must pardon them for it, for poverty and not the want of goodwill was the cause of it. He made many complaints of Montezuma and his allies who were all hostile to them and made war on them, but they had defended themselves very well. Now they had thought to do the same against us, but they could not do it although they had gathered against us three times with all their warriors, and we must be invincible, and when they found this out about our persons they wished to become friends with us and the vassals of the great prince the Emperor Don Carlos, for they felt sure that in our company they and their women and children would be guarded and protected, and would not live in dread of the Mexican traitors, and he said many other words placing themselves and their city at our disposal.

Xicotenga was tall, broad shouldered and well made; his face was long, pockmarked and coarse, he was about thirty-five years old and of a dignified deportment.

Cortés thanked him very courteously, in a most flattering manner, and said that he would accept them as vassals of our King and Lord, and as our own friends. Then Xicotenga begged us to come to his city, for all the Caciques, elders and priests were waiting to receive us with great rejoicing. Cortés replied that he would go there promptly, and would start at once, were it not for some negotiations which he was carrying on with the great Montezuma, and that he would come after he had despatched the messengers. Then Cortés spoke somewhat more sharply and severely about the attacks they had made on us both by day and night, adding that as it could not now be amended he would pardon it. Let them see to it that the peace we now were granting them was an enduring one, without any change, for otherwise he would kill them and destroy their city and that he [Xicotenga] should not expect further talk about peace, but only of war.

When Xicotenga and all the chieftains who had come with him heard these words they answered one and all, that the peace would be firm and true, and that to prove it they would all remain with us as hostages.

The Mexican Ambassadors were present during all these discussions and heard all the promises that were made, and the conclusion of peace weighed on them heavily, for they fully understood that it boded them no good. And when Xicotenga had taken his leave these Ambassadors of Montezuma half laughingly asked Cortés whether he believed any of those promises which were made on behalf of all Tlaxcala [alleging] that it was all a trick which deserved no credence, and the words were those of traitors and deceivers; that their object was to attack and kill us as soon as they had us within their city in a place where they could do so in safety; that we should bear in mind how often they had put forth all their strength to destroy us and had failed to do so, and had lost many killed and wounded, and that now they offered a sham peace so as to avenge themselves. Cortés answered them, with a brave face, that their alleged belief that such was the case did not trouble him, for even if it were true he would be glad of it so as to punish them [the Tlaxcalans] by taking their lives, that it did not matter to him whether they attacked him by day or by night, in the city or in the open, he did not mind one way or the other, and it was for the purpose of seeing whether they were telling the truth that he was determined to go to their city.

The Ambassadors seeing that he had made up his mind begged him to wait six days in our camp as they wished to send two of their companions with a message to their Lord Montezuma, and said that they would return with a reply within six days. To this Cortés agreed, on the one hand because, as I have said he was suffering from fever, and on the other because, although when the Ambassadors had made these statements he had appeared to attach no importance to them he thought that there was a chance of their being true and that until there was greater certainty of peace, they were of a nature requiring much consideration.

As at the time that this peace was made the towns all along the road that we had traversed from our Villa Rica de Vera Cruz were allied to us and friendly, Cortés wrote to Juan de Escalante who, as I have said, remained in the town to finish building the fort, and had under his command the sixty old or sick soldiers who had been left behind. In these letters he told them of the great mercies which our Lord Jesus Christ had vouchsafed to us in the victories which we had gained in our battles and encounters since we had entered the province of Tlaxcala, which had now sued for peace with us, and asked that all of them would give thanks to God for it. He also told them to see to it that they always kept on good terms with our friends in the towns of the Totonacs, and he told him to send at once two jars of wine which had been left behind, buried in a certain marked place in his lodgings, and some sacred wafers for the Mass, which had been brought from the Island of Cuba for those which we had brought on this expedition were already finished.

These letters were most welcome, and Escalante wrote in reply to say what had happened in the town, and all that was asked for arrived very quickly.

About this time we set up a tall and sumptuous cross in our camp, and Cortés ordered the Indians of Tzumpantzingo and those who dwelt in the houses near our camp to whitewash it, and it was beautifully finished.

I must cease writing about this and return to our new friends the Caciques of Tlaxcala, who when they saw that we did not go to their city, came themselves to our camp and brought poultry and tunas [tuna = the prickly pear, the fruit of the Nopal cactus (*Opuntia* sp.)], which were then in season, each one brought some of the food which he had in his house and gave it to us with the greatest goodwill without asking anything in return, and they always begged Cortés to come with them soon to their city. As we had promised to wait six days for the return of the Mexicans, Cortés put off the Tlaxcalans with fair speeches. When the time expired, according to their word, six chieftains, men of great importance, arrived from Mexico, and brought a rich present from the great Montezuma consisting of valuable gold jewels wrought in various shapes worth three thousand pesos in gold, and two hundred pieces of cloth, richly worked with feathers and other patterns. When they offered this present the Chieftains said to Cortés that their Lord Montezuma was delighted to hear of our success, but that he prayed him most earnestly on no account to go with the people of Tlaxcala to their town, nor to place any confidence in them, that they wished to get him there to rob him of his gold and cloth, for they were very poor, and did not possess a decent cotton cloak among them, and that the knowledge that Montezuma looked on us as friends, and was sending us gold and jewels and cloth, would still more induce the Tlaxcalans to rob us.

Cortés received the present with delight, and said that he thanked them for it, and would repay their Lord Montezuma with good works, and if he should perceive that the Tlaxcalans had that in mind against which Montezuma had sent them to warn him, they would pay for it by having all their lives taken, but he felt sure they would be guilty of no such villainy, and he still meant to go and see what they would do.

Cortés begged the Mexican Ambassadors to wait for three days for the reply to their prince, as he had at present to deliberate and decide about the past hostilities and the peace which was now offered, and the Ambassadors said that they would wait.

When the old Caciques from all Tlaxcala saw that we did not come to their city, they decided to come to us, some in litters, others in hammocks or carried on men's backs, and others on foot. These were the Caciques already mentioned by me, named Mase Escasi, Xicotenga the elder, Guaxolocingo, Chichimecatecle, and Tecapaneca of Topeyanco. They arrived at our camp with a great company of chieftains, and with every sign of respect made three obeisances to Cortés and to all of us, and they burnt copal and touched the ground with their hands and kissed it, and Xicotenga the elder began to address Cortés in the following words:

"Malinche, Malinche, we have sent many times to implore you to pardon us for having attacked you and to state our excuse, that we did it to defend ourselves from the hostility of Montezuma and his powerful forces, for we believed that you belonged to his party and were allied to him. If we had known what we now know, we should not only have gone out to receive you on the roads with supplies of food, but would even have had them swept for you, and we would even have gone to you to the sea where you keep your acales (which are the ships). Now that you have pardoned us, what I and all these Caciques have come to request is, that you will come at once with us to our City, where we will give you of all that we possess and will serve you with our persons and property. Look to it Malinche that you do not decide otherwise or we will leave you at once, for we fear that perchance these Mexicans may have told you some of the falsehoods and lies that they are used to tell about us. Do not believe them nor listen to them, for they are false in everything, and we well know that it is on their account that you have not wished to come to our City."

Cortés answered them with cheerful mien and said, that it was well-known, many years before we had come to these countries, what a good people they were and that it was on this account that he wondered at their attacking us.

He said that the Mexicans who were there were [merely] awaiting a reply which he was sending to their Lord Montezuma.

He thanked them heartily for what they said about our going at once to their City and for the food which they were continually sending and for their other civilities, and he would repay them by good deeds. He said that he would already have set out for their City if he had had anyone to carry the *tepuzques* (that is, the cannon). As soon as they heard these words the Tlaxcalans were so pleased that one could see it in their faces, and they said: "So this is the reason why you have delayed, and never mentioned it." And in less than half an hour they provided over five hundred Indian carriers.

The next day, early in the morning we began our march along the road to the Capital of Tlaxcala.

The messengers of Montezuma had already begged Cortés that they might go with us to see how affairs were settled at Tlaxcala and that he would despatch them from there, and that they should be quartered in his own lodgings so as not to receive any insults, for, as they said, they feared such from the Tlaxcalans.

Before going on any further I wish to say that in all the towns we had passed through, and in others where they had heard of us, Cortés was called Malinche, and so I will call him Malinche from now henceforth in all the accounts of conversations which were held with any of the Indians.

The reason why he was given this name is that Doña Marina, our interpreter, was always in his company, particularly when any Ambassadors arrived, and she spoke to them in the Mexican language. So that they gave Cortés the name of "Marina's Captain" and for short Malinche.

I also wish to say that from the time we entered the territory of Tlaxcala until we set out for the city, twenty-four days had elapsed, and we entered the city on the 23rd September, 1519.

When the Caciques saw that our baggage was on the way to their city, they at once went on ahead to see that everything was ready for our reception and that our quarters were decked with garlands.

Many of the chieftains came near to Cortés and accompanied him, and when we entered the town there was not space in the streets and on the roofs for all the Indian men and women with happy faces who came out to see us. They brought us about twenty cones made of sweet scented native roses of various colours, and gave them to Cortés and to the other soldiers whom they thought were Captains, especially to the horsemen. When we arrived at some fine courts where our quarters were, Xicotenga the elder and Mase Escasi took Cortés by the hand and led him into his lodging. For each one of us had been prepared a bed of matting such as they use, and sheets of henequen. Our friends whom we had brought from Cempoala and Xocotlan were lodged near to us, and Cortés asked that the messengers from the great Montezuma might also be given quarters close to his lodging.

Although we could see clearly that we were in a land where they were well disposed towards us, and were quite at peace, we did not cease to be very much on the alert as was always our custom, and it appears that one captain whose duty it was to station the scouts and spies and watchmen said to Cortés, "It seems, sir, that the people are very peaceful and we do not need so many guards, nor to be so circumspect as we are accustomed to be." Cortés replied, "Well, gentlemen, I can myself see all that you have brought to my notice, but it is a good custom always to be prepared, and although these may be very good people, we must not trust to their peacefulness, but must be as alert as we should be if they intended to make war on us and we saw them coming on to the attack, and whether it was done in good faith or bad, we must remember that the great Montezuma has sent to warn us." Xicotenga the elder and Mase Escasi were greatly annoyed with Cortés, and said to him through our interpreters: "Malinche, either you take us for enemies or you show signs in what we see you doing that you have no confidence in us or in the peace which you promised to us and we promised to you, and we say this to you because we see that you keep watch, and travelled along the road all ready for action in the same way as when you attacked our squadrons, and we believe that you, Malinche, do this on account of the treasons and abominations which the Mexicans had told you in secret so as to turn you against us. See to it that you do not believe them, for you are established here, and we will give you all that you desire, even ourselves and our children, and we are ready to die for you, so you can demand as hostages whatever you may wish."

Cortés and all of us marvelled at the courtesy and affection with which they spoke, and Cortés answered them that he had always believed them, and there was no need of hostages, it was enough to note their goodwill, and that as to being on the alert, it was always our custom, and they must not be offended at it. When this conversation was over, other chiefs arrived with a great supply of poultry and maize bread, and tunas and other fruits and vegetables which the country produced, and supplied the camp very liberally, and during the twenty days that we stayed there there was always more than enough to eat.

Baptizing Tlaxcalan Women

It appears that it had been arranged among all the Caciques to give us from among their daughters and nieces the most beautiful of the maidens who were ready for marriage, and Xicotenga the elder said: "Malinche, so that you may know more clearly our goodwill towards you and our desire to content you in everything, we wish to give you our daughters, to be your wives, so that you may have children by them, for we wish to consider you as brothers as you are so good and valiant. I have a very beautiful daughter who has not been married, and I wish to give her to you," so also Mase Escasi and all the other Caciques said that they would bring their daughters, and that we should accept them as wives, and they made many other speeches and promises. Throughout the day Mase Escasi and Xicotenga the elder never left Cortés' immediate neighbourhood. As Xicotenga the elder was blind from old age, he felt Cortés all over his head and face and beard and over all his body.

Cortés replied to them that, as to the gift of the women, he and all of us were very grateful and would repay them with good deeds as time went on. The Padre de la Merced was present and Cortés said to him: "Señor Padre, it seems to me that this would be a good time to make an attempt to induce these Caciques to give up their Idols and their sacrifices, for they will do anything we tell them to do on account of the great fear they have of the Mexicans." The friar replied: "Sir, that is true, but let us leave the matter until they bring their daughters and then there will be material to work upon, and your honour can say that you do not wish to accept them until they give up sacrifices—if that succeeds, good, if not we shall do our duty."

The next day the same old Caciques came and brought with them five beautiful Indian maidens, and for Indians they were very good-looking and well adorned, and each of the Indian maidens brought another

Indian girl as her servant, and all were the daughters of Caciques, and Xicotenga said to Cortés: "Malinche, this is my daughter who has never been married and is a maiden, take her for your own," and he gave her to him by the hand, "and let the others be given to the captains." Cortés expressed his thanks, and with every appearance of gratification said that he accepted them and took them as our own, but that for the present they should remain in the care of their parents. The Chiefs asked him why he would not take them now, and Cortés replied that he wished first to do the will of God our Lord, and that for which our Lord the King had sent us, which was to induce them to do away with their Idols, and no longer to kill and sacrifice human beings, and to lead them to believe in that which we believed, that is in one true God, and he told them much more touching our holy faith, and in truth he expressed it very well, for Doña Marina and Aguilar, our interpreters, were already so expert at it that they explained it very clearly. He also told them that if they wished to be our brothers and to have true friendship with us, so that we should willingly accept their daughters and take them, as they said, for our wives, that they should at once give up their evil Idols and believe in and worship our Lord God and things would prosper with them, and when they died their souls would go to Heaven to enjoy glory everlasting; but that if they went on making sacrifices as they were accustomed to do to their Idols, they would be led to Hell where they would burn forever in live flames, and what they replied to it all is as follows:

"Malinche, we have already understood from you before now, and we thoroughly believe that this God of yours and this great Lady are very good, but look you, you have only just come to our homes, as time goes on we shall understand your beliefs much more clearly, and see what they are, and will do what is right. But how can you ask us to give up our Teules which for many years our ancestors have held to be gods and have made sacrifices to them and have worshipped them? Even if we, who are old men, might wish to do it to please you, what would our priests say, and all our neighbours, and the youths and children throughout the province?

They would rise against us, especially as the priests have already consult the greatest of our Teules, and he told them not to forget the sacrifice of men and all the rites they were used to practise, otherwise the gods would destroy the whole province with famine, pestilence and war." Thus they spoke and gave as their answer that we should not trouble to talk of them on that subject again for they were not going to leave off making sacrifices even if they were killed for it.

When we heard that reply which they gave so honestly and without fear, the Padre de la Merced, who was a wise man, and a theologian, said: "Sir, do not attempt to press them further on this subject, for it is not just to make them Christians by force, and I would not wish that you should do what we did in Cempoala, that is, destroy their Idols, until they have some knowledge of our Holy Faith." Furthermore two gentlemen, namely Juan Velásquez de Leon and Francisco de Lugo, spoke to Cortés and said: "The Padre is right in what he says, you have fulfilled your duty with what you have done, and do not touch again on this matter when speaking to these Caciques," and so the subject dropped. What we induced the Caciques to do, by entreaty, was at once to clear out one of the cues, which was close by and had been recently built, and after removing the Idols, to clean it and whitewash it so that we could place a cross in it and the image of Our Lady, and this they promptly did. Then Mass was said there and the Cacicas were baptized. The daughter of the blind Xicotenga was given the name of Doña Luisa, and Cortés took her by the hand and gave her to Pedro de Alvarado, and said to Xicotenga that he to whom he gave her was his brother and his Captain, and that he should be pleased at it as she would be well treated by him, and Xicotenga was contented that it should be so. The daughter or niece of Mase Escasi was named Doña Elvira and she was very beautiful and it seems to me that she was given to Juan Velásquez de Leon. The others were given baptismal names, always with the title of nobility (doña) and Cortés gave them to Gonzalo de Sandoval and Cristóbal de Olid and Alonzo de Ávila. When this had been done Cortés told them the reason why he put up two crosses, and that it was because their Idols were afraid of them, and that wherever we were encamped or wherever we slept they were placed in the roads; and at all this they were quite content.

Before I go on any further I wish to say about the Cacica the daughter of Xicotenga, who was named Doña Luisa and was given to Pedro de Alvarado, that when they gave her to him all the greater part of Tlaxcala paid reverence to her, and gave her presents, and looked on her as their mistress, and Pedro de Alvarado, who was then a bachelor, had a son by her named Don Pedro and a daughter named Doña Leonor, who is now the wife of Don Francisco de la Cueva, a nobleman, and a cousin of the Duke of Alburquerque, who had by her four or five sons, very good gentlemen.

Cortés then took those Caciques aside and questioned them very fully about Mexican affairs. Xicotenga, as he was the best informed and a great chieftain, took the lead in talking, and from time to time he was helped by Mase Escasi who was also a great chief.

He said that Montezuma had such great strength in warriors that when he wished to capture a great city or make a raid on a province, he could place a hundred and fifty thousand men in the field, and this they knew well from the experience of the wars and hostilities they had had with them for more than a hundred years past.

Cortés asked them how it was that with so many warriors as they said came down on them they had never been entirely conquered. They answered that although, the Mexicans sometimes defeated them and killed them, and carried off many of their vassals for sacrifice, many of the enemy were also left dead on the field and others were made prisoners, and that they never could come so secretly that they did not get some warning, and that when they knew of their approach they mustered all their forces and with the help of the people of Huexotzingo they defended themselves and made counterattacks. That as all the provinces which had been raided by Montezuma and placed under his rule were ill disposed towards the Mexicans, and that as their inhabitants were carried off by force to the wars, they did not fight with goodwill; indeed, it was from these very men that they received warnings, and for this reason they had defended their country to the best of their ability.

The place from which the most continuous trouble came to them was a very great city a day's march distant, which is called Cholula, whose inhabitants were most treacherous. It was there that Montezuma secretly mustered his companies and, as it was nearby, they made their raids by night. Moreover, Mase Escasi said that Montezuma kept garrisons of many warriors stationed in all the provinces in addition to the great force he could bring from the city, and that all the provinces paid tribute of gold and silver, feathers, stones, cloth and cotton, and Indian men and women for sacrifice and others for servants, that he [Montezuma] was such a great prince that he possessed everything he could desire, that the houses where he dwelt were full of riches and [precious] stones and chalchihuites which he had robbed and taken by force from those who would not give them willingly, and that all the wealth of the country was in his hands.

Then they spoke of the great fortifications of the city, and what the lake was like, and the depth of water, and about the causeways that gave access to the city, and the wooden bridges in each causeway, and how one can go in and out [by water] through the opening that there is in each bridge, and how when the bridges are raised one can be cut off between bridge and bridge and not be able to reach the city. How the greater part of the city was built in the lake, and that one could not pass from house to house except by drawbridges and canoes which they had ready. That all the houses were flat roofed and all the roofs were provided with parapets so that they could fight from them.

They brought us pictures of the battles they had fought with the Mexicans painted on large henequen cloths, showing their manner of fighting.

As our captain and all of us had already heard about all that these Caciques were telling us, we changed the subject, and started them on another more profound, which was, how was it that they came to inhabit that land, and from what direction had they come? and how was it that they differed so much from and were so hostile to the Mexicans, seeing that their countries were so close to one another?

They said that their ancestors had told them, that in times past there had lived among them men and women of giant size with huge bones, and because they were very bad people of evil manners that they had fought with them and killed them, and those of them who remained died off. So that we could see how huge and tall these people had been they brought us a leg bone of one of them which was very thick and the height of a man of ordinary stature, and that was the bone from the hip to the knee. I measured myself against it and it was as tall as I am although I am of fair size. They brought other pieces of bone like the first but they were already eaten away and destroyed by the soil. We were all amazed at seeing those bones and felt sure that there must have been giants in this country, and our Captain Cortés said to us that it would be well to send that great bone to Castile so that His Majesty might see it, so we sent it with the first of our agents who went there.

These Caciques also told us that they had learnt from their forefathers that one of their Idols, to which they paid the greatest devotion, had told them that men would come from distant lands in the direction of the rising sun to subjugate them and govern them, and that if we were those men, they were rejoiced at it, as we were so good and brave, and that when they made peace with us they had borne in mind what their Idols had said, and for this reason they had given us their daughters so as to obtain relations who would defend them against the Mexicans.

When they had finished their discourse we were all astounded and said can they possibly have spoken the truth? Then our Captain Cortés replied to them and said that certainly we came from the direction of the sunrise and that our Lord the King had sent us for this very purpose that we should become as brothers to them; for he had heard of them, and that he prayed God to give us grace, so that by our hands and our intercession they would be saved, and we all said Amen.

I feel bound to dwell on one other thing which they discussed with us, and that is the volcano near Huexotzingo which at the time we were in Tlaxcala was throwing out much fire, much more than usual. Our Captain Cortés and all of us were greatly astonished as we had never seen such a thing before. One of our Captains named Diego de Ordás was very anxious to go and see what sort of a thing it was, and asked leave of the general to ascend the mountain, and leave was given [this account of the ascent of Popocatepetl appears to be given in the wrong place by Bernal Díaz: it probably took place when the Spaniards left Cholula—see Cortés's Second Letter], and he even expressly ordered him to do it. He took with him two of our soldiers and certain Indian chiefs from Huexotzingo, and the chiefs that he took with him frightened him by saying that when one was halfway up Popocatepetl, for so the volcano is called, one could not endure the shaking of the ground and the flames and stones and ashes which were thrown out of the mountain, and that they would not dare to ascend further than where stood the cues of the Idols which are called the Teules of Popocatepetl. Nevertheless Diego de Ordás and his two companions went on up until they reached the summit, and the Indians who had accompanied them remained below and did not dare to make the ascent. It appears from what Ordás and the two soldiers said afterwards, that, as they ascended, the volcano began to throw out great tongues of flame, and half-burnt stones of little weight and a great quantity of ashes, and that the whole of the mountain range where the volcano stands was shaken, and that they stopped still without taking a step in advance for more than an hour, when they thought that the outburst had passed and not so much smoke and ashes were being thrown out; then they climbed up to the mouth which was very wide and round, and opened to the width of a quarter of a league. From this summit could be seen the great city of Mexico, and the whole of the lake, and all the towns which were built in it. This volcano is distant twelve or thirteen leagues from Mexico.

Ordás was delighted and astonished at the sight of Mexico and its cities and after having had a good look at the view he returned to Tlaxcala with his companions, and the Indians of Huexotzingo and of Tlaxcala looked on it as a deed of great daring. When he told his story to Captain Cortés and all of us, we were greatly astonished at it, for at that time we had not seen nor heard of such things as we have today, when we know all about it, and many Spaniards and even some Franciscan friars have made the ascent to the crater.

When Diego de Ordás went to Castile he asked the King for it [the mountain] as his [coat of] arms and his nephew, who lives at Puebla, now bears them.

Since we have been settled in this land we have never known the volcano to throw out so much fire or make such a noise as it did when we first arrived, and it has even remained some years without throwing out any fire, up to the year 1539 when it threw up great flames and stones and ashes.

I must tell how in this town of Tlaxcala we found wooden houses furnished with gratings, full of Indian men and women imprisoned in them, being fed up until they were fat enough to be sacrificed and eaten. These prisons we broke open and destroyed, and set free the prisoners who were in them, and these poor Indians did not dare to go in any direction, only to stay there with us and thus escape with their lives. From now on, in all the towns that we entered, the first thing our Captain ordered us to do was to break open these prisons and set free the prisoners.

These prisons are common throughout the land and when Cortés and all of us saw such great cruelty, he showed that he was very angry with the Caciques of Tlaxcala, and they promised that from that time forth they would not kill and eat any more Indians in that way. I said [to myself] of what benefit were all those promises, for as soon as we turned our heads they would commit the same cruelties.

When our Captain remembered that we had already been resting in Tlaxcala for seventeen days, and that we had heard so much said about the great wealth of Montezuma and his flourishing city, he arranged to take counsel with all those among our captains and soldiers whom he could depend on as wishing to advance, and it was decided that our departure should take place without delay, but there was a good deal of dissent expressed in camp about this decision, for some soldiers said that it was a very rash thing to go and enter into such a strong city, as we were so few in number, and they spoke of the very great strength of Montezuma. Our Captain Cortés replied that there was now no other course open to us, for we had constantly asserted and proclaimed that we were going to see Montezuma, so that other counsels were useless.

When Xicotenga and Mase Escasi, the lords of Tlaxcala, saw that we were determined to go to Mexico, their spirits were weighed down, and they were constantly with Cortés advising him not to enter on such an undertaking.

Our captain said to them that he thanked the Caciques for their good counsel, and he showed them much affection, and made them many promises, and he gave as presents to Xicotenga the elder, and to Mase Escasi and most of the other Caciques a great part of the fine cloth which Montezuma had presented, and told them that it would be a good thing to make peace between them and the Mexicans, so that they should become friends and they could then obtain salt and cotton and other merchandise. Xicotenga replied that peace was useless, and that enmity was deeply rooted in their hearts, for such were the Mexicans that, under cover of peace, they would only be guilty of greater treachery, for they never told the truth in anything that they promised, and that he was not to trouble about saying more on the subject, and that they could only again implore us to take care not to fall into the hands of such bad people.

We went on to talk about the road which we should take to reach Mexico, for the ambassadors from Montezuma, who remained with us and were to be our guides, said that the most level and the best road was by the city of Cholula, where the people were vassals of Montezuma and there we should receive proper attention. To all of us this appeared to be good advice, that we should go by that city. When however the Caciques of Tlaxcala heard that we wished to go by a road which the Mexicans were choosing for us, they became very sorrowful, and begged us in any case to go by Huexotzingo, where the people were their relations and our friends, and not by way of Cholula, for in Cholula Montezuma always kept his double dealings concealed.

For all that they talked and advised us not to enter into that city, our Captain (in accordance with our counsel which had been well talked over) still determined to go by Cholula, on the one hand, because all agreed that it was a large town, and well furnished with towers, and fine and tall cues, and situated on a beautiful plain, and on the other hand, because it was almost surrounded by other considerable towns and could provide ample supplies, and our friends of Tlaxcala were near at hand. We intended to stay there until we could decide how to get to Mexico without having to fight for it, for the great power of the Mexicans was a thing to be feared, and unless God our Lord, by His Divine mercy which always helped us and gave us strength, should first of all so provide, we could not enter Mexico in any other manner.

After much discussion it was settled that we should take the road by Cholula, and Cortés at once sent messengers to ask the people of Cholula how it happened that being so near to us they had not come to visit us, and pay that respect which was due to us as the messengers of so great a prince as the King who had sent us to the country to tell them of their salvation. He then requested all the Caciques and priests of that city to come and see us and give their fealty to our Lord and King, and if they did not come he would look upon them as ill disposed towards us.

While Cortés was talking to us all and to the Caciques of Tlaxcala about our departure and about warfare, they came to tell them that four Ambassadors, all four chieftains who were bringing presents, had arrived in the town.

Cortés ordered them to be called, and when they came before him they paid the greatest reverence to him and to all of us soldiers who were there with him, and presented their gift of rich jewels of gold and many sorts of workmanship, well worth two thousand dollars, and ten loads of cloth beautifully embroidered with feathers.

Cortés received them most graciously, and the Ambassadors said, on behalf of their Lord Montezuma, that he greatly wondered that we should stay so many days among a people who were so poor and ill bred, who were so wicked, and such traitors and thieves that they were not fit even to be slaves, and that when either by day or night we were most off our guard they would kill us in order to rob us. That he begged us to come at once to his city, and he would give us of all that he possessed, although it would not be as much as we deserved or he would like to give, and that although all the supplies had to be carried into the city, he would provide for us as well as he was able.

Montezuma did this so as to get us out of Tlaxcala, for he knew of the friendship we had made, and how, to perfect it, the Tlaxcalans had given their daughters to Malinche, and the Mexicans fully understood that our confederation could bring no good to them.

Cortés thanked the messengers with many caressing expressions and signs of affection, and gave as his answer that he would go very soon to see their Lord Montezuma, and he begged them to remain a few days with us.

At that time Cortés decided that two of our Captains should go and see and speak to the great Montezuma, and see the great city of Mexico and Pedro de Alvarado and Bernaldino Vásquez de Tápia had already set out on the journey, accompanied by some of the ambassadors of the great Montezuma who were used to being with us, and the four ambassadors who had brought the present remained with us as hostages. However, we did not think it well advised, so he wrote to them telling them to return at once.

The ambassadors with whom they had been travelling gave an account of their doings to Montezuma, and he asked them what sort of faces and general appearance had these two Teules who were coming to Mexico, and whether they were Captains, and it seems that they replied that Pedro de Alvarado was of very perfect grace both in face and person, that he looked like the Sun, and that he was a Captain, and in addition to this they brought with them a picture of him with his face very naturally portrayed, and from that time forth they gave him the name of Tonatio, which means the Sun or the child of the Sun, and so they called him ever after. Of Bernaldino Vásquez de Tápia, they said that he was a robust man, and of a very pleasant disposition, and that he also was a captain, and Montezuma was much disappointed that they had turned back again.

I have already said how our Captain sent messengers to Cholula to tell the Caciques of that City to come and see us at Tlaxcala. When the Caciques understood what Cortés ordered them to do, they thought that it would be sufficient to send four unimportant Indians to make their excuses. The Caciques of Tlaxcala were present when these messengers arrived, and they said to our Captain that the people of Cholula had sent those Indians to make a mock of him and of all of us, for they were only commoners of no standing; so Cortés at once sent them back with four other Cempoala Indians to tell the people of Cholula that they must send some chieftains, and as the distance was only five leagues that they must arrive within three days, otherwise he should look on them as rebels; that when they came he wished to receive them as friends and brothers as he had received their neighbours and people of Tlaxcala, and that if they did not wish for our friendship that we should take measures which would displease them and anger them.

When the Caciques of Cholula had listened to that embassy they answered that they were not coming to Tlaxcala, for the Tlaxcalans were their enemies, and they knew that they [the Tlaxcalans] had said many evil things about them and about their Lord Montezuma; that it was for us to come to their city and to leave the confines of Tlaxcala, and that then if they did not do what they ought to do we could treat them as such as we had sent to say they were.

When our Captain saw that the excuse that they made was a just one we resolved to go to Cholula, and as soon as the Caciques of Tlaxcala perceived that we were determined to go there, they said to Cortés: "So you wish to trust to the Mexicans and not to us who are your friends, we have already told you many times that you must beware of the people of Cholula and of the power of Mexico, and so that you can receive all the support possible from us, we have got ready ten thousand warriors to accompany you." Cortés thanked them very heartily for this, but after consultation with all of us it was agreed that it would not be advisable to take so many warriors to a country in which we were seeking friends, and that it would be better to take only one thousand, and this number we asked of the Tlaxcalans and said that the rest should remain in their houses.

violent resistance

THE MASSACRE AT CHOLULA

One morning we started on our march to the city of Cholula and that day we went on to sleep at a river which runs within a short league of the city, and there they put up for us some huts and ranchos. This same night the Caciques of Cholula sent some chieftains to bid us welcome to their country, and they brought supplies of poultry and maize bread, and said that in the morning all the Caciques and priests would come out to receive us, and they asked us to forgive their not having come sooner. Cortés thanked them both for the food they had brought and for the goodwill which they showed us.

At dawn we began to march and the Caciques and priests and many other Indians came out to receive us, most of them were clothed in cotton garments made like tunics. They came in a most peaceful manner and willingly, and the priests carried braziers containing incense with which they fumigated our Captain and us soldiers who were standing near him. When these priests and chiefs saw the Tlaxcalan Indians who came with us, they asked Doña Marina to tell the General that it was not right that their enemies with arms in their hands should enter their city in that manner. When our Captain understood this, he ordered the soldiers and the baggage to halt, and, when he saw us all together and that no one was moving, he said: "It seems to me, Sirs, that before we enter Cholula these Caciques and priests should be put to the proof with a friendly speech, so that we can see what their wishes may be; for they come complaining of our friends the Tlaxcalans and they have much cause for what they say, and I want to make them understand in fair words the reason why we come to their city, and as you gentlemen already know, the Tlaxcalans have told us that the Cholulans are a turbulent people, and, as it would be a good thing that by fair means they should render their obedience to His Majesty, this appears to me to be the proper thing to do."

Then he told Doña Marina to call up the Caciques and priests to where he was stationed on horseback with all of us around him, and three chieftains and two priests came at once, and they said: "Malinche, forgive us for not coming to Tlaxcala to see you and to bring food, it was not for want of goodwill but because Mase Escasi and Xicotenga and all Tlaxcala are our enemies, and have said many evil things of us and of the Great Montezuma our Prince, and as though what they said were not enough, they now have the boldness, under your protection, to come armed into our city, and we beg you as a favour to order them to return to their own country, or at least to stay outside in the fields and not to enter our city in such a manner." But as for us they said that we were very welcome.

As our Captain saw that what they said was reasonable, he at once sent Pedro de Alvarado and Cristóbal de Olid to ask the Tlaxcalans to put up their huts and ranchos there in the fields, and not to enter the city with us, excepting those who were carrying the cannon, and our friends from Cempoala, and he told them to explain to the Tlaxcalans that the reason why he asked them to do so was that all the Caciques and priests were afraid of them, and that when we left Cholula on our way to Mexico we would send to summon them, and that they were not to be annoyed at what he was doing. When the people of Cholula knew what Cortés had done, they appeared to be much more at ease.

Then Cortés began to make a speech to them, saying that our Lord and King had sent us to these countries to give them warning and command them not to worship Idols, nor sacrifice human beings, or eat their flesh, and as the road to Mexico, whither we were going to speak with the Great Montezuma, passed by there, and there was no other shorter road, we had come to visit their city and to treat them as brothers. As other great Caciques had given their obedience to His Majesty, it would be well that they should give theirs as the others had done.

They replied that we had hardly entered into their country, yet we already ordered them to give up their Teules, and that they could not do it. As to giving their obedience to our King they were content to do so.

And thus they pledged their word, but it was not done before a notary. When this was over we at once began our march towards the City, and so great was the number of people who came out to see us that both the streets and housetops were crowded, and I do not wonder at this for they had never seen men such as we are, nor had they ever seen horses.

They lodged us in some large rooms where we were all together with our friends from Cempoala and the Tlaxcalans who carried the baggage, and they fed us on that day and the next very well and abundantly.

After the people of Cholula had received us in the festive manner already described, and most certainly with a show of goodwill, it presently appeared that Montezuma sent orders to his ambassadors, who were still in our company, to negotiate with the Cholulans that an army of twenty thousand men which Montezuma had sent and equipped should, on entering the city, join with them in attacking us by night or by day, get us into a hopeless plight and bring all of us that they could capture bound to Mexico. And he sent many presents of jewels and cloths, also a golden drum, and he also sent word to the priests of the city that they were to retain twenty of us to sacrifice to their Idols.

The warriors whom Montezuma sent were stationed in some ranchos and some rocky thickets about half a league from Cholula and some were already posted within the houses.

They fed us very well for the first two days, but on the third day they neither gave us anything to eat nor did any of the Caciques or priests make their appearance, and if any Indians came to look at us, they did not approach us, but remained some distance off, laughing at us as though mocking us. When our Captain saw this, he told our interpreters to tell the Ambassadors of the Great Montezuma to order the Caciques to bring some food, but all they brought was water and firewood, and the old men who brought it said there was no more maize.

That same day other Ambassadors arrived from Montezuma, and joined those who were already with us and they said to Cortés, very impudently, that their Prince had sent them to say that we were not to go by his city because he had nothing to give us to eat, and that they wished at once to return to Mexico with our reply. When Cortés saw that their speech was unfriendly, he replied to the Ambassadors in the blandest manner, that he marvelled how such a great Prince as Montezuma should be so vacillating, and he begged them not to return to Mexico, for he wished to start himself on the next day, to see their Prince, and act according to his orders, and I believe that he gave the Ambassadors some strings of beads and they agreed to stay.

When this had been done, our Captain called us together, and said to us: "I see that these people are very much disturbed, and it behoves us to keep on the alert, in case some trouble is brewing among them," and he at once sent for the principal Cacique, telling him either to come himself or to send some other chieftains. The Cacique replied that he was ill and could not come.

When our Captain heard this, he ordered us to bring before him, with kindly persuasion, two of the numerous priests who were in the great Cue near our quarters. We brought two of them, without doing them any disrespect, and Cortés ordered each of them to be given a Chalchihuite, and addressing them with friendly words he asked them what was the reason that the Cacique and chieftains and most of the priests were frightened, for he had sent to summon them and they did not want to come. It seems that one of these priests was a very important personage among them, who had charge of or command over all the Cues in the City, and was a sort of Bishop among the priests and was held in great respect. He replied that they, who were priests, had no fear of us, and if the Cacique and chieftain did not wish to come, he would go himself and summon them, and that if he spoke to them he believed they would do as he told them and would come.

Cortés at once told him to go, and that his companion should await his return. So the priest departed and summoned the Cacique and chieftains who returned in his company to Cortés' quarters. Cortés asked them what it was they were afraid of, and why they had not given us anything to eat, and said that if our presence in their city were an annoyance to them, we wished to leave the next day for Mexico to see and speak to the Lord

Montezuma, and he asked them to provide carriers for the transport of the baggage and tepusques and to send us some food at once.

The Cacique was so embarrassed that he could hardly speak, he said that they would look for the food, but their Lord Montezuma had sent to tell them not to give us any, and was not willing that we should proceed any further.

While this conversation was taking place, three of our friends, the Cempoala Indians, came in and said secretly to Cortés, that close by where we were quartered they had found holes dug in the streets, covered over with wood and earth, so that without careful examination, one could not see them, that they had removed the earth from above one of the holes and found it full of sharp pointed stakes to kill the horses when they galloped, and that the *Azoteas* had breastworks of adobes [sundried bricks] and were piled up with stones, and certainly this was not done with good intent for they also found barricades of thick timbers in another street. At this moment eight Tlaxcalans arrived, from the Indians whom we had left outside in the fields with orders that they were not to enter Cholula, and they said to Cortés: "Take heed, Malinche, for this City is ill disposed, and we know that this night they have sacrificed to their Idol, which is the God of War, seven persons, five of them children, so that the God may give them victory over you, and we have further seen that they are moving all their baggage and women and children out of the city." When Cortés heard this, he immediately sent these Tlaxcalans back to their Captains, with orders to be fully prepared if we should send to summon them, and he turned to speak to the Caciques, priests and chieftains of Cholula and told them to have no fear and show no alarm, but to remember the obedience which they had promised to him, and not to swerve from it, lest he should have to chastise them. That he had already told them that we wished to set out on the morrow and that he had need of two thousand warriors from the city to accompany us, just as the Tlaxcalans had provided them, for they were necessary on the road. They replied that the men would be given, and asked leave to go at once to get them ready, and they went away very well contented,

for they thought that between the warriors with whom they were to supply us, and the regiments sent by Montezuma, which were hidden in the
rocky thickets and barrancas, we could not escape death or capture, for
the horses would not be able to charge on account of certain breastworks
and barricades which they immediately advised the troops to construct, so
that only a narrow lane would be left through which it would be impossible for us to pass. They warned the Mexicans to be in readiness as we
intended to start on the next day and told them that our capture would
be sure, for they had made sacrifices to their War Idols who had promised
them victory.

As our Captain wished to be more thoroughly informed about the
plot and all that was happening, he told Doña Marina to take more chalchihuites to the two priests who had been the first to speak, for they were
not afraid, and to tell them with friendly words that Malinche wished
them to come back and speak to him, and to bring them back with her.
Doña Marina went and spoke to the priests in the manner she knew so
well how to use, and thanks to the presents they at once accompanied her.
Cortés addressed them and asked them to say truly what they knew, for
they were the priests of Idols and chieftains and ought not to lie, and that
what they should say would not be disclosed in any manner, for we were
going to leave the next morning, and he would give them a large quantity
of cloth. They said the truth was that their Lord Montezuma knew that
we were coming to their city, and that every day he was of many minds
and could not come to any decision on the matter, that sometimes he sent
orders to pay us much respect when we arrived and to guide us on the way
to his city, and at other times he would send word that it was not his wish
that we should go to Mexico, and now recently his Gods Tescatepuca and
Huichilobos, to whom he paid great devotion, had counselled him that
we should either be killed here in Cholula or should be sent, bound, to
Mexico. That the day before he had sent out twenty thousand warriors,
and half of them were already within this city, and the other half were
stationed nearby in some gullies, and that they already knew that we were
about to start tomorrow; they also told us about the barricades which they

had ordered to be made and the two thousand warriors that were to be given to us, and how it had already been agreed that twenty of us were to be kept to be sacrificed to the Idols of Cholula.

Cortés ordered these men to be given a present of richly embroidered cloth, and told them not to say anything about the information they had given us for, if they disclosed it, on our return from Mexico we would kill them. He also told them that we should start early the next morning, and he asked them to summon all the Caciques to come then so that he might speak to them.

That night Cortés took counsel of us as to what should be done, for he had very able men with him whose advice was worth having, but as in such cases frequently happens, some said that it would be advisable to change our course and go by Huexotzingo, others that we must manage to preserve the peace by every possible means and that it would be better to return to Tlaxcala, others of us gave our opinion that if we allowed such treachery to pass unpunished, wherever we went we should be treated to worse treachery, and that being there in the town, with ample provisions, we ought to make an attack, for the Indians would feel the effect of it more in their own homes than they would in the open, and that we should at once warn the Tlaxcalans so that they might join in it. All thought well of this last advice. As Cortés had already told them that we were going to set out on the following day, for this reason we should make a show of tying together our baggage, which was little enough, and then in the large courts within high walls, where we were lodged, we should fall on the Indian warriors, who well deserved their fate. As regards the Ambassadors of Montezuma, we should dissemble and tell them that the evil-minded Cholulans had intended treachery and had attempted to put the blame for it on their Lord Montezuma, and on themselves as his Ambassadors, but we did not believe Montezuma had given any such orders, and we begged them to stay in their apartments and not have any further converse with the people of the city, so that we should not have reason to think they were in league with them in their treachery, and we asked them to go with us as our guides to Mexico.

They replied that neither they themselves nor their Lord Montezuma knew anything about that which we were telling them. Although they did not like it, we placed guards over the Ambassadors, so that they could not go out without our permission.

All that night we were on the alert and under arms with the horses saddled and bridled, for we thought that for certain all the companies of the Mexicans as well as the Cholulans would attack us during the night.

There was an old Indian woman, the wife of a Cacique, who knew all about the plot and trap which had been arranged, and she had come secretly to Doña Marina, having noticed that she was young and good-looking and rich, and advised her, if she wanted to escape with her life, to come with her to her house, for it was certain that on that night or during the next day we were all going to be killed. Because she knew of this, and on account of the compassion she felt for Doña Marina, she had come to tell her that she had better get all her possessions together and come with her to her house, and she would there marry her to her son, the brother of a youth who accompanied her.

When Doña Marina understood this (as she was always very shrewd) she said to her: "O mother, thank you much for this that you have told me, I would go with you at once but that I have no one here whom I can trust to carry my clothes and jewels of gold of which I have many, for goodness sake, mother, wait here a little while, you and your son, and tonight we will set out, for now, as you can see, these Teules are on the watch and will hear us."

The old woman believed what she said, and remained chatting with her, and Doña Marina asked her how they were going to kill us all, and how and when and where the plot was made. The old woman told her neither more nor less than what the two priests had already stated, and Doña Marina replied: "If this affair is such a secret, how is it that you came to know about it?" and the old woman replied that her husband had told her, for he was a captain of one of the parties in the city; as to the plot she had known about it for three days, for a gilded drum had been sent to her husband from Mexico, and rich cloaks and jewels of gold had been sent to three other captains to induce them to bring us bound to their Lord Montezuma.

When Doña Marina heard this she deceived the old woman and said: "How delighted I am to hear that your son to whom you wish to marry me is a man of distinction. We have already talked a good deal, and I do not want them to notice us, so Mother you wait here while I begin to bring my property, for I cannot bring it all at once, and you and your son, my brother, will take care of it, and then we shall be able to go." The old woman believed all that was told her, and she and her son sat down to rest. Then Doña Marina went swiftly to the Captain and told him all that had passed with the Indian woman. Cortés at once ordered her to be brought before him, and questioned her about these treasons and plots, and she told him neither more nor less than the priests had already said, so he placed a guard over the woman so that she could not escape.

When dawn broke it was a sight to see the haste with which the Caciques and priests brought in the warriors, laughing and contented as though they had already caught us in their traps and nets, and they brought more Indian warriors than we had asked for, and large as they are (for they still stand as a memorial of the past) the courtyards would not hold them all.

We were already quite prepared for what had to be done. The soldiers with swords and shields were stationed at the gate of the great court so as not to let a single armed Indian pass out. Our Captain was mounted on horseback with many soldiers round him, as a guard, and when he saw how very early the Caciques and priests and warriors had arrived, he said: "How these traitors long to see us among the barrancas so as to gorge on our flesh, but Our Lord will do better for us." Then he asked for the two priests who had let out the secret, and he sent our interpreter, Aguilar, to tell them to go to their houses, for he had no need of their presence now. This was in order that, as they had done us a good turn, they should not suffer for it, and should not get killed. Cortés was on horseback and Doña Marina near to him, and he asked the Caciques why was it, as we had done them no harm whatever, that they had wished to kill us, and why should they turn traitors against us, when all we had said or done was to warn them against certain things of which we had already warned all the towns that we had passed through, and to tell them about matters concerning our holy faith, and this without compulsion of any kind? To what purpose then had they quite recently prepared many long and strong poles with collars and cords and placed them in a house near to the Great Temple, and why for the last three days had they been building barricades and digging holes in the streets and raising breastworks on the roofs of the houses, and why had they removed their children and wives and property from the city? Their ill will however had been plainly shown, and they had not been able to hide their treason. They had not even given us food to eat, and as a mockery had brought us firewood and water, and said that there was no maize. He knew well that in the barrancas nearby, there were many companies of warriors lying in wait for us, ready to carry out their treacherous plans, thinking that we should pass along that road towards Mexico. So in return for our having come to treat them like brothers and to tell them what Our Lord God and the King have ordained, they wished to kill us and eat our flesh, and had already prepared the pots with salt and peppers and tomatoes. If this was what they wanted it would have been better for them to make war on us in the open field like good and valiant warriors, as did their neighbours the Tlaxcalans. He knew for certain all that had been planned in the city and that they had even promised to their Idol, that twenty of us should be sacrificed before it, and that three nights ago they had sacrificed seven Indians to it so as to ensure victory, which was promised them; but as the Idol was both evil and false, it neither had, nor would have power against us, and all these evil and traitorous designs which they had planned and put into effect were about to recoil on themselves. Doña Marina told all this to them, and made them understand it very clearly, and when the priests, Caciques, and captains had heard it, they said that what had been stated was true but that they were not to blame for it, for the Ambassadors of Montezuma had ordered it at the command of their Prince.

Then Cortés told them that the royal laws decreed that such treasons as those should not remain unpunished and that for their crime they must die. Then he ordered a musket to be fired, which was the signal that we had agreed upon for that purpose, and a blow was given to them which they will remember forever, for we killed many of them, so that they gained nothing from the promises of their false idols.

Not two hours had passed before our allies, the Tlaxcalans, arrived, and they had fought very fiercely where the Cholulans had posted other companies to defend the streets and prevent their being entered, but these were soon defeated. The Tlaxcalans went about the city, plundering and making prisoners and we could not stop them, and the next day more companies from the Tlaxcalan towns arrived, and did great damage, for they were very hostile to the people of Cholula, and when we saw this, both Cortés and the captains and the soldiers, on account of the compassion that we had felt, restrained the Tlaxcalans from doing further damage, and Cortés ordered Cristóbal de Olid to bring him all the Tlaxcalan captains together so that he could speak to them, and they did not delay in coming; then he ordered them to gather together all their men and go and camp in the fields, and this they did, and only the men from Cempoala remained with us.

Just then certain Caciques and priests of Cholula who belonged to other districts of the town, and said that they were not concerned in the treasons against us (for it is a large city and they have parties and factions among themselves), asked Cortés and all of us to pardon the provocation of the treachery that had been plotted against us, for the traitors had already paid with their lives. Then there came the two priests who were our friends and had disclosed the secret to us, and the old woman, the wife of the captain, who wanted to be the mother-in-law of Doña Marina, and all prayed Cortés for pardon.

When they spoke to him, Cortés made a show of great anger and ordered the Ambassadors of Montezuma, who were detained in our company, to be summoned. He then said that the whole city deserved to be destroyed, but that out of respect for their Lord Montezuma, whose vassals they were, he would pardon them, and that from now on they must be well behaved, and let them beware of such affairs as the last happening again, lest they should die for it.

Then, he ordered the Chiefs of Tlaxcala, who were in the fields, to be summoned, and told them to return the men and women whom they had taken prisoners, for the damage they had done was sufficient. Giving up the prisoners went against the grain with the Tlaxcalans, and they said that the Cholulans had deserved far greater punishment for the many treacheries they had constantly received at their hands. Nevertheless as Cortés ordered it, they gave back many persons, but they still remained rich, both in gold and mantles, cotton cloth, salt and slaves. Besides this Cortés made them and the people of Cholula friends, and, from what I have since seen and ascertained, that friendship has never been broken.

Furthermore, Cortés ordered all the priests and Caciques to bring back the people to the city, and to hold their markets and fairs, and not to have any fear, for no harm would be done to them. They replied that within five days the city would be fully peopled again, for at that time nearly all the inhabitants were in hiding. They said it was necessary that Cortés should appoint a Cacique for them, for their ruler was one of those who had died in the Court, so he asked them to whom the office ought to go, and they said to the brother of the late Cacique, so Cortés at once appointed him to be Governor.

In addition to this, as soon as he saw the city was reinhabited, and their markets were carried on in safety, he ordered all the priests, captains and other chieftains of that city to assemble, and explained to them very clearly all the matters concerning our holy faith, and told them that they could see how their Idols had deceived them, and were evil things not speaking the truth; he begged them to destroy the Idols and break them in pieces. That if they did not wish to do it themselves we would do it for them. He also ordered them to whitewash a temple, so that we might set up a cross there.

They immediately did what we asked them in the matter of the cross, and they said that they would remove their Idols, but although they were many times ordered to do it, they delayed. Then the Padre de la Merced said to Cortés that it was going too far, in the beginning, to take away their Idols until they should understand things better, and should see how our expedition to Mexico would turn out, and time would show us what we ought to do in the matter, that for the present the warnings we had given them were sufficient, together with the setting up of the Cross.

The city is situated on a plain, in a locality where there were many neighbouring towns, such as Tepeaca, Tlaxcala, Chalco, Tecamachalco, Huexotzingo and many others, and it is a land fruitful in maize and other vegetables, and much Chili pepper, and the land is full of Magueys from which they make their wine. They make very good pottery in the city of red and black and white clay with various designs, and with it supply Mexico and all the neighbouring provinces as, so to say, do Talavera or Placencia in Spain. At that time there were many high towers in the city where the Idols stood, especially the Great Cue which was higher than that of Mexico, although the Mexican Cue was very lofty and magnificent.

As soon as the Squadrons sent by the Great Montezuma, which were already stationed in the ravines near Cholula, learned what had taken place they returned, faster than at a walk, to Mexico and told Montezuma how it all happened. But fast as they went the news had already reached him, through the two Chieftains who had been with us and who went to him posthaste. We learned on good authority that when Montezuma heard the news he was greatly grieved and very angry, and at once sacrificed some Indians to his Idol Huichilobos, whom they looked on as the God of War, so that he might tell him what was to be the result of our going to Mexico, or if he should permit us to enter the city. We even knew that he was shut in at his devotions and sacrifices for two days in company with ten of the Chief Priests, and that a reply came from those Idols which was, that they advised him to send messengers to us to disclaim all blame for the Cholulan affair, and that with demonstrations of peace we should be allowed to enter into Mexico, and that when we were inside, by depriving us of food and water, or by raising some of the bridges, they would kill us.

This affair and punishment at Cholula became known throughout the provinces of New Spain and if we had a reputation for valour before, from now on they took us for sorcerers, and said that no evil that was planned against us could be so hidden from us that it did not come to our knowledge, and on this account they showed us goodwill.

I think that the curious reader must be already satiated hearing this story about Cholula and I wish that I had finished writing about it, but I cannot avoid calling to mind the prisons of thick wooden beams which we found in the city, which were full of Indians and boys being fattened so that they could be sacrificed and their flesh eaten. We broke open all these prisons, and Cortés ordered all the Indian prisoners that were confined within them to return to their native countries, and with threats he ordered the Caciques and captains and priests of the city not to imprison any more Indians in that way, and not to eat human flesh. They promised not to do so, but what use were such promises? as they never kept them.

Let us anticipate and say that these were the great cruelties that the Bishop of Chiapas, Fray Bartolomé de las Casas, wrote about and never ceased talking about, asserting that for no reason whatever, or only for our pastime and because we wanted to, we inflicted that punishment, and he even says it so artfully in his book that he would make those believe, who neither saw it themselves, nor know about it, that these and other cruelties about which he writes were true (as he states them) while it is altogether the reverse of true. [Blotted out in the original: "I beg your Lordship's pardon for stating it so clearly."—G. G.] It did not happen as he describes it. Let the monks of the order of Santo Domingo see what they can read in the book in which he has written it, and they will find it to be very different the one from the other. I also wish to say that some good Franciscan monks, who were the first friars whom his Majesty sent to this New Spain after the Conquest of Mexico, as I shall relate further on, went to Cholula to inform themselves and find out how and in what way that punishment was carried out, and for what reason, and the enquiry that they made was from the same priests and elders of the city, and after fully informing themselves from these very men, they found it to be neither more nor less than what I have written down in this narrative, and not as the Bishop has related it. If perchance we had not inflicted that punishment, our lives would have been in great danger on account of the squadrons and companies of Mexican and Cholulan warriors who were there, and the barricades and breastworks, and if to our misfortune they had killed us there, this New Spain would not have been so speedily conquered, nor would another Armada have dared to have come, and if it did, it would have been under greater difficulty, for the Mexicans would have defended their ports, and they would still have continued in a state of Idolatry.

I have heard a Franciscan Friar called Fray Toribio Motolinea, who led a good life, say that it would have been better if that punishment could have been prevented, and they had not given cause for its being carried out but, as it had been carried out, it was a good thing that all the Indians of the provinces of New Spain should see and understand that those Idols and all the rest of them were evil and lying, for it showed that all their promises turned out false, and they lost the adoration which the people had hitherto given them, and thenceforth they would not sacrifice to them, nor come on pilgrimages to them from other parts, as they used to do. From that time they did not care for it [the principal Idol] and removed it from the lofty cue where it had stood, and either hid it or broke it up, so that it never appeared again, and they have put up another Idol in its place.

Fourteen days had already passed since we had come to Cholula and we had nothing more to do there, for we saw that the city was again fully peopled, and we had established friendship between them and the people of Tlaxcala. But as we knew that the Great Montezuma was secretly sending spies to our camp to enquire and find out what our plans were, our Captain determined to take counsel of certain captains and soldiers, whom he knew to be well disposed towards him, because he never did anything without first asking our advice about it. It was agreed that we should send to tell the Great Montezuma, gently and amicably, that in order to carry out the purpose for which our Lord and King had sent us to these parts, we had crossed many seas and distant lands, and that while we were marching towards his city, his ambassadors had guided us by way of Cholula, where the people had plotted a treason with the intention of killing us, and we had punished some of those who intended to carry out the plot. As our Captain knew that the Cholulans were his subjects, it was only out of respect for his person, and on account of our great friendship, that he refrained from destroying and killing all those who were concerned in the treason. However, the worst of it all is that the priests and Caciques say it was done on misadvice and command. This of course we never believed, that such a great prince as he is could issue such orders, especially as he had declared himself our friend, and we had inferred from his character that since his Idols had put such an evil thought as making war on us into his head, he would surely fight us in the open field. But as we look upon him as our great friend and wish to see and speak to him, we are setting out at once for his city to give him a more complete account of what Our Lord the King had commanded us to do.

The March to Mexico

When Montezuma heard this message and learned through the people of Cholula that we did not lay all the blame on him, we heard it said that he returned again with his priests to fast and make sacrifices to his Idols, to know if they would again repeat their permission to allow us to enter into the city or no, and whether they would reiterate the commands they had already given him. The answer which they gave was the same as the first, that he should allow us to enter and that once inside the city he could kill us when he chose. His captains and priests also advised him that if he should place obstacles in the way of our entry, we would make war on him through his subject towns, seeing that we had as our friends the Tlaxcalans, and all the Totonacs of the hills, and other towns which had accepted our alliance, and to avoid these evils the best and most sensible advice was that which Huichilobos had given.

When Montezuma heard the message which we sent to him concerning our friendship and the other fearless remarks, after much deliberation he despatched six chieftains with a present of gold and jewels of a variety of shapes which were estimated to be worth over two thousand pesos, and he sent certain loads of very rich mantles beautifully worked.

When the Chiefs came before Cortés with the present they touched the ground with their hands and with great reverence, such as they use among themselves, they said: "Malinche, Our Lord the Great Montezuma, sends thee this present, and asks thee to accept it with the great affection which he has for thee and all thy brethren, and he says that the annoyance that the people of Cholula have caused him weighs heavily on him, and he wishes to punish them more in their persons, for they are an evil and a lying people in that they have thrown the blame of the wickedness which they wished to commit upon him and his ambassadors," that we might take it as very certain that he was our friend, and that we could go to his City whenever we liked, for he wished to do us every honour as very valiant men, and the messengers of such a great King. But because he had nothing to give us to eat, for everything has to be carried into the city by carriers as it is built on the lake, he could not entertain us very satisfactorily, but he would endeavour to do us all the honour that was possible, and he had ordered all the towns through which we had to pass to give us what we might need. Cortés received the present with demonstrations of affection and embraced the messengers, and ordered them to be given certain twisted-cut glass beads.

Cortés gave the ambassadors a suitable and affectionate reply and ordered the messengers who had come with the present to remain with us as guides and the other three to return with the answer to their Prince, and to advise him that we were already on the road.

When the Chief Caciques of Tlaxcala understood that we were going, their souls were afflicted and they sent to say to Cortés that they had already warned him many times that he should be careful what he was about, and should refrain from entering such a strong city where there was so much warlike preparation and such a multitude of warriors, for one day or the other we would be attacked, and they feared that we would not escape alive, and on account of the goodwill that they bore us, they wished to send ten thousand men under brave captains to go with us and carry food for the journey.

Cortés thanked them heartily for their good wishes and told them that it was not just to enter into Mexico with such a host of warriors, especially when one party was so hostile to the other, that he only had need of one thousand men to carry the tepusques and the baggage, and to clear some of the roads, and they at once sent us the thousand Indians very well equipped.

Just as we were ready to set out, there came to Cortés all the Caciques and all the principal warriors whom we had brought from Cempoala, who had marched in our company and served us well and loyally, and said that they wanted to go back to Cempoala and not to proceed beyond Cholula in the direction of Mexico, for they felt certain that if they went there it would be for them and for us to go to our deaths. The Great Montezuma would order them to be killed because they had broken their fealty by refusing to pay him tribute and by imprisoning his tax-gatherers.

When Cortés observed the determination with which they demanded permission, he answered that they need not have the slightest fear that they would come to any harm, for, as they would go in our company, who would dare to annoy either them or us? and he begged them to change their minds and stay with us, and he promised to make them rich. Although Cortés pressed them to stay, and Doña Marina put it in the most warm-hearted manner, they never wished to stay, but only to return to their homes. When Cortés perceived this he said: "God forbid that these Indians who have served us so well should be forced to go," and he sent for many loads of rich mantles and divided them among them, and he also sent to our friend the fat Cacique two loads of mantles for himself and for his nephew the other great Cacique named Cuesco.

We set out from Cholula in carefully arranged order as we were always accustomed to do, and arrived that day at some ranchos standing on a hill about four leagues from Cholula, they are peopled from Huexotzingo, and I think they are called the Ranchos of Yscalpan. To this place soon came the Caciques and priests of the towns of Huexotzingo which were nearby, and people from other small towns, which stand on the slopes of the volcano near their boundary line, who brought us food and a present of golden jewels of small value, and they asked Cortés to accept them and not consider the insignificance of the gift but the good-will with which it was offered. They advised him not to go to Mexico as it was a very strong city and full of warriors, where we should run much risk. They also told us to look out, if we had decided upon going, for when we had ascended to the pass we should find two broad roads, one leading to a town named Chalco, and the other to another town called Tlamanalco [Bernal Díaz writes "Tlamanalco" in error—Cortés says it was Amecameca], both of them subject to Mexico; that the one road was well swept and cleared so as to induce us to take it, and that the other road had been closed up and many great pines and other trees had been cut down so that horses could not use it and we could not march along it. That a little way down the side of the mountain along the road that had been cleared, the Mexicans (thinking that we must take that road) had cut away a piece of the hillside, and had made ditches and barricades, and that certain squadrons of Mexicans had waited at that point so as to kill us there. So they counselled us not to go by the road which was clear, but by the road where the felled trees were, saying that they would send many men with us to clear it.

Cortés thanked them for the counsel they had given him, and said that with God's help he would not abandon his march but would go the way they advised him. Early the next morning we began our march, and it was nearly midday when we arrived at the ridge of the mountain where we found the roads just as the people of Huexotzingo had said. There we rested a little and began to think about the Mexican squadrons on the intrenched hillside where the earthworks were that they had told us about.

Then Cortés ordered the Ambassadors of the great Montezuma who came in our company to be summoned, and he asked them how it was that those two roads were in that condition, one very clean and swept and the other covered with newly felled trees. They replied that it was done so that we should go by the cleared road which led to a city named Chalco, where the people would give us a good reception, for it belonged to their Prince Montezuma, and that they had cut the trees and closed up the other road to prevent our going by it, for there were bad passes on it, and it went somewhat round about before going to Mexico, and came out at another town which was not as large as Chalco. Then Cortés said that he wished to go by the blocked-up road, and we began to ascend the mountain with the greatest caution, our allies moving aside the huge thick tree trunks with great labour, and some of them still lie by the roadside to this very day. As we rose higher it began to snow and the snow caked on the ground. Then we descended the hill and went to sleep at a group of houses which they build like inns or hostels where the Indian traders lodge, and we supped well, but the cold was intense, and we posted our watchmen, sentinels and patrols and even sent out scouts. The next day we set out on our march, and, about the hour of high Mass, arrived at a town (Amecameca), where they received us well and where there was no scarcity of food.

When the other towns in the neighbourhood heard of our arrival, people soon came from Chalco and from Chimaloacan and from Ayotzingo, where the canoes are, for it is their port. All of them together brought a present of gold and two loads of mantles and eight Indian women and the gold was worth over one hundred and fifty pesos and they said: "Malinche, accept these presents which we give you and look on us in the future as your friends." Cortés received them with great goodwill and promised to help them in whatever they needed and when he saw them together he told the Padre de la Merced to counsel them regarding matters touching our holy faith, and that they should give up their Idols. Cortés also explained to them about the great power of our Lord, the Emperor, and how we had come to right wrongs and to stop robbery.

When they heard this, all these towns that I have named, secretly, so that the Mexican Ambassadors should not hear them, made great complaints about Montezuma, and his tax-gatherers, who robbed them of all they possessed, and carried off their wives and daughters, and made the men work as though they were slaves, and made them carry pine timber and stone and firewood and maize either in their canoes or over land, and many other services such as planting cornfields, and they took their lands for the service of the Idols.

Cortés comforted them with kindly words which he knew well how to say to them through Doña Marina, but added that at the present moment he could not undertake to see justice done them and they must bear it awhile and he would presently free them from that rule. The Caciques replied: "We are of opinion that you should stay here with us, and we will give you what we possess, and that you should give up going to Mexico, as we know for certain it is very strong and full of warriors, and they will not spare your lives."

Cortés replied to them, with a cheerful mien, that we had no fear that the Mexicans, or any other nation, could destroy us and, as we wished to start at once, he asked them to give him twenty of their principal men to go in his company, and they brought us the twenty Indians.

Just as we were starting on our march to Mexico there came before Cortés four Mexican chiefs sent by Montezuma who brought a present of gold and cloths. After they had made obeisance according to their custom, they said: "Malinche, our Lord the Great Montezuma sends you this present and says that he is greatly concerned for the hardships you have endured in coming from such a distant land in order to see him, and that he has already sent to tell you that he will give you much gold and silver and chalchihuites as tribute for your Emperor and for yourself and the other Teules in your company, provided you do not come to Mexico, and now again he begs as a favour, that you will not advance any further but return whence you have come, and he promises to send you to the port a great quantity of gold and silver and rich stones for that King of yours, and, as for you, he will give you four loads of gold and for each of your brothers one load, but as for going on to Mexico your entrance into it is forbidden, for all his vassals have risen in arms to prevent your entry, and besides this there is no road thither, only a very narrow one, and there is no food for you to eat." And he used many other arguments about the difficulties to the end that we should advance no further.

Cortés with much show of affection embraced the Ambassadors, although the message grieved him, and he accepted the present, and said that he marvelled how the Lord Montezuma, having given himself out as our friend, and being such a great Prince, should be so inconstant; that one time he says one thing and another time sends to order the contrary, and regarding what he says about giving gold to our Lord the Emperor and to ourselves, he is grateful to him for it, and what he sends him now he will pay for in good works as time goes on. How can he deem it befitting that being so near to his city, we should think it right to return on our road without carrying through what our Prince has commanded us to do? If the Lord Montezuma had sent his messengers and ambassadors to some great prince such as he is himself, and if, after nearly reaching his house, those messengers whom he sent should turn back without speaking to the Prince about that which they were sent to say, when they came back into his [Montezuma's] presence with such a story, what favour would he show them? He would merely treat them as cowards of little worth; and this is what our Emperor would do with us; so that in one way or another we were determined to enter his city, and from this time forth he must not send any more excuses on the subject, for he [Cortés] was bound to see him, and talk to him and explain the whole purpose for which we had come, and this he must do to him personally. When after he understood it all, if our presence in the city did not seem good to him, we would return whence we had come. As for what he said about there being little or no food, not enough to support us, we were men who could get along even if we have but little to eat, and we were already on the way to his city, so let him take our coming in good part.

As soon as the messengers had been despatched, we set out for Mexico, and as the people of Huexotzingo and Chalco had told us that Montezuma had held consultations with his Idols and priests, who had said he was to allow us to enter and that then he could kill us, and as we are but human and feared death, we never ceased thinking about it. As that country is very thickly peopled we made short marches, and commended ourselves to God and to Our Lady his blessed Mother, and talked about how and by what means we could enter the City, and it put courage into our hearts to think that as our Lord Jesus Christ had vouchsafed us protection through past dangers, he would likewise guard us from the power of the Mexicans.

We went to sleep at a town called Iztapalatengo [this is clearly a mistake; the town was Ayotzingo] where half the houses are in the water and the other half on dry land, and there they gave us a good supper.

The Great Montezuma, when he heard the reply which Cortés had sent to him, at once determined to send his nephew named Cacamatzin, the Lord of Texcoco, with great pomp to bid welcome to Cortés and to all of us, and one of our scouts came in to tell us that a large crowd of friendly Mexicans was coming along the road clad in rich mantles. It was very early in the morning when this happened, and we were ready to start, and Cortés ordered us to wait in our quarters until he could see what the matter was.

At that moment four chieftains arrived, who made deep obeisance to Cortés and said that close by there was approaching Cacamatzin, the great Lord of Texcoco, a nephew of the Great Montezuma, and he begged us to have the goodness to wait until he arrived.

He did not tarry long, for he soon arrived with greater pomp and splendour than we had ever beheld in a Mexican Prince, for he came in a litter richly worked in green feathers, with many silver borderings, and rich stones set in bosses made out of the finest gold. Eight Chieftains, who, it was said were all Lords of Towns, bore the litter on their shoulders. When they came near to the house where Cortés was quartered, the Chieftains assisted Cacamatzin to descend from the litter, and they swept the ground, and removed the straws where he had to pass, and when they came before our Captain they made him deep reverence, and Cacamatzin said:

"Malinche, here we have come, I and these Chieftains to place ourselves at your service, and to give you all that you may need for yourself and your companions and to place you in your home, which is our city, for so the Great Montezuma our Prince has ordered us to do, and he asks your pardon that he did not come with us himself, but it is on account of ill health that he did not do so, and not from want of very goodwill which he bears towards you."

When our Captain and all of us beheld such pomp and majesty in those chiefs, especially in the nephew of Montezuma, we considered it a matter of the greatest importance, and said among ourselves, if this Cacique bears himself with such dignity, what will the Great Montezuma do?

When Cacamatzin had delivered his speech, Cortés embraced him, and gave many caresses to him and all the other Chieftains, and gave him three stones which are called Margaritas, which have within them many markings of different colours, and to the other Chieftains he gave blue glass beads, and he told them that he thanked them and when he was able he would repay the Lord Montezuma for all the favours which every day he was granting us.

As soon as the speech-making was over, we at once set out, and as the Caciques whom I have spoken about brought many followers with them, and as many people came out to see us from the neighbouring towns, all the roads were full of them.

Arrival in the Splendid City of Tenochtitlan

During the morning, we arrived at a broad Causeway*and continued our march towards Iztapalapa, and when we saw so many cities and villages built in the water and other great towns on dry land and that straight and level Causeway going towards Mexico, we were amazed and said that it was like the enchantments they tell of in the legend of Amadis, on account of the great towers and cues and buildings rising from the water, and all built of masonry. And some of our soldiers even asked whether the things that we saw were not a dream. It is not to be wondered at that I here write it down in this manner, for there is so much to think over that I do not know how to describe it, seeing things as we did that had never been heard of or seen before, not even dreamed about.

Thus, we arrived near Iztapalapa, to behold the splendour of the other Caciques who came out to meet us, who were the Lord of the town named Cuitlahuac, and the Lord of Culuacan, both of them near relations of Montezuma. And then when we entered the city of Iztapalapa, the appearance of the palaces in which they lodged us! How spacious and well built they were, of beautiful stonework and cedar wood, and the wood of other sweet-scented trees, with great rooms and courts, wonderful to behold, covered with awnings of cotton cloth.

When we had looked well at all of this, we went to the orchard and garden, which was such a wonderful thing to see and walk in, that I was never tired of looking at the diversity of the trees, and noting the scent which each one had, and the paths full of roses and flowers, and the many fruit trees and native roses, and the pond of freshwater. There was another thing to observe, that great canoes were able to pass into the garden from the lake through an opening that had been made so that

---

*The Causeway of Cuitlahuac separating the lake of Chalco from the lake of Xochimilco.

there was no need for their occupants to land. And all was cemented and very splendid with many kinds of stone [monuments] with pictures on them, which gave much to think about. Then the birds of many kinds and breeds which came into the pond. I say again that I stood looking at it and thought that never in the world would there be discovered other lands such as these, for at that time there was no Peru, nor any thought of it. Of all these wonders that I then beheld today all is overthrown and lost, nothing left standing.

Let us go on, and I will relate that the Caciques of that town and of Coyoacan brought us a present of gold, worth more than two thousand pesos.

Early next day we left Iztapalapa with a large escort of those great Caciques whom I have already mentioned. We proceeded along the Causeway which is here eight paces in width and runs so straight to the City of Mexico that it does not seem to me to turn either much or little, but, broad as it is, it was so crowded with people that there was hardly room for them all, some of them going to and others returning from Mexico, besides those who had come out to see us, so that we were hardly able to pass by the crowds of them that came; and the towers and cues were full of people as well as the canoes from all parts of the lake. It was not to be wondered at, for they had never before seen horses or men such as we are.

Gazing on such wonderful sights, we did not know what to say, or whether what appeared before us was real, for on one side, on the land, there were great cities, and in the lake ever so many more, and the lake itself was crowded with canoes, and in the Causeway were many bridges at intervals, and in front of us stood the great City of Mexico, and we—we did not even number four hundred soldiers! and we well remembered the words and warnings given us by the people of Huexotzingo and Tlaxcala, and the many other warnings that had been given that we should beware of entering Mexico, where they would kill us, as soon as they had us inside.

Let the curious readers consider whether there is not much to ponder over in this that I am writing. What men have there been in the world who have shown such daring? But let us get on, and march along the Causeway. When we arrived where another small causeway branches off [Acachinango, leading to Coyoacan, which is another city] where there were some buildings like towers, which are their oratories, many more chieftains and Caciques approached clad in very rich mantles, the brilliant liveries of one chieftain differing from those of another, and the causeways were crowded with them. The Great Montezuma had sent these great Caciques in advance to receive us, and when they came before Cortés they bade us welcome in their language, and as a sign of peace, they touched their hands against the ground, and kissed the ground with the hand.

There we halted for a good while, and Cacamatzin, the Lord of Texcoco, and the Lord of Iztapalapa and the Lord of Tacuba and the Lord of Coyoacan went on in advance to meet the Great Montezuma, who was approaching in a rich litter accompanied by other great Lords and Caciques, who owned vassals. When we arrived near to Mexico, where there were some other small towers, the Great Montezuma got down from his litter, and those great Caciques supported him with their arms beneath a marvellously rich canopy of green-coloured feathers with much gold and silver embroidery and with pearls and chalchihuites suspended from a sort of bordering, which was wonderful to look at. The Great Montezuma was richly attired according to his usage, and he was shod with sandals, the soles were of gold and the upper part adorned with precious stones. The four Chieftains who supported his arms were also richly clothed according to their usage, in garments which were apparently held ready for them on the road to enable them to accompany their prince, for they did not appear in such attire when they came to receive us. Besides these four Chieftains, there were four other great Caciques who supported the canopy over their heads, and many other Lords who walked before the Great Montezuma, sweeping the ground where he would tread and spreading cloths on it, so that he should not tread on the earth. Not one of these Chieftains dared even to think of looking him in the face, but kept their eyes lowered with great reverence, except those four relations, his nephews, who supported him with their arms.

When Cortés was told that the Great Montezuma was approaching, and he saw him coming, he dismounted from his horse, and when he was near Montezuma, they simultaneously paid great reverence to one another. Montezuma bade him welcome and our Cortés replied through Doña Marina wishing him very good health. And it seems to me that Cortés, through Doña Marina, offered him his right hand, and Montezuma did not wish to take it, but he did give his hand to Cortés and then Cortés brought out a necklace which he had ready at hand, made of glass stones, which I have already said are called Margaritas, which have with them many patterns of diverse colours, these were strung on a cord of gold and with musk so that it should have a sweet scent, and he placed it round the neck of the Great Montezuma and when he had so placed it he was going to embrace him, and those great Princes who accompanied Montezuma held back Cortés by the arm so that he should not embrace him, for they considered it an indignity.

Then Cortés through the mouth of Doña Marina told him that now his heart rejoiced at having seen such a great Prince, and that he took it as a great honour that he had come in person to meet him and had frequently shown him such favour.

Then Montezuma spoke other words of politeness to him, and told two of his nephews who supported his arms, the Lord of Texcoco and the Lord of Coyoacan, to go with us and show us to our quarters, and Montezuma with his other two relations, the Lord of Cuitlahuac and the Lord of Tacuba who accompanied him, returned to the city, and all those grand companies of Caciques and chieftains who had come with him returned in his train. As they turned back after their Prince we stood watching them and observed how they all marched with their eyes fixed on the ground without looking at him, keeping close to the wall, following him with great reverence. Thus space was made for us to enter the streets of Mexico, without being so much crowded. But who could now count the multitude of men and women and boys who were in the streets and on the azoteas, and in canoes on the canals, who had come out to see us. It was indeed wonderful, and, now that I am writing about it, it all comes before my eyes as though it had happened but yesterday. Coming to think it over it seems to be a great mercy that our Lord Jesus Christ was pleased to give us grace and courage to dare to enter into such a city; and for the many times He has saved me from danger of death, as will be seen later on, I give Him sincere thanks, and in that He has preserved me to write about it, although I cannot do it as fully as is fitting or the subject needs. Let us make no words about it, for deeds are the best witnesses to what I say here and elsewhere.

Let us return to our entry to Mexico. They took us to lodge in some large houses, where there were apartments for all of us, for they had belonged to the father of the Great Montezuma, who was named Axayaca, and at that time Montezuma kept there the great oratories for his idols, and a secret chamber where he kept bars and jewels of gold, which was the treasure that he had inherited from his father Axayaca, and he never disturbed it. They took us to lodge in that house, because they called us Teules, and took us for such, so that we should be with the Idols or Teules which were kept there. However, for one reason or another, it was there they took us, where there were great halls and chambers canopied with the cloth of the country for our Captain, and for every one of us beds of matting with canopies above, and no better bed is given, however great the chief may be, for they are not used. And all these palaces were coated with shining cement and swept and garlanded.

As soon as we arrived and entered into the great court, the Great Montezuma took our Captain by the hand, for he was there awaiting him, and led him to the apartment and saloon where he was to lodge, which was very richly adorned according to their usage, and he had at hand a very rich necklace made of golden crabs, a marvellous piece of work, and Montezuma himself placed it round the neck of our Captain Cortés, and greatly astonished his [own] Captains by the great honour that he was bestowing on him. When the necklace had been fastened, Cortés thanked Montezuma through our interpreters, and Montezuma replied—"Malinche, you and your brethren are in your own house, rest awhile," and then he went to his palaces, which were not far away, and we divided our lodgings by companies, and placed the artillery pointing in a convenient direction, and the order which we had to keep was clearly explained to us, and that we were to be much on the alert, both the cavalry and all of us soldiers. A sumptuous dinner was provided for us according to their use and custom, and we ate it at once. So this was our lucky and daring entry into the great city of Tenochtitlan Mexico on the 8th day of November the year of our Saviour Jesus Christ, 1519.

When the Great Montezuma had dined and he knew that some time had passed since our Captain and all of us had done the same, he came in the greatest state to our quarters with a numerous company of chieftains, all of them his kinsmen. When Cortés was told that he was approaching he came out to the middle of the Hall to receive him, and Montezuma took him by the hand, and they brought some seats, made according to their usage and very richly decorated and embroidered with gold in many designs, and Montezuma asked our Captain to be seated, and both of them sat down each on his chair. Then Montezuma began a very good speech, saying that he was greatly rejoiced to have in his house and his kingdom such valiant gentlemen as were Cortés and all of us. That two years ago he had received news of another Captain who came to Champoton and likewise last year they had brought him news of another Captain who came with four ships, and that each time he had wished to see them, and now that he had us with him he was at our service, and would give us of all that he possessed; that it must indeed be true that we were those of whom his ancestors in years long past had spoken, saying that men would come from where the sun rose to rule over these lands, and that we must be those men, as we had fought so valiantly in the affairs at Champoton and Tabasco and against the Tlaxcalans; for they had brought him pictures of the battles true to life.

Cortés answered him through our interpreters who always accompanied him, especially Doña Marina, and said to him that he and all of us did not know how to repay him the great favours we received from him every day. It was true that we came from where the sun rose, and were the vassals and servants of a great Prince called the Emperor Don Carlos, who held beneath his sway many and great princes, and that the Emperor having heard of him and what a great prince he was, had sent us to these parts to see him, and to beg them to become Christians, the same as our Emperor and all of us, so that his soul and those of all his vassals might be saved. Later on he would further explain how and in what manner this should be done, and how we worship one only true God, and who He is, and many other good things which he should listen to, such as he had already told to his ambassadors Tendile and Pitalpitoque and Quintalbor when we were on the sand dunes. When this conference was over, the Great Montezuma had already at hand some very rich golden jewels, of many patterns, which he gave to our Captain, and in the same manner to each one of our Captains he gave trifles of gold, and three loads of mantles of rich feather work, and to the soldiers also he gave to each one two loads of mantles, and he did it cheerfully and in every way he seemed to be a great Prince. When these things had been distributed, he asked Cortés if we were all brethren and vassals of our great Emperor, and Cortés replied yes, we were brothers in affection and friendship, and persons of great distinction, and servants of our great King and Prince. Further polite speeches passed between Montezuma and Cortés, and as this was the first time he had come to visit us, and so as not to be wearisome, they ceased talking. Montezuma had ordered his stewards that, according to our own use and customs in all things, we should be provided with maize and grinding stones, and women to make bread, and fowls and fruit, and much fodder for the horses. Then Montezuma took leave of our Captain and all of us with the greatest courtesy, and we went out with him as far as the street. Cortés ordered us not to go far from our quarters for the present, until we knew better what was expedient.

The next day Cortés decided to go to Montezuma's palace, and he first sent to find out what he intended doing and to let him know that we were coming. He took with him four captains, namely Pedro de Alvarado, Juan Velásquez de Leon, Diego de Ordás, and Gonzalo de Sandoval, and five of us soldiers also went with him.

When Montezuma knew of our coming he advanced to the middle of the hall to receive us, accompanied by many of his nephews, for no other chiefs were permitted to enter or hold communication with Montezuma where he then was, unless it were on important business. Cortés and he paid the greatest reverence to each other and then they took one another by the hand and Montezuma made him sit down on his couch on his right hand, and he also bade all of us to be seated on seats which he ordered to be brought.

Then Cortés began to make an explanation through Doña Marina and Aguilar, and said that he and all of us were rested, and that in coming to see and converse with such a great prince as he was, we had completed the journey and fulfilled the command which our great King and Prince had laid on us. But what he chiefly came to say on behalf of our Lord God had already been brought to his [Montezuma's] knowledge through his ambassadors, Tendile, Pitalpitoque and Quintalbor, at the time when he did us the favour to send the golden sun and moon to the sand dunes; for we told them then that we were Christians and worshipped one true and only God, that we believe in Him and worship Him, but that those whom they look upon as gods are not so, but are devils, which are evil things, and if their looks are bad their deeds are worse, and they could see that they were evil and of little worth, for where we had set up crosses such as those his ambassadors had seen, they dared not appear before them, through fear of them, and that as time went on they would notice this.

He also told them that, in course of time, our Lord and King would send some men who among us lead very holy lives, much better than we do, who will explain to them all about it, for at present we merely came to give them due warning, and so he prayed him to do what he was asked and carry it into effect.

As Montezuma appeared to wish to reply, Cortés broke off his argument, and to all of us who were with him he said: "With this we have done our duty considering it is the first attempt."

Montezuma replied: "Señor Malinche, I have understood your words and arguments very well before now, from what you said to my servants at the sand dunes, this about three Gods and the Cross, and all those things that you have preached in the towns through which you have come. We have not made any answer to it because here throughout all time we have worshipped our own gods, and thought they were good, as no doubt yours are, so do not trouble to speak to us anymore about them at present. Regarding the creation of the world, we have held the same belief for ages past, and for this reason we take it for certain that you are those whom our ancestors predicted would come from the direction of the sunrise. As for your great King, I feel that I am indebted to him, and I will give him of what I possess, for as I have already said, two years ago I heard of the Captains who came in ships from the direction in which you came, and they said that they were the servants of this your great King, and I wish to know if you are all one and the same."

Cortés replied: Yes, that we were all brethren and servants of our Emperor, and that those men came to examine the way and the seas and the ports so as to know them well in order that we might follow as we had done. Montezuma was referring to the expeditions of Francisco Hernández de Córdova and of Grijalva, and he said that ever since that time he had wished to capture some of those men who had come so as to keep them in his kingdoms and cities and to do them honour, and his gods had now fulfilled his desires, for now that we were in his home, which we might call our own, we should rejoice and take our rest, for there we should be well treated. And if he had on other occasions sent to say that we should not enter his city, it was not of his free will, but because his vassals were afraid, for they said that we shot our flashes of lightning, and killed many Indians with our horses, and that we were angry Teules, and other childish stories, and now that he had seen our persons and knew we were of flesh and bone, and had sound sense, and that we were very valiant, for these reasons he held us in much higher regard than he did from their reports, and he would share his possessions with us. Then Cortés and all of us answered that we thanked him sincerely for such signal goodwill, and Montezuma said, laughing, for he was very merry in his princely way of speaking: "Malinche, I know very well that these people of Tlaxcala with whom you are such good friends have told you that I am a sort of God or Teule, and that everything in my houses is made of gold and silver and precious stones, I know well enough that you are wise and did not believe it but took it as a joke. Behold now, Señor Malinche, my body is of flesh and bone like yours, my houses and palaces of stone and wood and lime; that I am a great king and inherit the riches of my ancestors is true, but not all the nonsense and lies that they have told you about me, although of course you treated it as a joke, as I did your thunder and lightning."

Cortés answered him, also laughing, and said that opponents and enemies always say evil things, without truth in them, of those whom they hate, and that he well knew that he could not hope to find another Prince more magnificent in these countries, and that not without reason had he been so vaunted to our Emperor.

While this conversation was going on, Montezuma secretly sent a great Cacique, one of his nephews who was in his company, to order his stewards to bring certain pieces of gold, which it seems must have been put apart to give to Cortés, and ten loads of fine cloth, which he apportioned, the gold and mantles between Cortés and the four captains, and to each of us soldiers he gave two golden necklaces, each necklace being worth ten pesos, and two loads of mantles. The gold that he then gave us was worth in all more than a thousand pesos and he gave it all cheerfully and with the air of a great and valiant prince. As it was now past midday, so as not to appear importunate, Cortés said to him: "Señor Montezuma, you always have the habit of heaping load upon load in every day conferring favours on us, and it is already your dinner time." Montezuma replied that he thanked us for coming to see him, and then we took our leave with the greatest courtesy and we went to our lodgings.

And as we went along we spoke of the good manners and breeding which he showed in everything, and that we should show him in all ways the greatest respect, doffing our quilted caps when we passed before him, and this we always did.

The Great Montezuma was about forty years old, of good height and well proportioned, slender and spare of flesh, not very swarthy, but of the natural colour and shade of an Indian. He did not wear his hair long, but so as just to cover his ears, his scanty black beard was well shaped and thin. His face was somewhat long, but cheerful, and he had good eyes and showed in his appearance and manner both tenderness and, when necessary, gravity. He was very neat and clean and bathed once every day in the afternoon. He had many women as mistresses, daughters of Chieftains, and he had two great Cacicas as his legitimate wives. He was free from unnatural offences. The clothes that he wore one day, he did not put on again until four days later. He had over two hundred Chieftains in his guard, in other rooms close to his own, not that all were meant to converse with him, but only one or another, and when they went to speak to him they were obliged to take off their rich mantles and put on others of little worth, but they had to be clean, and they had to enter barefoot with their eyes lowered to the ground, and not to look up in his face. And they made him three obeisances, and said: "Lord, my Lord, my Great Lord," before they came up to him, and then they made their report and with a few words he dismissed them, and on taking leave they did not turn their backs, but kept their faces towards him with their eyes to the ground, and they did not turn their backs until they left the room. I noticed another thing, that when other great chiefs came from distant lands about disputes or business, when they reached the apartments of the Great Montezuma, they had to come barefoot and with poor mantles, and they might not enter directly into the Palace, but had to loiter about a little on one side of the Palace door, for to enter hurriedly was considered to be disrespectful.

For each meal, over thirty different dishes were prepared by his cooks according to their ways and usage, and they placed small pottery braziers beneath the dishes so that they should not get cold. They prepared more than three hundred plates of the food that Montezuma was going to eat, and more than a thousand for the guard. When he was going to eat, Montezuma would sometimes go out with his chiefs and stewards, and they would point out to him which dish was best, and of what birds and other things it was composed, and as they advised him, so he would eat, but it was not often that he would go out to see the food, and then merely as a pastime.

I have heard it said that they were wont to cook for him the flesh of young boys, but as he had such a variety of dishes, made of so many things, we could not succeed in seeing if they were of human flesh or of other things, for they daily cooked fowls, turkeys, pheasants, native partridges, quail, tame and wild ducks, venison, wild boar, reed birds, pigeons, hares and rabbits and many sorts of birds and other things which are bred in this country, and they are so numerous that I cannot finish naming them in a hurry; so we had no insight into it, but I know for certain that after our Captain censured the sacrifice of human beings, and the eating of their flesh, he ordered that such food should not be prepared for him thenceforth.

Let us cease speaking of this and return to the way things were served to him at mealtimes. It was in this way: if it was cold they made up a large fire of live coals of a firewood made from the bark of trees which did not give off any smoke, and the scent of the bark from which the fire was made was very fragrant, and so that it should not give off more heat than he required, they placed in front of it a sort of screen adorned with figures of idols worked in gold. He was seated on a low stool, soft and richly worked, and the table, which was also low, was made in the same style as the seats, and on it they placed the tablecloths of white cloth and some rather long napkins of the same material. Four very beautiful cleanly women brought water for his hands in a sort of deep basin which they call *xicales* [gourds], and they held others like plates below to catch the water, and they brought him towels. And two other women brought him tortilla bread, and as soon as he began to eat they placed before him a sort of wooden screen painted over with gold, so that no one should watch him eating. Then the four women stood aside, and four great chieftains who were old men came and stood beside them, and with these Montezuma now and then conversed, and asked them questions, and as a great favour he would give to each of these elders a dish of what to him tasted best. They say that these elders were his near relations, and were his counsellors and judges of lawsuits, and the dishes and food which Montezuma gave them they ate standing up with much reverence and without looking at his face. He was served on Cholula earthenware either red or black. While he was at his meal the men of his guard who were in the rooms near to that of Montezuma, never dreamed of making any noise or speaking aloud. They brought him fruit of all the different kinds that the land produced, but he ate very little of it. From time to time they brought him, in cup-shaped vessels of pure gold, a certain drink made from cacao, and the women served this drink to him with great reverence.

Sometimes at mealtimes there were present some very ugly humpbacks, very small of stature and their bodies almost broken in half, who are their jesters, and other Indians, who must have been buffoons, who told him witty sayings, and others who sang and danced, for Montezuma was fond of pleasure and song, and to these he ordered to be given what was left of the food and the jugs of cacao. Then the same four women removed the tablecloths, and with much ceremony they brought water for his hands. And Montezuma talked with those four old chieftains about things that interested him, and they took leave of him with the great reverence in which they held him, and he remained to repose.

As soon as the Great Montezuma had dined, all the men of the Guard had their meal and as many more of the other house servants, and it seems to me that they brought out over a thousand dishes of the food of which I have spoken, and then over two thousand jugs of cacao all frothed up, as they make it in Mexico, and a limitless quantity of fruit, so that with his women and female servants and bread makers and cacao makers his expenses must have been very great.

Let us cease talking about the expenses and the food for his household and let us speak of the Stewards and the Treasures and the stores and pantries and of those who had charge of the houses where the maize was stored. I say that there would be so much to write about, each thing by itself, that I should not know where to begin, but we stood astonished at the excellent arrangements and the great abundance of provisions that he had in all, but I must add what I had forgotten, for it is as well to go back and relate it, and that is, that while Montezuma was at table eating, as I have described, there were waiting on him two other graceful women to bring him tortillas, kneaded with eggs and other sustaining ingredients, and these tortillas were very white, and they were brought on plates covered with clean napkins, and they also brought him another kind of bread, like long balls kneaded with other kinds of sustaining food, and *pan pachol*, for so they call it in this country, which is a sort of wafer. There were also placed on the table three tubes much painted and gilded, which held liquidambar mixed with certain herbs which they call *tabaco*, and when he had finished eating, after they had danced before him and sung and the table was removed, he inhaled the smoke from one of those tubes, but he took very little of it and with that he fell asleep.

I remember that at that time his steward was a great Cacique to whom we gave the name of Tápia, and he kept the accounts of all the revenue that was brought to Montezuma, in his books which were made of paper which they call *amal*, and he had a great house full of these books. Now we must leave the books and the accounts for it is outside our story, and say how Montezuma had two houses full of every sort of arms, many of them richly adorned with gold and precious stones. There were shields great and small, and a sort of broadswords, and others like two-handed swords set with stone knives which cut much better than our swords, and lances longer than ours are, with a fathom of blade with many knives set in it, which even when they are driven into a buckler or shield do not come out, in fact they cut like razors so that they can shave their heads with them. There were very good bows and arrows and double-pointed lances and others with one point, as well as their throwing sticks, and many slings and round stones shaped by hand, and some sort of artful shields which are so made that they can be rolled up, so as not to be in the way when they are not fighting, and when they are needed for fighting they let them fall down, and they cover the body from top to toe. There was also much quilted cotton armour, richly ornamented on the outside with many coloured feathers, used as devices and distinguishing marks, and there were casques or helmets made of wood and bone, also highly decorated with feathers on the outside, and there were other arms of other makes which, so as to avoid prolixity, I will not describe, and there were artisans who were skilled in such things and worked at them, and stewards who had charge of the arms.

Let us leave this and proceed to the Aviary, and I am forced to abstain from enumerating every kind of bird that was there and its peculiarity, for there was everything from the Royal Eagle and other smaller eagles, and many other birds of great size, down to tiny birds of many-coloured plumage, also the birds from which they take the rich plumage which they use in their green feather work. The birds which have these feathers are about the size of the magpies in Spain, they are called in this country *Quezales* [*Trogon resplendens*], and there are other birds which have feathers of five colours—green, red, white, yellow and blue; I don't remember what they are called; then there were parrots of many different colours, and there are so many of them that I forget their names, not to mention the beautifully marked ducks and other larger ones like them. From all these birds they plucked the feathers when the time was right to do so, and the feathers grew again. All the birds that I have spoken about breed in these houses, and in the setting season certain Indian men and women who look after the birds, place the eggs under them and clean the nests and feed them, so that each kind of bird has its proper food. In this house that I have spoken of there is a great tank of freshwater and in it there are other sorts of birds with long stilted legs, with body, wings and tail all red; I don't know their names, but in the Island of Cuba they are called *Ypiris*, and there are others something like them, and there are also in that tank many other kinds of birds which always live in the water.

Let us leave this and go on to another great house, where they keep many Idols, and they say that they are their fierce gods, and with them many kinds of carnivorous beasts of prey, tigers and two kinds of lions, and animals something like wolves and foxes, and other smaller carnivorous animals, and all these carnivores they feed with flesh, and the greater number of them breed in the house. They give them as food deer and

religion

fowls, dogs and other things which they are used to hunt, and I have heard it said that they feed them on the bodies of the Indians who have been sacrificed. It is in this way: you have already heard me say that when they sacrifice a wretched Indian they saw open the chest with stone knives and hasten to tear out the palpitating heart and blood, and offer it to their Idols, in whose name the sacrifice is made. Then they cut off the thighs, arms and head and eat the former at feasts and banquets, and the head they hang up on some beams, and the body of the man sacrificed is not eaten but given to these fierce animals. They also have in that cursed house many vipers and poisonous snakes which carry on their tails things that sound like bells. These are the worst vipers of all, and they keep them in jars and great pottery vessels with many feathers, and there they lay their eggs and rear their young, and they give them to eat the bodies of the Indians who have been sacrificed, and the flesh of dogs which they are in the habit of breeding.

Let me speak now of the infernal noise when the lions and tigers roared and the jackals and foxes howled and the serpents hissed, it was horrible to listen to and it seemed like a hell. Let us go on and speak of the skilled workman Montezuma employed in every craft that was practised among them. We will begin with lapidaries and workers in gold and silver and all the hollow work, which even the great goldsmiths in Spain were forced to admire, and of these there were a great number of the best in a town named Atzcapotzalco, a league from Mexico. Then for working precious stones and chalchihuites, which are like emeralds, there were other great artists. Let us go on to the great craftsmen in feather work, and painters and sculptors who were most refined; then to the Indian women who did the weaving and the washing, who made such an immense quantity of fine fabrics with wonderful feather work designs; the greater part of it was brought daily from some towns of the province on the north coast near Vera Cruz called Cotaxtla.

In the house of the great Montezuma himself, all the daughters of chieftains whom he had as mistresses always wore beautiful things, and there were many daughters of Mexican citizens who lived in retirement

and wished to appear to be like nuns, who also did weaving but it was wholly of feather work. These nuns had their houses near the great Cue of Huichilobos and out of devotion to it, or to another idol, that of a woman who was said to be their mediatrix in the matter of marriage, their fathers placed them in that religious retirement until they married, and they were only taken out thence to be married.

Let us go on and tell about the great number of dancers kept by the Great Montezuma for his amusement, and others who used stilts on their feet, and others who flew when they danced up in the air, and others like Merry-Andrews, and I may say that there was a district full of these people who had no other occupation. Let us go on and speak of the workmen that he had as stonecutters, masons and carpenters, all of whom attended to the work of his houses, I say that he had as many as he wished for. We must not forget the gardens of flowers and sweet-scented trees, and the many kinds that there were of them, and the arrangement of them and the walks, and the ponds and tanks of freshwater where the water entered at one end and flowed out of the other; and the baths which he had there, and the variety of small birds that nested in the branches, and the medicinal and useful herbs that were in the gardens. It was a wonder to see, and to take care of it there were many gardeners. Everything was made in masonry and well cemented, baths and walks and closets, and apartments like summerhouses where they danced and sang. There was as much to be seen in these gardens as there was everywhere else, and we could not tire of witnessing his great power. Thus as a consequence of so many crafts being practised among them, a large number of skilled Indians were employed.

As we had already been four days in Mexico and neither the Captain nor any of us had left our lodgings except to go to the houses and gardens, Cortés said to us that it would be well to go to the great Plaza of Tlaltelolco and see the great Temple of Huichilobos, and that he wished to consult the Great Montezuma and have his approval. For this purpose he sent Jerónimo de Aguilar and the Doña Marina as messengers, and with them went our Captain's small page named Orteguilla, who already understood something of the language. When Montezuma knew his wishes he sent to say that we were welcome to go; on the other hand, as he was afraid that we might do some dishonour to his Idols, he determined to go with us himself with many of his chieftains. He came out from his Palace in his rich litter, but when half the distance had been traversed and he was near some oratories, he stepped out of the litter, for he thought it a great affront to his idols to go to their house and temple in that manner. Some of the great chieftains supported him with their arms, and the tribal lords went in front of him carrying two staves like sceptres held on high, which was the sign that the Great Montezuma was coming. (When he went in his litter he carried a wand half of gold and half of wood, which was held up like a wand of justice.) So he went on and ascended the great Cue accompanied by many priests, and he began to burn incense and perform other ceremonies to Huichilobos.

Our Captain and all of those who had horses went to Tlaltelolco on horseback, and nearly all of us soldiers were fully equipped, and many Caciques whom Montezuma had sent for that purpose went in our company. When we arrived at the great marketplace, called Tlaltelolco, we were astounded at the number of people and the quantity of merchandise that it contained, and at the good order and control that was maintained, for we had never seen such a thing before. The chieftains who accompanied us acted as guides. Each kind of merchandise was kept by itself and had its fixed place marked out. Let us begin with the dealers in gold, silver, and precious stones, feathers, mantles and embroidered goods. Then there were other wares consisting of Indian slaves both men and women; and I say that they bring as many of them to that great market for sale as the Portuguese bring negroes from Guinea; and they brought them along tied to long poles, with collars round their necks so that they could not escape, and others they left free. Next there were other traders who sold great pieces of cloth and cotton, and articles of twisted thread, and there were *cacahuateros* who sold cacao. In this way one could see every sort of merchandise that is to be found in the whole of New Spain, placed in arrangement in the same manner as they do in my own country, which is Medina del Campo, where they hold the fairs, where each line of booths has its particular kind of merchandise, and so it is in this great market.

There were those who sold cloths of henequen and ropes and the sandals with which they are shod, which are made from the same plant, and sweet cooked roots, and other tubers which they get from this plant, all were kept in one part of the market in the place assigned to them. In another part there were skins of tigers and lions, of otters and jackals, deer and other animals and badgers and mountain cats, some tanned and others untanned, and other classes of merchandise.

Let us go on and speak of those who sold beans and sage and other vegetables and herbs in another part, and to those who sold fowls, cocks with wattles, rabbits, hares, deer, mallards, young dogs and other things of that sort in their part of the market, and let us also mention the fruiterers, and the women who sold cooked food, dough and tripe in their own part of the market; then every sort of pottery made in a thousand different forms from great water jars to little jugs, these also had a place to themselves; then those who sold honey and honey paste and other dainties like nut paste, and those who sold lumber, boards, cradles, beams, blocks and benches, each article by itself, and the vendors of *ocote* [pitch pine for torches] firewood, and other things of a similar nature. But why do I waste so many words in recounting what they sell in that great market?— for I shall never finish if I tell it all in detail. Paper, which in this country is called amal, and reeds scented with liquidambar, and full of tobacco, and yellow ointments and things of that sort are sold by themselves, and much cochineal is sold under the arcades which are in that great marketplace, and there are many vendors of herbs and other sorts of trades. There are also buildings where three magistrates sit in judgment, and there are executive officers like *Alguacils* who inspect the merchandise. I am forgetting those who sell salt, and those who make the stone knives, and how they split them off the stone itself; and the fisherwomen and others who sell some small cakes made from a sort of ooze which they get out of the great lake, which curdles, and from this they make a bread having a flavour something like cheese. There are for sale axes of brass and copper and tin, and gourds and gaily painted jars made of wood. I could wish that I had finished telling of all the things which are sold there, but they are so numerous and of such different quality and the great marketplace with its surrounding arcades was so crowded with people, that one would not have been able to see and inquire about it all in two days.

Then we went to the great Cue, and when we were already approaching its great courts, before leaving the marketplace itself, there were many more merchants, who, as I was told, brought gold for sale in grains, just as it is taken from the mines. The gold is placed in the quills of the geese of the country, white quills, so that the gold can be seen through, and according to the length and thickness of the quills they arrange their accounts with one another, how much so many mantles or so many gourds full of cacao were worth, or how many slaves, or whatever other thing they were exchanging.

Before reaching the great Cue there is a great enclosure of courts, it seems to me larger than the plaza of Salamanca, with two walls of masonry surrounding it, and the court itself all paved with very smooth great white flagstones. And where there were not these stones it was cemented and burnished and all very clean, so that one could not find any dust or a straw in the whole place.

When we arrived near the Great Cue and before we had ascended a single step of it, the Great Montezuma sent down from above, where he was making his sacrifices, six priests and two chieftains to accompany our Captain. On ascending the steps, which are one hundred and fourteen in number, they attempted to take him by the arms so as to help him to ascend (thinking that he would get tired) as they were accustomed to assist their lord Montezuma, but Cortés would not allow them to come near him. When we got to the top of the great Cue, on a small plaza which has been made on the top where there was a space like a platform with some large stones placed on it, on which they put the poor Indians for sacrifice, there was a bulky image like a dragon and other evil figures and much blood shed that very day.

When we arrived there Montezuma came out of an oratory where his cursed idols were, at the summit of the great Cue, and two priests came with him, and after paying great reverence to Cortés and to all of us he said: "You must be tired, Señor Malinche, from ascending this our great Cue," and Cortés replied through our interpreters who were with us that he and his companions were never tired by anything. Then Montezuma took him by the hand and told him to look at his great city and all the other cities that were standing in the water, and the many other towns on the land round the lake, and that if he had not seen the great marketplace well, that from where they were they could see it better.

So we stood looking about us, for that huge and cursed temple stood so high that from it one could see over everything very well, and we saw the three causeways which led into Mexico, that is the causeway of Iztapalapa by which we had entered four days before, and that of Tacuba, and that of Tepeaquilla [Guadelupe], and we saw the freshwater that comes from Chapultepec which supplies the city, and we saw the bridges on the three causeways which were built at certain distances apart through which the water of the lake flowed in and out from one side to the other, and we beheld on that great lake a great multitude of canoes, some coming with supplies of food and others returning loaded with cargoes of merchandise; and we saw that from every house of that great city and of all the other cities that were built in the water it was impossible to pass from house to house, except by drawbridges which were made of wood or in canoes; and we saw in those cities Cues and oratories like towers and fortresses and all gleaming white, and it was a wonderful thing to behold; then the houses with flat roofs, and on the causeways other small towers and oratories which were like fortresses.

After having examined and considered all that we had seen we turned to look at the great marketplace and the crowds of people that were in it, some buying and others selling, so that the murmur and hum of their voices and words that they used could be heard more than a league off. Some of the soldiers among us who had been in many parts of the world, in Constantinople, and all over Italy, and in Rome, said that so large a marketplace and so full of people, and so well regulated and arranged, they had never beheld before.

Let us leave this, and return to our Captain, who said to Fray Bartolomé de Olmedo, who happened to be nearby him: "It seems to me, Señor Padre, that it would be a good thing to throw out a feeler to Montezuma, as to whether he would allow us to build our church here"; and the Padre replied that it would be a good thing if it were successful, but it seemed to him that it was not quite a suitable time to speak about it, for Montezuma did not appear to be inclined to do such a thing.

Then our Cortés said to Montezuma: "Your Highness is indeed a very great prince and worthy of even greater things. We are rejoiced to see your cities, and as we are here in your temple, what I now beg as a favour is that you will show us your gods and Teules." Montezuma replied that he must first speak with his high priests, and when he had spoken to them he said that we might enter into a small tower and apartment, a sort of ball, where there were two altars, with very richly carved boardings on the top of the roof. On each altar were two figures, like giants with very tall bodies and very fat, and the first which stood on the right hand they said was the figure of Huichilobos their god of War; it had a very broad face and monstrous and terrible eyes, and the whole of his body was covered with precious stones, and gold and pearls, and with seed pearls stuck on with a paste that they make in this country out of a sort of root, and all the body and head was covered with it, and the body was girdled by great snakes made of gold and precious stones, and in one hand he held a bow and in the other some arrows. And another small idol that stood by him, they said was his page, and he held a short lance and a shield richly decorated with gold and stones. Huichilobos had round his neck some Indians' faces and other things like hearts of Indians, the former made of gold and the latter of silver, with many precious blue stones.

There were some braziers with incense which they call copal, and in them they were burning the hearts of the three Indians whom they had sacrificed that day, and they had made the sacrifice with smoke and copal. All the walls of the oratory were so splashed and encrusted with blood that they were black, the floor was the same and the whole place stank vilely. Then we saw on the other side on the left hand there stood the other great image the same height as Huichilobos, and it had a face like a bear and eyes that shone, made of their mirrors which they call *Tezcat*, and the body plastered with precious stones like that of Huichilobos, for they say that the two are brothers; and this Tezcatepuca was the god of Hell and had charge of the souls of the Mexicans, and his body was girt with figures like little devils with snakes' tails. The walls were so clotted with blood and the soil so bathed with it that in the slaughterhouses of Spain there is not such another stench.

They had offered to this Idol five hearts from the day's sacrifices. In the highest part of the Cue there was a recess of which the woodwork was very richly worked, and in it was another image half man and half lizard, with precious stones all over it, and half the body was covered with a mantle. They say that the body of this figure is full of the seeds that there are in the world, and they say that it is the god of seedtime and harvest, but I do not remember its name, and everything was covered with blood, both walls and altar, and the stench was such that we could hardly wait the moment to get out of it.

They had an exceedingly large drum there, and when they beat it the sound of it was so dismal and like, so to say, an instrument of the infernal regions, that one could hear it a distance of two leagues, and they said that the skins it was covered with were those of great snakes. In that small place there were many diabolical things to be seen, bugles and trumpets and knives, and many hearts of Indians that they had burned in fumigating their idols, and everything was so clotted with blood, and there was so much of it, that I curse the whole of it, and as it stank like a slaughterhouse we hastened to clear out of such a bad stench and worse sight. Our Captains said to Montezuma through our interpreter, half laughing: "Señor Montezuma, I do not understand how such a great Prince and wise man as you are has not come to the conclusion, in your mind, that these idols of yours are not gods, but evil things that are called devils, and so that you may know it and all your priests may see it clearly, do me the favour to approve of my placing a cross here on the top of this tower, and that in one part of these oratories where your Huichilobos and Tezcatepuca stand we may divide off a space where we can set up an image of Our Lady (an image which Montezuma had already seen) and you will see by the fear in which these Idols hold it that they are deceiving you."

Montezuma replied half angrily (and the two priests who were with him showed great annoyance), and said: "Señor Malinche, if I had known that you would have said such defamatory things I would not have shown you my gods, we consider them to be very good, for they give us health and rains and good seedtimes and seasons and as many victories as we desire, and we are obliged to worship them and make sacrifices, and I pray you not to say another word to their dishonour."

When our Captain heard that and noted the angry looks he did not refer again to the subject, but said with a cheerful manner: "It is time for your Excellency and for us to return," and Montezuma replied that it was well, but that he had to pray and offer certain sacrifices on account of the great *tatacul*, that is to say sin, which he had committed in allowing us to ascend his great Cue, and being the cause of our being permitted to see his gods, and of our dishonouring them by speaking evil of them, so that before he left he must pray and worship.

Then Cortés said: "I ask your pardon if it be so," and then we went down the steps, and as they numbered one hundred and fourteen, and as some of our soldiers were suffering from tumours and abscesses, their legs were tired by the descent.

I will leave off talking about the oratory, and I will give my impressions of its surroundings, and if I do not describe it as accurately as I should do, do not wonder at it, for at that time I had other things to think about, regarding what we had on hand, that is to say my soldier's duties and what my Captain ordered me to do, and not about telling stories. To go back to the facts, it seems to me that the circuit of the great Cue was equal to that of six large sites [*solares*—a *solar* is a town lot for house building], such as they measure in this country, and from below up to where a small tower stood, where they kept their idols, it narrowed, and in the middle of the lofty Cue up to its highest point, there were five hollows like barbicans, but open, without screens, and as there are many Cues painted on the banners of the conquerors, and on one which I possess, anyone who has seen them can infer what they looked like from outside, better than I myself saw and understood it. There was a report that at the time they began to build that great Cue, all the inhabitants of that mighty city had placed as offerings in the foundations, gold and silver and pearls and precious stones, and had bathed them with the blood of the many Indian prisoners of war who were sacrificed, and had placed there every sort and kind of seed that the land produces, so that their Idols should give them victories and riches, and large crops. Some of my inquisitive readers will ask, how could we come to know that into the foundations of that great Cue they cast gold and silver and precious chalchihuites and seeds, and watered them with the human blood of the Indians whom they sacrificed, when it was more than a thousand years ago that they built and made it? The answer I give to this is that after we took that great and strong city, and the sites were apportioned, it was then proposed that in the place of that great Cue we should build a church to our patron and guide Señor Santiago, and a great part of the site of the great temple of Huichilobos was occupied by the site of the holy church, and when they opened the foundations in order to strengthen them, they found much gold and silver and chalchihuites and pearls and seed pearls and other stones. And a settler in Mexico who occupied another part of the same site found the same things, and the officers of His Majesty's treasury demanded them saying that they belonged by right to His Majesty, and there was a lawsuit about it. I do not remember what happened except that they sought information from the Caciques and Chieftains of Mexico, and from Guatémoc, who was then alive, and they said that it was true that all the inhabitants of Mexico at that time cast into the foundations those jewels and all the rest of the things, and that so it was noted in their books and pictures of ancient things, and from this cause those riches were preserved for the building of the holy church of Santiago.

Let us leave this and speak of the great and splendid Courts which were in front of the temple of Huichilobos, where now stands the church of Señor Santiago, which was called Tlaltelolco, for so they were accustomed to call it.

I have already said that there were two walls of masonry which had to be passed before entering, and that the court was paved with white stones, like flagstones, carefully whitewashed and burnished and clean, and it was as large and as broad as the plaza of Salamanca. A little way apart from the great Cue there was another small tower which was also an Idol house, or a true hell, for it had at the opening of one gate a most terrible mouth such as they depict, saying that such there are in hell. The mouth was open with great fangs to devour souls, and here too were some groups of devils and bodies of serpents close to the door, and a little way off was a place of sacrifice all blood-stained and black with smoke, and encrusted with blood, and there were many great ollas and *cántaros* and *tinajas* [names of various large pottery vessels for holding water and cooking] of water inside the house, for it was here that they cooked the flesh of the unfortunate Indians who were sacrificed, which was eaten by the priests. There were also near the place of sacrifice many large knives and chopping blocks, such as those on which they cut up meat in the slaughterhouses. Then behind that cursed house, some distance away from it, were some great piles of firewood, and not far from them a large tank of water which rises and falls, the water coming through a tube from the covered channel which enters the city from Chapultepec. I always called that house "the Infernal Regions."

Let us go on beyond the court to another Cue where the great Mexican princes were buried, where also there were many Idols, and all was full of blood and smoke, and it had other doorways with hellish figures, and then near that Cue was another full of skulls and large bones arranged in perfect order, which one could look at but could not count, for there were too many of them. The skulls were by themselves and the bones in separate piles. In that place there were other Idols, and in every house or Cue or oratory that I have mentioned there were priests with long robes of black cloth and long hoods like those of the Dominicans and slightly resembling those of the Canons. The hair of these priests was very long and so matted that it could not be separated or disentangled, and most of them had their ears scarified, and their hair was clotted with blood. Let us go on; there were other Cues, a little way from where the skulls were, which contained other Idols and places of sacrifice decorated with other evil paintings. And they said that those idols were intercessors in the marriages of men. I do not want to delay any longer telling about idols, but will only add that all round that great court there were many houses, not lofty, used and occupied by the priests and other Indians who had charge of the Idols. On one side of the great Cue there was another much larger pond or tank of very clear water dedicated solely to the service of Huichilobos and Tezcatepuca, and the water entered that pond through covered pipes which came from Chapultepec. Near to this were other large buildings such as a sort of nunnery where many of the daughters of the inhabitants of Mexico were sheltered like nuns up to the time they were married, and there stood two Idols with the figures of women, which were the intercessors in the marriages of women, and women made sacrifices to them and held festivals so that they should give them good husbands.

I have spent a long time talking about this great Cue of Tlaltelolco and its Courts, but I say that it was the greatest temple in the whole of Mexico although there were many others, very splendid. Four or five par- ishes or districts possessed, between them, an oratory with its Idols, and as they were very numerous I have not kept count of them all. I will go on and say that the great oratory that they had in Cholula was higher than that of Mexico, for it had one hundred and twenty steps, and according to what they say they held the Idol of Cholula to be good, and they went to it on pilgrimages from all parts of New Spain to obtain absolution, and for this reason they built for it such a splendid Cue; but it is of another form from that of Mexico although the courts are the same, very large with a double wall. I may add that the Cue in the City of Texcoco was very lofty, having one hundred and seventeen steps, and the Courts were broad and fine, shaped in a different form from the others. It is a laughable matter that every province had its Idols and those of one province or city were of no use to the others, thus they had an infinite number of Idols and they made sacrifices to them all.

After our Captain and all of us were tired of walking about and seeing such a diversity of Idols and their sacrifices, we returned to our quarters, all the time accompanied by many Caciques and chieftains whom Montezuma sent with us.

Montezuma in Captivity

When our Captain and the Friar of the Order of Mercy saw that Montezuma was not willing that we should set up a cross on the Temple of Huichilobos nor build a church there, and because, ever since we entered this city of Mexico, when Mass was said, we had to place an altar on tables and then to dismantle it again, it was decided that we should ask Montezuma's stewards for masons so that we could make a church in our quarters.

The stewards said that they would tell Montezuma of our wishes, and Montezuma gave his permission and ordered us to be supplied with all the material we needed. In two days we had our church finished and the holy cross set up in front of our apartments, and Mass was said there every day until the wine gave out. As Cortés and some of the other Captains and the Friar had been ill during the war in Tlaxcala, they made the wine that we had for Mass go too fast, but after it was all finished we still went to the church daily and prayed on our knees before the altar and images, for one reason, because we were obliged to do so as Christians and it was a good habit, and for another reason, in order that Montezuma and all his Captains should observe it, and should witness our adoration and see us on our knees before the Cross, especially when we intoned the Ave Maria, so that it might incline them towards it.

When we were all assembled in those chambers, as it was our habit to inquire into and want to know everything while we were looking for the best and most convenient site to place the altar, two of our soldiers, one of whom was a carpenter named Alonzo Yañes, noticed on one of the walls marks showing that there had been a door there, and that it had been closed up and carefully plastered over and burnished. Now as there was a rumour and we had heard the story that Montezuma kept the treasure of his father Axayaca in that building, it was suspected that it might be in this chamber which had been closed up and cemented only a few days before. Yañes spoke about it to Juan Velásquez de Leon and Francisco de Lugo, and those Captains told the story to Cortés, and the door was secretly opened. When it was opened Cortés and some of his Captains went in first, and they saw such a number of jewels and slabs and plates of gold and chalchihuites and other great riches, that they were quite carried away and did not know what to say about such wealth. The news soon spread among all the other Captains and soldiers, and very secretly we went in to see it. When I saw it I marvelled, and as at that time I was a youth and had never seen such riches as those in my life before, I took it for certain that there could not be another such store of wealth in the whole world. It was decided by all our captains and soldiers, that we should not dream of touching a particle of it, but that the stones should immediately be put back in the doorway and it should be sealed up and cemented just as we found it, and that it should not be spoken about, lest it should reach Montezuma's ears, until times should alter.

Let us leave this about the riches, and say that four of our captains took Cortés aside in the church, with a dozen soldiers in whom he trusted and confided, and I was one of them, and we asked him to look at the net and trap in which we found ourselves, and to consider the great strength of that city, and observe the causeways and bridges, and to think over the words of warning that we had been given in all the towns we had passed through, that Montezuma had been advised by his Huichilobos to allow us to enter into the city, and when we were there, to kill us. That he [Cortés] should remember that the hearts of the men are very changeable, especially those of Indians, and he should not repose trust in the goodwill and affection that Montezuma was showing us, for at some time or other, when the wish occurred to him, he would order us to be attacked, and by the stoppage of our supplies of food or of water, or by the raising of any of the bridges, we should be rendered helpless. Then, considering the great multitude of Indian warriors that Montezuma had as his guard, what should we be able to do either in offence or defence? and as all the houses were built in the water, how could our friends the Tlaxcalans enter and come to our aid? He should think over all this that we had said, and if we wished to safeguard our lives, that we should at once, without further delay, seize Montezuma and should not wait until next day to do it. He should also remember that all the gold that Montezuma had given us and all that we had seen in the treasury of his father Axayaca, and all the food which we ate, all would be turned to arsenic poison in our bodies, for we could neither sleep by night nor day nor rest ourselves while these thoughts were in our minds, and that if any of our soldiers should give him other advice short of this, they would be senseless beasts who were dazed by the gold, incapable of looking death in the face.

When Cortés heard this he replied: "Don't you imagine, gentlemen, that I am asleep, or that I am free from the same anxiety, you must have felt that it is so with me; but what possibility is there of our doing a deed of such great daring as to seize such a great prince in his own palace, surrounded as he is by his own guards and warriors, by what scheme or artifice can we carry it out, so that he should not call on his warriors to attack us at once?" Our Captains replied (that is Juan Velásquez de Leon and Diego de Ordás, Gonzalo de Sandoval and Pedro de Alvarado) that with smooth speeches he should be got out of his halls and brought to our quarters, and should be told that he must remain a prisoner, and if he made a disturbance or cried out, that he would pay for it with his life; that if Cortés did not want to do this at once, he should give them permission to do it, as they were ready for the work, for, between the two great dangers in which we found ourselves, it was better and more to the purpose to seize Montezuma than to wait until he attacked us; for if he began the attack, what chance should we have? Some of us soldiers also told Cortés that it seemed to us that Montezuma's stewards, who were employed in providing us with food, were insolent and did not bring it courteously as during the first days. Also two of our Allies the Tlaxcalan Indians said secretly to Jerónimo de Aguilar, our interpreter, that the Mexicans had not appeared to be well disposed towards us during the last two days. So we stayed a good hour discussing the question whether or not we should take Montezuma prisoner, and how it was to be done, and to our Captain this last advice seemed opportune, that in any case we should take him prisoner, and we left it until the next day. All that night we were praying to God that our plan might tend to His Holy service.

The next morning after these consultations, there arrived, very secretly, two Tlaxcalan Indians with letters from Villa Rica and what they contained was the news that Juan de Escalante, who had remained there as Chief Alguacil, and six of our soldiers had been killed in a battle against the Mexicans, that his horse had also been slain, and many Totonacs who were in his company. Moreover, all the towns of the Sierra and Cempoala and its subject towns were in revolt, and refused to bring food or serve in the fort. They [the Spaniards] did not know what to do, for as formerly they had been taken to be Teules, that now after this disaster, both the Totonacs and Mexicans were like wild animals, and they could hold them to nothing, and did not know what steps to take.

When we heard this news, God knows what sorrow affected us all, for this was the first disaster we had suffered in New Spain.

As we had determined the day before to seize Montezuma, we were praying to God all that night that it would turn out in a manner redounding to His Holy service, and the next morning the way it should be done was settled.

Cortés took with him five captains who were Pedro de Alvarado, Gonzalo de Sandoval, Juan Velásquez de Leon, Francisco de Lugo and Alonzo de Ávila, and he took me and our interpreters Doña Marina and Aguilar, and he told us all to keep on the alert, and the horsemen to have their horses saddled and bridled. As for our arms I need not call them to mind, for by day or night we always went armed and with our sandals on our feet, for at that time such was our footgear, and Montezuma had always seen us armed in that way when we went to speak to him, so did not take it as anything new, nor was he disturbed at all.

When we were all ready, our Captain sent to tell Montezuma that we were coming to his Palace, for this had always been our custom, and so that he should not be alarmed by our arriving suddenly.

Montezuma understood more or less that Cortés was coming because he was annoyed about the Villa Rica affair, and he was afraid of him, but sent word for him to come and that he would be welcome.

When Cortés entered, after having made his usual salutations, he said to him through our interpreters: "Señor Montezuma, I am very much astonished that you, who are such a valiant Prince, after having declared that you are our friend, should order your Captains, whom you have stationed on the coast near to Tuxpan, to take arms against my Spaniards, and that they should dare to rob the towns which are in the keeping and under the protection of our King and master and to demand of them Indian men and women for sacrifice, and should kill a Spaniard, one of my brothers, and a horse." (He did not wish to speak of the Captain nor of the six soldiers who died as soon as they arrived at Villa Rica, for Montezuma did not know about it, nor did the Indian Captains who had attacked them), and Cortés went on to say: "Being such a friend of yours I ordered my Captains to do all that was possible to help and serve you, and you have done exactly the contrary to us. Also in the affair at Cholula your Captains and a large force of warriors had received your own commands to kill us. I forgave it at the time out of my great regard for you, but now again your vassals and Captains have become insolent, and hold secret consultations stating that you wish us to be killed. I do not wish to begin a war on this account nor to destroy this city, I am willing to forgive it all, if silently and without raising any disturbance you will come with us to our quarters, where you will be as well served and attended to as though you were in your own house, but if you cry out or make any disturbance you will immediately be killed by these my Captains, whom I brought solely for this purpose." When Montezuma heard this he was terrified and dumbfounded, and replied that he had never ordered his people to take arms against us, and that he would at once send to summon his Captains so that the truth should be known, and he would chastise them, and at that very moment he took from his arm and wrist the sign and seal of Huichilobos, which was only done when he gave an important and weighty command which was to be carried out at once. With regard to being taken prisoner and leaving his Palace against his will, he said that he was not the person to whom such an order could be given, and that he would not go. Cortés replied to him with very good arguments and Montezuma answered him with even better, showing that he ought not to leave his house. In this way more than half an hour was spent over talk, and when Juan Velásquez de Leon and the other Captains saw that they were wasting time over it and could not longer await the moment when they should remove him from his house and hold him a prisoner, they spoke to Cortés somewhat angrily and said: "What is the good of your making so many words, let us either take him prisoner, or stab him, tell him once more that if he cries out or makes an uproar we will kill him, for it is better at once to save our lives or to lose them," and as Juan Velásquez said this with a loud and rather terrifying voice, for such was his way of speaking, Montezuma, who saw that our Captains were angered, asked Doña Marina what they were saying in such loud tones. As Doña Marina was very clever, she said: "Señor Montezuma, what I counsel you, is to go at once to their quarters without any disturbance at all, for I know that they will pay you much honour as a great Prince such as you are, otherwise you will remain here a dead man, but in their quarters you will learn the truth." Then Montezuma said to Cortés: "Señor Malinche, if this is what you desire, I have a son and two legitimate daughters, take them as hostages, and do not put this affront on me, what will my chieftains say if they see me taken off as a prisoner?" Cortés replied to him that he must come with them himself and there was no alternative. At the end of much more discussion that took place, Montezuma said that he would go willingly, and then Cortés and our Captains bestowed many caresses on him and told him that they begged him not to be annoyed, and to tell his captains and the men of his guard that he was going of his own free will, because he had spoken to his Idol Huichilobos and the priests who attended him, and that it was beneficial for his health and the safety of his life that he should be with us. His rich litter, in which he was used to go out with all the Captains who accompanied him was promptly brought, and he went to our quarters where we placed guards and watchmen over him.

All the attentions and amusements which it was possible for him to have, both Cortés and all of us did our best to afford him, and he was not put under any personal restraint, and soon all the principal Mexican Chieftains, and his nephews came to talk with him, and to learn the reason of his seizure, and whether he wished them to attack us. Montezuma answered them, that he was delighted to be here some days with us of his own free will and not by force, and that when he wished for anything he would tell them so, and that they must not excite themselves nor the City, nor were they to take it to heart, for what had happened about his being there was agreeable to his Huichilobos, and certain priests who knew had told him so, for they had spoken to the Idol about it. In this way which I have now related the capture of the Great Montezuma was effected.

There, where he remained, he had his service and his women and his baths in which he bathed himself, and twenty great chiefs always stayed in his company holding their ancient offices, as well as his councillors and captains, and he stayed there a prisoner without showing any anger at it, and Ambassadors from distant lands came there with their suites, and brought him his tribute, and he carried on his important business.

I will not say anything more at present about this imprisonment, and will relate how the messengers whom Montezuma sent with his sign and seal to summon the Captains who had killed our soldiers, brought them before him as prisoners and what he said to them I do not know, but he sent them on to Cortés, so that he might do justice to them, and their confession was taken when Montezuma was not present and they confessed that what I have already stated was true, that their Prince had ordered them to wage war and to extract tribute, and that if any Teules should appear in defence of the towns, they too should be attacked or killed. When Cortés heard this confession he sent to inform Montezuma how it implicated him in the affair, and Montezuma made all the excuses he could, and our captain sent him word that he believed the confession himself, but that although Montezuma deserved punishment in conformity with the ordinances of our King, to the effect that any person causing others, whether guilty or innocent, to be killed, shall

die for it, yet he was so fond of him and wished him so well, that even
if that crime lay at his door, he, Cortés, would pay the penalty with his
own life sooner than allow Montezuma's to pass away. With all this that
Cortés sent to tell him, Montezuma felt anxious, and without any further
discussion Cortés sentenced those captains to death and to be burned in
front of Montezuma's palace. This sentence was promptly carried out,
and, so that there could be no obstruction while they were being burned,
Cortés ordered shackles to be put on Montezuma himself, and when this
was done Montezuma roared with rage, and if before this he was scared,
he was then much more so. After the burning was over our Cortés with
five of our captains went to Montezuma's apartment and Cortés himself
took off the fetters, and he spoke such loving words to him that his anger
soon passed off, for our Cortés told him that he not only regarded him
as a brother, but much more, and that, as he was already Lord and King
of so many towns and provinces, if it were possible he would make him
Lord of many more countries as time went on, such as he had not been
able to subdue, and which did not now obey him, and he told him that
if he now wished to go to his Palace, that he would give him leave to go.
Cortés told him this through our interpreters and while Cortés was saying it the tears apparently sprang to Montezuma's eyes. He answered with
great courtesy, that he thanked him for it (but he well knew that Cortés'
speech was mere words), and that now at present it was better for him to
stay there a prisoner, for there was danger, as his chieftains were numerous, and his nephews and relations came every day to him to say that
it would be a good thing to attack us and free him from prison, that as
soon as they saw him outside they might drive him to it. He did not wish
to see revolutions in his city, but if he did not comply with their wishes
possibly they would want to set up another Prince in his place. And so he
was putting those thoughts out of their heads by saying that Huichilobos
had sent him word that he should remain a prisoner. (From what we
understood and there is no doubt about it, Cortés had told Aguilar to
tell Montezuma secretly, that although Malinche wished to release him
from his imprisonment, that the rest of our captains and soldiers would

not agree to it.) When he heard this reply, Cortés threw his arms round him and embraced him and said: "It is not in vain Señor Montezuma that I care for you as I care for myself." Then Montezuma asked Cortés that a Spanish page named Orteguilla who already knew something of his language might attend on him, and this was very advantageous both for Montezuma and for us, for through this page Montezuma asked and learned many things about Spain, and we learned what his captains said to him, and in truth this page was so serviceable that Montezuma got to like him very much.

Games with Montezuma

Let us cease talking about how Montezuma became fairly contented with the great flattery and attention he received and the conversation that he had with us, and whenever we passed before him, even if it was Cortés himself, we doffed our mailed caps or helmets, for we always went armed, and he treated us all with politeness. The name of the principal captain who was punished by being burned was Quetzalpopoca. I may say that when the news of this punishment spread about throughout the provinces of New Spain, they were terrified, and the towns of the Coast, where they had killed our soldiers, returned again and rendered good service to the settlers who remained in Villa Rica.

As our captain was careful in all things, and seeing that Montezuma was a prisoner, and fearing that he might become depressed at being shut in and confined, he endeavoured every day, after prayers (for we had no wine for Mass) to go and pay court to him, and he went accompanied by four Captains, usually by Pedro de Alvarado, Juan Velásquez and Diego de Ordás, and with much reverence they asked Montezuma how he was, and that he should issue his orders and they would all be carried out, so that he should not be weary of his confinement. He answered that on the contrary, being a prisoner rested him, and this was because our gods gave us power to confine him or his Huichilobos permitted it, and in one conversation after another they gave him to understand more fully the things about our holy faith, and the great power of the Emperor our Lord.

Then sometimes Montezuma and Cortés would play at Totoloque, which is the name they give to a game played with some very smooth small pellets made of gold for this game, and they toss these pellets to some distance as well as some little slabs which were also made of gold, and in five strokes [tries] they gained or lost certain pieces of gold or rich jewels that they staked. I remember that Pedro de Alvarado was keeping the score for Cortés, and one of his nephews, a great cacique, was marking for Montezuma, and Pedro de Alvarado always marked one point more than Cortés gained, and when Montezuma saw it he said courteously and laughingly that he did not like Tonatio (for so they called Pedro de Alvarado) to keep the score for Cortés, because he made so much *yxoxol* in what he marked, which in their language means to say that he cheated, in that he always marked one point too many. Cortés and all of us soldiers who were on guard at the time, could not restrain our laughter at what the great Montezuma said, because Pedro de Alvarado, although he was so handsome and well mannered, had a mania for excessive talking, and we knew his temperament. To return to the game, if Cortés won, he gave the jewels to those nephews and favourites of Montezuma who attended on him, and if Montezuma won he divided them among us soldiers on guard, and in addition to what he gave us from the game, he never omitted giving us every day presents of gold and cloth, both to us and to the captain of the Guard, who, at that time, was Juan Velásquez de Leon, who showed himself in every way to be the friend and servant of Montezuma.

A soldier named Pedro López was placed as sentinel over Montezuma, and on the question whether it was time to change the watch during the night, he had words with an officer and said, "Oh! curse this dog, I am sick to death of keeping constant guard over him." Montezuma heard the expression, and weighed it in his mind, and when Cortés came to pay his court to him, he heard of it, and was so angry about it, that he had Pedro López, good soldier as he was, flogged in our quarters, and from that time on all the soldiers who came on guard, went through their watch in silence and good manners. However it was not necessary to give orders to many of us who stood guard over him about the civility that we ought to show to this great cacique; he knew each one of us and even knew our names and our characters and he was so kind that to all of us he gave jewels and to some mantles, and handsome Indian women. As I was a young man in those days, whenever I was on guard, or passed in front of him, I doffed my headpiece with the greatest respect, and the page Orteguilla had told him that I had been on two expeditions to discover New Spain before the time of Cortés, so I asked Orteguilla to beg Montezuma to do me the favour of giving me a very pretty Indian woman, and when Montezuma heard this he told them to call me, and he said to me: "Bernal Diaz del Castillo, they tell me that you have quantities of cloth and gold, and I will order them to give you today a pretty maid. Treat her very well for she is the daughter of a chieftain, and they will also give you gold and mantles," and I answered him with much reverence, that I kissed his hands for his great favour, and might God our Lord prosper him, and it seems that he asked the page what I had replied to him, and he told him; and Montezuma said to him: "Bernal Diaz seems to me to be a gentleman," for as I have said, he knew all our names, and he told them to give me three small slabs of gold and two loads of mantles.

Let us stop talking of this and tell how of a morning after saying his prayers and making sacrifices to his idols, he took his breakfast, which was a small matter, for he ate no meat, only chili peppers, then he was occupied for an hour in hearing suits from many parts brought by Caciques who came to him from distant lands.

As all the materials for building the two sloops had arrived, Cortés at once went to tell the great Montezuma that he wished to build two small ships so as to take pleasure trips on the lake, and asked him to send his carpenters to cut the wood, together with our experts in boat-building, who were named Martin López and Andrés Nuñez. As the oak timber was distant about four leagues, it was soon brought and shaped, and as there were many Indian carpenters, the boats were soon built and caulked and tarred, and their rigging was set up and their sails cut to the right size and measurement, and an awning provided for each one, and they turned out to be as good and fast as though they had taken a month to set up the models, for Martin López was a past master of the art.

Let us leave this and say that Montezuma told Cortés that he wished to go to his temples and make sacrifices, and pay the devotion to his gods that it was his duty to do, so that his Captains and chieftains might observe it, especially certain nephews of his, who came every day to tell him that they wished to free him and to attack us, and he answered them, that it pleased him to be with us, so they should think it was as he had told them, that his God Huichilobos had commanded him to stay with us, as he had made them believe before. Cortés replied that as to this permission he asked for, he should beware not to do anything for which he might lose his life, and so as to prevent any disorders, or commands to his Captains or priests either to release him, or attack us, he would send Captains and soldiers with him who would immediately stab him to death, should any change be noticed in his bearing. He might go and welcome, but must not sacrifice any human beings, for that was a great offence against the true God, that was to the God we were preaching to him about, and there stood our altars and the image of Our Lady, before whom he could pray. Montezuma said that he would not sacrifice a single human being, and he set off in his rich litter in great state with many great Caciques in his company as was his custom, and they carried his insignia in front of him in the form of a sort of staff or rod, which was the sign that his royal presence was going that way (just as they do now to the Viceroys of New Spain). There went with him as a guard four of our Captains, and one hundred and fifty soldiers, and the Padre de la Merced also went with us to stop the sacrifice if he should offer human beings. So we went to the Cue of Huichilobos and when we came near to that cursed temple, Montezuma ordered them to take him from his litter and he was carried on the shoulders of his nephews and of other Caciques until he arrived at the temple; as I have already stated, as he went through the streets all the chieftains cast down their eyes and never looked at his face. When we arrived at the foot of the steps leading to the oratory there were many priests waiting to help him with their arms in the ascent.

There had already been sacrificed the night before four Indians, and in spite of what our Captain said and the dissuasions of the Padre de la Merced, he paid no heed but persisted in killing men and boys to accomplish his sacrifice, and we could do nothing at that time only pretend not to notice it, for Mexico and the other great cities were very ready to rebel under the nephews of Montezuma, as I shall explain further on.

When Montezuma had completed his sacrifices, and he did not tarry much in making them, we returned with him to our quarters, and he was very cheerful, and gave presents of golden jewels to us soldiers who had accompanied him.

When the two sloops were finished building and had been launched and the masts and rigging had been set up and adorned with the Royal and Imperial banners, and the sailors had been got ready to navigate them, they went out in them both rowing and sailing, and they sailed very well. When Montezuma heard of it, he said to Cortés that he wished to go hunting on a rocky Island [the Peñon de Tepepolco or del Marques], standing in the lake which was preserved so that no one dared to hunt there, however great a chief he might be, under pain of death. Cortés replied that he was very welcome to go, but he must remember what he had told him on the former occasion when he went to visit his Idols, that to raise any disturbances was more than his life was worth; moreover, he could go in the sloops, as it was better sailing in them than in the canoes and pirogues however large they might be. Montezuma said that he would be delighted to sail in the sloop that was the swiftest, and he took with him many lords and chieftains, and advised his huntsmen to follow in canoes and pirogues. A son of Montezuma and many Caciques went in the other sloop. Then Cortés ordered Velásquez de Leon who was captain of the Guard and Pedro de Alvarado and Cristóbal de Olid, Alonzo de Ávila with two hundred soldiers, to accompany Montezuma, and to remember the great responsibility he was placing on them in looking after him, and as all those Captains whom I have named were very alert, they took on board all the soldiers I have spoken about, and four bronze cannon and all the powder that we possessed, and our gunners, and they put up a highly decorated awning as a protection from the weather, and Montezuma and his chieftains went under it. As at that time there was a strong breeze blowing, and the sailors were delighted to please and content Montezuma, they worked the sails so well that they went flying along, and the canoes which held his huntsmen and chieftains were left far behind in spite of the large number of rowers they carried. Montezuma was charmed, and said that it was a great art this of combining sails and oars together. So he arrived at the Peñol, which was not very far off, and Montezuma killed all the game he wanted, deer and hares and rabbits, and returned very contented to the city. When we arrived near Mexico, Pedro de Alvarado and Juan Velásquez de Leon and the other Captains ordered the cannon to be discharged, and this delighted Montezuma, and as we saw him so frank and kind, we treated him with the respect in which the Kings of these countries are held, and he behaved in the same manner to us. If I were to relate the traits and qualities that he showed as a great Prince, and the reverence and service that all the Lords of New Spain paid to him, I should never come to an end. There was not a thing that he ordered to be brought that was not immediately there.

I must leave him now and state how, in the discussion that Montezuma held with the Caciques of all the territory whom he had called together, after he had made a speech without Cortés or any of us, excepting Orteguilla the page, being present, it was reported that he had told them to consider how for many years past they had known for certain, through the traditions of their ancestors, which they had noted down in their books of records, that men would come from the direction of the sunrise to rule these lands, and that then the lordship and kingdom of the Mexicans would come to an end. Now he believed, from what his Gods had told him, that we were these men, and the priests had consulted Huichilobos about it and offered up sacrifices, but their Gods would no longer answer them as they had been accustomed to do.

All that Huichilobos would give them to understand was that what he had told them before he now again gave as his reply, and they were not to ask him again, so that they took it to mean that they should give their fealty to the King of Spain whose vassals these Teules say that they are. He went on to say: "As for the present it does not imply anything, and as in time to come we shall see whether we receive another and better reply from our Gods, so we will act according to the time. For the present, what I order and beg you all to do with goodwill is to give and contribute some sign of vassalage, and I will soon tell you what is most suitable, and as just now I am importuned about it by Malinche, I beg that no one will refuse it. During the eighteen years that I have been your Prince, you have always been very loyal to me, and I have enriched you and have broadened your lands, and have given you power and wealth, and if at this present time, our Gods permit me to be held captive here, it would not have happened, unless, as I have told you many times, my great Huichilobos had commanded it."

When they heard these arguments, all of them gave as an answer that they would do as he had ordered them, and they said it with many tears and sighs, and Montezuma more tearful than any of them. Then he sent a chieftain to say that on the following day they would give their fealty and vassalage to His Majesty.

Montezuma returned after this to talk about the matter with his Caciques, and in the presence of Cortés and our Captains and many of our soldiers, and of Pedro Hernández, Cortés' secretary, they gave their fealty to His Majesty, and they showed much emotion in doing so, and Montezuma could not keep back his tears. He was so dear to us, and we were so much affected at seeing him weep, that our own eyes were softened and one soldier wept as much as Montezuma, such was the affection we had for him. I will leave off here, and say that Cortés and the Fraile de la Merced, who was very wise, were constantly in Montezuma's palace, trying to amuse him and to persuade him to give up his Idols.

As Captain Diego de Ordás and the other soldiers [who had been sent by Cortés on an exploring expedition] arrived with samples of gold and the report that all the land was rich, Cortés by the advice of Ordás and the other Captains and soldiers, decided to speak to, and demand of Montezuma, that all the Caciques and towns of the land should pay tribute to His Majesty, and that he himself as the greatest Chieftain, should also contribute from his treasure. Montezuma replied that he would send to all his towns to ask for gold, but that many of them did not possess any, only some jewels of little worth which had come to them from their ancestors. He at once despatched chieftains to the places where there were mines and ordered each town to give so many ingots of fine gold, of the same size and thickness as others that they were used to pay as tribute, and the messengers carried with them as samples two small ingots. From other parts they only brought small jewels of little worth.

He also sent to the province whose Cacique and Lord was that near kinsman of his who would not obey him. This province was distant from Mexico about twelve leagues, and the reply the messengers brought back was to the effect that neither would he give any gold nor obey Montezuma, that he also was Lord of Mexico, and that the dominion belonged to him as much as to Montezuma himself, who was sending to ask him to pay tribute.

When Montezuma heard this he was so enraged that he immediately sent his seal and sign by some faithful captains with orders to bring him as a prisoner. When this kinsman was brought into Montezuma's presence he spoke to him very disrespectfully, and without any fear, and very valiantly, and they say, that he had intervals of madness, for he was as though thunderstruck. Cortés came to know all about this, and he sent to beg Montezuma as a favour, to give this man to him as he wished to place a guard over him, for he had been told that Montezuma had ordered him to be killed. When the Cacique was brought before him Cortés spoke to him in a most amiable manner and told him not to act like a madman against his prince, and wished to set him free. However, when Montezuma heard this he said that he should not be set free but should be attached to the great chain like the other Kinglets already named by me.

Let us go back to say that within twenty days all the chieftains whom Montezuma had sent to collect the tribute of gold, came back again. And as they arrived Montezuma sent to summon Cortés and our captains and certain soldiers whom he knew, who belonged to his guard, and said these formal words, or others of like meaning:—

"I wish you to know, Señor Malinche and Señores Captains and soldiers, that I am indebted to your great King, and I bear him goodwill both for being such a great Prince and for having sent to such distant lands to make inquiries about me; and the thought that most impresses me is that he must be the one who is to rule over us, as our ancestors have told us, and as even our gods have given us to understand in the answers we have received from them. Take this gold which has been collected; on account of haste no more has been brought. That which I have got ready for the emperor is the whole of the Treasure which I have received from my father, which is in your possession and in your apartments."

"I know well enough that as soon as you came here you opened the chamber and beheld it all, and that you sealed it up again as it was before. When you send it to him, tell him in your papers and letters, 'This is sent to you by your true vassal Montezuma.' I will also give you some very valuable stones which you will send to him in my name; they are Chalchihuites, and are not to be given to anyone else but only to him, your Great Prince. Each stone is worth two loads of gold. I also wish to send him three blowguns with their bags and pellet moulds for they have such good jewel work on them that he will be pleased to see them, and I also wish to give him of what I possess although it is but little, for all the rest of the gold and jewels that I possessed I have given you from time to time."

When Cortés and all of us heard this we stood amazed at the great goodness and liberality of the Great Montezuma, and with much reverence we all doffed our helmets, and returned him our thanks, and with words of the greatest affection Cortés promised him that we would write to His Majesty of the magnificence and liberality of this gift of gold which he gave us in his own royal name. After some more polite conversation Montezuma at once sent his Mayordomos to hand over all the treasure and gold and wealth that was in that plastered chamber, and in looking it over and taking off all the embroidery with which it was set, we were occupied for three days, and to assist us in undoing it and taking it to pieces, there came Montezuma's goldsmiths from the town named Azcapotzalco, and I say that there was so much, that after it was taken to pieces there were three heaps of gold, and they weighed more than six hundred thousand pesos, as I shall tell further on, without the silver and many other rich things, and not counting in this the ingots and slabs of gold, and the gold in grains from the mines. We began to melt it down with the help of the Indian goldsmiths, and they made broad bars of it, each bar measuring three fingers of the hand across. When it was already melted and made into bars, they brought another present separately which the Grand Montezuma had said that he would give, and it was a wonderful thing to behold the wealth of gold and the richness of the other jewels that were brought, for some of the Chalchihuites were so fine that among these Caciques they were worth a vast quantity of gold. The three blowguns with their pellet moulds, and their coverings of jewels and pearls, and pictures in feathers of little birds covered with pearl shell and other birds, all were of great value. I will not speak of the plumes and feathers and other rich things for I shall never finish calling them to mind.

The gold I have spoken about was marked with an iron stamp, and the stamp was the royal arms. The mark was not put on the rich jewels which it did not seem to us should be taken to pieces.

As we had neither marked weights nor scales, some iron weights were made, some as much as an *arroba* [an arroba is twenty-five pounds], others of half an arroba, two pounds, one pound and half a pound, and of four ounces, not that they would turn out very exact, but within half an ounce more or less in each lot that was weighed.

After the weight was taken the officers of the King said that there was gold worth more than six hundred thousand pesos, and this was without counting the silver and many other jewels which were not yet valued.

Some soldiers said that there was more. As there was now nothing more to do than to take out the royal fifth, and to give to each captain and soldier his share, and to set aside the shares of those who remained at the port of Villa Rica, it seems that Cortés endeavoured not to have it divided up so soon, but to wait until there was more gold, and there were good weights, and proper accounts of how it turned out. But most of us captains and soldiers said that it should be divided up at once, for we had seen that at the time when the pieces were given out of the Treasury of Montezuma, there was much more gold in the heaps, and that a third part of it was missing, which they had taken and hidden both on behalf of Cortés, as well as of the Captains and the Fraile de la Merced, and it went on diminishing. The next day they were to distribute the shares, and I will tell how it was divided, and the greater part remained with Captain Cortés and other persons, and what was done about it I will go on to relate.

First of all the royal fifth was taken out, then Cortés said that they should take out for him another fifth, the same as for His Majesty, for we had promised it to him at the sand dunes when we elected him Captain General and Chief Justice. After that, he said that he had been put to certain expenses in the Island of Cuba and that what he had spent on the expedition should be taken from the heap, and in addition to this that there should be taken from the same heap the expenses incurred by Diego Velásquez in the ships which we had destroyed, and we all agreed to it, and beside this the expenses of the procurators who were sent to Spain. Then there were the shares of those who remained in Villa Rica, and there were seventy of them, and for his horse that had died, and for the mare which had belonged to Juan Sedeño which the Tlaxcalans had killed with a sword cut; then for the Fraile de la Merced, and the priest Juan Diaz and the Captains and for those who had brought horses, double shares, and for musketeers and crossbowmen the same, and other trickeries, so that very little was left to each as a share, and it was so little that many of the soldiers did not want to take it, and Cortés was left with it all. At that time we could do nothing but hold our tongues, for to ask for justice in the matter was useless. There were other soldiers who took their shares at the rate of one hundred pesos and clamored for the rest, and to content them Cortés secretly gave to one and the other, apparently bestowing favours so as to satisfy them, and with the smooth speeches that he made to them they put up with it.

At that time many of our Captains ordered very large golden chains to be made by the Great Montezuma's goldsmiths. Cortés, too, ordered many jewels to be made, and a great service of plate. Some of our soldiers had their hands so full, that many ingots of gold, marked and unmarked, and jewels of a great diversity of patterns were openly in circulation. Heavy gaming was always going on with some playing cards which were made from drum skins by Pedro Valenciano and were as well made and painted as the originals. So this was the condition we were in, but let us stop talking of the gold and of the bad way it was divided, and worse way in which it was spent.

As Cortés heard that many of the soldiers were discontented over their share of the gold and the way the heaps had been robbed, he determined to make a speech to them all with honeyed words, and he said that all he owned was for us, and he did not want the fifth but only the share that came to him as Captain General, and that if anyone had need of anything he would give it to him, and that the gold we had collected was but a breath of air, that we should observe what great cities there were there and rich mines, and that we should be lords of them all and very prosperous and rich, and he used other arguments very well expressed which he knew well how to employ.

One day Montezuma said: "Look here, Malinche, I love you so much that I want to give you one of my daughters, who is very beautiful, so that you can marry her and treat her as your legitimate wife"; Cortés doffed his cap in thanks, and said that it was a great favour that Montezuma was conferring on him, but that he was already married and had a wife, and that among us we were not permitted to have more than one wife, he would however, keep her [Montezuma's daughter] in the rank to which the daughter of so great a prince was entitled, but that first of all he desired her to become a Christian, as other ladies, the daughters of Chieftains, already were; and to this Montezuma consented.

The Great Montezuma always showed goodwill to us, but he never ceased his sacrifices at which human beings were killed, and Cortés tried to dissuade him from this but met with no success. So Cortés took counsel with his captains as to what should be done in the matter, for he did not dare to put an end to it for fear of a rising in the City and of the priests who were in charge of Huichilobos. On the advice of his Captains, Cortés went to the Palace where Montezuma was imprisoned and took seven captains and soldiers with him, and said to Montezuma: "Señor, I have often asked you not to sacrifice any more human beings to your gods who are deceiving you, and you will not cease doing it, I wish you to know that all my companions and these captains who are with me have come to beg you to give them leave to remove the gods from your temple and put our Lady Santa Maria and a Cross in their place, and, if you will not give them leave now, they will go and remove them, and I would not like them to kill any priests."

When Montezuma heard those words, and saw that the Captains were rather angry, he said: "Oh! Malinche, how can you wish to destroy the city entirely! for our gods are very angry with us, and I do not know that they will stop even at your lives, what I pray you to do for the present is to be patient, and I will send to summon all the priests and I will see their reply." When Cortés heard this he made a sign that he wished to speak quite privately to Montezuma. When they were left alone he said to Montezuma, that in order to prevent this affair from becoming known and causing a disturbance and becoming an offence to the priests on account of their idols being overturned, that he would arrange with these Captains to the effect that they should do nothing of the sort, provided they were given an apartment in the Great Cue where they might make an altar on which to place the Image of Our Lady and set up a Cross. Then Montezuma, with sighs and a very sorrowful countenance, said that he would confer with his priests. After much discussion had taken place, it was agreed to, and our altars and an image of Our Lady and a Cross were set up, apart from their cursed Idols, with great reverence and with thanks to God from all of us, and the Padre de la Merced chanted Mass assisted by the priest Juan Diaz and many of our soldiers. Our Captain ordered an old soldier to be stationed there as guardian, and begged Montezuma to order the priests not to touch the altar, but only to keep it swept and to burn incense and keep wax candles burning there by day and night, and to decorate it with branches and flowers.

There was never a time when we were not subject to surprises of such a kind, that had our Lord God not assisted us, they would have cost us our lives. Thus as soon as we had placed the image of Our Lady and the Cross on the Altar which we had made on the Great Cue and the Holy Gospel had been preached and Mass said, it seems that Huichilobos and Tezcatepuca spoke to the priests, and told them that they wished to leave their country as they were so badly treated by the Teules, and they did not wish to stay where those figures and the Cross had been placed, nor would they remain there unless we were killed, and this was their answer and they need not expect any other, and they should inform Montezuma and all his Captains, so that they might at once go to war and kill us. The Idols further told them that they could see how all the gold that used to be kept for their honour, had been broken up by us and made into ingots, and let them beware how we were making ourselves lords over the country, and were holding five great Caciques prisoners, and they told them of other misdeeds so as to induce them to attack us. In order that Cortés and all of us should know about this, the Great Montezuma sent word to tell Cortés that he wished to speak to him on very important matters, and the page Orteguilla came and said to him that Montezuma was very sad and much disturbed, and that during the previous night and part of the day many priests and leading Captains had been with him and had said things to him privately that he [the page] could not understand.

When Cortés heard this he went in haste to the palace where Montezuma was staying and took with him Cristóbal de Olid, who was Captain of the Guard, and four other Captains and Doña Marina and Jerónimo de Aguilar, and, after they had paid much respect to him, Montezuma said: "Oh! Señor Malinche and Captains, how distressed I am at the reply and command which our Teules have given to our priests and to me and all my Captains, which is that we should make war on you and kill you, and drive you back across the sea. I have thought it over, and what seems to me best is that you should at once leave this city before you are attacked, and that not one of you should remain here. This, Señor Malinche, I say that you should not fail to do, for it is to your interest, if not you will be killed, remember it is a question of your lives." Cortés and our Captains felt grief at what he said and were even a good deal disquieted, and it was not to be wondered at, the affair coming so suddenly and with such insistence that our lives were at once placed in the greatest danger by it, for the warning was given us with the greatest urgency. Cortés replied that he thanked Montezuma sincerely for the warning, and that at the present time there were two things that troubled him, one was that he had no vessels in which to sail, for he had ordered those in which he had come to be broken up, and the other was that Montezuma would be forced to come with us so that our great Emperor might see him, and that he begged as a favour that he would place restraint on his priests and captains while three ships were being built at the sand dunes, as it would be more advantageous to them, for if they began the war they would all of them be killed.

He also asked, so that Montezuma might see that he wished to carry out what he had said without delay, that carpenters might be sent with two of our soldiers who were great experts in ship building, to cut wood near the sand dunes.

Montezuma was even more sorrowful than before because Cortés told him that he would have to come with us before the Emperor; he said that he would send the carpenters, and that they should hurry and not waste time in talk, but work, and that meanwhile he would command the priests and captains not to ferment disturbances in the city and he would order Huichilobos to be appeased with sacrifices, but not of human lives. After this exciting conversation Cortés and his captains took leave of Montezuma, and we were all in the greatest anxiety wondering when they would begin the attack.

Then Cortés ordered Martin López, the ship carpenter, to be summoned and Andrés Nuñez, and the Indian carpenters whom the Great Montezuma had given him and after some discussion as to the size of the three vessels to be built he ordered him at once to set about the work and to get them ready, for in Villa Rica there was everything necessary in the way of iron and blacksmiths, tackle, tow, and calkers and pitch. So they set out and cut the wood on the coast near Villa Rica, and in haste began to build ships.

Let us leave him building the ships and say how we all went about in that city very much depressed, fearing that at any moment they might attack us; and our friends from Tlaxcala and Doña Marina also told the captain that an attack was probable, and Orteguilla, Montezuma's page, was always in tears. We all kept on the alert and placed a strong Guard over Montezuma, and we slept shod and armed and with all our weapons to hand, and our horses stood saddled and bridled all day long. There is another thing I must say, but not with the intention of boasting about it, that I grew so accustomed to go about armed, and to sleep in the way I have said, that after the conquest of New Spain I kept to the habit of sleeping in my clothes and without a bed, and I slept thus better than on a mattress.

Cortés Struggles with Narváez

At this point in Díaz del Castillo's longer version, the narrative focuses on intensive infighting among the Spaniards triggered by the arrival on the coast of nineteen ships carrying fourteen hundred soldiers under the command of Panfilo de Narváez. Sent by Diego Velásquez in Cuba, Narváez is joined by three Spanish soldiers left behind in Mexico by the explorer Pizarro and who are familiar with recent campaigns and movements by Cortés's troops. Secret envoys bring gifts from Montezuma for Narváez and an anti-Cortés alliance is formed. Some days later Cortés learns of this threat and Montezuma's secret negotiations on the coast. Narváez demands the surrender of Villa Rica de la Vera Cruz. Narváez's envoys to Villa Rica are captured by Cortés's representatives in Villa Rica and secretly sent with other Narváez men to Cortés in Mexico. Dazzled by the countryside and the city of Tenochtitlan and bribed by Cortés, they return to Narváez's camp with the intention of persuading others to desert Narváez. Cortés writes Narváez from Tenochtitlan promising and pleading for Spanish solidarity in the face of the natives. Not persuaded, Narváez moves to Cempoala and takes away the treasure that Cortés had left in the control of the Fat Cacique and begins a march toward Mexico. Cortés leaves Montezuma and the capital under Pedro de Alvarado's charge and plans to attack Narváez's troops. Cortés successfully sends a few envoys to win friends in Narváez's camp while at the same time launching a surprise attack in which Narváez is wounded and loses an eye. Many of Narváez's men join Cortés—some unwillingly—but are allowed to settle in the country. Their horses and goods are returned to them, causing dissension among Cortés's followers. According to Bernal Díaz, a black man in Narváez's troops has smallpox and accidentally unleashes a terrible epidemic among the natives. Suddenly, bad news comes to Cortés from Mexico.

Let me say how ill luck suddenly turns the wheel, and after great good fortune and pleasure follows sadness; it so happened that at this moment came the news that Mexico was in revolt, and that Pedro de Alvarado was besieged in his fortress and quarters, and that they had set fire to this same fortress in two places, and had killed seven of his soldiers and wounded many others, and he sent to demand assistance with great urgency and haste. This news was brought by two Tlaxcalans without any letter, but a letter soon arrived by two other Tlaxcalans sent by Pedro de Alvarado in which he told the same story. When we heard this bad news, God knows how greatly it depressed us.

By forced marches we began our journey to Mexico, Narvaez and Salvatierra remaining as prisoners in Villa Rica.

Just at this moment, as we were ready to start, there arrived four great chieftains sent to Cortés by the great Montezuma to complain to him of Pedro de Alvarado, and what they said, with tears streaming from their eyes, was that Pedro de Alvarado sallied out from his quarters with all the soldiers that Cortés had left with him, and, for no reason at all, fell on their chieftains and Caciques who were dancing and celebrating a feast in honour of their Idols Huichilobos and Tezcatepuca, Pedro de Alvarado having given them leave to do so. He killed and wounded many of them and in defending themselves they had killed six of his soldiers. Thus they made many complaints against Pedro de Alvarado, and Cortés, somewhat disgusted, replied to the messengers that he would go to Mexico and put it all to rights. So they went off with that reply to their great Montezuma, who it is said, resented it as a very bad one and was enraged at it.

Cortés also promptly despatched letters to Pedro de Alvarado in which he advised him to look out that Montezuma did not escape, and that we were coming by forced marches, and he informed him about the victory we had gained over Narvaez, which Montezuma knew about already, and I will leave off here and tell what happened later on.

Spanish Massacre of the Dancers

We were soon on our way by forced marches until we reached Tlaxcala, where we learnt that up to the time that Montezuma and his captains heard that we had defeated Narvaez they did not cease to attack, and had already killed seven of Alvarado's soldiers and burnt his quarters, but as soon as they heard of our victory they ceased attacking him; but they added that Alvarado's company were much exhausted through want of water and food, for Montezuma had failed to order food to be given to them.

Some Tlaxcalan Indians brought this news at the very moment we arrived, and Cortés at once ordered a muster to be made of the men he had brought with him and found over thirteen hundred soldiers counting both our people and the followers of Narvaez, and over ninety-six horses and eighty crossbowmen, and as many musketeers, and with these it seemed to Cortés that he had force enough to enter Mexico in safety. In addition to this the Caciques of Tlaxcala gave us two thousand Indian warriors, and we at once set out by forced marches to Texcoco, and they paid no honour to us there and not a single chieftain made his appearance, for all were hidden away and ill disposed.

We arrived at Mexico on the day of Señor San Juan de Junio [Midsummer Day] 1520, and no Caciques or Captains or Indians whom we knew appeared in the streets, and all the houses were empty when we reached the quarters where we used to lodge. The great Montezuma came out to the courtyard to embrace and speak to Cortés and bid him welcome, and congratulate him on his victory over Narvaez, and as Cortés was arriving victorious he refused to listen to him, and Montezuma returned to his quarters very sad and depressed.

When each one of us was lodged in the quarters he had occupied before we set out from Mexico, and the following of Narvaez were lodged in other quarters, we then saw and talked with Pedro de Alvarado and the soldiers who had stayed with him; they gave us an account of the attacks made on them, and the straits in which the Mexicans had placed them, and we told them the story of our victory over Narvaez.

Cortés tried to find out what was the cause of the revolt in Mexico, for we clearly understood that it made Montezuma unhappy if we should think it had been his desire or had been done by his advice. Many of the soldiers who had remained with Pedro de Alvarado through that critical time said, that if Montezuma had had a hand in it, all of them would have been killed, but Montezuma calmed his people until they ceased to attack.

What Pedro de Alvarado told Cortés about the matter was that it was done by the Mexicans in order to liberate Montezuma, and because their Huichilobos ordered it, on account of our having placed the image of our Lady the Virgin Santa Maria and the Cross in his house. Moreover he said that many Indians had come to remove the holy image from the altar where we placed it, and were not able to move it, and that the Indians looked upon it as a great miracle and had said so to Montezuma, who had told them to leave it in the place and altar in which it stood, and not to attempt to do otherwise, and so it was left.

Pedro de Alvarado further stated that because Narvaez' message to Montezuma, that he was coming to release him from prison and to capture us, had not turned out to be true, and because Cortés had told Montezuma that as soon as we possessed ships we should go and embark and leave the country entirely, and we were not going, and it was nothing but empty words, and because it was evident that many more Teules were arriving, it seemed well to the Mexicans to kill him (Pedro de Alvarado) and his soldiers and release the great Montezuma before the followers of Narvaez or our own men re-entered Mexico, and afterwards not to leave one of us or of the followers of Narvaez alive.

Cortés turned and asked Pedro de Alvarado what was the reason that he attacked them when they were dancing and holding a festival.

He replied that he knew for certain that as soon as they had finished the festivals and dances and the sacrifices that they were offering to their Huichilobos and Tezcatepuca, they would at once come and make an attack according to the agreement they had made between themselves, and this and all the rest he learned from a priest and from two chieftains and from other Mexicans.

Cortés said to him: "But they have told me that they asked your permission to hold festivals and dances"; he replied that it was true, and it was in order to take them unprepared and to scare them, so that they should not come to attack him, that he hastened to fall on them.

When Cortés heard this he said to him, very angrily, that it was very ill done and a great mistake and that he wished to God that Montezuma had escaped and not heard such an account from his Idols. So he left him and spoke no more to him about it.

Pedro de Alvarado himself also said that when he advanced against them in that conflict, he ordered a cannon, that was loaded with one ball and many small shot, to be fired, for as many squadrons of Indians were approaching to set fire to his quarters he sallied forth to fight them, and he ordered the cannon to be fired, but it did not go off, and after he had made a charge against the squadrons which were attacking him, and many Indians were bearing down on him, while he was retreating to the fortress and quarters, then, without fire being applied to the cannon, the ball and the small shot were discharged and killed many Indians; and had it not so happened the enemy would have killed them all, and they did on that occasion carry off two of his soldiers alive.

Another thing Pedro de Alvarado stated, and this was the only thing that was also reported by the other soldiers, for the rest of the stories were told by Alvarado alone, and it is that they had no water to drink, and they dug in the courtyard, and made a well and took out freshwater, all around being salt; in all it amounted to many gifts that our Lord God bestowed on us.

When Cortés saw that they had given us no sort of a reception in Texcoco, and had not even given us food, except bad food and with bad grace, and that we found no chieftains with whom to parley, and he saw that all were scared away and ill disposed, and observed the same condition on coming to Mexico, how no market was held and the whole place was in revolt, and he heard from Pedro de Alvarado about the disorderly manner in which he made his attack, and as it appears that on the march Cortés had spoken to the Captains of Narvaez glorifying himself on the great veneration and command that he enjoyed, and how on the road the Indians would turn out to receive him and celebrate the occasion and give him gold, and that in Mexico he ruled as absolutely over the great Montezuma as over all his Captains, and that they would give him presents of gold, as they were used to do, and when everything turned out contrary to his expectations and they did not even give us food to eat, he was greatly irritated, and haughty towards the numerous Spaniards that he was bringing with him, and very sad and fretful. At this moment the great Montezuma sent two of his chieftains to beg our Cortés to go and see him, for he wished to speak to him, and the answer that Cortés gave them was "Go to, for a dog, who will not even keep open a market, and does not order food to be given us." Then when our Captains, that is Juan Velásquez de Leon, Cristóbal de Olid, Alonzo de Ávila and Francisco de Lugo, heard Cortés say this, they exclaimed: "Señor, moderate your anger and reflect how much good and honour this king of these countries has done us, who is so good that had it not been for him we should all of us already be dead, and they would have eaten us, and remember that he has even given you his daughters."

When Cortés heard this he was more angry than ever at the words they said to him, as they seemed to be a reproof, and he said: "Why should I be civil to a dog who was treating secretly with Narvaez, and now you can see that he does not even give us food to eat." Our Captains replied: "That is to our minds what he ought to do and it is good advice." As Cortés had so many Spaniards there with him in Mexico, both of our own party and of the followers of Narvaez he did not trouble himself a whit about anything, and he spoke angrily and rudely again, addressing the chieftains and telling them to say to their Lord Montezuma that he should at once order the markets and sales to be held, if not he would see what would happen.

The chieftains well understood the offensive remarks that Cortés made about their Lord and even the reproof that our Captains gave to Cortés about it, for they knew them well as having been those who used to be on guard over their Lord, and they knew that they were good friends of their Montezuma, and according to the way they understood the matter they repeated it to Montezuma. Either from anger at this treatment, or because it had already been agreed on that we were to be attacked, it was not a quarter of an hour later that a soldier arrived in great haste and badly wounded. He came from a town close by Mexico named Tacuba and was escorting some Indian women who belonged to Cortés, one of them a daughter of Montezuma, for it appears that Cortés had left them there in charge of the Lord of Tacuba, for they were relations of this same Lord, when we went off on the expedition against Narvaez. This soldier said that all the city and road by which he had come was full of warriors fully armed, and that they had taken from him the Indian women he was bringing and had given him two wounds and that if he had not let the women go, the Mexicans would have captured him, and would have put him in a canoe and carried him off to be sacrificed, and that they had broken down a bridge.

Let me go on and say that Cortés promptly ordered Diego de Ordás to go with four hundred soldiers, and among them most of the crossbowmen and musketeers and some horsemen, and examine into what the soldier had reported, and that if he found that he could calm the Indians without fighting and disturbance that he should do so.

Diego de Ordás set out in the way that he was ordered with his four hundred soldiers, but he had hardly reached the middle of the street along which he was to march, when so many squadrons of Mexican warriors fell on him and so many more were on the roofs of the houses, and they made such fierce attacks that on the first assault they killed eight soldiers and wounded all the rest, and Diego de Ordás himself was wounded in three places, and in this manner he could not advance one step further but had to return little by little to his quarters. During the retreat they killed another good soldier named Lyscano who, with a broadsword, had done the work of a very valiant man.

At that moment, while many squadrons came out against Ordás, many more approached our quarters and shot off so many javelins and stones from slings, and arrows, that they wounded on that occasion alone over forty-six of our men, and twelve of them died of their wounds; and such a number of warriors fell upon us that Diego de Ordás, who was coming in retreat, could not reach our quarters on account of the fierce assaults they made on him, some from the rear and others in front and others from the roofs.

Little availed our cannon, or our muskets, crossbows and lances, or the thrusts we gave them, or our good fighting, for although we killed and wounded many of them, yet they managed to reach us by pushing forward over the points of our swords and lances, and closing up their squadrons never desisted from their brave attack, nor could we push them away from us.

At last, what with cannon and muskets and the damage we did them with our sword thrusts, Ordás found an opportunity to enter our quarters, and not until then, much as he desired it, could he force a passage with his badly wounded soldiers, fourteen fewer in number. Still many of the squadrons never ceased from attacking us, and telling us that we were like women, and they called us rogues and other abusive names. But the damage they had done us up to this time was as nothing to what they did afterwards, for such was their daring that, some attacking on one side and some on the other, they penetrated into our quarters and set fire to them, and we could not endure the smoke and the fire until it was remedied by flinging much earth over it, and cutting off other rooms whence the fire came. In truth, they believed that they would burn us alive in there. These conflicts lasted all day long, and even during the night so many squadrons of them fell on us, and hurled javelins, stones and arrows in masses, and random stones so that what with those that fell during the day and those that then fell in all the courts and on the ground, it looked like chaff on a threshing floor.

We passed the night in dressing wounds and in mending the breaches in the walls that the enemy had made, and in getting ready for the next day. Then, as soon as it was dawn, our Captain decided that all of us and Narvaez' men should sally out to fight with them and that we should take the cannon and muskets and crossbows and endeavour to defeat them, or at least to make them feel our strength and valour better than the day before. I may state that when we came to this decision, the Mexicans were arranging the very same thing. We fought very well, but they were so strong, and had so many squadrons which relieved each other from time to time, that even if ten thousand Trojan Hectors and as many more Roldans had been there, they would not have been able to break through them.

We noted their tenacity in fighting, but I declare that I do not know how to describe it, for neither cannon nor muskets nor crossbows availed, nor hand-to-hand fighting, nor killing thirty or forty of them every time we charged, for they still fought on in as close ranks and with more energy than in the beginning. Sometimes when we were gaining a little ground or a part of the street, they pretended to retreat, but it was merely to induce us to follow them and cut us off from our fortress and quarters, so as to fall on us in greater safety to themselves, believing that we could not return to our quarters alive, for they did us much damage when we were retreating.

Then, as to going out to burn their houses, I have already said that between one house and another they have wooden drawbridges, and these they raised so that we could only pass through deep water. Then we could not endure the rocks and stones hurled from the roofs, in such a way that they damaged and wounded many of our men. I do not know why I write thus, so lukewarmly, for some three or four soldiers who were there with us and who had served in Italy, swore to God many times that they had never seen such fierce fights, not even when they had taken part in such between Christians and against the artillery of the King of France, or of the Great Turk, nor had they seen men like those Indians with such courage in closing up their ranks.

With great difficulty we withdrew to our quarters, many squadrons of warriors still pressing on us with loud veils and whistles, and trumpets and drums, calling us villains and cowards who did not dare to meet them all day in battle, but turned in flight.

On that day they killed ten or twelve more soldiers and we all returned badly wounded. What took place during the nights was the arrangement that in two days' time all the soldiers in camp, as many as were able, should sally out with four engines like towers built of strong timber, in such a manner that five and twenty men could find shelter under each of them, and they were provided with apertures and loopholes through which to shoot, and musketeers and crossbowmen accompanied them, and close by them were to march the other soldiers, musketeers and crossbowmen and the guns, and all the rest, and the horsemen were to make charges.

When this plan was settled, as we spent all that day in carrying out the work and in strengthening many breaches that they had made in the walls, we did not go out to fight.

I do not know how to tell of the great squadrons of warriors who came to attack us that day in our quarters, not only in ten or twelve places, but in more than twenty, for we were distributed over them all and in many other places, and while we built up and fortified ourselves, as I have related, many other squadrons openly endeavoured to penetrate into our quarters, and neither with guns, crossbows nor muskets, nor with many charges and sword thrusts could we force them back, for they said that not one of us should remain alive that day and they would sacrifice our hearts and blood to their gods, and would have enough to glut their appetites and hold feasts on our arms and legs, and would throw our bodies to the tigers, lions, vipers and snakes, which they kept caged, so that they might gorge on them, and for that reason they had ordered them not to be given food for the past two days. As for the gold we possessed, we would get little satisfaction from it or from all the cloths; and as for the Tlaxcalans who were with us, they said that they would place them in cages to fatten, and little by little they would offer their bodies in sacrifice; and, very tenderly, they said that we should give up to them their great Lord Montezuma, and they said other things. Night by night, in like manner, there were always many yells and whistles and showers of darts, stones and arrows.

As soon as dawn came, after commending ourselves to God, we sallied out from our quarters with our towers, with the cannon, muskets and crossbows in advance, and the horsemen making charges, but, as I have stated, although we killed many of them it availed nothing towards making them turn their backs, indeed if they had fought bravely on the two previous days, they proved themselves far more vigorous and displayed much greater forces and squadrons on this day. Nevertheless, we determined, although it should cost the lives of all of us, to push on with our towers and engines as far as the great Cue of Huichilobos.

I will not relate at length the fights we had with them in a fortified house, nor will I tell how they wounded the horses, nor were the horses of any use to us, because although the horsemen charged the squadrons to break through them, so many arrows, darts and stones were hurled at them, that they, well protected by armour though they were, could not prevail against the enemy, and if they pursued and overtook them, the Mexicans promptly dropped for safety into the canals and lagoons where they had raised other walls against the horsemen, and many other Indians were stationed with very long lances to finish killing them. Thus it benefited us nothing to turn aside to burn or demolish a house, it was quite useless, for, as I have said, they all stood in the water, and between house and house there was a movable bridge, and to cross by swimming was very dangerous, for on the roofs they had such store of rocks and stones and such defences, that it was certain destruction to risk it. In addition to this, where we did set fire to some houses, a single house took a whole day to burn, and the houses did not catch fire one from the other; thus it was useless toil to risk our persons in the attempt, so we went towards the great Cue of their Idols. Then, all of a sudden, more than four thousand Mexicans ascended it [this was the Great Teocalli of Tenochtitlan, quite close to the Spanish Quarters; Cortés says that five hundred Mexicans ascended the Teocalli itself to defend it], not counting other Companies that were posted on it with long lances and stones and darts, and placed themselves on the defensive, and resisted our ascent for a good while, and neither the towers nor the cannon or crossbows, nor the muskets were of any avail, nor the horsemen, for, although they wished to charge, the whole of the courtyard was paved with very large flagstones, so that the horses lost their foothold, and the stones were so slippery that the horses fell. While from the steps of the lofty Cue they forbade our advance, we had so many enemies both on one side and the other that although our cannon shots carried off ten or fifteen of them and we slew many others by sword thrusts and charges, so many men attacked us that we were not able to ascend the lofty Cue. However with great unanimity we persisted in the attack, and without taking the towers (for they were already destroyed) we made our way to the summit.

Here Cortés showed himself very much of a man, as he always was. Oh! what a fight and what a fierce battle it was that took place; it was a memorable thing to see us all streaming with blood and covered with wounds and others slain. It pleased our Lord that we reached the place where we used to keep the image of Our Lady, and we did not find it, and it appears, as we came to know, that the great Montezuma paid devotion to Her, and ordered the image to be preserved in safety.

We set fire to their Idols and a good part of the chamber with the Idols Huichilobos and Tezcatepuca was burned. On that occasion the Tlaxcalans helped us very greatly. After this was accomplished, while some of us were fighting and others kindling the fire, as I have related, oh! to see the priests who were stationed on this great Cue, and the three or four thousand Indians, all men of importance. While we descended, oh! how they made us tumble down six or even ten steps at a time! And so much more there is to tell of the other squadrons posted on the battlements and recesses of the great Cue discharging so many darts and arrows that we could face neither one group of squadrons nor the other. We resolved to return, with much toil and risk to ourselves, to our quarters, our castles being destroyed, all of us wounded and sixteen slain, with the Indians constantly pressing on us and other squadrons on our flanks.

However clearly I may tell all this, I can never fully explain it to anyone who did not see us. So far, I have not spoken of what the Mexican squadrons did who kept on attacking our quarters while we were marching outside, and the great obstinacy and tenacity they displayed in forcing their way in.

In this battle, we captured two of the chief priests, whom Cortés ordered us to convey with great care.

Many times I have seen among the Mexicans and Tlaxcalans, paintings of this battle, and the ascent that we made of the great Cue, as they look upon it as a very heroic deed. And although in the pictures that they have made of it, they depict all of us as badly wounded and streaming with blood and many of us dead they considered it a great feat, this setting fire to the Cue, when so many warriors were guarding it both on the battlements and recesses, and many more Indians were below on the ground and the Courts were full of them and there were many more on the sides; and with our towers destroyed, how was it possible to scale it?

Let us stop talking about it and I will relate how with great labour we returned to our quarters and if many men were then following us, as many more were in our quarters, for they had already demolished some walls so as to gain an entry, but on our arrival they desisted. Nevertheless, during all the rest of the day they never ceased to discharge darts, stones and arrows, and during the night yells and stones and darts.

That night was passed in dressing wounds and in burying the dead, in preparations for going out to fight the following day, in strengthening and adding parapets to the walls they had pulled down, and to other breaches they had made, and in consulting how and in what way we could fight without suffering such great damage and death, and throughout the discussion we found no remedy at all.

Then I also wish to speak of the maledictions that the followers of Narvaez hurled at Cortés, and the words that they used, cursing him and the country and even Diego Velásquez who had sent them there when they were peacefully settled in their homes in the Island of Cuba, and they were crazy and out of their minds.

Let us go back to our story. It was decided to sue for peace so that we could leave Mexico, and as soon as it was dawn many more squadrons of Mexicans arrived and very effectually surrounded our quarters on all sides, and if they had discharged many stones and arrows before, they came much thicker and with louder howls and whistles on this day, and other squadrons endeavoured to force an entrance in other parts, and cannon and muskets availed nothing, although we did them damage enough.

When Cortés saw all this, he decided that the great Montezuma should speak to them from the roof and tell them that the war must cease, and that we wished to leave his city. When they went to give this message from Cortés to the great Montezuma, it is reported that he said with great grief: "What more does Malinche want from me? I neither wish to live nor to listen to him, to such a pass has my fate brought me because of him." And he did not wish to come, and it is even reported that he said he neither wished to see nor hear him, nor listen to his false words, promises or lies. Then the Padre de la Merced and Cristóbal de Olid went and spoke to him with much reverence and in very affectionate terms, and Montezuma said: "I believe that I shall not obtain any result towards ending this war, for they have already raised up another Lord and have made up their minds not to let you have this place alive, therefore I believe that all of you will have to die."

Montezuma was placed by a battlement of the roof with many of us soldiers guarding him, and he began to speak to his people, with very affectionate expressions telling them to desist from the war, and that we would leave Mexico. Many of the Mexican Chieftains and Captains knew him well and at once ordered their people to be silent and not to discharge darts, stones or arrows, and four of them reached a spot where Montezuma could speak to them, and they to him, and with tears they said to him: "Oh! Señor, and our great Lord, how all your misfortune and injury and that of your children and relations afflicts us, we make known to you that we have already raised one of your kinsmen to be our Lord," and there he stated his name, that he was called Cuitlahuac, the Lord of Ixtapalapa, and moreover they said that the war must be carried through, and that they had vowed to their Idols not to relax it until we were all dead, and that they prayed every day to their Huichilobos and Tezcatepuca to guard him free and safe from our power, and that should it end as they desired, they would not fail to hold him in higher regard as their Lord than they did before, and they begged him to forgive them. They had hardly finished this speech when suddenly such a shower of stones and darts were discharged that (our men who were shielding him having neglected for a moment their duty, because they saw how the attack ceased while he spoke to them) he was hit by three stones, one on the head, another on the arm and another on the leg, and although they begged him to have the wounds dressed and to take food, and spoke kind words to him about it, he would not. Indeed, when we least expected it, they came to say that he was dead. Cortés wept for him, and all of us Captains and soldiers, and there was no man among us who knew him and was intimate with him, who did not bemoan him as though he were our father, and it is not to be wondered at, considering how good he was. It was stated that he had reigned for seventeen years and that he was the best king there had ever been in Mexico, and that he had conquered in person, in three wars which he had carried on in the countries he had subjugated.

I have already told about the sorrow that we all of us felt about it when we saw that Montezuma was dead. We even thought badly of the Fraile de la Merced because he had not persuaded him to become a Christian, and he gave as an excuse that he did not think that he would die of those wounds, but that he ought to have ordered them to give him something to stupefy him. At the end of much discussion Cortés ordered a priest and a chief from among the prisoners to go and tell the Cacique whom they had chosen for Lord, who was named Cuitlahuac, and his Captains, that the great Montezuma was dead, and they had seen him die, and about the manner of his death and the wounds his own people had inflicted on him, and they should say how grieved we all were about it, and that they should bury him as the great king that he was, and they should raise the cousin of Montezuma who was with us, to be king, for the inheritance was his, or one of Montezuma's other sons, and that he whom they had raised to be king was not so by right, and they should negotiate a peace so that we could leave Mexico; and if they did not do so, now that Montezuma was dead, whom we held in respect and for that reason had not destroyed their city, we should sally out to make war on them and burn all their houses and do them much damage. So as to convince them that Montezuma was dead, he ordered six Mexicans who were high chieftains, and the priests whom we held as prisoners, to carry him out on their shoulders, and to hand the body over to the Mexican Captains, and to tell them what Montezuma had commanded at the time of his death, for those who carried him out on their backs were present at his death; and they told Cuitlahuac the whole truth, how his own people killed him with blows from three stones.

Spanish Defeat and the Noche Triste

When they beheld him thus dead, we saw that they were in floods of tears and we clearly heard the shrieks and cries of distress that they gave for him, but for all this, the fierce assault they made on us never ceased, and then they came on us again with greater force and fury, and said to us: "Now for certain you will pay for the death of our King and Lord, and the dishonour to our Idols; and as for the peace you sent to beg for, come out here and we will settle how and in what way it is to be made," and they said that they had already chosen a good king, and he would not be so fainthearted as to be deceived with false speeches like their good Montezuma, and as for the burial, we need not trouble about that, but about our own lives, for in two days there would not be one of us left—so much for the messages we had sent them. With these words they fell on us with loud yells and whistles and showers of stones, darts and arrows, while other squadrons were still attempting to set fire to our quarters in many places.

When Cortés and all of us observed this, we agreed that next day we would all of us sally out from our camp and attack in another direction, where there were many houses on dry land, and we would do all the damage we were able and go towards the causeway, and that all the horsemen should break through the squadrons and spear them with their lances or drive them into the water, even though the enemy should kill the horses. This was decided on in order to find out if by chance, with the damage and slaughter that we should inflict on them, they would abandon their attack and arrange some sort of peace, so that we could go free without more deaths and damage. Although the next day we all bore ourselves very manfully and killed many of the enemy and burned a matter of twenty houses and almost reached dry land, it was all of no use, because of the great damage and deaths and wounds they inflicted on us, and we could not hold a single bridge, for they were all of them half broken down. Many Mexicans charged down on us, and they had set up walls and barricades in places which they thought could be reached by the horses, so that if we had met with many difficulties up to this time, we found much greater ones ahead of us.

Now we saw our forces diminishing every day and those of the Mexicans increasing, and many of our men were dead and all the rest wounded, and although we fought like brave men we could not drive back nor even get free from the many squadrons which attacked us both by day and night, and the powder was giving out, and the same was happening with the food and water, and the great Montezuma being dead, they were unwilling to grant the peace and truce which we had sent to demand of them. In fact we were staring death in the face, and the bridges had been raised. It was therefore decided by Cortés and all of us captains and soldiers that we should set out during the night. That very afternoon we sent to tell them, through one of their priests whom we held prisoner and who was a man of great importance among them, that they should let us go in peace within eight days and we would give up to them all the gold; and this was done to put them off their guard so that we might get out that night.

The order was given to make a bridge of very strong beams and planks, so that we could carry it with us and place it where the bridges were broken. Four hundred Tlaxcalan Indians and one hundred and fifty soldiers were told off to carry this bridge and place it in position and guard the passage until the army and all the baggage had crossed. Two hundred Tlaxcalan Indians and fifty soldiers were told off to carry the cannon, and Gonzalo de Sandoval, Diego de Ordás, Francisco de Sauzedo, Francisco de Lugo and a company of one hundred young and active soldiers were selected to go in the van to do the fighting. It was agreed that Cortés himself, Alonzo de Ávila, Cristóbal de Olid and other Captains should go in the middle and support the party that most needed help in fighting. Pedro de Alvarado and Juan Velásquez de Leon were with the rearguard, and placed in the middle between them and the preceding section were two captains and the soldiers of Narvaez, and three hundred Tlaxcalans and thirty soldiers were told off to take charge of the prisoners and of Doña Marina and Doña Luisa; by the time this arrangement was made, it was already night.

In order to bring out the gold and divide it up and carry it, Cortés ordered his steward named Cristóbal de Guzman and other soldiers who were his servants to bring out all the gold and jewels and silver, and he gave them many Tlaxcalan Indians for the purpose, and they placed it in the Hall. Then Cortés told the King's officers named Alonzo Dávila and Gonzalo Mejia to take charge of the gold belonging to His Majesty, and he gave them seven wounded and lame horses and one mare, and many friendly Tlaxcalans, more than eighty in number, and they loaded them with parcels of it, as much as they could carry, for it was put up into very broad ingots, and much gold still remained in the Hall piled up in heaps. Then Cortés called his secretary and the others who were King's Notaries, and said: "Bear witness for me that I can do no more with this gold. We have here in this apartment and Hall over seven hundred thousand pesos in gold, and, as you have seen, it cannot be weighed nor placed in safety. I now give it up to any of the soldiers who care to take it, otherwise it will be lost among these dogs of Mexicans."

When they heard this many of the soldiers of Narvaez and some of our people loaded themselves with it. I declare that I had no other desire but the desire to save my life, but I did not fail to carry off from some small boxes that were there, four chalchihuites, which are stones very highly prized among the Indians, and I quickly placed them in my bosom under my armour, and, later on, the price of them served me well in healing my wounds and getting me food.

After we had learnt the plans that Cortés had made about the way in which we were to escape that night and get to the bridges, as it was somewhat dark and cloudy and rainy, we began before midnight to bring along the baggage, and the horses and mare began their march, and the Tlaxcalans who were laden with the gold. Then the bridge was quickly put in place, and Cortés and the others whom he took with him in the first detachment and many of the horsemen, crossed over it. While this was happening, the voices, trumpets, cries and whistles of the Mexicans began to sound and they called out in their language to the people of Tlaltelolco, "Come out at once with your canoes for the Teules are leaving; cut them off so that not one of them may be left alive." When I least expected it, we saw so many squadrons of warriors bearing down on us, and the lake so crowded with canoes that we could not defend ourselves. Many of our soldiers had already crossed the bridge, and while we were in this position, a great multitude of Mexicans charged down on us with the intention of removing the bridge and wounding and killing our men who were unable to assist each other; and as fortune is perverse at such times, one mischance followed another, and as it was raining, two of the horses slipped and fell into the lake. When I and others of Cortés' Company saw that, we got safely to the other side of the bridge, and so many warriors charged on us, that despite all our good fighting, no further use could be made of the bridge, so that the passage or water opening was soon filled up with dead horses, Indian men and women, servants, baggage and boxes.

Fearing that they would not fail to kill us, we thrust ourselves ahead along the causeway, and we met many squadrons armed with long lances waiting for us, and they used abusive words to us, and among them they cried: "Oh! villains, are you still alive?"—and with the cuts and thrusts we gave them, we got through, although they then wounded six of those who were going along with me. Then if there was some sort of plan such as we had agreed upon it was an accursed one; for Cortés and the captains and soldiers who passed first on horseback, so as to save themselves and reach dry land and make sure of their lives, spurred on along the causeway, and they did not fail to attain their object, and the horses with the gold and the Tlaxcalans also got out in safety. I assert that if we had waited (the horsemen and the soldiers one for the other) at the bridges, we should all have been put an end to, and not one of us would have been left alive; the reason was this, that as we went along the causeway, charging the Mexican squadrons, on one side of us was water and on the other *azoteas* [the flat roofs of the houses], and the lake was full of canoes so that we could do nothing. Moreover the muskets and crossbows were all left behind at the bridge, and as it was nighttime, what could we do beyond what we accomplished? which was to charge and give some sword thrusts to those who tried to lay hands on us, and to march and get on ahead so as to get off the causeway.

Had it been in the daytime, it would have been far worse, and we who escaped did so only by the Grace of God. To one who saw the hosts of warriors who fell on us that night and the canoes full of them coming along to carry off our soldiers, it was terrifying. So we went ahead along the causeway in order to get to the town of Tacuba where Cortés was already stationed with all the Captains. Gonzalo de Sandoval, Cristóbal de Olid and others of those horsemen who had gone on ahead were crying out: "Señor Captain, let us halt, for they say that we are fleeing and leaving them·to die at the bridges; let us go back and help them, if any of them survive"; but not one of them came out or escaped. Cortés' reply was that it was a miracle that any of us escaped. However, he promptly went back with the horsemen and the soldiers who were unwounded, but they did not march far, for Pedro de Alvarado soon met them, badly wounded, holding a spear in his hand, and on foot, for the enemy had already killed his sorrel mare, and he brought with him four soldiers as badly wounded as he was himself, and eight Tlaxcalans, all of them with blood flowing from many wounds.

While Cortés was on the causeway with the rest of the Captains, we repaired to the courtyard in Tacuba. Many squadrons had already arrived from Mexico, shouting out orders to Tacuba and to the other town named Atzcapotzalco, and they began to hurl darts, stones and arrows and attack with their long lances. We made some charges and both attacked them and defended ourselves.

Let us go back to Pedro de Alvarado. When Cortés and the other Captains met him in that way, and saw that no more soldiers were coming along the causeway, tears sprang to his eyes. Pedro de Alvarado said that Juan Velásquez de Leon lay dead with many other gentlemen both of our own company and that of Narvaez, and that more than eighty of them were at the bridge; that he and the four soldiers whom he brought with him, after their horses had been killed, crossed the bridge in great peril, over the dead bodies, horses and boxes with which that passage at the bridge was choked. Moreover, he said that all the bridges and causeways were crowded with warriors. At the bridge of sorrow, which they afterwards called "Alvarado's leap," I assert that at the time not a single soldier stopped to see if he leaped much or little, for we could hardly save our own lives, as we were in great danger of death on account of the multitude of Mexicans charging down on us. I never heard of this leap of Alvarado until after Mexico was captured, and it was in some satirical verses made by a certain Gonzalo de Ocampo, which, as they were somewhat nasty, I will not fully quote here, except that he says: "Thou shouldst remember the leap that thou tookest from the bridge"; but I will not dwell on this subject.

Let us go on and I will relate how, when we were waiting in Tacuba, many Mexican warriors came together from all those towns and they killed three of our soldiers, so we agreed to get out of that town as quickly as we could, and five Tlaxcalan Indians, who found out a way towards Tlaxcala without following the main road, guided us with great precaution until we reached some small houses placed on a hill, and near to them a Cue or Oratory built like a fort, where we halted.

As we marched along we were followed by the Mexicans who hurled arrows and darts at us and stones from their slings, and the way in which they surrounded us and continually attacked us, was terrifying, as I have already said many times and am tired of repeating it.

We defended ourselves in that Cue and fortress, where we lodged and attended to the wounded and made many fires, but as for anything to eat, there was no thought of it. At that Cue or Oratory, after the great city of Mexico was captured, we built a church, which is called "Nuestra Señora de los Remedios," and is very much visited, and many of the inhabitants and ladies from Mexico now go there on pilgrimages and to hold novenas [religious exercises extending over nine days].

It was pitiable to see our wounds being dressed and bound up with cotton cloths, and as they were chilled and swollen they were very painful. However what was more to be wept over was the loss of the gentlemen and brave soldiers who were missing, namely, Juan Velásquez de Leon, Francisco de Sauzedo, Francisco de Morla, Lares the good horseman and many others of us followers of Cortés. I name these few only because it would be a long business to write the names of the great number of our companions who were missing. Of the followers of Narvaez, the greater number were left at the bridges weighed down with gold.

Let us go on to say how there were left dead at the bridges the sons and daughters of Montezuma as well as the prisoners we were bringing with us, also Cacamatzin the Lord of Texcoco and other kings of provinces. Let us stop relating all these hardships and say how we were thinking of what we had in front of us, for we were all wounded, and only twenty-three horses escaped; then of the cannon and artillery and powder, we saved nothing; the crossbows were few in number and we promptly mended their cords and made arrows but the worst of all was that we did not know what we should find the disposition of our friends the Tlaxcalans would be towards us. In addition to this, always surrounded by Mexicans who fell on us with yells, we determined to get out of that place at midnight with the Tlaxcalans in front as guides, taking every precaution. We marched with the wounded in the middle and the lame supported with staffs, and some, who were very bad and could not walk, on the croups of the horses that were lame and were not fit for fighting. Those horsemen who were not wounded went in front or were divided some on one side, some on the other, and marching in this manner all of us who were most free from wounds kept our faces towards the enemy. The wounded Tlaxcalans went in the body of our squadron and the rest of them who were sufficiently sound faced the enemy in company with us. The Mexicans were always harassing us with loud cries, yells and whistles, shouting out, "You are going where not one of you will be left alive," and we did not understand why they said so, but it will be seen later on. But I have forgotten to write down how happy we were to see Doña Marina still alive, and Doña Luisa the daughter of Xicotenga, whose escape at the bridges was due to some Tlaxcalans, and also a woman named Maria de Estrada, who was the only Spanish woman in Mexico. Those who escaped and got away first from the bridges were some sons of Xicotenga, the brothers of Doña Luisa. Most of our servants who had been given to us in Tlaxcala and in the city of Mexico itself were left behind dead.

That day we reached some farms and huts belonging to a large town named Cuautitlan. Thence we went through some farms and hamlets with the Mexicans always in pursuit of us, and as many of them had got together, they endeavoured to kill us and began to surround us, and hurled many stones with their slings and javelins and arrows, and with their broadswords they killed two of our soldiers in a bad pass, and they also killed a horse and wounded many of our men, and we also with cut and thrust killed some of them, and the horsemen did the same. We slept in those houses and we ate the horse they had killed, and the next day very early in the morning we began our march, with the same and even greater precautions than we observed before, half of the horsemen always going ahead. On a plain a little more than a league further on (when we began to think that we could march in safety) our scouts, who were on the lookout, returned to say that the fields were full of Mexican warriors waiting for us. When we heard this we were indeed alarmed but not so as to be fainthearted or to fail to meet them and fight to the death. There we halted for a short time and orders were given how the horsemen were to charge and return at a hard gallop, and were not to stop to spear the enemy but to keep their lances aimed at their faces until they broke up their squadrons; and that all the soldiers, in the thrusts they gave, should pass their swords through the bodies of their opponents, and that we should act in such a way as to avenge thoroughly the deaths and wounds of our companions, so that if God willed it we should escape with our lives.

After commending ourselves to God and the Holy Mary, full of courage, and calling on the name of Señor Santiago, as soon as we saw that the enemy began to surround us, and that the horsemen, keeping in parties of five, broke through their ranks, we all of us charged at the same time.

Oh! what a sight it was to see this fearful and destructive battle, how we moved all mixed up with them foot to foot, and the cuts and thrusts we gave them, and with what fury the dogs fought, and what wounds and deaths they inflicted on us with their lances and macanas. Then, as the ground was level, to see how the horsemen speared them as they chose, charging and returning, and although both they and their horses were wounded, they never stopped fighting like very brave men. As for all of us who had no horses, it seemed as if we all put on double strength, for although we were wounded and again received other wounds, we did not trouble to bind them up so as not to halt to do so, for there was not time, but with great spirit we closed with the enemy so as to give them sword thrusts. I wish to tell about Cortés and Cristóbal de Olid, Gonzalo de Sandoval, Gonzalo Dominguez and a Juan de Salamanca who although badly wounded rode on one side and the other, breaking through the squadrons; and about the words that Cortés said to those who were in the thick of the enemy, that the cuts and thrusts that we gave should be aimed at distinguished chieftains, for they all of them bore great golden plumes and rich arms and devices. Then to see how the valiant and spirited Sandoval encouraged us and cried: "Now, gentlemen, this is the day when we are bound to be victorious; have trust in God and we shall come out of this alive for some good purpose." They killed and wounded a great number of our soldiers, but it pleased God that Cortés and the Captains whom I have already named who went in his Company reached the place where the Captain General of the Mexicans was marching with his banner displayed, and with rich golden armour and great gold and silver plumes. When Cortés saw him with many other Mexican Chieftains all wearing great plumes, he said to our Captains: "Now, Señores, let us break through them and leave none of them unwounded"; and commending themselves to God, Cortés, Cristóbal de Olid, Sandoval, Alonzo de Avila, and the other horsemen charged, and Cortés struck his horse against the Mexican Captain, which made him drop his banner, and the rest of our Captains succeeded in breaking through the squadron which consisted of many Indians following the Captain who carried the banner, who nevertheless had not fallen at the shock that Cortés had given him, and it was Juan de Salamanca, who rode with Cortés on a good piebald mare, who gave him a lance thrust and took from him the rich plume that he wore, and afterwards gave it to Cortés, saying that as it was he who first met him and made him lower his banner and deprived his followers of the courage to fight, that the plume belonged to him (Cortés). However, three years afterwards, the King gave it to Salamanca as his coat of arms, and his descendants bear it on their tabards.

Let us go back to the battle. It pleased Our Lord that when that Captain who carried the Mexican banner was dead (and many others were killed there) their attack slackened, and all the horsemen followed them and we felt neither hunger nor thirst, and it seemed as though we had neither suffered nor passed through any evil or hardship, as we followed up our victory killing and wounding. Then our friends the Tlaxcalans were very lions, and with their swords and broadswords which they there captured from the enemy behaved very well and valiantly. When the horsemen returned from following up the victory we all gave many thanks to God for having escaped from such a great multitude of people, for there had never been seen or found throughout the Indies such a great number of warriors together in any battle that was fought, for there was present there the flower of Mexico and Texcoco and all the towns around the lake, and others in the neighbourhood, and the people of Otumba and Tepetexcoco and Saltocan, who all came in the belief that this time not a trace of us would be left. Then what rich armour they wore, with so much gold and plumes and devices, and nearly all of them were captains and chieftains. Near the spot where this hard-fought and celebrated battle took place, and where one can say God spared our lives, there stands a town named Otumba.

Our escape from the City of Mexico was on the tenth of the month of July [1520], and this celebrated battle of Otumba was fought on the fourteenth of the month of July.

In recalling this terrible defeat at the hands of the Mexica squadrons, Bernal writes that *"within a matter of five days over eight hundred and sixty soldiers were killed and sacrificed"* plus five Spanish women and over a thousand Tlaxcalans. He criticizes Narváez's followers, who died in greater numbers, *"because they went forth laden with gold, and owing to its weight they could neither escape nor swim."*

Depleted in numbers and spirit, the Spaniards flee in retreat toward Tlaxcala where they spend twenty-two days recovering and making plans. They discover that the gold they had stored in Tlaxcala had been retaken by the Mexicas, thus leaving the settlers in Villa Rica empty-handed for their previous efforts with Cortés. Warmly welcomed by the Tlaxcalans, who also mourned the huge loss of their warrior elites, they tell Cortés, *"Do not think Malinche, that it is a small thing you have done to escape with your lives from that impregnable city and its bridges."* Xicotenga the Younger had continued to rebel against his father's alliance with the Spaniards but with little effect though he was still at large.

A number of Narváez's men petition to abandon the war and return home. Cortés seeks reinforcements and with a sizable force of Tlaxcalan warriors eventually attacks and defeats the Mexica garrison of Tepeaca after which the Tepeacans join Cortés's forces. The garrison town is renamed *Villa Segura de la Frontera* and becomes a *"slave town,"* that is, a base for raiding nearby communities, the collection of slaves, and their branding with a special design Ƅ that, according to Bernal Díaz, *"means Guerra."*

The populace in the Aztec capital is also in great distress. A smallpox epidemic has killed many including Montezuma's successor, leading to the ascension to the throne of *"Guatemoc,"* one of Montezuma's nephews. Bernal Díaz claims that Guatemoc sent squadrons to reinforce other garrison towns so as to avoid a repeat of the Tepeaca defeat. These reinforcements abuse the people of Guacachula and Izucar, and they turn against the Mexicas and ally with the Spaniards.

Reinforcements for Narváez arrive on the coast (the governor of Cuba not having heard of Narváez's defeat by Cortés), and Cortés persuades them to turn over their supplies and loyalty to him. Several other contingents of *reinforcements arrive from Jamaica and elsewhere on the mainland, swelling Cortés's Spanish numbers by 150 soldiers and twenty more horses.*

When Gonzalo de Sandoval arrived at the town of Segura de la Frontera after having made the expeditions I have spoken of, we had all the people of that province pacified. So Cortés decided, with the officials of the King, that all the slaves that had been taken should be branded so that his fifth might be set aside after the fifth had been taken for His Majesty, and to this effect he had a proclamation made in the town and camp, that all the soldiers should bring to a house chosen for the purpose all the women whom we were sheltering, to be branded, and the time allowed for doing this was the day of the proclamation and one more.

We all came with all the Indian women and girls and boys whom we had captured, but the grown-up men we did not trouble about as they were difficult to watch and we had no need of their services, as we had our friends the Tlaxcalans. When they had all been brought together and had been marked with the iron which was like this 𝕲, which stands for *guerra* [war], when we were not expecting it they set aside the Royal fifth, and then took another fifth for Cortés, and, in addition to this, the night before, after we had placed the women in that house as I have stated, they took away and hid the best-looking Indian women, and there was not a good-looking one left, and when it came to dividing them, they allotted us the old and ugly women, and there was a great deal of grumbling about it against Cortés and those who ordered the good-looking Indian women to be stolen and hidden; so much so that some of the soldiers of Narvaez said to Cortés himself, that they took God to witness that such a thing had never happened as to have two Kings in the country belonging to our Lord the King, and to deduct two-fifths. One of the soldiers who said this to him was Juan Bono de Quejo, and moreover he said that they would not remain in such a country, and that he would inform His Majesty in Spain about it, and the Royal Council of the Indies. Another soldier told Cortés very clearly that it did not suffice to divide the gold which had been secured in Mexico in the way in which he had done it for when he was dividing it he said that it was three hundred thousand pesos that had been collected, and when we were fleeing from Mexico, he had ordered witness to be taken that there remained more than seven hundred thousand; and that now the poor soldier who had done all the hard work and was covered with wounds could not even have a good-looking Indian woman; besides the soldiers had given the Indian women skirts and chemises, and all those women had been taken and hidden away. Moreover when the proclamation had been issued that they were to be brought and branded, it was thought that each soldier would have his women returned to him, and they would be appraised according to the value of each in pesos, and that when they had been valued a fifth would be paid to His Majesty and there would not be any fifth for Cortés; and other complaints were made worse than these.

When Cortés saw this, he said with smooth words that he swore on his conscience (for that was his usual oath) that from that time forward he would not act in that way, but that good or bad, all the Indian women should be put up to auction and that the good-looking ones should be sold for so much, and those that were not good-looking for a lower price, so that there should be no cause of quarrel with him. However, here in Tepeaca no more slaves were made, but afterwards in Texcoco it was done nearly in this manner, as I will relate further on.

I will stop talking about this and will refer to another matter almost worse than this of the slaves, which was that when on that night of sorrow [the noche triste] we were fleeing from Mexico, Cortés declared before a King's Notary that whoever should wish to take gold from what was left there, might carry it off and welcome, for their own, as otherwise it would be lost. As in our camp and town of Segura de la Frontera Cortés got to know that there were many bars of gold, and that they were changing hands at play, and as the proverb has it: "*El oro y amores eran malos de encubrir*" (gold and love affairs are difficult to hide), he ordered a proclamation to be made, that under heavy penalty they should bring and declare the gold that they had taken, and that a third part of it should be returned to them, and that if they did not bring it, all would be seized. Many of the soldiers who possessed gold did not wish to give it up, and some of it Cortés took as a loan, but more by force than by consent, and as nearly all the Captains possessed gold and even the officials of the King, the proclamation was all the more ignored and no more spoken of; however, this order of Cortés' seemed to be very wrong.

Once the Tepeaca countryside is pacified, the Spaniards return to Tlaxcala and are saddened to learn that Mase Escasi has died of smallpox. While all are in mourning Cortés settles a dispute among the Tlaxcalans as to who should succeed Mase Escasi on the throne. The Tlaxcalans reassert their loyalty to Cortés and do the majority of the labor when he orders the building of thirteen launches to be used in the siege and attack of Mexico. Cortés recovers the rigging, bolts, and anchors that had been taken from the ships he had ordered burned near Villa Rica and "with the help of more than a thousand Indians" transported them to Tlaxcala. While a debate goes on about the best place from which to launch the ships against the Mexican capital (Texcoco or Ayotzingo), a large ship from Spain and the Canary Islands arrives "laden with a great variety of merchandise, muskets, powder, crossbows and crossbow cords, and three horses and other arms." These goods and the ship's passengers come into Cortés's hands.

The Return to the Valley and the Alliance with Texcoco

When Cortés saw that he possessed such a goodly store of muskets and powder and crossbows and realized the strong desire of all of us, both Captains and soldiers, again to attack the great City of Mexico, he decided to ask the Caciques of Tlaxcala to give him ten thousand Indian warriors to join us on an expedition to Texcoco; which after Mexico is one of the largest cities in the whole of New Spain. Xicotenga the elder promptly said that he would give him with the utmost willingness not only ten thousand men but many more if he chose to take them, and that another valiant Cacique, our great friend Chichimecatecle would go as their captain. On the day after the feast of the Nativity in the year 1520 we began our march, and slept at (Tesmelucan) a pueblo subject to Tlaxcala, and the people of the town gave us what we needed. From there onward it was Mexican territory, and we went more cautiously, for it was well-known in Mexico and Texcoco that we were marching towards their city. That day we met no obstacles whatever and camped at the foot of the Sierra, a march of about three leagues. The night was very cold, but we got through it safely thanks to our patrols, and scouts. When the dawn came we began to ascend a small pass and in some difficult places like barrancas the hillside had been cut away so that we could not pass, and many pine trees and other timber had been placed across the track, but having so many friendly Tlaxcalans with us, a clearing was soon made, and sending a company of musketeers and crossbowmen in advance we marched on with the utmost caution, our allies cutting and pushing aside trees to enable the horsemen to pass, until we got to the top of the range. Then we descended a little and caught sight of the lake of Mexico and its great cities standing in the water, and when we saw it we gave great thanks to God for allowing us to see it again.

We descended the mountain to where we saw great smoke signals, and marching onward we came upon a large squadron of Mexican and Texcocan warriors who were waiting for us at a pass through a rocky thicket where there was an apparently broken-down wooden bridge, and a deep gulch and waterfall below it. However, we soon defeated the squadron and passed in perfect safety. To hear the shouts that they gave from the farms and from the barrancas! However they did nothing else, and shouted only from places where the horsemen could not reach them. Our friends the Tlaxcalans carried off fowls and whatever else they could steal, and they did not abstain from this although Cortés had ordered them not to make war on the people if they were not attacked. The Tlaxcalans answered that if the people were well disposed and peaceable they would not come out on the road and attack us as they did at the passage of the barranca and bridge, where they tried to stop our advance.

We went to sleep that night at (Coatepec) a deserted pueblo subject to Texcoco, and took every precaution lest we should be attacked during the darkness.

As soon as dawn came we began our march towards Texcoco, which was about two leagues distant from where we slept. However, we had not advanced half a league when we saw our scouts returning at a breakneck pace and looking very cheerful, and they told Cortés that ten Indians were approaching unarmed and carrying golden devices and banners, and that yells and shouts no longer came from the huts and farms they had passed on the road as had happened the day before.

Then Cortés ordered a halt until seven Indian Chieftains, natives of Texcoco, came up to us. They carried a golden banner, and a long lance, and before reaching us they lowered the banner and knelt down (which is a sign of peace), and when they came before Cortés who had our interpreters standing by him, they said: "Malinche, our Lord and Chieftain of Texcoco, Coanacotzin sends to beg you to receive him into your friendship, and he is awaiting you peaceably in the City, and in proof thereof accept this banner of gold, and he begs as a favour that you will order your Tlaxcalans and your brethren not to do any harm to his land, and that you will come and lodge in the city where he will provide you with all that you need." Moreover they said that the troops which had been stationed in the ravines and bad passes did not belong to Texcoco, but were Mexicans sent by Guatemoc.

When the message had been considered Cortés at once sent for the Tlaxcalan Captains and ordered them, in the most friendly way, not to do any damage nor to take anything whatever in this country because peace had been made, and they did as he told them, but he did not forbid their taking food if it were only maize and beans, or even fowls and dogs, of which there was an abundance, all the houses being full of them.

Then Cortés took counsel with his Captains, and it seemed to them all that this begging for peace was a trick, for if it had been true it would not have been done so suddenly, and they would have brought food. Nevertheless, Cortés accepted the banner, which was worth about eighty pesos, and thanked the messengers and said to them, that he was not in the habit of doing evil or damage to any vassals of His Majesty, and if they kept the peace which they had announced he would protect them against the Mexicans; that as they might have seen, he had already ordered the Tlaxcalans not to do any damage in their country, and they would avoid doing so for the future, although they knew how in that city over forty Spaniards our brethren, and two hundred Tlaxcalans had been killed at the time when we were leaving Mexico, and many loads of gold and other spoil which belonged to them had been stolen, and that he must beg their chieftain Coanacotzin and the other chiefs and captains of Texcoco to restore to us the gold and the cloths, but as to the death of the Spaniards, there was no remedy for it, he would therefore not ask them for any.

The messengers replied that they would report to their Lord as he ordered them to do, but that he who had ordered the Spaniards to be killed and who took all the spoil was a chieftain named Cuitlahuac who had been chosen King of Mexico after Montezuma's death, and that they took to him in Mexico nearly all the Teules and they had been promptly sacrificed to Huichilobos.

When Cortés heard that reply, he made no answer, lest he should lose his temper or threaten them, but he bade them Godspeed. One of the ambassadors remained in our company, and we went on to a suburb of Texcoco called Coatlinchan, and there they gave us plenty to eat and all that we had need of, and we cast down some Idols that were in the houses where we lodged, and early the next day we went to the city of Texcoco. In none of the streets nor houses did we see any women, boys or children, only terrified-looking men. We took up our quarters in some great rooms and halls, and Cortés at once summoned the captains and most of us soldiers and told us not to leave the precincts of the great courts, and to keep well on the alert until we could see how things were going, for it did not seem to him that the city was friendly. He ordered Pedro de Alvarado and Cristóbal de Olid and some other soldiers, and me among them, to ascend the great Cue which was very lofty, and to look from the lofty Cue over the City and the lake, and what we saw was that all the inhabitants were moving off with their goods and chattels, and women and children, some to the hills and others to the reed thickets in the lake, and that the lake was thronged with canoes great and small.

As soon as Cortés knew this he wanted to capture the Lord of Texcoco who had sent him the golden banner, and when certain priests whom Cortés sent as messengers went to summon him, he had already placed himself in safety, for he was the very first to flee to Mexico with many other chieftains. We passed that night with great precautions, and very early the next day Cortés ordered all the Indian chieftains who had remained in Texcoco to be summoned before him, for as it was a very large city there were many other chieftains of the parties opposing the Cacique who had fled, with whom there had been discussions and disputes about the command and Kingship of that city. When they came before Cortés he learned from them how and since when Coanacotzin had ruled over the city. They told him that Coanacotzin in his desire to seize the power had infamously killed his elder brother Cuicuitzcatzin with the assistance given him for that purpose by Cuitlahuac, the Prince of Mexico, the one that made war on us when we were fleeing after the death of Montezuma. Furthermore,

there were among them other Lords who had a better right to the kingdom of Texcoco than he who now held it, and that it should go to a youth
who at that time became a Christian with much religious pomp, and was
named Don Hernando Cortés, for our Captain was his Godfather. They
said that this youth was the legitimate son of Nezahualpilli, the Lord
and King of Texcoco, and presently without any further delay, and with
the greatest festive celebration and rejoicing throughout Texcoco, they
appointed him their natural Lord and King, with all the ceremonies which
they were accustomed to render to their so-called Kings; and in perfect
peace and with the love of all his vassals, and of the neighbouring towns,
he governed absolutely and was obeyed. For his better instruction in the
matters of our faith and to improve his manners, and so that he should
learn our language, Cortés ordered that he should have as his tutors
Antonio de Villa Real, and a Bachelor of Arts named Escobar; Cortés
then asked for a large force of Indian labourers to broaden and deepen
the canals and ditches through which we were to draw the launches to
the lake when they were finished and ready to sail. He also explained to
Don Hernando himself and the other chieftains what was the reason and
purpose in having the launches built, and how we were going to blockade
Mexico. Don Hernando offered all the assistance within his power, and
of his own accord promised to send messengers to all the neighbouring
pueblos and tell them to become vassals of His Majesty, and accept our
friendship and authority against Mexico.

After spending twelve days in Texcoco the Tlaxcalans had exhausted
their provisions, and they were so numerous that the people of Texcoco
were unable to furnish them with sufficient food. As we were unwilling
that they should become a burden to the people of Texcoco and as the
Tlaxcalans themselves were most desirous of fighting the Mexicans and
avenging the death of the many Tlaxcalans who had been killed and
offered as sacrifices during their past defeats, Cortés determined that we
should set out on our march to Iztapalapa with himself as Commander
in Chief, and with Andrés de Tápia, Cristóbal de Olid and thirteen horsemen, twenty crossbowmen, six musketeers and two hundred and twenty

soldiers, and our Tlaxcalan allies, besides twenty chieftains from Texcoco given us by Don Hernando. I have already said that more than half the houses in Iztapalapa were built in the water and the other half on dry land. We kept on our way in good order, and as the Mexicans always held watchmen and garrisons and warriors ready to oppose us and to reinforce any of their towns, when they knew that we were going to attack them, they warned the people of Iztapalapa to be prepared, and sent over eight thousand Mexicans to help them. Like good warriors they awaited our coming on dry land, and for a good while they fought very bravely against us. Then the horsemen broke through their ranks, followed by the cross-bows and muskets, and all our Tlaxcalan allies who charged on them like mad dogs, and the enemy quickly abandoned the open ground and took refuge in the town. However, they had arranged a stratagem, and this was the way they did it; they fled and got into their canoes which were in the water, and into the houses which stood in the lake, others retired among the reeds, and as it was a dark night, they gave us a chance to take up quarters in the town, well contented with the spoil we had taken and still more with the victory we had gained. While we were in this situation, when we least expected it such a flood of water rushed through the whole town, that if the chieftains whom we had brought from Texcoco had not cried out, and warned us to get out of the houses to dry land as quickly as we could, we should all have been drowned, for the enemy had burst open the canals of fresh- and salt water and torn down a causeway, so that the water rose up all of a sudden. As our allies the Tlaxcalans were not accustomed to water and did not know how to swim, two of them were drowned, and we, at great risk to our lives, all thoroughly drenched and with our powder spoilt, managed to get out without our belongings, and in that condition, very cold, and without any supper, we passed a bad night. Worst of all were the jeers and the shouts and whistles which the people of Iztapalapa and the Mexicans uttered from their houses and canoes. However, there was still a worse thing to happen to us, for as they knew in Mexico about the plan that had been made to drown us by breaking down the causeway and canals, we found waiting for us on land

and in the lake many battalions of warriors, and, as soon as day dawned, they made such an attack on us that we could hardly bear up against it; but they did not defeat us, although they killed two soldiers and one horse, and wounded many both of us and the Tlaxcalans. Little by little the attack slackened and we returned to Texcoco, half ashamed at the trick and stratagem to throw us into the water, and also because we gained very little credit in the battle they fought against us afterwards, as our powder was exhausted. Nevertheless, it frightened them, and they had enough to do in burying and burning their dead, and curing their wounds and rebuilding their houses.

Though difficult to discern in the text, this next section narrates Cortés's circumambulation of the five lakes (and Tenochtitlan) in order to probe Mexica defenses, form alliances with some native communities, and plan the siege of the capital. The Spaniards attack or make contact with Xochimilco, Chalco, Tacuba, and Tenayuca before returning to Texcoco, from which the attack will be launched. This journey around the lake begins from Texcoco.

When we had been two days in Texcoco after our return from the expedition to Iztapalapa, three pueblos came peaceably to Cortés to beg pardon for the past wars and the deaths of Spaniards whom they had killed.

As Cortés saw that there was nothing else to be done at the time, he pardoned them, but he gave them a severe reprimand, and they bound themselves by many promises always to be hostile to the Mexicans and to be the vassals of His Majesty, and to serve us, and so they did.

About the same time the inhabitants of the pueblo named Mixquic, which is also called Venezuela, which stands in the lake, came to beg for peace and friendship. These people had apparently never been on good terms with the Mexicans, and in their hearts they detested them. Cortés and all of us were greatly pleased at these people coming to seek our friendship, because their pueblo was in the lake, and through them we hoped to get at their neighbours who were likewise established on the water, so Cortés thanked them greatly and dismissed them with promises

and gentle speeches. While this was taking place they came to tell Cortés
that great squadrons of Mexicans were advancing on the four pueblos
which had been the first to seek our friendship, one named Coatlinchan
and others whose names I forget, and they told Cortés that they did not
dare to stay in their houses and that they wished to flee to the mountains
or to come to Texcoco where we were, and they said so many things to
Cortés to induce him to help them, that he promptly got ready twenty
horsemen and two hundred soldiers, thirteen crossbowmen, and ten
musketeers and took with him Pedro de Alvarado and Cristóbal de Olid,
and went to the pueblos, a distance from Texcoco of about two leagues.
It appeared to be true that the Mexicans had sent to threaten them and
warn them that they would be destroyed for accepting our friendship, but
the point of dispute over which they uttered the worst threats concerned
some large maize plantations lying near the lake which were ready for
the harvest, whence the people of Texcoco were providing our camp. The
Mexicans wanted to take the maize, for they said that it was theirs, for it
had been the custom for those four pueblos to sow and harvest the maize
plantations on that plain for the priests of the Mexican Idols. Over this
question of the maize field many Indians had been killed. When Cortés
understood about it, he promised the people that when the time came for
them to go and gather maize, he would send a Captain and many horsemen and soldiers to protect those who went to fetch it. They were well
pleased with what Cortés had said to them, and we returned to Texcoco.
From that time forward, whenever we had need of maize in our camp, we
mustered the Indian warriors from all those towns and with our Tlaxcalan
allies and ten horsemen and a hundred soldiers, with some musketeers
and crossbowmen, we went after the maize. I say this because I went twice
for it myself and on one occasion we had a capital skirmish with some
powerful Mexican Squadrons which had come in more than a thousand
canoes, and awaited us in the maize fields, and as we had our allies with
us, although the Mexicans fought like brave men we made them take to
their canoes, but they killed one of our soldiers and wounded twelve, and
they also wounded some Tlaxcalans, but the enemy had not much to brag

about for fifteen or twenty of them were lying dead, and we carried off five of them as prisoners.

The next day we heard the news that the people of Chalco and Tlamanalco and their dependencies wished to make peace, but on account of the Mexican garrisons stationed in their towns, they had no opportunity to do so, and that these Mexicans did much damage in their country and took their women, especially if they were handsome.

We had also heard that the timber for building the launches had been cut and prepared at Tlaxcala, and as the time was passing, and none of the timber had yet been brought to Texcoco, most of the soldiers were a good deal worried about it. Then, in addition to this, the people came from the pueblo of Mixquic and from other friendly pueblos to tell Cortés that the Mexicans were coming to attack them because they had accepted our friendship. Moreover some of our friends the Tlaxcalans, who had already grabbed clothing and salt and gold and other spoil, wished to return home, but they did not dare to do so because the road was not safe.

As Cortés had told the people of Chalco that he was coming to help them so that the Mexicans should no longer come and attack them (for we had been going there and back every week to assist them) he ordered a force of soldiers to be prepared and they were three hundred soldiers, thirty horsemen, twenty crossbowmen and fifteen musketeers, and the Treasurer Julian de Alderete, Pedro de Alvarado, Andrés de Tápia, Cristóbal de Olid, and the Friar Pedro Melgarejo went also, and Cortés ordered me to go with him, and there were many Tlaxcalans and allies from Texcoco in his company. He left Gonzalo de Sandoval behind with a good company of soldiers and horsemen to guard Texcoco and the launches.

On the morning of Friday the 5th April, 1521, after hearing Mass we set out for Tlamanalco, where we were well received, and we slept there. The next day we went to Chalco for the one town is quite close to the other, and there Cortés ordered all the Caciques of the province to be called together and he made them a speech, in which he gave them to understand that we were now going to try whether we could bring to peace some of the towns in the neighbourhood of the lake, and also to view the land and position before blockading Mexico, and that we were going to place thirteen launches on the lake, and he begged them to be ready to accompany us on the next day with all their warriors. When they understood this, all with one voice promised that they would willingly do what we asked.

The next day we went to sleep at Chimaluacan, and there we met more than twenty thousand allies from Chalco, Texcoco, and Huexotzingo and from Tlaxcala and other towns, and in all the expeditions in which I have been engaged in New Spain, never have I known so many of our allied warriors to accompany us as joined us now.

As I have already said before, many of them came in hope of gathering spoil, and it is also true that they came to gorge on human flesh, if there should be any fighting, for they knew for certain that we should have to fight battles. It was the same, so to say, as when in Italy an army marches from one place to another it is followed by crows and kites and other birds of prey which live on the dead bodies that are left in the field after a bloody battle, so I believe it was for the same reason that we were followed by so many thousand Indians.

About this time we received news, that in a plain nearby, there were many companies and squadrons of Mexicans and all their allies from the country round about waiting to attack us. So Cortés held us in readiness and after hearing Mass we set out early in the morning from the pueblo of Chimaluacan, and marched among some high rocks between two hills where there were fortifications and barricades, where many Indians both men and women were safely sheltered, and from these strongholds they yelled and shouted at us, but we did not care to attack them, but kept quietly on our way, and arrived at a plain where there were some springs with very little water. On one side was a high rocky hill [probably Tlayacapan] with a fortress very difficult to subdue, as the attempt soon proved, and we saw that it was crowded with warriors, and from the summit they shouted at us and threw stones and shot darts and arrows, and wounded three of our soldiers. Then Cortés ordered us to halt there, and said: "It seems that all these Mexicans who shut themselves up in fortresses make mock of us as long as we do not attack them," and he ordered some horsemen and crossbowmen to go round to the other side of the hill and see if there was a more convenient opening whence to attack them. They returned to say that the best approach was where we then were, for there was no other place where it was possible to climb up, for it was all steep rock. Then Cortés ordered us to make an attack. The Standard-Bearer Cristóbal del Corral led the way with other ensigns and all of us followed him while Cortés and the horsemen kept guard on the plain, so that no other troops of Mexicans should fall on the baggage or on us during our attack on the stronghold. As we began to climb up the hill, the Indians who were posted above rolled down so many huge stones and rocks that it was terrifying to see them hurtling and bounding down, and it was a miracle that we were not all of us killed. One soldier named Martínez fell dead at my feet; he had a helmet on his head but he gave no cry and never spoke another word. Still we kept on, but as the great *Galgas*, as we call these big rocks in this country, came rolling and tearing and bounding down and breaking in pieces, they soon killed two more good soldiers, Gaspar Sánchez, nephew of the Treasurer of Cuba, and a man named Bravo, but still we kept on. Then another valiant soldier named Alonzo Rodriguez was killed, and two others were wounded in the head, and nearly all the rest were wounded in the legs, and still we persevered and pushed on ahead.

As I was active in those days, I kept on following the Standard-Bearer Corral, and we got beneath some hollows and cavities which there were in the hillside so as to avoid a chance rock hitting us and I clambered up from hollow to hollow to escape being killed. The Standard-Bearer Cristóbal del Corral sheltered himself behind some thick trees covered with thorns which grow in these hollows, his face was streaming with blood and his banner was broken, and he called out: "Oh Señor Bernal Diaz del Castillo, it is impossible to go on any further, keep in the shelter of the hollow and take care that none of those galgas or boulders strike you, for one can hardly hold on with one's hands and feet, much less climb any higher." Just then I saw that Pedro Barba, a captain of the crossbowmen, and two other soldiers were coming up in the same way that Corral and I had done, climbing from hollow to hollow. I called out from above: "Señor Capitan, don't come up any further, for you can't hold on with hands and feet, but will roll down again." When I said this to him he replied as though he were very valiant, or some great lord and could make no other reply: "Go ahead." I took that reply as a personal insult, and answered him: "Let us see you come to where I am," and I went up still higher. At that very moment such a lot of great stones came rolling down on us from above where they had stored them for the purpose, that Pedro Barba was wounded and one soldier killed, and they could not climb a single step higher.

Then the Standard-Bearer Corral cried out that they should pass the word to Cortés, from mouth to mouth, that we could not get any higher, and that to retreat was equally dangerous.

When Cortés heard this he understood what was happening, for there below where he stood on the level ground two or three soldiers had been killed and seven of them wounded by the great impetus of the boulders which were hurled down on them, and Cortés thought for certain that nearly all of us who had made the ascent must have been killed or badly wounded, for from where he stood, he could not see the folds in the hill. So by signs and shouts and by the shots that they fired, we up above knew that they were meant as signals for us to retreat, and in good order we descended from hollow to hollow, our bodies bruised and streaming with blood, the banners rent, and eight men dead. When Cortés saw us he gave thanks to God and they related to him what had happened between Pedro Barba and me. Pedro Barba himself and the Standard-Bearer Corral were telling him about the great strength of the hill and that it was a marvel that the boulders did not carry us away as they flew down, and the story was soon known throughout the camp.

Let us leave these empty tales and say how there were many companies of Mexicans lying in wait in places where we could neither see nor observe them, hoping to bring help and succour to those posted on the hill, for they well knew that we should not be able to force our way into the stronghold, and they had arranged while we were fighting to attack us in the rear. When Cortés knew that they were approaching, he ordered the horsemen and all of us to go and attack them, and this we did, for the ground was level in places as there were fields lying between the small hills, and we pursued the enemy until they reached another very strong hill.

We killed very few Indians during the pursuit for they took refuge in places where we could not reach them. So we returned to the stronghold which we had attempted to scale, and seeing that there was no water there, and that neither we nor the horses had had anything to drink that day, for the springs which I have spoken about as being there contained nothing but mud, because the many allies whom we had brought with us crowded into them and would not let them flow. For this reason orders were given to shift our camp, and we went down through some fields to another hill which was distant from the first about a league and a half, thinking that we should find water there, but we found very little of it. Near this hill were some native mulberry trees and there we camped, and there were some twelve or thirteen houses at the foot of the stronghold. As soon as we arrived the Indians began to shout and shoot darts and arrows and roll down boulders from above.

There were many more people in this fortress than there were in the first hill, and it was much stronger, as we afterwards found out.

Our musketeers and crossbowmen fired up at them but they were so high up and protected by so many barricades that we could not do them any harm, besides there was no possibility of climbing up and forcing our way in. Although we made two attempts, from the houses that stood there, over some steps by which we could mount up for two stages, beyond that it was worse than the first hill, so that we did not increase our reputation at this stronghold any more than at the first, and the victory lay with the Mexicans and their allies.

That night we slept in the mulberry grove and were half dead with thirst. It was arranged that on the next day all the musketeers and cross-bowmen should go to another hill which was close by the large one, and should climb up it, for there was a way up although it was not an easy one,

to see if from that hill their muskets and crossbows would carry as far as
the stronghold on the other, so that they could attack it. Cortés ordered
Francisco Verdugo and the Treasurer Juan de Aldecrete, who boasted that
they were good crossbowmen, and Pedro Barba who was a Captain, to
go as leaders, and all the rest of the soldiers to attack from the steps and
tracks above the houses which I have already spoken of, and to climb up
as best we could. So we began the ascent, but they hurled down so many
stones both great and small that many of the soldiers were wounded,
and in addition to this it was quite useless to attempt the ascent, for
even using both our hands and feet we could climb no further. While
we were making these attempts the musketeers and crossbowmen from
the other hill of which I have spoken, managed to reach the enemy with
their muskets and crossbows but they could only just do it, however they
killed some and wounded others. In this way we went on attacking them
for about half an hour when it pleased our Lord God that they agreed to
make peace. The reason why they did so was that they had not got a drop
of water, and there was a great number of people on the level ground on
the hilltop and the people from all the neighbourhood round had taken
refuge there both men, women and children and slaves. So that we down
below should understand that they wished for peace, the women on the
hill waved their shawls and clapped the palms of their hands together as a
sign that they would make bread or tortillas for us and the warriors ceased
shooting arrows and darts and hurling down stones.

When Cortés observed this he ordered that no more harm should be
done to them, and by signs he made them understand that five of their
chiefs should come down to treat for peace. When they came down with
much reverence they asked Cortés to pardon them for having protected
and defended themselves by taking refuge in that stronghold. Cortés
replied somewhat angrily that they deserved death for having begun the
war, but as they had come to make peace, they must go at once to the
other hill and summon the Caciques and chiefs who were stationed there
and bring in the dead bodies, and that if they came in peace he would
pardon what had happened, if not, that we should attack them and besiege

them until they died of thirst, for we knew well that there too they had no water, for there is very little in all that part of the country. So they went off at once to summon the Caciques as they were told to do.

Cortés sent the Standard-Bearer Corral, and two other captains namely Juan Jaramillo and Pedro de Ircio and me, who happened to be there with them, to ascend the hill and see what the stronghold was like, whether there were many Indians wounded or killed by the arrows and muskets and how many people were gathered there.

When he gave us these orders he said, "Look to it, Sirs, that you do not take from them a single grain of maize," and as I understood it he meant that we should help ourselves, and it was for that reason that he sent us and told me to go with the others. We ascended the hill by a track, and I must say that it was stronger than the first for it was sheer rock, and when we reached the top the entrance into the stronghold was no wider than the two mouths of a silo or an oven. At the very top it was level ground and there was a great breadth of meadowland all crowded with people, both warriors and many women and children, and we found twenty dead men and many wounded, and they had not a drop of water to drink. All their clothes and other property was done up in bundles and there were many bales of cloaks which were the tribute they paid to Guatemoc, and when I saw so many loads of cloths and knew that it was intended for tribute I began to load four Tlaxcalans, my free servants whom I had brought with me, and I also put four other bales on the backs of four other Indians who were guarding the tribute, one bale on each man's back. When Pedro de Ircio saw this he said that the bales should not be taken and I contended that they should, but as he was Captain, I did as he ordered, for he threatened to tell Cortés about it. Pedro de Ircio said to me that I had heard what Cortés had said, that we should not take a single grain of maize, and I replied that was true, and that it was on account of those very words I wished to carry off these robes. However, he would not let me carry off anything at all, and we went down to tell Cortés what we had seen. Then Pedro de Ircio said to Cortés: "I took nothing from them although Bernal Diaz del Castillo had already laden eight Indians with cloth and would have brought them away loaded had I not stopped him." Then Cortés replied, half angrily: "Why did he not bring them, you ought to have stayed there with the cloth and the Indians," and he added: "See how they understand me, I send them to help themselves, and from Bernal Diaz, who did understand me, they took away the spoil which he was taking from those dogs who will sit there laughing at us in the company of those whom we have killed and wounded."

When Pedro de Ircio heard this he wished to go up to the stronghold again, but he was told that there was no reason for his going, and that on no account should he return there.

Let us leave this talk and say that the people from the other hill came in, and, after much discussion about their being pardoned for their past deeds, all gave their fealty to His Majesty. As there was no water in that place we went at once to a fine pueblo already mentioned by me in the last chapter called Oaxtepec, where is the garden which I have said is the best that I have ever seen in all my life, and so said the Treasurer Alderete and the monk Fray Pedro Melgarejo and our Cortés. When they saw it and walked about in it they admired it greatly and said that they had never seen a better garden in Spain. I must add that we all found quarters in the garden that night. The Caciques of the town came to speak and offer their services to Cortés, for Gonzalo de Sandoval had already brought them to peace when he entered the town. That night we slept there and the next morning very early we left for Yautepec and we met some squadrons of Mexicans who had come out from that town and the horsemen pursued them more than a league and a half until they took refuge in another large pueblo called Tepostlan where the inhabitants were so completely off their guard that we fell upon them before their spies whom they had sent to watch us could reach them.

The next day very early in the morning we began our march again and about eight o'clock we arrived at Xochimilco. I cannot estimate the great number of the warriors who were waiting for us, some on the land and others in a passage by a broken bridge, and the great number of breastworks and barricades which had been thrown up, and the lances which they carried made from the swords captured from us during the great slaughter on the causeways at Mexico. I say that all the mainland was covered with warriors, and at the passage of that bridge we were fighting them for more than half an hour and could not get through, neither muskets nor crossbows nor the many great charges that we made were of any avail, and the worst of all was that many other squadrons of them were already coming to attack us on our flanks. When we saw that, we dashed through the water and bridge, some half swimming and others jumping, and here some of our soldiers, much against their will, had perforce to drink so much of the water beneath the bridge that their bellies were swollen up from it.

To go back to the battle, at the passage of the bridge many of our soldiers were wounded, but we soon brought the enemy to the sword's point along some streets where there was solid ground ahead of us. Cortés and the horsemen turned in another direction on the mainland where they came on more than ten thousand Indians, all Mexicans, who had come as reinforcements to help the people in the city, and they fought in such a way with our troops that, with their lances in rest, they awaited the attack of the horsemen and wounded four of them. Cortés was in the middle of the press and the horse he was riding, which was a very good one, a dark chestnut called "el Romo" [the Flat-Nosed] either because he was too fat or was tired (for he was a pampered horse) broke down, and the Mexican warriors who were around in great numbers laid hold of Cortés and dragged him from the horse; others say that by sheer strength they threw the horse down. Whichever way it may have happened, Cortés and the horse fell to the ground and at that very moment many more Mexican warriors pressed up to see if they could carry him off alive. When some Tlaxcalans and also a very valiant soldier named Cristóbal de Olea saw what had happened, they at once came up and with good cuts and thrusts they cleared a space so that Cortés could mount again although he was badly wounded in the head. Olea was also very badly wounded with three sword cuts. By that time all of us soldiers who were anywhere near came to their help. At that time, as every street in the City was crowded with squadrons of warriors and as we were obliged to follow their banners, we were not able all to keep together, but some of us to attack in some places and some of us in others as Cortés commanded us. However we all knew from the shouts and cries, yells and whistles that we heard, that where Cortés and the horsemen were engaged the fight was hottest, and, without further explanation, although there were swarms of warriors round us, we went at great risk to ourselves to join Cortés. Fifteen horsemen had already joined him and were fighting near some canals where the enemy had thrown up breastworks and barricades. When we came up we put the Mexicans to flight, but not all of them turned their backs on us, and because the soldier Olea who had helped our Cortés was very badly wounded with three sword cuts and was bleeding, and because the streets of the city were crowded with warriors, we advised Cortés to turn back to some barricades, so that he and Olea and the horse might be attended to.

So we turned back, but not without anxiety on account of the stones, arrows and javelins which they fired at us from the barricades, for the Mexicans thought that we were turning to retreat and they followed us with great fury. At this moment Andrés de Tápia and Cristóbal de Olid came up, and all the rest of the horsemen who had gone off with them in other directions. Blood was streaming down Olid's face, and from his horse and from all the rest of them, for everyone was wounded; and they said that they had been fighting against such a host of Mexicans in the open fields that they could make no headway against them, for when we had passed the bridge which I have mentioned it seems that Cortés had divided the horsemen so that half went in one direction and half in the other, one half following one set of squadrons and the other half another set of squadrons.

While we were treating the wounds by searing them with oil, there was a great noise of yells, trumpets, shells and drums from some of the streets on the mainland, and along them came a host of Mexicans into the court where we were tending the wounded, and they let fly such a number of javelins and stones that they at once wounded many of our soldiers.

However, the enemy did not come very well out of that incursion for we charged on them and with good cuts and thrusts we left most of them stretched out on the ground.

The horsemen too were not slow in riding out to the attack and killed many of them, but two of the horses were wounded. We drove them out of that court, and when Cortés saw that there were no more of the enemy we went to rest in another great court where stood the great oratories of the city.

Many of our soldiers ascended the highest temple where the Idols were kept, and from thence looked over the Great City of Mexico and the lakes, for one had a commanding view of it all, and they could see approaching more than two thousand canoes full of warriors who were coming straight towards us from Mexico. Later on we learnt that Guatemoc had sent them to attack us that night or next day, and at the same time he sent another ten thousand warriors by land so that by attacking us both on one side and the other, not one of us should go out of that city alive. He had also got ready another ten thousand men as a reinforcement when the attack was made. All this we found out on the following day from five Mexican captains who were captured during the battle.

However, our Lord ordained that it should be otherwise, for when that great fleet of canoes was observed and it was known that they were coming to attack us, we agreed to keep a very good watch throughout the camp, especially at the landing places and canals where they had to disembark. The horsemen were waiting very much on the alert all night through, with the horses saddled and bridled on the causeway and on the mainland, and Cortés and all his captains were keeping watch and going the rounds all night long. I and two other soldiers were posted as sentinels on some masonry walls, and we had got together many stones where we were posted, and the soldiers of our company were provided with crossbows and muskets and long lances, so that if the enemy should reach the landing place on the canals we could resist them and make them turn back.

While my companions and I were watching we heard a sound of many canoes being paddled, although they approached with muffled paddles, to disembark at the landing place where we were posted, and with a good shower of stones and with the lances we opposed them so that they did not dare to disembark. We sent one of our companions to give warning to Cortés, and while this was happening there again approached many more canoes laden with warriors, and they began to shoot darts and stones and arrows at us, and as we again opposed them, two of our soldiers were wounded in the head but as it was nighttime and very dark the canoes went to join the captains of the whole fleet of canoes and they all went off together to disembark at another landing place where the canals were deeper. Then as they were not used to fighting during the night, they all went to join the squadrons that Guatemoc had sent by land which already numbered more than fifteen thousand Indians.

It appears that in this city there were many rich men who had very large houses full of mantles and cloth and Indian cotton shirts, and they possessed gold and feather work and much other property. It so happened that while we were occupied as I have described, the Tlaxcalans and some of our soldiers chanced to find out in what part of the town these houses were situated, and some of the Xochimilco prisoners went with them to point them out. These houses stood in the freshwater lake and one could reach them by a causeway but there were two or three small bridges in the causeway where it crossed some deep canals, and as our soldiers went to the houses and found them full of cloth and no one was guarding them, they loaded themselves and many of the Tlaxcalans with the cloth and the gold ornaments and came with it to the camp. Some of the other soldiers when they saw this, also set out for the houses, but while they were inside taking the cloth out of some huge wooden boxes, at that very moment a great flotilla of canoes arrived full of Indians from Mexico who fell upon them and wounded many of the soldiers, and carried off four of them alive and took them to Mexico, but the rest escaped.

When these four soldiers were taken to Guatemoc he learnt how few of us we were who had come with Cortés and that many of us were wounded, and all that he wished to know about our journey. When he had thoroughly informed himself about all this, he ordered the arms, feet and heads of our unfortunate companions to be cut off and sent them to the towns of our allies, to those that had already made peace with us, and he sent to tell them that he did not think there would be one of us left alive to return to Texcoco. The hearts and blood were offered to the Idols.

Let us leave this and say how he at once sent many fleets of canoes full of warriors, and other companies by land, and told them to see to it that we did not leave Xochimilco alive. As I am tired of writing about the many battles and encounters which we fought against the Mexicans in those days, and yet cannot omit to mention them, I will say that as soon as dawn broke there came such a host of Mexicans by the waterways and others by the causeways and by the mainland, that we could hardly break them up. So we then went out from the city to a great Plaza which stood at a little distance from the town, where they were used to hold their markets, and halted there with all our baggage ready for the march. Cortés then began to make us a speech about the danger in which we were placed, for we knew for certain that in the bad passes on the roads, at the creeks and on the canals the whole power of Mexico and its allies would be lying in wait for us, and he told us that it would be a good thing, and it was his command, that we should march unencumbered and should leave the baggage and the cloths so that it should not impede us when it came to fighting. When we heard this with one voice we answered that, please God we were men enough to defend our property and persons and his also, and that it would show great cowardice to do such a thing. When Cortés knew our wishes and heard our reply he said that he prayed God to help us, and then, knowing the strength and power of the enemy, we arranged the order of march, the baggage and the wounded in the middle, the horsemen divided so that half of them marched ahead and half as a rearguard. The crossbowmen and our native allies we also placed near the middle as a security, for the Mexicans were accustomed to attack the baggage. Of the musketeers we did not take much count for they had no powder left.

In this order we began our march, and when the squadrons of Mexicans whom Guatemoc had sent out that day saw us retreating from

Xochimilco they thought that it was from fear and that we did not dare to meet them, which was true, and so great a host of them started off at once and came directly against us that they wounded eight soldiers of whom two died within eight days, and they thought to defeat us and break into the baggage, but as we marched in the order I have described they were not able to do it. However, all along the road until we reached a large town called Coyoacan, about two leagues distant from Xochimilco, the warriors never ceased to make sudden attacks on us from positions where we could not well get at them, but whence they could assail us with javelins and stones and arrows, and then take refuge in the neighbouring creeks and ditches.

When we arrived at Coyoacan about ten o'clock in the morning we found it deserted.

As this large town stands on level ground, we determined to rest there that day and the next so as to attend to the wounded and to make arrows, for we understood very well that we should have to fight more battles before returning to our camp at Texcoco.

Next day but one early in the morning we began our march, following the road to Tacuba, which stands about two leagues from our starting place. At one place on the road many squadrons of warriors divided into three parties came out to attack us, but we resisted all three attacks, and the horsemen followed the enemy over the level ground until they took refuge in the creeks and canals.

As we kept on our way Cortés left us with ten horsemen and four pages, intending to prepare an ambush for the Mexicans who came out from the creeks and made attacks on us. The Mexicans pretended that they were running away and Cortés with the horsemen and servants followed them. Then Cortés saw that there was a large force of the enemy placed in ambush who fell upon him and his horsemen and wounded some horses, and if they had not retreated at once they would all have been killed or taken prisoner. As it was, the Mexicans carried off two alive out of the four soldiers who were pages to Cortés, and they carried them to Guatemoc who had them sacrificed.

We arrived at Tacuba with our banners flying and with all the army and the baggage. The rest of the horsemen had come in with Pedro de Alvarado and Cristóbal de Olid, but Cortés and the ten horsemen who were with him did not appear, and we had an uncomfortable suspicion that some disaster might have overtaken him. Then Pedro de Alvarado and Cristóbal de Olid and other horsemen went in search of him, in the direction of the creeks where we had seen him turn off. At that moment the other two pages who had gone with Cortés and who had escaped with their lives came into camp, and they told us all that I have already related, and said that they had escaped because they were fleet of foot, and that Cortés and the others were following slowly because their horses were wounded. While we were talking Cortés appeared, at which we all rejoiced, although he had arrived very sad and almost tearful.

When we reached Tacuba it rained heavily and we took shelter for nearly two hours in some large courts, and Cortés with some other captains and many of us soldiers ascended the lofty temple of that town whence one had a good view of the city of Mexico which is quite near, and of the lake and the other cities which are built in the water.

We continued our march, and passed by Atzcapotzalco, which we found to be deserted, and went on to Tenayuca. This town was also deserted. From thence we went to Guatitlan, and throughout the day it never ceased raining with heavy rainstorms, and as we marched with our arms shouldered and never took off our harness by day or night, what with the weight and the soaking we got, we were quite broken down. We arrived at that large town when night was falling but it also was deserted. It never ceased raining all night long and the mud was very deep. The natives of the place and some squadrons of Mexicans yelled at us all night from the canals and other places where we could do them no harm. As it was raining and very dark no sentinels could be posted or rounds made, and no order was kept, nor could we find those who were posted, and this I can myself assert for they stationed me as a watchman for the first watch, and neither officer nor patrol visited me, and so it was throughout the camp.

Let us leave this carelessness and say that the next day we continued our march to another large pueblo [Citlaltepec] of which I do not remember the name; the mud was very deep in it, and we found it deserted. The following day we passed by other deserted pueblos and the day after we reached a pueblo called Aculman, subject to Texcoco. When they knew in Texcoco that we were coming, they came out to receive Cortés, and there were many Spaniards who had lately come from Spain. Captain Gonzalo de Sandoval with many soldiers also came out to receive us and with him came the Lord of Texcoco.

The Siege Begins from Texcoco

After Antonio de Villafaña had been punished, and those who had joined with him in the conspiracy had quieted down, Cortés examined the sloops which were already built and had their rigging, sails and oars in place, and spare oars for each sloop. Moreover the canal by which the sloops were to pass out to the lake was already broad and deep. So Cortés sent to advise all the friendly pueblos near Texcoco to make eight thousand arrowheads of copper in each pueblo, and he also ordered them to make and trim for him in each pueblo eight thousand arrows of a very good kind of wood, and for these they also carried away a sample, and messengers and letters were then sent to our friend Xicotenga the elder, and to his son Xicotenga the younger and to his brothers, and to Chichimecatecle, informing them that when the day of Corpus Christi was passed, we were going to leave this city to proceed against Mexico and to invest it. He told them to send him twenty thousand warriors from their own people at Tlaxcala, and from those of Huexotzingo and Cholula, for all were now friends and brothers in arms, and they all knew the time of meeting and the plan, as he had informed them by their own Indians who were continually leaving our camp laden with the spoils from the expeditions we had made.

He also gave warning to the people of Chalco and Tlamanalco and their vassals, to be prepared when we should send to summon them, and he gave them to understand that we were about to invest Mexico, and the time when we should set out, and he said the same to Don Fernando the Lord of Texcoco and to his chieftains and to all his vassals, and to all the other towns friendly to us. One and all replied that they would do exactly what Cortés sent to order them, and that they would come.

After the orders were given, Cortés decided with our Captains and soldiers that on the second day of the feast of Espíritu Santo (this was the year one thousand five hundred and twenty-one) a review should be held. This review was held in the great Courts of Texcoco and there were present eighty-four horsemen, six-hundred-and-fifty soldiers with swords and shields and many with lances, and one-hundred-and-ninety-four crossbowmen and musketeers. From these there were chosen to man the thirteen launches those that I will now mention—For each launch, twelve crossbowmen and musketeers; in addition to them there were also set apart another twelve men, six on each side as rowers for each launch. And besides these there was a Captain for each launch and an artilleryman.

Cortés also divided among them all the boat guns and falconets we possessed and the powder he thought they would need. When this was done, he ordered the following rules, which we all had to observe, to be proclaimed.

First, no man should dare to blaspheme Our Lord Jesus Christ, nor Our Lady, His Blessed Mother, nor the Sainted Apostles, nor any other saints under heavy penalty.

Second, no soldier should ill treat our allies, since they went to help us, or should take anything away from them even if they should be spoils gained by war, whether Indian men or women or gold or silver or Chalchihuites.

Another was, no soldier should dare to depart either by day or night from our camp to go to any pueblo of our allies, or anywhere else, either to fetch food or for any other matter, under heavy penalties.

Another, all the soldiers should wear very good armour, well quilted, a neck guard, head piece, leggings and shield, for we knew about the great number of javelins and stones and arrows and lances, and for all of them it was necessary to wear the armour which the proclamation mentioned.

Another, no one should gamble for a horse or arms on any account, under heavy penalty.

Another, no soldier, horseman, crossbowman, or musketeer should go to sleep unless he were fully armed and shod with his sandals, unless it were under the stress of wounds or because he was suffering from illness, so that we might be fully prepared whatsoever time the Mexicans might come to attack us.

In addition to these, the laws were proclaimed which were ordered to be observed in soldiering; that is, that anyone who sleeps when on guard or leaves his post should be punished with death, and it was proclaimed that no soldier should go from one camp to another without leave from his Captain under pain of death.

Another, that any soldier deserting his Captain in war or battle, should suffer death.

After the review had taken place, Cortés saw that not enough men who knew how to row could be found for the launches, although those who had been brought in the ships which we destroyed when we came with Cortés were thoroughly experienced and the sailors from the ships of Narvaez and those from Jamaica also knew how to row, and all of them were placed on the list and had been warned. Yet counting all of them, there was not a full supply, as many of the men refused to row. So Cortés made enquiries to find out who were seamen, or had been seen to go out fishing, and if they came from Palos or Triana or from any other port or place where there were sailors, and he ordered them under pain of heavy penalties to go on board the launches. However highborn they might say they were, he made them go and row, and in this way he got together one hundred and fifty men as rowers, and they were much freer from hardships than we were who were stationed on the causeways fighting, and they became rich from plunder as I will relate further on.

After Cortés had decided who should go in the launches, he divided the crossbowmen and musketeers and the powder, cannon and arrows and everything else that was necessary among them and ordered them to place in each launch the royal banners and other banners with the name that was given to each launch, besides other things which were needed, and he named as Captains of the launches those whom I will now mention here:—Garcí Holguin, Pedro Barba, Juan de Linpias, Carvajal the deaf, Juan Jaramillo, Jerónimo Ruiz de la Mota, his companion Caravajal, and one Portillo who had just come from Castile, a good soldier who had a handsome wife and a Zamora who was a ship's mate, a Colmenero who was a seaman and a good soldier, a Lema, a Jínes Nórtes, one Briones a native of Salamanca, another Captain whose name I do not remember, and Miguel Diaz de Auz.

After he had named them, he gave instructions to each Captain what he was to do, and to what part of the causeways he was to go, and with which one of the Captains who were on land he was to cooperate.

The next day [Thursday, 23 May] the two Divisions continued their March together and we went to sleep at a large town [Zitlaltepec] which was deserted, for we were already in Mexican territory. The day following we went to sleep at Cuautitlan, and it also was without inhabitants, and the next day we passed through Tenayuca and Atzcapotzalco, which were also deserted, and at the hour of vespers we arrived at Tacuba and at once took up our quarters in some large houses and rooms, for this town also was deserted, and there, too, all our friends the Tlaxcalans found quarters, and that very afternoon we went through the farms belonging to those towns and brought in food to eat. We slept there that night after stationing good watchmen, sentinels and scouts, for as I have already said, Mexico was close by Tacuba, and when night fell we heard great shouts which the Mexicans raised at us from the lake, crying out much abuse, that we were not men enough to come out and fight them. They had many of their canoes full of warriors and the causeways also were crowded with fighting men, and these words were said with the idea of provoking us to come out that night and fight; but as we had gained experience from the affair of the causeways and bridges we would not go out until the next day, which was Sunday [26 May].

After hearing Mass, which was said by Father Juan Díaz, and commending ourselves to God, we agreed that with the two Divisions together, we should go out and cut off the water of Chapultepec by which the city was supplied which was about half a league distant from Tacuba.

As we were marching to break the pipes, we came on many warriors who were waiting for us on the road, for they fully understood that would be the first thing by which we could do them damage, and so when they met us near some bad ground, they began to shoot arrows at us and hurl javelins and stones from slings, and they wounded three of our soldiers, but we quickly made them turn their backs and our friends the Tlaxcalans followed them so that they killed twenty and we captured eighteen of them.

As soon as these squadrons had been put to flight we broke the conduits through which the water flowed to the city, and from that time onwards it never flowed into Mexico so long as the war lasted. When we had accomplished this, our Captains agreed that we should go at once to reconnoitre and advance along the causeway from Tacuba, and do what was possible towards gaining possession of a bridge. When we had reached the causeway, there were so many canoes on the lake full of warriors, and the causeways also were so crowded with them, that we were astounded at it; and they shot so many arrows and javelins and stones from slings that at the first encounter they wounded over thirty soldiers. Still we went on marching along the causeway towards the bridge, and from what I understand they gave way for us to reach it, so as to get us on the other side of the bridge. When they had got us there, I declare that such a host of warriors charged down on us, that we could not hold out against them; for on the causeway, which was eight paces wide, what could we do against such a great force as was stationed on one side and the other of the causeway, and struck at us as at a mark, for although our musketeers and crossbowmen never ceased loading and firing at the canoes, they did them but very little damage for they brought the canoes very well protected with bulwarks of wood. Then when we attacked the squadrons that fought on the causeway itself, they promptly threw themselves into the water, and there were so many of them that we could not prevail against them. Those on horseback did not make any progress whatever, for the Indians wounded their horses from one side and from the other, and as soon as they charged after the squadrons the Indians threw themselves in the water. The enemy had raised breastworks where other warriors were stationed in waiting, with long lances which they had made like scythes from the weapons which had been captured from us when they drove us fleeing out of Mexico.

In this manner we stood fighting with them about an hour, and so many stones were showered on us that we could not bear up against them, and we even saw that there was approaching us in another direction a great fleet of canoes to cut off our passage, so as to turn our flanks, and knowing this, and because we saw that our friends the Tlaxcalans whom we had brought with us were greatly obstructing the causeway, and, if they went off of it, it was clear enough that they could not fight in the water, our Captains and all of us soldiers agreed to retreat in good order and not to go further ahead.

When the Mexicans saw us retreating and the Tlaxcalans escaping beyond the causeway what shouts and howls and whistles they gave us, and how they came on to join us foot to foot. I declare that I do not know how to describe it, for all the causeway was heaped up with javelins, arrows, and stones that had been hurled at us, and many more of them must have fallen in the water. When we found ourselves on dry land we gave thanks to God for having freed us from that battle, for by that time eight of our soldiers had fallen dead, and more than fifty were wounded. Through all this, they yelled out at us and shouted abuse from the canoes, and our friends the Tlaxcalans told them to come on land and even if they were double the number they would fight them. These were the first things that we did to cut off the water and reconnoitre the lake, although we gained no honour by them. That night we stayed in our camp while the wounded were attended to, and one horse died, and we posted a good force of sentinels and scouts.

The next morning Captain Cristóbal de Olid said that he wished to go to his station at Coyoacan, a league and a half away, and notwithstanding that Pedro de Alvarado and other gentlemen begged him not to separate the two divisions, but to keep them together, he would not do so; for as Cristóbal de Olid was very courageous, and in the reconnaissance which we made of the lake, the day before, we had not done well, he said that it was Pedro de Alvarado's fault that we had advanced so rashly, so that he would not stay and went off to Coyoacan where Cortés had sent him. We remained in our camp, for it was not right to separate one division from the other at that time, and if the Mexicans had known how few soldiers we were during the four or five days that we were there apart before the launches could come, and had fallen on us and on the division of Cristóbal de Olid separately, we should have incurred great hardship and they would have done us great damage. So we stayed in Tacuba and Cristóbal de Olid in his camp, without daring to reconnoitre any further nor to advance along the causeways, and every day we had skirmishes with many squadrons of Mexicans who came on land to fight with us, and even challenged us so as to place us in situations where they could master us and we could do them no damage.

I will leave them there and I will tell how Gonzalo de Sandoval set out from Texcoco four days after the feast of Corpus Christi [Friday, 31 May] and came to Iztapalapa; almost all the march was among friends, subjects of Texcoco, and when he reached the town of Iztapalapa he at once began to make war and to burn many of the houses that stood on dry land, for all the rest of the houses stood in the lake. However, not many hours passed before great squadrons of Mexicans came promptly to the aid of that city and Sandoval had a good battle with them and great encounters when they fought on land; and when they had taken refuge in their canoes they shot many javelins, arrows and stones at him and wounded his soldiers. While they were thus fighting they saw that on a small hill [Cerro de la Estrella] that was close to Iztapalapa on dry land, great smoke signals were being made, and they were answered by other smoke signals from other towns standing in the lake, and it was a sign to assemble all the canoes from Mexico and all the towns around the lake, for they saw that Cortés had already set out from Texcoco with the thirteen launches.

I will now relate what we did in our camp at Tacuba, for, as we knew that Cortés was going about the lake, we advanced along our causeway with great caution, and not like the first time, and we reached the first bridge, the crossbowmen and musketeers acting in concert some firing while others loaded. Pedro de Alvarado ordered the horsemen not to advance with us but to remain on dry land to guard our rear, fearing lest the pueblos I have mentioned through which we had passed, should attack us on the causeway. In this way we stood sometimes attacking, at others on the defensive so as to prevent the Mexicans reaching land from the causeway, for every day we had encounters and in them they killed three soldiers, and we were also engaged in filling up the bad places.

When we saw ourselves reinforced with the four launches sent by Cortés, Pedro de Alvarado ordered two of them to go on one side of the causeway and two on the other side, and we began to fight very successfully, for the launches vanquished the canoes which were wont to attack us from the water, and so we had an opportunity to capture several bridges and barricades, and while we were fighting, so numerous were the stones from the slings and the javelins and arrows that they shot at us that although all the soldiers were well protected by armour they were injured and wounded, and not until night parted us did we cease contending and fighting.

From time to time the Mexicans changed about and relieved their squadrons as we could tell by the devices and distinguishing marks on their armour. Whenever we left a bridge or barricade unguarded after having captured it with much labour, the enemy would retake and deepen it that same night, and construct stronger defences and even make hidden pits in the waters, so that the next day when we were fighting, and it was time for us to retire, we should get entangled among the defences. To prevent the launches from coming to our assistance, they had fixed many stakes hidden in the water so that they should get impaled on them.

When we drew off in the night we treated our wounds by searing them with oil, and a soldier named Juan Catalan blessed them for us and made charms, and truly we found that our Lord Jesus Christ was pleased to give us strength in addition to the many mercies he vouchsafed us every day, for the wounds healed rapidly.

Wounded and tied up in rags as we were we had to fight from morning until night, for if the wounded had remained in camp without coming out to fight, there would not have been twenty men in each company well enough to go out.

Then I wish to speak of our captains and ensigns and our standard-bearers, who were covered with wounds and their banners ragged, and I declare that we had need of a fresh standard-bearer every day for we all came out in such a condition that they were not able to advance fighting and carry the banners a second time.

Then with all this did we perchance have enough to eat? I do not speak of want of maize cakes, for we had enough of them, but of some refreshing food for the wounded. The cursed stuff that kept life in us was some herbs that the Indians eat, and the cherries of the country while they lasted, and afterwards tunas [fruit of the nopal cactus, prickly pears], which came into season at that time.

Tlatelolco and the towns on the Lake had been warned by Guatemoc that on seeing a signal on the great Cue of Tlatelolco they should hasten to assist some in canoes and others by land; and the Mexican captains had been fully prepared and advised how and when and to what points they were to bring assistance.

When we saw that however many water openings we captured by day the Mexicans returned and closed them up again, we agreed that we should all go and station ourselves on the causeway [about Thursday, 20 June; Alvarado must have turned off from the Tacuba Causeway to the left on entering the outskirts of the city and followed a causeway leading directly to Tlatelolco, making his camp about halfway between the Tacuba Causeway and the great Teocalli of Tlatelolco] in a small plaza where there were some Idol towers which we had already taken, and where there was space to erect our "ranchos," although they were very poor ones and when it rained we all got wet, and they were fit for nothing but to cover us from the dew.

We left the Indian women who made bread for us in Tacuba, and all the horsemen and our friends the Tlaxcalans were left to guard them, and to watch and guard the passes so that the enemy should not come from the neighbouring pueblos and attack our rearguard on the causeway while we were fighting.

So when once we had set up our ranchos where I have stated, thenceforward we endeavoured quickly to destroy the houses and blocks of buildings and to fill up the water openings that we captured. We levelled the houses to the ground, for if we set fire to them they took too long to burn, and one house would not catch fire from another, for each house stood in the water, and one could not pass from one to the other without crossing bridges or going in canoes. If we wanted to cross the water by swimming they did us much damage from the azoteas, so that we were more secure when the houses were demolished. As soon as we had captured some barrier or bridge or bad pass where they offered much resistance, we endeavoured to guard it by day and by night. This was the way in which all our companies kept guard together during the night. The first company, which numbered more than forty soldiers, kept watch from nightfall until midnight, and from midnight until two hours before dawn another company, also of forty men, kept watch, and the first company did not leave their post but we slept there on the ground; this second watch is called the *modorra* [the drowsy time, before dawn] and soon another forty soldiers came and kept the *alba* [dawn] watch, which is the two hours until daylight, but those who watched the modorra could not leave, but had to stay there, so that when dawn came there were over one hundred and twenty soldiers all on watch together. Moreover on some nights, when we judged that there was special danger we kept watch together, from nightfall until dawn, awaiting a great sally of the Mexicans in fear lest they should break through.

On several nights great squadrons came to attack us and break through at midnight, and others during the modorra and others during the dawn watch, and they came sometimes without commotion and at others with loud yells and whistles, and when they arrived where we were keeping night watch, what javelins and stones and arrows they let fly, and there were many others with lances, and although they wounded some of us, yet we resisted them, and sent back many of them wounded. Then, notwithstanding all the precautions we took, they would turn on us and open some bridge or causeway which we had captured, and we could not defend it from them in the night so as to prevent them doing it, and the next day it was our turn again to capture it and stop it up, and then they would come again to open it and strengthen it with walls, until the

Mexicans changed their method of fighting which I will tell about in its proper time.

The Mexicans still brought in much food and water from the nine towns built on the lake, so to prevent these supplies being brought to them, it was arranged between all the three camps that two launches should cruise in the lake by night and should capture all the canoes they were able, and destroy or bring them to our camps. But even with all this, many laden canoes did not fail to get in, and as the Mexicans went about in their canoes carrying supplies, yet there was never a day when the launches did not bring in a prize of canoes and many Indians hanging from the yards.

The Mexicans then armed thirty piraguas, which are very large canoes, with specially good rowers and warriors, and by night they posted all thirty amongst some reed beds in a place where the launches could not see them; then they sent out before nightfall, with good rowers, two or three canoes covered over with branches as though they were carrying provisions or bringing in water. In the track which, in the opinion of the Mexicans, the launches would follow them when they were fighting with them, they had driven numerous strong timbers made pointed like stakes so that they should get impaled on them. Then as the canoes were going over the lake showing signs of being afraid and drew near to the reed beds, two of our launches set out after them, and the two canoes made as though they were retreating to the land, to the place where the thirty piraguas were posted in ambush, and the launches followed them and as soon as they reached the ambush all the piraguas together sallied out and made for the launches and quickly wounded all the soldiers, rowers and captains, and the launches could go neither in one direction or another on account of the stakes that had been fixed. In this way the Mexicans killed a captain named de Portilla, an excellent soldier who had been in Italy, and they wounded Pedro Barba who was another very good captain, and they captured his launch, and within three days he died of his wounds. These two launches belonged to the camp of Cortés, and he was greatly distressed about it.

Let us leave this and say that when the Mexicans saw that we were levelling all the houses to the ground and were filling up the bridges and openings they decided on another way of fighting, and that was, to open a bridge and a very wide and deep channel which we had to pass wading through the water, and it was sometimes out of our depth, and they had dug many pits which we could not see under the water and had made walls and barricades both on the one side and the other of the opening, and had driven in many pointed stakes of heavy timber in places where our launches would run onto them if they should come to our assistance when we were fighting to capture this fort, for they well knew that the first thing we must do was to destroy the barricade and pass through that open space of water so as to reach the City. At the same time they had prepared in hidden places many canoes well manned with warriors and good rowers. One Sunday morning [23 June] great squadrons of warriors began to approach from three directions and attacked us in such a way that it was all we could do to hold our own and prevent them from defeating us.

At that time Pedro de Alvarado had ordered half the horsemen who used to stay in Tacuba to sleep on the causeway, for there was not so much risk as at the beginning, as there were no longer any azoteas, for nearly all the houses had been demolished. To go back to my story, three squadrons of the enemy came on very fearlessly, the one from the direction of the great open space of water, the other by way of some houses that we had pulled down, and the other squadron had taken us in the rear from the direction of Tacuba, and we were surrounded. The horsemen with our Tlaxcalan friends broke through the squadron that had taken us in the rear and we all of us fought very valiantly with the other two squadrons until we forced them to retreat. However, that seeming flight that they made was a pretence, but we captured the first barricade where they made a stand, and we, thinking that we were victorious, crossed that water at a run, for where we passed there were no pits and we followed up our advance among some great houses and temple towers. The enemy acted as though they were still retreating, but they did not cease to shoot javelins and stones from slings and many arrows and when we were least expecting it a great multitude of warriors who were hidden in a place we were not able to see, and many others from the azoteas and houses joined the combat, and those who at first acted as though they were retreating, turned round on us all at once and dealt us such treatment that we could not withstand them. We then decided to retreat with great caution, but at the water opening which we had captured, that is to say at the place where we had crossed the first time, where there were no pits, they had stationed such a fleet of canoes that we were not able to cross at that ford, and they forced us to go across in another direction, where the water was very deep, and they had dug many pits. As such a multitude of warriors were coming against us, and we were in retreat, we crossed the water by swimming and wading, and nearly all the soldiers fell in the pits; then the canoes came down upon us and there the Mexicans carried off five of our companions, and took them alive to Guatemoc, and they wounded nearly all of us. Moreover, the launches which were guarding us could not come to our assistance because they were impaled on the stakes which had been fixed there, and from the canoes and azoteas the Mexicans attacked them so fiercely with javelins and arrows that they killed three soldiers and rowers and wounded many of us. To go back to the pits and the opening, I declare it was a wonder that we were not all killed in them. Concerning myself, I may say that many Indians had already laid hold of me, but I managed to get my arm free, and our Lord Jesus Christ gave me strength so that by some good sword thrusts that I gave them I saved myself, but I was badly wounded in one arm, and when I found myself out of that water in safety, I became insensible and without power to stand on my feet and altogether breathless, and this was caused by the great strain that I exerted in getting away from that rabble and from the quantity of blood I had lost. I declare that when they had me in their clutches, that in my thoughts I was commending myself to our Lord God and to our Lady His Blessed Mother and He gave me the strength I have spoken of by which I saved myself; thank God for the mercy that He vouchsafed me.

There is another thing I wish to mention, that Pedro de Alvarado and the horsemen, when they had thoroughly routed the squadrons that came on our rear from Tacuba, did not any of them pass that water or the barricades, with the exception of one horseman who had come only a short time before from Spain, and there they killed him, both him and his horse. The horsemen were already advancing to our assistance when they saw us coming back in retreat, and if they had crossed there, and should have then had to retreat, there would not have been one of them, nor of the horses, nor of us left alive. Flushed with the victory they had gained, the Mexicans continued during that whole day, which as I have said was a Sunday, to send so vast a host of warriors against our camp, that we could not prevail against them, and they expected for certain to rout us, but we held our own against them by the help of some bronze cannon and hard fighting, and by all the companies together keeping guard every night.

Indian Allies and Spanish Disasters

Let us leave this and say when Cortés heard of it he was very angry. Then when we saw that it was our fault that great disaster had happened, we began then and there to fill in that opening, and although it meant great labour and many wounds which the enemy inflicted while we were at work, and the death of six soldiers, in four days we had it filled in [by Friday, 28 June], and at night we kept watch on the place itself, all three companies in the order I have already mentioned.

Let me now say that the towns situated in the lake when they saw how day by day we were victorious both on water and on land, and that the people of Chalco, Tlaxcala and other pueblos had made friends with us, decided to sue Cortés for peace and with great humility they asked pardon if in any way they had offended us, and said that they had been under orders and could not do otherwise. [From Cortés's account the submission of these towns appears to have taken place about 18 June.] The towns that came in were Iztapalapa, Churubusco, Culuacan and Mixquic and all those of the freshwater lake, and Cortés told them that we should not move the camp until the Mexicans sued for peace or he had destroyed them by war. He ordered them to aid us with all the canoes that they possessed to fight against Mexico, and to come and build ranchos for Cortés and to bring him food, and they replied that they would do so, and they built the ranchos but brought very little food. However, our ranchos where we were stationed were never rebuilt so we remained in the rain, for those who have been in this country know that through the months of June, July and August it rains every day in these parts.

We made attacks on the Mexicans every day and succeeded in capturing many idol towers, houses, canals and other openings and bridges which they had constructed from house to house, and we filled them all up with adobes and the timbers from the houses that we pulled down and destroyed and we kept guard over them, but notwithstanding all this trouble that we took, the enemy came back and deepened them and widened the openings and erected more barricades. And because our three companies considered it a dishonour that some should be fighting and facing the Mexican squadrons and others should be filling up passes and openings and bridges, Pedro de Alvarado, so as to avoid quarrels as to who should be fighting or filling up openings, ordered that one company should have charge of the filling in and look after that work one day, while the other two companies should fight and face the enemy, and that this should be done in rotation one day one company, and another day another company, until each company should have had its turn, and owing to this arrangement there was nothing captured that was not razed to the ground, and our friends the Tlaxcalans helped us. So we went on penetrating into the City, but at the hour for retiring all three companies had to fight in union, for that was the time when we ran the greatest risk. First of all we sent all the Tlaxcalans off the causeway, for it was clear that they were considerable embarrassment when we were fighting.

Guatemoc now ordered us to be attacked at all three camps at the same time by all his troops and with all the energy that was possible both on land and by water, and he ordered them to go by night during the modorra watch, so that the launches should not be able to assist us on account of the stakes. They came on with so furious an impetus that had it not been for those who were on the watch, who were over one hundred and twenty soldiers well used to fighting, they would have penetrated into our camp, and we ran a great risk as it was, but by fighting in good order we withstood them; however, they wounded fifteen of our men and two of them died of their wounds within eight days.

Also in the camp of Cortés they placed our troops in the greatest straits and difficulties and many were killed and wounded, and in the camp of Sandoval the same thing happened, and in this way they came on two successive nights and many Mexicans also were killed in these encounters and many more wounded. When Guatemoc and his captains and priests saw that the attack that they made on those two nights profited them nothing, they decided to come with all their combined forces at the dawn watch and attack our camp, and they came on so fearlessly that they surrounded us on two sides, and had even half defeated us and cut us off, when it pleased our Lord Jesus Christ to give us strength to turn and close our ranks, and we sheltered ourselves to a certain degree with the launches, and with good cut and thrust, and advancing shoulder to shoulder, we drove them off. In that battle they killed eight and wounded many of our soldiers and they even injured Pedro de Alvarado. If the Tlaxcalans had slept on the causeway that night we should have run great risk from the embarrassment they would have caused us on account of their numbers, but the experience of what had happened before made us get them off the causeway promptly and send them to Tacuba, and we remained free from care. To go back to our battle, we killed many Mexicans and took prisoner four persons of importance. I well understand that interested readers will be surfeited with seeing so many fights every day but one cannot do less, for during the ninety and three days that we besieged this strong and great City we had war and combats every day and every night as well. However, when it seemed to us that we were victorious, great disasters were really coming upon us, and we were in the greatest danger of perishing in all three camps, as will be seen later on.

As Cortés saw that it was impossible to fill in all the openings, bridges and canals of water that we captured day by day, which the Mexicans reopened during the night and made stronger than they had been before with barricades, and that it was very hard work fighting and filling in bridges and keeping watch all of us together (all the more as we were most of us wounded and twenty had died), he decided to consult his captains and soldiers who were in his camp, that is Cristóbal de Olid, Francisco Verdugo, Andrés de Tápia, the ensign Corral and Francisco de Lugo, and he also wrote to us in the camp of Pedro de Alvarado and to the camp of Sandoval to take the opinion of all us captains and soldiers. The question he asked was, whether it seemed good to us to make an advance into the City with a rush, so as to reach Tlatelolco, which is the great market of Mexico, and is much broader and larger than that of Salamanca, and that if we could reach it, whether it would be well to station all our three camps there, as from thence we should be able to fight through the streets of Mexico without having such difficulty in retreating and should not have so much to fill in, or have to guard the bridges. As was likely to happen in such discussions and consultations, some of us said that it was not good advice or a good idea to intrude ourselves so entirely into the heart of the City, but that we should remain as we were, fighting and pulling down and levelling the houses. We who held the latter opinion gave as the most obvious reason for it that if we stationed ourselves in Tlatelolco and left the causeways and bridges unguarded and deserted, the Mexicans—having so many warriors and canoes—would reopen the bridges and causeways and we would no longer be masters of these. They would attack us with their powerful forces by night and day, and as they always had many impediments made with stakes ready prepared, our launches would not be able to help us, thus by the plan that Cortés was proposing we would be the besieged and the enemy would have possession of the land, the country and the lake, and we wrote to him about his proposal so that "it should not happen to us as it had happened before" (as the saying of the Mazegatos runs), when we went fleeing out of Mexico.

After Cortés had heard our opinions and the good reasons we gave for them the only result of all the discussion was that on the following day we were to advance with all the energy we could from all three camps, horsemen as well as crossbowmen, musketeers and soldiers and to push forward until we reached the great marketplace at Tlatelolco. When all was ready in all the three camps and our friends the Tlaxcalans had been warned as well as the people of Texcoco and those from the towns of the lake who had again given their fealty to His Majesty, who were to come with their canoes to help the launches, one Sunday morning (30th June) after having heard Mass, we set out from our camp with Pedro de Alvarado, and Cortés set out for his camp, and Sandoval with his companies, and in full force each company advanced capturing bridges and barricades, and the enemy fought like brave warriors and Cortés on his side gained many victories, so too did Gonzalo de Sandoval on his side. Then we on our side had already captured another barricade and a bridge, which was done with much difficulty because Guatemoc had great forces guarding them, and we came out of the fight with many of our soldiers wounded, and one soon died of his wounds, and more than a thousand of our Tlaxcalan friends alone came out of it injured; however, we still followed up our victory very cheerfully.

Let us cease speaking about Cortés and his defeat and return to our army, that of Pedro de Alvarado, and say how we advanced victoriously, and, when we least expected it, we saw advancing against us with loud yells very many squadrons of Mexicans with very handsome ensigns and plumes, and they cast in front of us five heads streaming with blood which they had just cut off the men whom they had captured from Cortés, and they cried:—"Thus will we kill you as we have killed Malinche and Sandoval, and all whom they had brought with them, and these are their heads and by them you may know them well," and saying these words they closed in on us until they laid hands on us and neither cut nor thrust nor crossbows nor muskets availed to stop them, all they did was to rush at us as at a mark. Even so we lost nothing of our order in retreating, for we at once commanded our friends the Tlaxcalans to clear off quickly from the causeways and bad passages, and this time they did it with a will, for when they saw the five heads of our companions dripping with blood and heard the Mexicans say that they had killed Malinche and Sandoval and all the Teules whom they had brought with them, and that so they would do to us also and to the Tlaxcalans, they were thoroughly frightened, thinking it was true, and for this reason, I say, they cleared off the causeway very completely.

As we were retreating we heard the sound of trumpets from the great Cue, which from its height dominates the whole City, and also a drum a most dismal sound indeed it was, like an instrument of demons, as it resounded so that one could hear it two leagues off, and with it many small tambourines and shell trumpets, horns and whistles. At that moment, as we afterwards learnt, they were offering the hearts of ten of our comrades and much blood to the idols.

Simultaneously there came against us many squadrons which Guatemoc had newly sent out, and he ordered his horn to be sounded. When this horn was sounded it was a signal that his captains and warriors must fight so as to capture their enemies or die in the attempt, and the sound that it made echoed in their ears, and when his captains and squadrons heard it, the fury and courage with which they threw themselves on us, in order to lay hold of us, was terrifying, and I do not know how to describe it here; even now when I stop to remember, it is as though I could see it all at this minute, and were present again in that fight and battle. But I reassert that our Lord Jesus Christ saved us, for if he had not given us strength, seeing that we were all wounded, we should never otherwise have been able to reach our ranchos, and I give thanks and praise to God for it, that I escaped that time with many others from the power of the Mexicans.

To go back to our story, the horsemen made charges, and with two heavy cannon that we placed near our ranchos with some loading while others fired we held our own, for the causeway was crowded to the utmost with the enemy and they came after us up to the houses, as though we were already conquered, and shot javelins and stones at us, and as I have said, with those cannon we killed many of them. The man who was most helpful that day was a gentleman named Pedro Moreno Medrano, for he acted as gunner because the artillerymen we used to have with us were some of them dead and the others wounded, and Pedro Moreno besides always being a brave soldier was on that day a great help to us. Being as we were in that condition, thoroughly miserable and wounded, we knew nothing of either Cortés or Sandoval nor of their armies, whether they had been killed or routed, as the Mexicans told us they were when they cast before us the five heads which they brought tied together by the hair and the beards, saying that Malinche and all the Teules were already dead, and that thus they were going to kill all of us that very day. We were not able to get news from them because we were fighting half a league apart one from the other, and for this very reason we were much distressed, but by all of us both wounded and sound keeping together in a body we held out against the shock of the fury of the Mexicans who came against us, and who did not believe that there would be a trace of us left after the attack that they made upon us.

Then they had already captured one of our launches and killed three soldiers and wounded the captain and most of the soldiers who were in it, and it was rescued by another launch of which Juan Jaramillo was captain. Yet another launch was impaled in a place from which it could not move, and its captain was Juan de Linpias Caravajal, who went deaf at that time. He himself fought most valiantly and so encouraged his soldiers, who were rowing the launch that day, that they broke the stakes on which they were impaled and got away, all badly wounded, and saved their launch. This Linpias was the first to break the stakes and it was a great thing for all of us.

Cortés sent Andrés de Tápia with three horsemen posthaste by land [round by Coyoacan], at the risk of their lives, to our camp, to find out if we were alive. The Captain Andrés de Tápia made great haste, although he and two of those who came with him were wounded. When they reached our camp and found us fighting with the Mexican force which was still close to us, they rejoiced in their hearts and related to us what had happened about the defeat of Cortés. However, they did not care to state that so many were dead, and said that about twenty-five had been killed and that all the rest were well.

Let us stop talking of this and turn to Sandoval and his captains and soldiers, who marched on victoriously in the part and streets they had captured, and when the Mexicans had defeated Cortés they turned on Sandoval and his army and captains so effectively that he could make no headway, and they killed six soldiers and wounded all whom he had brought with him, and gave Sandoval himself three wounds one in the thigh, another in the head and another in the left arm. While Sandoval was battling with the enemy they placed before him six heads of Cortés' men whom they had killed, and said they were the heads of Malinche and of Tonatio and other Captains, and that they meant so to do with Sandoval and those who were with him, and they attacked him fiercely. When Sandoval saw this he ordered all his captains and soldiers to show a brave spirit and not be dismayed, and to take care that in retreating there should not be any confusion on the causeway which was narrow, and first of all he ordered his allies, who were numerous, to clear off the causeway so as not to embarrass him, and with the help of his two launches and of his musketeers and crossbowmen, with great difficulty he retired to his quarters, with all his men badly wounded and even discouraged and six of them dead. When he found himself clear of the causeway, although he was surrounded by Mexicans, he encouraged his people and their captains and charged them all to be sure to keep together in a body by day and by night so as to guard the camp and avoid defeat. Then when he learned from the captain Luis Marin, that they were well able to do it, wounded and bound up in rags as he was, he took two other horsemen with him and rode posthaste to the camp of Cortés. When Sandoval saw Cortés he said: "Oh Sir Captain, what is this? Are these the counsels and stratagems of warfare that you have always impressed on us, how has this disaster happened?" Cortés replied, with tears springing to his eyes: "Oh my son Sandoval, for my sins this has been permitted; however, I do not deserve as much blame in the matter as all my captains and soldiers impute, but the Treasurer Julian de Alderete to whom I gave the order to fill in that passage where they defeated us, and he did not do it."

The Treasurer in turn blamed Cortés for not ordering the many allies that he had with him to clear off the causeway in good time, and there were many other discussions and replies from Cortés to the Treasurer which as they were spoken in anger, will be left untold. At that moment there arrived two launches which Cortés kept in the lake and by the causeway, and they had not come in nor had anything been known about them since the defeat. It seems that they had been detained and impaled on some stakes, and, according to what the captains reported, they had been kept there surrounded by canoes which attacked them, and they all came in wounded, and said that God in the first place aided them with a

wind, and thanks to the great energy with which they rowed they broke
the stakes; at this Cortés was well pleased, for up to that time, although
he did not publish it so as not to dishearten the soldiers, he knew nothing
about the launches and had held them as lost.

Cortés strongly advised Sandoval to proceed at once posthaste to
our camp of Pedro de Alvarado, and see whether we were routed, or how
we stood, and if we were alive to help us to keep up the defence so that
they should not break into our camp, and he told Francisco de Lugo,
who accompanied Sandoval (for he well knew that there were Mexican
squadrons on the road), that he had already sent Andrés de Tápia with
three horsemen to get news of us, and he feared that they had been killed
on the road. After saying this to him and taking leave of him he went to
embrace Sandoval, and said: "Look here, my son, as I am not able to go
everywhere, for you can see that I am wounded, I commit this work to
your care so that you may inspire confidence in all three camps. I know
well that Pedro de Alvarado and all his captains and brothers and soldiers
have fought valiantly and acted like gentlemen, but I fear the great forces
of these dogs may have defeated him, and as for me and my army, you
observe in what condition I am."

Sandoval and Francisco de Lugo came posthaste [by way of Coyoacan
and Tacuba to the camp on the causeway] to where we were and when he
arrived it was a little after dusk and it seems that the defeat of Cortés took
place before noon. When Sandoval arrived he found us fighting with the
Mexicans who wanted to get into our camp by way of some houses which
we had pulled down, and others by the causeway, and many canoes by
the lake, and they had already got one launch stranded on the land, and
of the soldiers who were in it two were dead and most of them wounded.
Sandoval saw me and six other soldiers standing more than waist high in
the water helping the launch to get off into deep water, and many Indians
attacking us with swords which they had captured from us (and they gave
me an arrow wound and a sword cut in the leg) so as to prevent us helping the launch, which, judging from the energy they were displaying, they
intended to carry off with their canoes. They had attached many ropes to

it with which to tow it off and place it inside the City. When Sandoval saw us in that position he said to us: "Oh! Brothers put your strength into it and prevent them carrying off the launch," and we exerted so much strength that we soon hauled it out in safety, although as I have said, all of the sailors came out wounded and two dead.

At that time many companies of Mexicans came to the causeway and wounded the horsemen as well as all of us, and they gave Sandoval a good blow with a stone in the face. Then Pedro de Alvarado and other horsemen went to his assistance. As so many squadrons approached I and twenty other soldiers faced them, and Sandoval ordered us to retreat little by little so that they should not kill the horses, and because we did not retreat as quickly as he wished he said to us with fury: "Do you wish that through your selfishness they should kill me and all these horsemen? For the love of me, dear brothers, do fall back"—at that moment the enemy again wounded him and his horse. Just then we cleared our allies off the causeway, and we retreated little by little keeping our faces to the enemy and not turning our backs, as though to form a dam. Notwithstanding the number of Mexicans that the balls were sweeping away, we could not fend them off, on the contrary they kept on following us thinking that this very night they would carry us off to be sacrificed.

Dismal Drums and Human Sacrifices

When we had retreated near to our quarters and had already crossed a great opening where there was much water the arrows, javelins and stones could no longer reach us. Sandoval, Francisco de Lugo and Andrés de Tápia were standing with Pedro de Alvarado each one relating what had happened to him and what Cortés had ordered, when again there was sounded the dismal drum of Huichilobos and many other shells and horns and things like trumpets and the sound of them all was terrifying, and we all looked towards the lofty Cue where they were being sounded, and saw that our comrades whom they had captured when they defeated Cortés were being carried by force up the steps, and they were taking them to be sacrificed. When they got them up to a small square in front of the oratory, where their accursed idols are kept, we saw them place plumes on the heads of many of them and with things like fans in their hands they forced them to dance before Huichilobos, and after they had danced they immediately placed them on their backs on some rather narrow stones which had been prepared as places for sacrifice, and with stone knives they sawed open their chests and drew out their palpitating hearts and offered them to the idols that were there, and they kicked the bodies down the steps, and Indian butchers who were waiting below cut off the arms and feet and flayed the skin off the faces, and prepared it afterwards like glove leather with the beards on, and kept those for the festivals when they celebrated drunken orgies, and the flesh they ate in *chilmole*. In the same way they sacrificed all the others and ate the legs and arms and offered the hearts and blood to their idols, as I have said, and the bodies, that is their entrails and feet, they threw to the tigers and lions which they kept in the house of the carnivores which I have spoken about in an earlier chapter.

When we saw those cruelties all of us in our camp said the one to the other: "Thank God that they are not carrying me off today to be sacrificed."

It should also be noted that we were not far away from them [they must have been at their camp on the causeway—they could not have seen this from Tacuba], yet we could render them no help, and could only pray God to guard us from such a death.

Then, at the moment that they were making the sacrifices, great squadrons of Mexicans fell on us suddenly and gave us plenty to do on all sides and neither in one way or the other could we prevail against them.

And they cried: "Look, that is the way in which you will all have to die, for our gods have promised it to us many times." Then the words and threats which they said to our friends the Tlaxcalans were so injurious and evil that they disheartened them, and they threw them roasted legs of Indians and the arms of our soldiers and cried to them: "Eat of the flesh of these Teules and of your brothers, for we are already glutted with it, and you can stuff yourselves with this which is over, and observe that as for the houses which you have destroyed we shall have to bring you to rebuild them much better with white stone and well-worked masonry, so go on helping the Teules, for you will see them all sacrificed."

There was another thing that Guatemoc ordered to be done when he won that victory, he sent to all the towns of our allies and friends and to their relations, the hands and feet of our soldiers and the flayed faces with the beards, and the heads of the horses that they had killed, and he sent word that more than half of us were dead and he would soon finish us off, and he told them to give up their friendship with us and come to Mexico and if they did not give it up promptly, he would come and destroy them, and he sent to tell them many other things to induce them to leave our camp and desert us, and then we should be killed by his hands.

As they still went on attacking us both by day and by night, all of us in our camp kept watch together, Gonzalo de Sandoval and Pedro de Alvarado and the other captains keeping us company during our watch, and although during the night great companies of warriors came against us we withstood them. Both by day and night half the horsemen remained in Tacuba and the other half were on the causeway.

There was another greater evil that they did us; no matter how carefully we had filled in the water spaces since we advanced along the causeway, they returned and opened them all and constructed barricades stronger than before. Then our friends of the cities of the lake who had again accepted our friendship and had come to aid us with their canoes believed that they "came to gather wool and went back shorn," for many of them lost their lives and many more returned wounded, and they lost more than half of the canoes they had brought with them, but, even with all this, thenceforth they did not help the Mexicans for they were hostile to them, but they carefully watched events as they happened.

Let us cease talking about misfortunes and once again tell about the caution, and the manner of it, that from now on we exercised, and how Gonzalo de Sandoval and Francisco de Logo and Andrés de Tápia and the other soldiers who had come to our camp thought it would be well to return to their posts and to give a report to Cortés as to how and in what position we stood. So they went posthaste and told Cortés that Pedro de Alvarado and all his soldiers were using great caution both in fighting as well as in keeping watch, and moreover Sandoval, as he considered me a friend, said to Cortés that he had found me and the soldiers fighting more than waist high in water defending a stranded launch, and that if it had not been for us the enemy would surely have killed the captain and soldiers who were on board, and because he said other things in my praise about when he ordered me to retreat, I am not going to repeat them here, for other persons told of it, and it was known throughout the camp of Cortés and in our own, but I do not wish to recite it here. When Cortés clearly understood the great caution that we observed in our camp it greatly eased his heart, and from that time onwards he ordered all three camps not to fight with the Mexicans either too much or too little, meaning that we were not to trouble about capturing any bridge or barricade, and, except in defence of our camps, we were not to go out to fight with the enemy.

Nevertheless the day had hardly dawned when they were attacking our camp, discharging many stones from slings, and javelins and arrows and shouting out hideous abuse, and as we had near the camp a very broad and deep opening of water we remained for four days in succession without crossing it. Cortés remained as long in his camp and Sandoval in his. This determination not to go out and fight and endeavour to capture the barricades which the Mexicans had returned to open and fortify, was because we were all badly wounded and worn out with hardships, both from keeping watch and bearing arms without anything sustaining to eat; and because we had lost the day before over sixty and odd soldiers from all the camps, and eight horses and so that we might obtain some rest, and take mature counsel as to what should be done. From that time onwards, Cortés ordered us to remain quiet, as I have said, so I will leave off here and tell how and in what way we fought and everything else that happened in our camp.

The Mexicans continued with their attacks every day, and our friends, the people of Tlaxcala and Cholula and Huexotzingo, and even those of Texcoco and Chalco and Tlamanalco, decided to return to their own Countries, and nearly all of them went off without Cortés or Pedro de Alvarado or Sandoval knowing about it. There only remained in Cortés' camp Ixtlixochitl, who was afterwards baptized and named Don Carlos (he was the brother of Don Fernando the Lord of Texcoco and was a very valiant man) and about forty of his relations and friends. In Sandoval's camp there remained another cacique from Huexotzingo with about fifty men, and in our camp there remained two sons of Lorenzo de Vargas and the brave Chichimecatecle with about eighty Tlaxcalans, his relations and vassals. When we found ourselves with so few allies we were distressed, and Cortés and Sandoval each of them asked the allies that remained in his camp, why the others had gone off in that way, and they replied that they had observed Mexicans speaking with their Idols during the night who promised them that they should kill us, and they believed it to be true; so it was through fear that they left, and what made it more credible was seeing us all wounded and many of us dead, and of their own people more than twelve hundred were missing, and they feared that we should all be killed. In conversations which Cortés had with Ixtlixochitl, he said to him: "Señor Malinche, do not be distressed because you cannot fight every day with the Mexicans, get your foot well, and take my advice, and that is to stay some days in your camp, and tell Tonatio to do the same and stay in his camp and Sandoval in Tepeaquilla, and keep the launches on the move night and day to prevent supplies of provisions or water from getting to the enemy for there are within this great City so many thousand *xiquipeles* [a division numbering eight thousand men] of warriors that they must of necessity eat up the food that they possess, and the water they are now drinking is from some springs they have made, and it is half salt, and as it rains every day and sometimes at night they catch the water and live on that, but what can they do if you stop their food and water? They will suffer more from hunger and thirst than from war." When Cortés understood this advice, he threw his arms round him and thanked him for it and made him promises that he would give him pueblos. This advice many of us soldiers had already discussed, but, such is our nature, that we did not wish to wait so long a time, but to advance into the city. When Cortés had well considered what the cacique had said, he ordered two launches to go to our camp and to that of Sandoval to tell us that he ordered us to remain another three days without advancing into the city. As at that time the Mexicans were victorious he did not dare to send out one launch alone. There was one thing that helped us much, which was that our launches now ventured to break the stakes that the Mexicans had placed in the lake to impale them, and they did it in this way, they rowed with all their strength, and so that the rowing should carry greater impetus they set about it from some distance back and got wind into their sails and rowed their best, so they became masters of the lake and even of a good many houses that stood apart from the city, and when the Mexicans saw this they lost some of their courage.

As now we had no allies, we ourselves began to fill in and stop up the great opening that, I have said before, was near our camp, and the first company on the rota worked hard at carrying adobes and timber to fill it in, while the other two companies did the fighting, and in the four days that all of us worked at it we had it filled in and levelled. Cortés did the same in his camp where the same arrangement prevailed, and even he himself was at work carrying adobes and timber, until the bridges and causeways and openings were secure so that a retreat could be effected in safety; and Sandoval did neither more nor less in his camp. With our launches close by us, and free from any fear of stakes we advanced in this manner little by little.

Let me say now what the Mexicans did during the night on their great and lofty Cues and that was to sound the cursed drum, which I again declare had the most accursed sound and the most dismal that it was possible to invent, and the sound carried far over the country, and they sounded other worse instruments and diabolical things, and they made great fires and uttered the loudest yells and whistles, for at that moment they were sacrificing our comrades whom they had captured from Cortés and we knew that it took them ten days in succession to complete the sacrificing of all our soldiers, and they left to the last Cristóbal de Guzman whom they kept alive for twelve or thirteen days, according to the report of the three Mexican captains whom we captured. Whenever they sacrificed them then their Huichilobos spoke to them and promised them victory, and that we should die by their hands within eight days, and told them to make vigorous attacks on us although many should die in them and in this way he kept them deluded.

Once more as soon as another day dawned all the greatest forces that Guatemoc could collect were already down upon us, and as we had filled up the opening and causeway and bridge they could pass it dry-shod. My faith! They had the daring to come up to our ranchos and hurl javelins and stones and arrows, but with the cannon we could always make them draw off, for Pedro Moreno, who had charge of the cannon, did much damage to the enemy. I wish to say that they shot our own arrows at us from crossbows, for while they held five crossbowmen alive, and Cristóbal de Guzman with them, they made them load the crossbows and show them how they were to be discharged, and either they or the Mexicans discharged those shots deliberately, but they did no harm with them.

Every day we had very hard fights, but we did not cease to advance, capturing barricades, bridges and water openings, and as our launches dared to go wherever they chose in the lake, and did not fear the stakes, they helped us very much. Let me say that as usual the launches that Cortés had at his camp cruised about giving chase to the canoes that were bringing in supplies and water and collecting in the lake a sort of ooze which when it was dried had the flavour of cheese, and these launches brought in many Indian prisoners. Twelve or thirteen days had gone by since the defeat of Cortés, and as soon as Ixtlixochitl observed that we had thoroughly recovered ourselves, and what the Mexicans said that they were sure to kill us within ten days was not true (which was what their Huichilobos and Tezcatepuca had promised them), he sent to advise his brother Don Fernando to send to Cortés, at once, the whole force of warriors that he could muster in Texcoco, and within two days of the time of his sending to tell him, more than two thousand warriors arrived.

When Cortés saw such a good reinforcement he was greatly delighted and said flattering words to them. At that time many Tlaxcalans with their captains also returned and a cacique from Topeyanco named Tecapaneca came as their general. Many Indians also came from Huexotzingo and a very few from Cholula. When Cortés knew that they had returned he ordered that all of them, as they arrived, should come to his camp so that he could speak to them. Before they arrived he ordered guards of our soldiers to be placed on the roads to protect them, in case the Mexicans should come out to attack them when they came before Cortés he made them a speech through Doña Marina and Jerónimo de Aguilar and told them that they had fully understood and knew for certain about the goodwill with which he had always regarded them and still bore them, both because they had served His Majesty, as well as for the good offices that we had received at their hands, and if he had, after reaching this city, commanded them to join us in destroying the Mexicans, he intended them to profit by it, and return to their land rich men, and to revenge themselves on their enemies, and not that we should capture that great

City solely for his benefit, and although he had always found them useful and they had helped us in everything, they must have seen clearly that we ordered them off the causeways every day, because we were less hampered when we fought without them, and that he who gave us victory and aided us in everything was Our Lord Jesus Christ, in whom we believe and whom we worship as he had already often told them and warned them at other times. Because they went away at the most critical time of the war they were deserving of death, for deserting their captains when they were fighting and for forsaking them, but as they did not understand our laws and ordinances he pardoned them, and in order to understand the situation better they should observe that without their help we still continued destroying houses and capturing barricades. From that time forward he ordered them not to kill any Mexicans, for he wished to conquer them by kindness. When he had made this speech to them he embraced Chichimecatecle and the two youthful Xicotengas, and Ixtlixochitl, and promised to give them territory and vassals in addition to what they now held. After the conversation with them he ordered them to depart, and each one went to his camp.

From all three camps we were now advancing into the City, Cortés on his side, Sandoval on his and Pedro de Alvarado on our side, and we reached the spot where the spring was, that I have already spoken about, where the Mexicans drank the brackish water, and we broke it up and destroyed it so that they might not make use of it. Some Mexicans were guarding it and we had a good skirmish with them. We could already move freely through all parts of the streets we had captured, for they were already levelled and free from water and openings and the horses could move very easily.

Thus the ten Companies of Pedro de Alvarado advanced fighting and reached Tlatelolco, and there were so many Mexicans guarding their Idols and lofty cues, and they had raised so many barricades that we were fully two hours before we were able to capture them and get inside. Now that the horses had space to gallop, although most of them were wounded, they helped us very much, and the horsemen speared many Mexicans. As the enemy were so numerous the ten [in the text "dos capitanias," evidently a mistake for "diez capitanias" as above] companies were divided into three parts to fight against them, and Pedro de Alvarado ordered the company commanded by a captain named Gutierre de Badajoz to ascend the lofty Cue of Huichilobos, which has one hundred and fourteen steps, and he fought very well against the enemy and against the many priests who were in the houses of the oratories, but the enemy attacked Gutierre de Badajoz and his company in such a way that they sent him rolling down ten or twelve steps, and we promptly went to his assistance.

As we advanced the squadrons with which we were fighting followed us, and we ran great risk of our lives, but nevertheless we ascended the steps which as I have said before were one hundred and fourteen in number. It is as well to mention here the great danger we were in, both one [company] and the other, in capturing those fortresses which were very lofty, and in those battles they once more wounded us all very badly, nevertheless we set the oratories on fire and burned the idols, and we planted our banners and were fighting on the level after we had set fire to the oratories until nighttime, but we could do nothing against so many warriors.

The Fall of Mexico and the Surrender of Guatemoc

As we were all of us now in Tlatelolco, Cortés ordered all the companies to take up their quarters, and keep watch there, because from our camp we had to come more than half a league to where we were now fighting. So we stayed there three days without doing anything worth mentioning, because Cortés ordered us not to advance any further into the City nor to destroy more houses, for he wished to stop and demand peace. During those days that we were waiting in Tlatelolco Cortés sent to Guatemoc begging him to surrender, and not to have any fear, and with many prom-ises he undertook that his (Guatemoc's) person should be much respected and honoured by him, and that he should govern Mexico and all his ter-ritory and cities as he was used to do, and he sent him food and presents such as tortillas, poultry, tunas and cacao, for he had nothing else to send. Guatemoc took counsel with his captains and what they advised him to reply was that he desired peace but that he would wait three days before giving an answer, and that at the end of three days Guatemoc and Cortés should meet and make arrangements about the peace, and that during those three days they would have time to know more fully the wishes and reply of their Huichilobos, and he might have added to mend bridges and to make openings in the causeway and prepare arrows, javelins and stones and make barricades.

Guatemoc sent four Mexican chieftains with that reply, and we believed that the promise of peace was true, and Cortés ordered the mes-sengers to be given plenty to eat and drink and then sent them back to Guatemoc, and with them he sent more refreshments the same as before. Then Guatemoc sent other messengers, and by them two rich mantles, and they said that Guatemoc would come when everything was ready. Not to waste more words about the matter he never intended to come (for they had counselled him not to believe Cortés and had reminded him of the end of his uncle the great Montezuma, and of his relations and the destruction of all the noble families of Mexico; and had advised him to say that he was ill) but intended that all should sally out to fight and that it would please their Gods to give them the victory they had so often promised them. As we were waiting for Guatemoc and he did not come, we understood their deceit and at that very moment so many battalions of Mexicans with their distinguishing marks sallied out and made an attack on Cortés that he could not withstand it, and as many more went in the direction of our camp and in that of Sandoval's. They came on in such a way that it seemed as though they had just then begun the fighting all over again, and as we were posted rather carelessly, believing that they had already made peace, they wounded many of our soldiers, three of them very severely, and two horses, but they did not get off with much to brag of, for we paid them out well. When Cortés saw this he ordered us again to make war on them and to advance into the City in the part where they had taken refuge. When they saw that we were advancing and capturing the whole City, Guatemoc sent two chiefs to tell Cortés that he desired to speak with him across a canal, Cortés to stand on one bank and Guatemoc on the other and they fixed the time for the morning of the following day. Cortés went, but Guatemoc would not keep the appointment but sent chieftains who said that their Lord did not dare to come out for fear lest, while they were talking, guns and crossbows should be discharged at him and should kill him. Then Cortés promised him on his oath that he should not be molested in any way that he did not approve of, but it was no use, they did not believe him and said "lest what happened to Montezuma should happen to him." At that time two of the chieftains who were talking to Cortés drew out from a bag which they carried some tortillas and the leg of a fowl and cherries, and seated themselves in a very leisurely manner and began to eat so that Cortés might observe it and believe that they were not hungry. When Cortés observed it he sent to tell them that as they did not wish to make peace, he would soon enter into all their houses to see if they had any maize and how much more poultry.

We went on in this way for another four or five days without attacking them, and about this time many poor Indians who had nothing to
eat, would come out every night, and they came to our camp worn out
by hunger. As soon as Cortés saw this he ordered us not to attack them
for perhaps they would change their minds about making peace, but they
would not make peace although we sent to entreat them.

In Cortés' camp there was a soldier who said that he had been in Italy
in the Company of the Great Captain [Gonzalvo de Córdova] and was in
the skirmish of Garallano and in other great battles, and he talked much
about engines of war and that he could make a catapult in Tlatelolco
by which, if they only bombarded the houses and part of the city where
Guatemoc had sought refuge, for two days, they would make them surrender peacefully. So many things did he say to Cortés about this, for he
was a very faithful soldier, that Cortés promptly set to work to make the
catapult and they brought lime and stone in the way the soldier required,
and carpenters and nails and all that was necessary for making the catapult, and they made two slings of strong bags and cords, and brought
him great stones, larger than an arroba jar. When the catapult was made
and set up in the way that the soldier ordered, and he said it was ready
to be discharged, they placed a suitable stone in the sling which had
been made and all this stone did was to rise no higher than the catapult
and fall back upon it where it had been set up. When Cortés saw this he
was angry with the soldier who gave the order for making it, and with
himself for believing him, and he said that he knew well that in war one
ought not to speak much about a thing that vexes one, and that the man
had only been talking for talking's sake, as had been found out in the
way that I have said. Cortés at once ordered the catapult to be taken to
pieces. Let us leave this and say that, when he saw that the catapult was
a thing to be laughed at, he decided that Gonzalo de Sandoval should go
in command of all the twelve launches and invade that part of the City
whither Guatemoc had retreated, which was in a part where we could not
reach the houses and palaces by land, but only by water. Sandoval at once
summoned all the captains of the launches and invaded that part of the

City where Guatemoc had taken refuge with all the flower of his Captains and the most distinguished persons that were in Mexico. Cortés ordered Sandoval not to kill or wound any Indians unless they should attack him, and even if they did attack him, he was only to defend himself and not do them any other harm, but he should destroy their houses and the many defences they had erected in the lake. Cortés himself ascended the great Cue of Tlatelolco to see how Sandoval advanced with the launches.

Sandoval advanced with great ardour upon the place where the Houses of Guatemoc stood, and when Guatemoc saw himself surrounded, he was afraid that they would capture him or kill him, and he had got ready fifty great piraguas with good rowers so that when he saw himself hard-pressed he could save himself by going to hide in some reed beds and get from thence to land and hide himself in another town, and those were the instructions he had given his captains and the persons of most importance who were with him in that fortified part of the city, so that they should do the same.

When they saw that the launches were getting among the houses they embarked in the fifty canoes, and they had already placed on board the property and gold and jewels of Guatemoc and all his family and women, and he had embarked himself and shot out into the lake ahead, accompanied by many Captains. As many other canoes set out at the same time, the lake was full of them, and Sandoval quickly received the news that Guatemoc was fleeing, and ordered all the launches to stop destroying the houses and fortifications and follow the flight of the canoes. As a certain García Holguin a friend of Sandoval, was captain of a launch which was very fast and a good sailor and was manned by good rowers Sandoval ordered him to follow in the direction in which they told him that Guatemoc was fleeing with his great piraguas, and instructed him not to do Guatemoc any injury whatever beyond capturing him in case he should overtake him, and Sandoval went in another direction with other launches which kept him company. It pleased our Lord God that Garcia Holguin should overtake the canoes and piraguas in which Guatemoc was travelling, and from the style and the awnings and the seat he was using he knew that it was Guatemoc the great Lord of Mexico, and he made signals for them to stop, but they would not stop, so he made as though he were going to discharge muskets and crossbows. When Guatemoc saw that, he was afraid, and said: "Do not shoot—I am the king of this City and they call me Guatemoc, and what I ask of you is not to disturb my things that I am taking with me nor my wife nor my relations, but carry me at once to Malinche." When Holguin heard him he was greatly delighted, and with much respect he embraced him and placed him in the launch, him and his wife and about thirty chieftains, and seated him in the poop on some mats and cloths, and gave him to eat of the food that he had brought with him, and he touched nothing whatever in the canoes that carried Guatemoc's property, but brought it along with the launch. By this time Gonzalo de Sandoval knew that Holguin had captured Guatemoc and was carrying him to Cortés, and he overtook Holguin and claimed the prisoner, and Holguin would not give him up and said that he had captured him and not Sandoval. When Cortés knew of this dispute he at once despatched Captain Luis Marin and Francisco de Verdugo to summon Sandoval and Holguin to come as they were in their launches without further discussion, and to bring Guatemoc and his wife and family with all signs of respect and that he would settle whose prisoner he was and to whom was due the honour of the capture.

While they were bringing him, Cortés ordered a guest chamber to be prepared as well as could be done at the time, with mats and cloths and seats, and a good supply of the food which Cortés had reserved for himself. Sandoval and Holguin soon arrived with Guatemoc, and the two captains between them led him up to Cortés, and when he came in front of him he paid him great respect, and Cortés embraced Guatemoc with delight, and was very affectionate to him and his captains. Then Guatemoc said to Cortés: "Señor Malinche, I have surely done my duty in defence of my City, and I can do no more and I come by force and a prisoner into your presence and into your power, take that dagger that you have in your belt and kill me at once with it," and when he said this he wept tears and sobbed and other great Lords whom he had brought with him also wept. Cortés answered him through Doña Marina and Aguilar very affectionately, that he esteemed him all the more for having been so brave as to defend the City, and he was deserving of no blame, on the contrary it was more in his favour than otherwise.

What he wished was that Guatemoc had made peace of his own free will before the city had been so far destroyed, and so many of his Mexicans had died, but now that both had happened there was no help for it and it could not be mended, let his spirit and the spirit of his Captains take rest, and he should rule in Mexico and over his provinces as he did before. Then Guatemoc and his Captains said that they accepted his favour, and Cortés asked after his wife and other great ladies, the wives of other Captains who, he had been told, had come with Guatemoc. Guatemoc himself answered and said that he had begged Gonzalo de Sandoval and García Holguin that they might remain in the canoes while he came to see what orders Malinche gave them. Cortés at once sent for them and ordered them all to be given of the best that at that time there was in the camp to eat, and as it was late and was beginning to rain, Cortés arranged for them to go to Coyoacan, and took Guatemoc and all his family and household and many chieftains with him and he ordered Pedro de Alvarado, Gonzalo de Sandoval and the other captains each to go to his own quarters and camp, and we went to Tacuba, Sandoval to Tepeaquilla and Cortés to Coyoacan. Guatemoc and his captains were captured on the thirteenth day of August at the time of vespers on the day of Señor San Hipólito in the year one thousand five hundred and twenty-one, thanks to our Lord Jesus Christ and our Lady the Virgin Santa Maria, His Blessed Mother. Amen.

The following selections from Bernal Díaz's longer narrative presented here, with the exception of a handful of pages, have not appeared in other abridgments. Reading them now gives crucial information about the severe difficulties of the "conquest," the ongoing resistance and rebellions of the indigenous peoples in many parts of Mesoamerica, infighting for wealth among the Spaniards, and the struggles of the author to write his place into history. We witness the murder of Cuauhtemoc by Cortés, who then falls into a deep depression for this deed, and the arrival of the twelve Franciscans, imitating the twelve apostles of Christ. We read of victories and defeats in Oaxaca, Chiapas, and Guatemala and realize that the Spaniards failed to actually "conquer" a number of towns that Bernal Díaz writes about. Readers will learn of the "great warriors of the Zapotecs," for as one soldier tells Bernal Díaz, he "would rather fight against cannon and great armies of enemies whether of Turks or Moors than against those Zapotecs." We read about the cruelty of Pedro de Alvarado during his expedition south to Guatemala. Finally we are amazed when the Spaniards stage their own version of a Roman gladiatorial drama held in the zocalo of Mexico near where the Great Temple stood. We gather a very different impression of the cultural and political encounters between Europeans and native Mesoamericans from reading these additional pages than we get from other abridgments ending at or close to the moment of Cuauhtemoc's surrender at Tlatelolco.

The City as a Wasteland
Taking Women

It rained and thundered and lightning flashed that afternoon and up to midnight heavier rain fell than usual. After Guatemoc had been captured all the soldiers turned as deaf as if some one had stood shouting from the top of a belfry with many bells clanging and in the midst of their ringing all of a sudden they had ceased to sound. I say this purposely, for during all the ninety-three days that we were besieging this city, both by night and day, some of the Mexican Captains kept on uttering so many shouts and yells, whilst they were mustering the squadrons and warriors who were to fight on the causeway, and others were calling out to those in the canoes who were to fight with the launches, and with us on the bridges, again others to those driving in piles and opening and deepening the water openings and bridges and making breastworks, or those who were making javelins and arrows, or to the women preparing rounded stones to hurl from the slings, while from the oratories and towers of the Idols, the accursed drums, trumpets and mournful kettledrums never ceased sounding, and in this way both by night and by day, there was such a great din that we could not hear one another. On the capture of Guatemoc, the shouts and all the clamour ceased, and it is for this reason I have said that up to then we seemed to be standing in a belfry.

Let us leave this and say that Guatemoc was of a very graceful make both in figure and features. His face was rather long, but cheerful, and when his eyes looked at you, they appeared rather grave than gentle, and there was no waver in them; he was twenty-one years of age [blotted out in the original, "twenty-three or twenty four years"], and his colour inclined rather more to white than the colour of the brown Indians, and they say that he was a nephew of Montezuma, the son of one of his sisters, and he was married to a daughter of this same uncle Montezuma, who was a young and beautiful woman.

Before we go any further, let me relate how the dispute between Sandoval and García Holguin came to an end. It was in this way; Cortés told them a story about the Romans having just such another dispute between Marius and Cornelius Sylla. It took place when Sylla brought Jugurtha a prisoner to Rome with his father-in-law, the King Bocos. When they entered Rome glorying over the deeds and exploits they had accomplished it seems that Sylla placed Jugurtha in his triumphal procession with an iron chain round his neck, and Marius said that he and not Sylla should have done this, and that before Sylla had thus placed him he must explain that Marius gave him the right to do so, and had sent him in his stead so that he might take Jugurtha prisoner in Marius's name, and that the King Bocos gave himself up to the name of Marius. Then as Marius was Captain General and he (Sylla) was fighting under his command and banner, and as Sylla was one of the Roman patricians and was held in high favour, and as Marius came from a town near Rome named Arpino and therefore a foreigner, although he had been several times Consul, he was not in as high favour as Sylla, and about this matter there were Civil Wars between Marius and Sylla, and it was never settled to whom should be given the honour of capturing Jugurtha.

Let me take up the thread of my story, which is that Cortés said that he would refer the matter to His Majesty as to which of the two he would favour by making it [the subject of] a grant of arms, and that the decision about it would be brought from Spain, and in two years' time there came a command from His Majesty that Cortés should have in the ornaments of his Coat of Arms, seven kings, who were Montezuma, the great Lord of Mexico, Cacamatzin, the Lord of Texcoco, and the Lords of Iztapalapa, Coyoacan, Tacuba and another great Lord who was a nephew of Montezuma, to whom they said would come the Caciqueship and Lordship of Mexico, (he was the Lord of Mataltzingo and of other provinces,) and this Guatemoc about whom the dispute arose.

Let us leave this and let us speak of the dead bodies and heads that were in the houses where Guatemoc had taken refuge. I say on my oath, Amen, that all the houses and the palisades in the lake were full of heads and corpses and I do not know how to describe it for in the streets and courts of Tlatelolco there was no difference, and we could not walk except among corpses and heads of dead Indians.

I have read about the destruction of Jerusalem but I know not for certain if there was greater mortality than this, for of the great number of the warriors from all the provinces and towns subject to Mexico who had crowded in [to the city] most of them died, and as I have already said, thus the land and the lake and the palisades were all full of dead bodies, and stank so much that no one could endure it, and for this reason, as soon as Guatemoc was captured, each one of the Captains went to his own camp, as I have already said, and even Cortés was ill from the stench which assailed his nostrils, and from headache, during the days we were in Tlatelolco.

Let us leave this and go on ahead and say that the soldiers who went about in the launches were the best off and gained much spoil because they were able to go to the houses in certain quarters in the lake where they knew that there was cloth and gold and other riches, and they also went to search in the reed beds whither the Mexicans had carried it [their property] so as to hide it when we gained possession of some houses or quarter [of the city]. Also because under pretext of giving chase to canoes which carried food or water, when they came on those in which some of the chieftains were fleeing to the mainland to get among the pueblos of the Otomies who were their neighbours, they robbed them of all they carried with them. I wish to say that we, the soldiers who were fighting on the causeways and on land gained no profit except arrow and lance wounds, and wounds from darts and stones, because when we captured any houses, the inhabitants had already carried off whatever property they possessed and we were not able to go through the water without first of all closing up the openings and bridges and, for this reason, I have said, in the chapter which tells of [the time] when Cortés was looking for sailors to go in the launches, that they were the best off, and not we who fought on land. This seems clear for the Mexican Captains and even Guatemoc, when Cortés demanded from them the treasure of Montezuma, told him that the crews of the launches had stolen the greater part of it.

Let us stop speaking of this until later on, and say that as there was so great a stench in the city, Guatemoc asked permission of Cortés for all the Mexican forces left in the city to go out to the neighbouring pueblos, and they were promptly told to do so. I assert that during three days and nights they never ceased streaming out and all three causeways were crowded with men, women and children, so thin, yellow, dirty and stinking, that it was pitiful to see them. When the city was free of them, Cortés went to examine it and we found the houses full of corpses and there were some poor Mexicans, who could not move out, still among them, and what they excreted from their bodies was a filth such as thin swine pass which have been fed upon nothing but grass, and all the city was as though it had been ploughed up and the roots of the herbs dug out and they had eaten them and even cooked the bark of some of the trees, and there was no freshwater to be found, only saltwater. I also wish to state that they did not eat the flesh of their own Mexicans, only that of our people and our Tlaxcalan allies whom they had captured, and there had been no births for a long time, as they had suffered so much from hunger and thirst and continual fighting.

Let us continue. Cortés ordered all the launches to assemble where some dockyards were built later on. To go back to my story, when this great and populous city so famed throughout the whole world had been captured, after giving many thanks to God our Lord and Our Lady His Blessed Mother, and having made certain offerings to Our Lord God, Cortés ordered a banquet to be held at Coyoacan in celebration of the capture of the city, and had already procured plenty of wine for the purpose out of a ship which had come from Spain to the port of Villa Rica, and he had pigs which they had brought him from Cuba and in order to make a festival of the occasion he ordered all the captains and soldiers whom he thought worth consideration from all three camps to be invited, and when we went to the banquet there were neither seats nor tables placed sufficient for a third part of the captains and soldiers who came, and there was much disorder, and it would have been better not to have given that banquet on account of many things which happened at it which were not creditable [blotted out in the original, "such as to get rid of all this supper and the kinds of dances and the . . . and other things that were not suitable and also because this plant of Noah's made some people behave crazily, and men walked on the top of the tables after they had eaten and could not find the way out to the patio. Others said that they must buy horses with golden saddles and there were crossbowmen who said that all the darts and guides that they would have in their quivers must be made of gold from the share which would be given them, and others went rolling down the steps. Then when they had cleared away the tables, such ladies as were present, went out to dance with the gallants who were weighted with, their (quilted) cotton armour and it seemed to me to be a thing to be laughed at. They were ladies whom I will not here describe for there were no others in camp nor in the whole of New Spain. First of all, the elderly Maria Destrada who afterwards married Pero Sanchez Farfan, and Francisca de Ordás who married a gentleman, Juan Gonzalo de Leon; la Bermuda, who married Olmos de Portillo, him of Mexico; another lady, the wife of Captain Portillo who died in (one of) the launches, but as she was a widow they did not bring her to the feast; and a somebody Gómez, who was the wife of Benito de Vargas; and another beautiful lady called La Bermuda—I don't remember her Christian name—who married one Hernan Martin and went to live in Oaxaca; and another elderly woman named Ysabel Rodriguez, who at that time, was the wife of a somebody Guadalupe, and another somewhat elderly woman who was called Mari Hernández who was the wife of the rich Juan de Cáceres. I cannot call to mind any others who were then in New Spain. Let us leave the banquet and capering and dances, for the next day that dawned, the tables . . ."]; and they gambled, and this also it would have been better not to have done, and all the gold should have been used for holy purposes and given with thanks to God for the many benefits and favours He had already shown us and continued to show us.

Let us cease to speak of this, for I wish to tell of other things that happened which I was forgetting, and which do not belong here, but should have been reported somewhat earlier, and it is that our friends Chichimecatecle and the two youthful Xicotengas, the sons of Don Lorenzo de Vargas, who used to be called Xicotenga the old and blind, fought very valiantly against the great forces of Mexico, and helped us very much, and so too did a brother of Don Fernando, the Lord of Texcoco, many times mentioned by me, who was called Ixtlixochitl ["Estesuchel" in the text], who was afterwards named Don Carlos; he did the deeds of a very daring and valiant man. There was another Indian Captain whose name I do not remember, a native of a pueblo on the lake, who performed wonders, and many other captains from the pueblos which assisted us. All fought very mightily, and Cortés gave them many thanks and much praise for having helped us, and made them many promises that he would make them rulers, and he would give them in time to come lands and vassals, and he bid them farewell, and as they were all rich and weighed down with the gold and spoil they had taken they went back to their lands and even carried with them the dried flesh of the Mexicans and divided it among their relations and friends as pertaining to their enemies, and they ate it at festivals.

Now that I am [far] away from the conflicts and arduous battles which we fought against the Mexicans by night and day, for which I give many thanks to God who delivered me from them, I wish to relate a thing that happened to me after seeing the sixty-two soldiers of Cortés, who were carried off alive, sacrificed and their chests cut open and their hearts offered to the Idols. What I shall say now will appear to some persons to be due to my want of any great inclination for fighting, but on the other hand, if it is well thought out, it arose out of the reckless daring and great courage with which in those days, I was obliged to expose myself in the thickest of the fights, for at that time it was expected of a good soldier and was necessary in order to maintain that reputation, that one should do whatever the boldest soldier was obliged to do. As each day I beheld my companions carried off to be sacrificed, and had seen how they sawed open their chests and tore out their still beating hearts and cut off their feet and arms and ate them, to the number of sixty-two, as I have already said, besides ten of our company whom they had captured before that, I feared that one day or another they would do the same to me, for they had already seized me twice to carry me off to be sacrificed, but it pleased God that I should escape from their power. When I called to mind those hideous deaths, and as the proverb says, "The little pitcher which goes many times to the fountain, &c," for this reason, from that time I always feared death more than ever. I say this because, before going into battle there was a horror and sadness in my heart, and I fasted once or twice, commending myself to God and His Blessed Mother, but on going into battle it was always the same, the fear promptly left me.

Let us leave this now and I will state and declare why in all these Mexican wars, when they killed our comrades, I have said, "they carried them off," and not "they killed them," and the reason was this, because the warriors who fought with us although they were able to kill those of our soldiers whom they carried off alive, did not kill them at once, but gave them dangerous wounds so that they could not defend themselves, and carried them off alive to sacrifice to their Idols, and they even first made them dance before Huichilobos, who was their Idol of War and this is the reason why I have said, "they carried them off." Let us leave this subject and I will relate what Cortés did after the capture of Mexico.

The first order that Cortés gave to Guatemoc was, that they [the Mexicans] should repair the water pipes from Chapultepec in the way they used to be, so that the water should at once come through the pipes and enter the City of Mexico; next, that all the streets should be cleared of the bodies and heads of the dead, and that they should be buried so that the city could be kept clean and free from any stench; that all the bridges and causeways should be thoroughly restored to their former condition, and that they should rebuild the palaces and houses, and within two months they should return to live in them, and he (Cortés) marked out where they were to settle and what part they were to leave clear so that we could settle there.

Let us leave these orders and others which I no longer remember and relate what Guatemoc and his captains told Cortés, that many of the captains and soldiers who went as crews of the launches as well as those who had marched along the causeways fighting, had carried off many of the daughters and wives of the chieftains, and they begged him as a favour that they should be given back to them and Cortés answered that it would be difficult to take the women from these who held them, but they might seek them out and bring them before him and he would see if they had become Christians or preferred to return to their homes to their fathers and husbands, [in the latter case] he would at once order them to be given up, and he gave them [the Mexicans], permission to go and look for them in all three camps, and an order that any soldier who might have any of them should at once give them up, if the Indian women of their free will wished to go back. Many chieftains went in search of the women from house to house and they were so persistent in their search that they found them, but there were many women who did not wish to go either with their fathers or mothers or husbands but to remain with the soldiers with whom they were, and others hid themselves and others said that they did not wish to return to Idolators, and some of them were already pregnant, and so they did not bring more than three of them whom Cortés especially ordered to be given up.

TORTURING GUATEMOC FOR TREASURE
Malicious Graffiti

Let us leave this and tell how [Cortés] at once ordered docks and a fort to be made where the launches could be stationed, and it seems to me that he appointed Pedro de Alvarado to be Alcaide to take charge of it, until Salazar de la Pedrada, who was appointed by his Majesty, came from Castile.

Let me speak of another matter: all were agreed that all the gold and silver and jewels that there were in Mexico should be collected together, and apparently it amounted to very little, for there was a report that Guatemoc had thrown all the rest into the lake four days before he was captured, and in addition to this the Tlaxcalans and the people of Texcoco, Huexotzingo, Cholula and all the rest of our friends who were present at the war, and the Teules who went about in the launches had stolen their share of it, so that the officers the Royal Treasury of the King our Lord alleged and proclaimed that Guatemoc had hidden it [the treasure] and that Cortés was delighted that he would not give it up that he might take it all for himself, and for this reason the Officers of the Royal Treasury determined to torture Guatemoc and the Lord of Tacuba who was his cousin and his great favourite, and certainly Cortés was much distressed that they should torture a Prince like Guatemoc for greed of gold, for they had already made many inquiries about it [the treasure] and all the Mayordomos of Guatemoc said that there was no more than the King's officers already had in their possession, which amounted to three hundred and eighty thousand gold pesos, which had already been melted and cast in bars, and from that was taken the Royal fifth, and another fifth for Cortés. When the conquistadores who bore Cortés ill will saw how little Gold there was, they told the treasurer Julian de Alderete (for he was called) that they suspected Cortés did not want Guatemoc or his captains to be captured or tortured, in order to keep the gold for himself, so, to avoid their imputing anything to Cortés about this matter and as he could not prevent it, they tortured (Guatemoc) by burning his feet with oil, and they did the same thing to the Lord of Tacuba, and what they confessed was that, four days before, they had thrown into the lake both the gold as well as the cannon and muskets which they had captured from us when they drove us out of Mexico, and when this last time, they defeated Cortés. They went to the place which Guatemoc pointed out as the spot where he had thrown it [the treasure], and good swimmers went in, but they found nothing at all.

What I myself saw was that we went with Guatemoc to the houses in which he used to live where there was a sort of reservoir of water, and from that tank we took out a golden sun, like the one Montezuma gave us and many jewels and pieces of little value which belonged to Guatemoc himself.

The Lord of Tacuba said that he had in some of his houses in Tacuba, about four leagues distant, certain objects of gold, and if we would take him there he would tell us where they were buried and would give them to us; so Pedro de Alvarado and six soldiers went and I went in his company. When we arrived the cacique said that it was so as to be killed on the road that he had told that story, and we were to kill him, for he possessed neither gold nor jewels, so we returned without them. Matters remained in this state, and we obtained no more gold to melt down. The truth is that the treasure of Montezuma which Guatemoc took possession of and held after his death, did not contain many jewels or ornaments of gold, for all [the best] had been especially selected to form the offering we made to His Majesty, and because it comprised many jewels of various shapes and different workmanship, all so excellent, if I should stop to describe each piece and its workmanship by itself it would be very tedious and I will omit the account from this story, but I assert that it was worth twice as much as the fifth which was taken out for His Majesty, and for Cortés, all of this we sent to our Lord the Emperor by Alonzo de Avila, who at that time came from the Island of

Santo Domingo, and Antonio de Quiñoes went in company with him to Castile, and further on I will relate how and in what way and when [this took place].

Let us stop talking about this and again state that in the lake where they said that Guatemoc had thrown the gold, I and other soldiers by diving were always able to fetch out small pieces of little value, which Cortés and the Treasurer Julian de Alderete promptly demanded of us as gold belonging to His Majesty, and they themselves went with us where we had taken it out, and took with them good swimmers and succeeded in getting out a matter of eighty or ninety pesos in small strings (of beads) and ducks and little dogs and pendants and small necklaces and other things of no value, for so one can express it considering the earlier report of what they had thrown into the lake.

Let us stop talking about it and relate how all of us captains and soldiers were somewhat thoughtful when we saw how little gold there was and how poor and unjust were our shares, and the Fraile de la Merced, Pedro de Alvarado, Cristóbal de Olid and other captains said to Cortés that as there was so little gold the [entire] share belonging to all of us should be given to and divided among those who were maimed and lame, blind, one eyed or deaf, and others who were crippled and had pains in their stomachs, and others who had been burned by the powder, and all those who were ill from pains in their sides, that to them all the gold should be given for to such like it would be right to give it, and all the rest of us who were fairly sound would look upon it as a good thing. This they said to Cortés after due consideration, believing that he would give us more than the [our] shares for there was a strong suspicion that he had it [gold] hidden away. What Cortés answered was that he would take care that we came out right, and would find means to attain that end. As all of us captains and soldiers wished to see what would fall to our share, we were in a hurry for the account to be issued, and a declaration made how many pesos would result for each of us, and after they had apportioned it they said that there fell to the horsemen eighty pesos and to a crossbowman, musketeer and shield-bearer sixty or fifty pesos, I do not remember well which, and when those shares were made known to us not a single soldier wanted to accept them. Then we grumbled against Cortés and they said that he had seized and hidden it, and the Treasurer Alderete in order to exculpate himself from our accusations, answered that he could do no more, for Cortés had taken another fifth (equal to that of His Majesty) from the heap for himself, and in repayment of the great cost of the horses that had died, moreover many pieces of gold which we ought to have sent to His Majesty had not been placed on the heap, and we had better take Cortés to task and not him. As in all three camps and in the launches there were soldiers who had been friends and comrades of Diego Velásquez the Governor of Cuba, [especially] among those who had come with Narvaez, who bore no goodwill towards Cortés but hated him, when they saw in the division of the gold that he did not give them the shares they desired, they would not take what he gave them, and said, "How came all the gold to be in the possession of him who held it?" and they were impertinent enough to say that Cortés had hidden it.

While Cortés was in Coyoacan lodging in some palaces which had their walls plastered and white-washed where it was easy to write on them with charcoal and other inks, numerous rather malicious sentences appeared [on them] every morning, some written in prose and others in verse, in the way lampoons are arranged. In some they said that the sun, moon and stars, the sea and land follow their [prescribed] courses, and if at any time they deviate beyond their limits from the plane for which they were created, they revert to their [original] elements, and thus it would be with the ambition of Cortés for power, and he would have to go back to his first condition. Others said he had given us a worse defeat than what we gave to Mexico, and that we were not to call ourselves conquerors of New Spain but the conquered of Hernando Cortés. Others said that a general's share had not satisfied him, but a king's share, not counting other profits, and others said how sad is my spirit until Cortés gives back all the gold that he has taken and hidden; and others said that Diego Velásquez spent his fortune and discovered all the North Coast as far as Panuco, and Cortés came to have the benefit of it and rose in revolt with the land and the gold and other things of a similar nature and even used expressions that cannot be put into this story. When Cortés came out of his quarters of a morning and read them, as they were both in verse and in prose and in very elegant style and rhyme, each sentence and couplet with pointed meaning, and at last got in its reproof, and not as simply as I have here stated, and as Cortés was something of a poet [himself] and took a pride in giving answers tending to the praise of his great and noteworthy deeds and belittling those of Diego Velásquez, Grijalva and Francisco Hernández de Córdova, and as he had taken Narvaez prisoner, he also answered by good rhymes much to the point. In all this writing the couplets and mottoes that they scored up became each day more impudent until Cortés wrote up "a blank wall is the paper of fools" and there appeared written further on "even of wise men and of Truths and His Majesty would soon know it." Cortés knew well that those who had written it were a certain Tirado, a friend of Diego Velásquez, who was [afterwards] son-in-law of Ramires the Elder and lived in Puebla, and one Villalobos who went to Castile, and another named Manzilla and several more who willingly aided in order that Cortés should feel to the full that they were thwarting him.

Cortés was enraged and said publicly that they should not write up malicious things, and that he would punish the shameless villains.

Let us leave this affair [and say] how there were many debts among us, some of us owed for crossbows fifty or sixty pesos, and others fifty for a sword, and in like manner all the things we had bought were dear; then there was a surgeon named Maestre Juan who tended some bad wounds and charged excessive prices for his cures, also a half quack named Múrcia who was an apothecary and barber who also doctored us, and thirty other traps and cheatings for which payment was demanded out of the shares that we were given.

The remedy that Cortés provided was the appointment of two trust-worthy persons who understood business and what each article that we had taken on credit was worth, so that they might be valued, and these valuers were named Santa Clara, a very honourable man, and another called something de Llerena also an honourable man; and it was ordered that the value they placed on the things that had been sold to us and the cures the surgeons had made should be accepted, and that if we did not possess the money they should wait for it for two years.

Another thing was also done; to all the gold that was melted down they added three carats more than its standard weight [that is, they debased the gold one-eighth] so as to help in the payments, and also because at that time ships and traders had come to Villa Rica, and they believed that in putting in the three carats they were helping us, [that is] the land and the conquistadores, but it did not help us in any way, on the contrary it was to our prejudice, for with the object of making a profit corresponding to the three carats, the merchants charged five carats more on the merchandise and articles they had for sale, and in this way the gold of the three carats was current for five or six years more, and for this reason the gold of the three carats was called Tepusque which means in the language of the Indians, copper, and we still have a way of saying when we mention any persons who are distinguished or meritorious. "Senor Don so and so of such a name, Juan, Martin or Alonso, but of other persons who are not of the same quality when we mention their names, so as to make a difference between the one and the other we say 'So and so of such a name Tepusque.'"

To go back to my story, considering that it was not just that the gold should be current in this way, information was sent to His Majesty in order to have the additional three carats removed and barred from currency in New Spain, and His Majesty was pleased to order that it should no longer be current and whatever had to be paid in export or import duties or fines to the Treasury should be paid in that base gold until it was used up and was no longer remembered, and in this way it was all taken to Castile and was there melted down and restored to the proper standard.

I wish to relate that at the time when this happened they hanged two Silversmiths who forged the royal carat marks and had put in much more pure copper. I have loitered on the way to tell these old stories, and have turned aside from my story, let us get back to it, and [I will relate] how when Cortés saw that many of the soldiers were insolent in demanding larger shares, saying that he had taken all for himself and had stolen it, and begged him to lend them money, he determined to free himself from this hold [that they had] over him and to send out and make settlements in all the provinces which he thought it would be advisable to settle. He ordered Gonzalo de Sandoval to go and settle at Tustepec and to chastise some Mexican garrisons which at the time we were driven out of Mexico had killed seventy-eight men and six Spanish women belonging to the followers of Narvaez, who had remained there to settle in a small town which they had called Medellin, and then to go on to Coatzacoalcos and form a settlement at that port. He also ordered a certain Pineda and Vicente Lopez to go and conquer the province of Panuco; and he ordered Rodrigo Rangel to stay in Villa Rica, as I have already stated, and Pedro de Ircio in his company, and [sent] Juan Álvarez the younger to Colima and a certain Villafuerte to Zacatula and Cristóbal de Olid to Michoacan. By this time Cristóbal de Olid was already married to a Portuguese lady named Doña Felipa de Arauz or Zarauz, who had come. . . . He also sent Francisco de Orozco to settle in Oaxaca, for at the time when we had captured Mexico, as it became known in all those provinces that I have mentioned that Mexico was destroyed, their caciques and Lords could not believe it, and as they were far off they sent chieftains to congratulate Cortés on his victories, and yield themselves as vassals to His Majesty, and to see if it were true that a place that was as dreaded among them as was Mexico had been levelled to the ground. They all brought great presents of gold which they gave to Cortés, and they even brought their small children with them and showed them Mexico and explained it to them much as we might say "Here stood Troy."

Let us leave this and make some remarks about what is well should be made clear; many interested readers have asked me what is the reason that the true conquistadores who won New Spain and the great and strong City of Mexico, did not remain to settle in it, but went to other provinces. I say that they have every reason and justification to ask it, I wish to state the cause of it, and it is this which I [now] relate; In the tribute books of Montezuma we saw whence they brought him tribute of gold and where there were mines and cacao, and garments of [cotton] cloth, and we wished to go to those places whence, we saw from the books and the accounts contained in them, they brought these things to Montezuma, all the more when we saw a captain so eminent and such a friend of Cortés as Sandoval start out from Mexico, and also because we observed that in the towns of the neighbourhood of Mexico they had neither gold, nor mines nor cotton, only much maize and maguey plantations from which they obtained their wine. On this account we considered it to be poor land and went off to settle in other provinces, and we were all thoroughly deceived.

I remember that when I went to ask Cortés to give me leave to go with Sandoval he said to me "On my conscience Señor Bernal Diaz del Castillo you are making a mistake, I would prefer your staying here with me, but if it is your wish to go with your friend Sandoval, go and good luck to you. I shall always consider your wishes but I know well that you will repent of having left me."

Let me turn back to the division of the gold and say that [finally] it all fell to the share of the king's officials on account of the slaves that had been sold by auction.

I do not wish to call to mind here the number of horsemen, musketeers, crossbowmen, and soldiers, nor on what day of what month Cortés despatched the captains mentioned by me, who went to settle in the provinces named by me above, for it would be a long story, except to state it took place a few days after the taking of Mexico and the Capture of Guatemoc, and two months later on Cortés sent other captains to other provinces.

Let us now cease to speak of Cortés and say that at the same time there arrived at the port of Villa Rica, with two ships, the Veedor of the smelting works which had been established in the Island of Santo Domingo, others said that he was Alcayde of the fortress in that Island, and he brought writs, and letters patent from Don Juan Rodrigo de Fonseca, Bishop of Burgos and Archbishop of Rosano, sent in His Majesty's name, to the effect that Cristóbal de Tápia should be governor of New Spain, and what happened about it I will go on to relate.

Let us leave this conversation and the promises which Narvaez made to Cortés, and I will relate how at that time Cortés went to settle the great City of Mexico, and he allotted the sites for the churches and monasteries and royal houses and plazas, and to all the settlers he gave lots, and let us not waste more time on the description of the way in which it is now built up, and according to the reports of many people who have been in many parts of Christendom, there had never been in the world another more populous or greater city of better houses inhabited by gentlemen, considering its character and the time at which it was settled (let it be understood) by the poor conquistadores. While Cortés, as I have stated, was occupied in the laying out of the city, and was somewhat recovered from his fatigue, they brought him letters from Panuco [to say] that the whole province had risen in revolt, and they were very belligerent warriors for they had killed many of the soldiers whom he had sent to make settlements, and he must without delay send all the assistance he could. Cortés promptly decided to go in person, for although he might have wished to send some of our other captains, there were none of them in Mexico, for, as I have stated, we had all of us gone to other provinces. He took all the soldiers he was able to collect, and horsemen, crossbowmen and musketeers, for there had already arrived in Mexico many men from among those whom the Veedor Tápia had brought with him, and others were there who had accompanied Vásquez de Ayllon to Florida, and others who by that time had come from the Islands.

Leaving a good garrison in Mexico with Diego de Soto a native of Toro as captain, Cortés set out from Mexico. At that time there were no horseshoes, or only a very few for the many horses he was taking with him, for there were over one hundred and thirty persons on horseback, and two hundred and fifty soldiers in all including musketeers and crossbowmen and the horsemen. He also took with him ten thousand Mexicans. At that time Cristóbal de Olid had already returned from Michoacan for he had established peace there, and he brought with him many Caciques and the son of Caçonçi, for so he was called, who was the Lord in chief of all those provinces, and he brought much low-grade gold, which was mixed with copper and silver. [Blotted out in the original: "and Cortés decided that from the low-grade silver horseshoes and nails should be made.—G. G."]

Cortés disbursed on that expedition to Panuco, a great quantity of pesos de oro and he afterwards demanded that His Majesty should repay him that expense, and the officials of His Majesty's treasury did not wish to receive the account nor to pay any of it, for they said that if he made that expedition and [incurred] that expense it was because he wished to gain possession of that province so that Don Francisco de Garay who was coming to conquer it should not have it, for the news had already been received that they were coming from the Island of Jamaica with a great fleet.

To go back to my story, I will relate how Cortés arrived with all his army at the province of Panuco and found the people at war, and he sent many times to summon them to peace and they would not come. He had many warlike encounters with them and in two battles in which they stood up to him, they killed three soldiers and wounded more than thirty and killed four horses, and many others were wounded, and more than two hundred of the Mexicans died, without counting another three hundred that were wounded. The Huastecs ["Guastecas" in the text], for so they call the Indians of these provinces, numbered over fifty thousand men when they gave battle to Cortés, but by the will of God they were defeated, and all the field where this battle took place, was closely strewn with dead and many wounded from among the natives of that province, so that they never rallied on that occasion to attack again.

Cortés remained for eight days in a town where those conflicts took place called [here the author has left a blank space—G. G.] . . . in order to cure the wounded and bury the dead, and supplies were plentiful.

In order to send once more and call the people to peace he despatched two Caciques, persons of importance from among those who had been taken prisoners in the battles and through Doña Marina and Gerónimo de Aguilar whom Cortés always took with him, he made them a speech and asked them, how could all the people of those provinces hope to avoid submitting themselves as vassals of His Majesty, when they had seen and had heard the news, how with all the power of Mexico and its strength in warriors, the city had been destroyed and razed to the ground, and [he told them] to make peace promptly, and to have no fear, for he pardoned them for the deaths that had taken place, and he spoke these words to them with kindness, but he also used threats. As [the Indians] were cowed and many had been killed in the last battle, and they saw their towns laid waste by fire, they made peace, and all brought jewels of gold, although they were of little value, and presented them to Cortés who received them in peace with affection and caresses.

From this place Cortés went with half his army to a river called Chila [Chila is to the north of the Río Panuco, about nineteen miles west of Tampico] about five leagues from the sea, and he again sent messengers to all the towns on the other side of the river to summon them to make peace and they would not come, for, made fierce by the blood of the numerous soldiers killed two years earlier, (who came under the captains whom Garay had sent to settle on that river, as I have already stated in the chapter which treats of that subject,) they thought they could do the same with our army. As they were posted by three great lagoons and rivers and swamps which served them as a strong fortress, the reply they made was to slay two of the messengers whom Cortés had sent to treat for peace, and to make prisoners of the others. Cortés waited some days to see if they would change from their evil purpose, and as they did not come, he sent for all the canoes that could be found in the river, and with them and some barges, made from the timbers of the old ships which had belonged to the captain whom Garay had sent and [the Indians] had killed, he sent one hundred and fifty soldiers, most of them musketeers and crossbowmen, across to the other side of the river by night, and fifty cavalry in canoes tied together two by two, so that they crossed over in a matter of . . . and as the natives of those provinces keep watch over the passes and rivers, when they saw them, they allowed them to pass with the intention of killing them, and they were waiting for them on the other side.

If many Huastec Indians, for so they are called, had come together in the first battles that they had fought against Cortés, far greater numbers had been massed on this occasion, and they came on like rabid lions to fall on our men, and on the first encounter they killed two soldiers and wounded over thirty, and they also killed three horses and wounded fifteen others and many of the Mexicans, but our men fell on them so quickly that they could not hold the field and they were soon put to flight leaving behind a great number of dead and wounded. When this battle was over our men went to sleep at a pueblo from which the inhabitants had fled, and they camped there after posting sentinels, watchmen, patrols and spies, and food for supper was not wanting. As soon as the dawn came, when walking through the pueblo [our men] saw hanging up in a Cue and oratory of the Idols, many clothes and faces that had been flayed off and cured like glove leather, with the beards and hair [still adhering], which had belonged to the soldiers of the captains sent by Garay to make a settlement on the Rio Panuco who had been killed, and many of them were recognised by our soldiers who said that they were their friends, and the hearts of all were broken with grief at seeing them in this state, and they took them down from where they were and carried them off for burial.

From that pueblo they went on to another place, and, as they knew how very warlike the people of that province were, they always marched with great caution and in fighting array so that they should not be taken unawares. It was reported by the scouts that some great squadrons of Indians were lying in ambush so that as soon as our men should dismount and go into the houses they might fall on the horses and on the men. As they had been found out, the Indians could not do as they intended, but all the same they sallied out very boldly and fought against our men like brave warriors and for more than half an hour the horsemen, musketeers, crossbowmen and the Mexican Indians, could not force them to retreat or drive them off. They killed two horses and wounded seven others and they also wounded fifteen soldiers of whom three died of their wounds.

There was one thing remarkable about these Indians, that even when they were beaten, they turned and rallied to fight three times, a thing one has seldom seen among these people. When they saw that our people were wounding and killing them they fled for refuge to a rapid and flowing river, and the horsemen and light infantry went in pursuit and wounded many of them, while others decided to scour the country and go to other pueblos which were deserted, and in them they found many large jars of the wine of the country stored underground in places like cellars. They spent five days among these villages scouring the country, and as all of these were deserted and abandoned by their inhabitants, they returned to the river Achile [Chila?]. Cortés again sent to summon all the pueblos on the other side of the river which were still at war to make peace, and, as our troops had already killed many of them, the Indians feared our falling on them again, and for this reason they sent to say that they would come within four days, that they were seeking jewels of gold to present to him. Cortés waited the four days when they said that they would come, and as they did not come then, he promptly ordered [an attack to be made] on a very large pueblo situated near a lagoon, which was very strong on account of its swamps and rivers, . . . they were to cross the lagoon on a dark and drizzling night in numerous canoes which he had promptly ordered to be collected and tied together two by two and in other single ones, and on well-made rafts [steering] towards a part of the pueblo where they could neither be seen nor heard from the town itself, and many of our Mexican allies crossed without being seen . . . and fell on the pueblo and destroyed it, and looted it and gained much spoil, and our allies carried off all the property that the natives possessed. When the Indians saw this, within five days nearly all the pueblos in the neighbourhood made peace, except some pueblos which were so far out of the way that our people were not able to go to them at that time.

Not to waste more words on this story I will omit telling of many things that happened and will only say that Cortés then founded a town with one hundred and twenty settlers, and among these he left twenty-seven horsemen and thirty-six musketeers and crossbowmen so that they numbered one hundred and twenty in all. This town was named Santistevan del Puerto and stands about a league from Chila. To the settlers who peopled that town he apportioned and gave in encomienda all the pueblos which had made peace, and he left as Captain of them and his representative one Pedro Vallejo.

While Cortés was in that town ready to start for Mexico, he learnt for certain that three pueblos which were at the head of the rebellion of that province and had been concerned in the death of many Spaniards, were on the move again, although they had given their fealty to His Majesty and made peace and they were persuading and luring the other pueblos in the neighbourhood and saying that after Cortés had returned to Mexico with the horsemen and soldiers, some day or night they would fall upon the settlers who remained behind and would have a good feast off them. When Cortés knew the whole truth, he ordered their houses to be completely destroyed by fire, but they soon made a new settlement.

About the same time that Cortés returned to Mexico from his expedition to Panuco, and occupied himself with the peopling and rebuilding of the city, Alonzo de Ávila already often mentioned by me in former chapters, had returned from the island of Santo Domingo and reported on the subjects he had been sent to negotiate with the Royal Audiencia and the Geronimite Friars who were the Governors of all the Islands, and the message he brought was that they gave us authority to conquer the whole of New Spain and to brand slaves according to the instructions that were sent, and to divide and make allotments of the Indians as was customary in the Islands of Española, Cuba and Jamaica ["Xamayca" in the text].

This permission which they gave was to be valid up to the time that His Majesty was informed of it, or should be pleased to send other orders, and the Geronimite Friars themselves at once wrote him an account of this and sent a ship posthaste to Castile, and at that time His Majesty who was still a youth, was in Flanders, and there he learnt what the Geronimite Friars were sending him.

They rendered no account of this to the Bishop of Burgos, for they were aware that he, in his position of President [of the Council] of the Indies, was very hostile to us, nor would they consult with him on many other matters of importance, for they were very ill pleased with his proceedings.

Let us leave this matter of the Bishop and repeat that as Cortés looked on Alonzo de Ávila as a very daring person, and was not on very good terms with him, he always wished to keep him at a distance, for truly if when Cristóbal de Tápia came with the commissions Alonzo de Ávila had been in Mexico (he was in the Island of Santo Domingo at the time) as he was a follower of the Bishop of Burgos and had been his servant, and Tápia had brought letters for him, he would have been a great opponent to Cortés and his affairs. For this reason Cortés always tried to keep him far from his person, and when he returned from this voyage he chose that occasion to allot Cuautitlan ["Gualtitan" in the text] to him so as to content and please him, and gave him certain pesos de oro, and with the fair words and promises, as well as the allotment of the town already mentioned which was a very good one and very profitable, he made so firm a friend and follower of him that he sent him to Castile, and with him his captain of the Guard named Antonio de Quiñones, and these two went as proctors of New Spain and of Cortés, and they took two ships and carried with them fifty eight thousand Castellanos [an ancient Spanish coin] in bars of gold. They also took with them what we called the private treasure of the great Montezuma which Guatemoc had in his keeping, and indeed it was a fine present for our great Caesar, for it contained many very rich jewels and some of the pearls were the size of filberts, and there were many chalchihuites which are fine stones like emeralds, and there was even one as broad as the palm of a hand, and many others so numerous that, so as to avoid delay, I will not stop to describe them or call them to mind. We also sent some pieces of the bones of giants which were found in a Cue or Oratory in Coyoacan, similar to those other great bones which were given to us in Tlaxcala which we had sent on the first occasion, and these were even larger. They also took three tigers [jaguars] and other things that I cannot now call to mind.

Zapotec Fury

When Gonzalo de Sandoval arrived at a pueblo named Tuxtepec all the province made peace except some Mexicans who were concerned in the deaths of sixty Spanish men and women from Castile who had remained behind ill in that pueblo when Narvaez came, and that was the time when we were defeated in Mexico, and then they [the Mexicans] slew them in this same pueblo. About two months after the people I have spoken about had been killed, I went [there] with Sandoval and I lodged in a small tower which had been a temple with Idols and which they [the Spaniards] had fortified when they were attacked, and there they were surrounded and perished of hunger and thirst and wounds. I mention that I lodged in that little tower because there were many mosquitoes in that pueblo of Tustepeque in the daytime, and as the tower was very lofty and exposed to the breeze there were not so many [mosquitoes] there as there were down below, and moreover it was near Sandoval's quarters.

To go back to our story, Sandoval endeavoured to seize the Mexican Captains who had attacked and killed them [the Spaniards] and he captured the chief of them and placed him on trial and for sentence ordered him to be burned, and there were many others who deserved the penalty of death as much as he did, but he let it pass and the one death paid for all.

When this was over he sent to summon to peace some pueblos of the Zapotecs, (another province about ten leagues distant from this town of Tuxtepec,) and they would not come, so he sent a Captain to bring them to peace. This was a man named Briones, often mentioned by me before, who was Captain of a sloop, and a good soldier in Italy according to his own account, and Sandoval gave him over one hundred soldiers, among them thirty musketeers and crossbowmen, and over a hundred allies from the pueblos which had made peace.

As Briones went on his way with his soldiers in good order, it seems that the Zapotecs were aware of his coming against their pueblos and they arranged an ambush on the road, which caused them [the Spaniards] to turn back in a hurry, rolling down some steep inclines, and more than a third of his soldiers were wounded and one of them died of his wounds. These hills where the Zapotecs live are so steep and difficult that horses cannot go among them, and the soldiers had to march on foot, one by one, in and out, along narrow paths, and there was always mist and dew and the paths were slippery. The Zapotecs were armed with very long lances, longer than ours are, with a fathom of cutting edge of stone knives which cut better than our swords, and with shields which cover the whole body, and many arrows, javelins and stones, and the natives were very daring and wonderfully lithe, and with a whistle or cry which they give among those hills the voice resounds and reverberates for a considerable time, as we should say like echoes.

So the Captain Briones returned with his men wounded and one of them dead, and he himself came back with an arrow wound.

The pueblo where he was defeated is called Tiltepec [San Miguel Tiltepec, District of Ixtlan, Northern Oaxaca, or Tiltepec, District of Choapam, Northern Oaxaca—"Teltepeque" in the text] and after it was brought to peace it was given in encomienda to a soldier named Ojeda the one eyed, who now lives in the town of Santo Alfonso. When Briones returned to make his report to Sandoval of what had happened, and told him what great warriors they [the Zapotecs] were, as Sandoval was in good spirits and Briones posed as being very valiant and was wont to tell how in Italy he had killed and wounded and cleft the heads and trunks of men, said Sandoval: "It seems to me Señor Capitan that these lands are different from those where you [formerly] went soldiering" and Briones, half angry, replied and said that he swore to the truth of his statements and that he would rather fight against cannon and great armies of enemies whether of Turks or Moors than against those Zapotecs and he gave reasons for it, that appeared acceptable. Still Sandoval told him he wished he had not sent him, since he was thus defeated, for he believed that he would have shown more valour, as he boasted he had done in Italy.

Let us leave this expedition which did more harm than good, and say how this same Gonzalo de Sandoval sent to summon to peace another province, which was called Xaltepec [Xaltepec or Jaltepec in the District of Choapam—"Xaltepeque" in the text]. These people were also Zapotecs and they border on other pueblos called those of the Mijes ["Minxes" in the text], a very active and warlike people who had disputes with the people of Xaltepec, the same who I say were now summoned. As many as twenty Caciques and chieftains made peace and brought a present of gold in the form of jewels of various workmanship and ten small tubes of gold in grains which they had just then extracted from the mines.

The Chieftains came clothed in very long cotton clothes which reached to the feet worked with much embroidery and they were, so to say, like Moorish burnooses. When they came before Sandoval they offered it [their present] with great reverence and he received it with pleasure, and ordered them to be given beads of Castile, and paid them honour and made much of them. They asked Sandoval to give them some Teules, for so they call the Spaniards in their language, to go with them against the pueblos of their enemies the Mijes who made war on them. As Sandoval could spare no soldiers at that time, to give them the help they asked for, because those who had gone with Briones were all wounded and others were sick and four were dead, for the country was very hot and unhealthy, he told them in pleasant phrases that he would send to Mexico to tell Malinche (for so they called Cortés) to send plenty of Teules, and that they must restrain themselves until they arrived, and meanwhile that ten of his companions would accompany them to examine the passes and the country so that they could go and make war against their enemies the Mijes. Sandoval only said this in order that we could go and see the pueblos and the mines where they extracted the gold they had brought, and in this way he dismissed all but three of them whom he ordered to stay and go with us.

Pedro de Alvarado Attacks in Guatemala

We must go back a little to recount the setting out of Pedro de Alvarado to found Tututepec, it was as Follows:—As soon as the City of Mexico was captured and it was known in all the districts and provinces that such a strong city had been razed to the ground, they sent to congratulate Cortés on his victory and to offer themselves as Vassals of His Majesty, and among the many great pueblos that came at that time there was one called Tehuantepec ["Teguantepeque" in the text] of the Zapotecs, and they brought a present of gold to Cortés and told him that there were other pueblos in their province somewhat remote named Tututepec which were their inveterate enemies and had come to make war on them because the people of Tehuantepec had given their fealty to His Majesty; that these towns were situated on the South Coast and that the people were very rich in gold in the form of jewels as well as in mines, and they begged Cortés with much importunity to give them horsemen, musketeers and crossbowmen to go against their enemies.

Cortés spoke to them very lovingly and told them that he wished to send Tonatio with them, for so they called Pedro de Alvarado, and he promptly gave him over one hundred and eighty soldiers, among them thirty-five horsemen, and instructions to demand another twenty soldiers, chiefly crossbowmen, from Francisco de Orozco who was captain of the province of Oaxaca ["Guaxaca" in the text], if that province were peaceable.

Carrying out his orders he [Alvarado] arranged his departure and set out from Mexico in the year [fifteen hundred and] twenty-two, and Cortés directed him to go and inspect certain rocky hills on the way, which were called Ulamo, where [the people] were said to be in revolt, but he found them all peaceful and well disposed at that time.

He delayed more than forty days before reaching Tututepec, and the Lord of the pueblo and other chieftains when they knew that he was approaching near to their pueblo went out to receive him peaceably, and took him off to lodge in the most thickly peopled part of the pueblo where the Cacique had his Oratories and his large apartments, and the houses were very close one to the other, and they were made of straw, for in that province they have no azoteas as it is a very hot country.

Alvarado took the advice of his Captains and soldiers that it was not a good thing to lodge in those houses so near one to the other, for if they were set on fire they could not protect themselves, and they agreed to go to the end of the pueblo. As soon as they were lodged the Cacique brought him very great presents of gold, and plenty to eat, and every day they stayed there he brought him very rich presents of gold.

As Alvarado saw that they possessed so much gold he ordered them to make some stirrups of fine gold like others which he gave them as patterns and they made and brought them to him. A few days later, he took the Cacique prisoner, because the people of Tehuantepec told Pedro de Alvarado that all that province intended to make war on him, and that when they lodged him among those houses where the Idols and chambers stood that it was in order to set fire to them, so that all of them [the Spaniards] should perish; and for this reason he made him prisoner. Other Spaniards of good faith and worthy of credence said that it was in order to extort much gold [from him] without bringing him to trial that he died in prison, and this is now accepted as certain, that one way or the other, that Cacique gave to Pedro de Alvarado over thirty thousand pesos, and he died from anger and from his imprisonment, and the Caciqueship went to his son, and he [Alvarado] got from him more gold than from his father. Then he sent to visit the pueblos in the neighbourhood and distributed them among the settlers and founded a town to which was given the name of Segura, because most of the settlers who peopled it had been formerly inhabitants of Segura de la Frontera, which was Tepeaca.

When this was accomplished and he had collected together a good sum in pesos de oro he took it to Mexico to give to Cortés.

It is also said that Cortés himself wrote to him that he should bring with him all the gold he was able to collect, in order to send it to His Majesty, because the Frenchmen had stolen all that he had sent by Alonzo de Ávila and Quiñones, and that he should give no share of it to any one of the soldiers who were in his company.

When Alvarado was already prepared to start for Mexico certain soldiers most of them musketeers and crossbowmen, formed a conspiracy to kill Pedro de Alvarado and his brothers on the following day, because he was carrying off the gold without giving them their share, although they had begged for it many times, but he would not give it up, also because he did not give them good assignments of Indians. If a soldier named Trebejo who was in the conspiracy had not revealed the plot to him, they would have attacked them the following night. When Alvarado knew about it, (and they told him about the hour of vespers) he went out hunting on horseback near some huts, and some of those who were in the plot went on horseback in his company. Then to deceive them he said "Señores I have got such a stitch in my side, let us go back to our quarters and call me a barber to bleed me."

As soon as he got back he sent to summon his brothers Jorge, Gonzalo and Gómez, all Alvarados, and the Alcaldes and Aguazils, and they seized those who were in the plot and according to verdict they hanged two of them, one named something de Salamanca a native of the county [of Salamanca], who had been a pilot, and the other named Bernaldino the Levantine, and with these two hangings he pacified the others, and he set off at once for Mexico with all the gold, and left the town settled. When the inhabitants who remained in the town saw that the allotments that had been given them were no good and that the country was unhealthy and very hot, and many of them were ill, and the servants and slaves they had brought with them had died, and that there were many bats and mosquitoes and even bedbugs, and above all that Alvarado had not divided the gold among them but had taken it with him, they decided to avoid wrangling and to abandon the settlement. Many of them went to Mexico, others to Oaxaca and they scattered over other parts.

When Cortés heard of this he sent to make enquiry about it, and he found out that the abandonment was agreed upon by the Alcades and Magistrates in Cabildo, and those who were concerned in it were condemned to death, and they appealed, and the punishment was [reduced to] banishment. This is what happened in the matter of Tututepec which was never afterwards peopled because it was unhealthy although the land was rich. When the natives of that country saw that the place was abandoned and what Alvarado had done was without reason or justice, they rebelled again, and Pedro de Alvarado returned to them and summoned them to make peace and without need to attack them they became peaceful.

Let us leave this and say that when Cortés had got together over eighty thousand pesos de oro to send to His Majesty together with the Phœnix tax he had invented, news came at that time that Francisco de Garay had arrived at Panuco with a great fleet, and what was done about it I will go on to relate.

Cortés always had lofty thoughts and in his ambition to command and rule wished in everything to copy Alexander of Macedon, and as he always had excellent Captains and accomplished soldiers about him, after he had established the great cities of Mexico, Oaxaca, Zacatula, Colima, la Vera Cruz, Panuco and Coatzacoalcos, as he had received news that in the Province of Guatemala there were strong towns with large populations, and that there were mines there, he determined to send Pedro de Alvarado to conquer and settle it; for although Cortés himself had already sent to that province to beg the people to come in peaceably, they would not come. So he gave to Alvarado for that expedition over three hundred soldiers and among them one hundred and twenty musketeers and crossbowmen. Moreover, he gave him one hundred and thirty-five horsemen and four cannon and much powder, and a gunner named something de Usagre and over two hundred Tlaxcalans and Cholulans, who went as auxiliaries. Then he gave him [Alvarado] his instructions, charging him to endeavour with the greatest care to bring the people to peace without making war on them, and to preach matters concerning our holy faith by means of certain interpreters and ecclesiastics whom he took with him, and not to permit sacrifices nor sodomy nor the robbing of one another; and that when he met with prisons and cages in which it was the custom to keep Indians confined in order to fatten them up for food, he should break them down, and liberate the captives from the prisons, and with kindness and goodwill he should bring the people to render obedience to His Majesty, and in all respects should treat them well.

Then after Pedro de Alvarado had said good-bye to Cortés and all the gentlemen who were his friends in Mexico, they took leave of one another and he set out from that city on the thirteenth day of the month of November in the year fifteen hundred and twenty-three.

Cortés ordered him to go by certain rocky hills in the province of Tehuantepec, which were near his road, where the people were in revolt. He brought [the inhabitants of] these rocky hills to peace. The hill was known as the Peñol de Guelamo because it was then in the encomienda of a soldier named Guelamo.

From thence he went to Tehuantepec, a large pueblo of the Zapotecs, where they received him very well for they were at peace, and they had already gone from that town (as I have stated in a former chapter which tells about it) to Mexico and given their fealty to His Majesty and had seen Cortés and moreover had taken him a good present of gold.

From Tehuantepec he [Alvarado] went to the province of Soconusco, which at that time was thickly peopled by more than fifteen thousand inhabitants [the word is *vecinos*, which here applied to natives probably means households, not individuals]; they also received him peaceably and gave him a present of gold and surrendered themselves as vassals to His Majesty. From Soconusco he arrived near to another group of villages named Zapotitlan ["Çapotitan" in the text (Zapote in the District of Soconusco, State of Chiapas?)], and on the road at a bridge over a river where there was a bad pass, he came across many squadrons of warriors who were waiting for him to prevent his passage, and he fought a battle with them in which they killed a horse and wounded many soldiers and two of them died of their wounds. So numerous were the Indians who had joined together against Alvarado, not only from Zapotitlan but from other towns in the neighbourhood, that in spite of the number that they [the Spaniards] wounded they were not able to drive them off. Three times they attacked Alvarado and it pleased Our Lord that he conquered them and they made peace.

From Zapotitlan the road led to a strong pueblo named Quetzalte-nango, and before reaching it he had other encounters with the natives of that pueblo and with others from a neighbouring pueblo called Utatlan ["Utlatan" in the text] which was the capital of certain pueblos which in their turn are in the neighbourhood of Quetzaltenango, and they wounded some soldiers and killed three horses, although Pedro de Alvarado and his people killed and wounded many of the Indians. Then there was a bad ascent for more than a league and a half through a defile. With the musketeers and crossbowmen and all his soldiers in good order he began the ascent, and at the top of the pass he found a fat Indian woman who was a witch, and a dog (one of those they breed because they are good to eat and do not know how to bark) that was sacrificed. Further on he came upon a vast number of warriors who were laying in wait for him, and they began to surround him; as the track was bad and among moun-tains the horsemen were not able to gallop or turn swiftly nor to make use of their mounts, but the musketeers and crossbowmen and soldiers with sword and shield fought stoutly with them hand to hand, and they went on fighting from the hill and pass downwards until they reached some barrancas where they had another but not very severe skirmish with other squadrons of warriors which were waiting for them in those bar-rancas. This was owing to a stratagem which they had arranged among themselves in this manner: that as Pedro de Alvarado advanced fighting, they should pretend to retreat, and as he would go on pursuing them to where over six thousand warriors, men from Utatlan and other pueblos subject to them were laying in wait there they intended to kill them (the Spaniards). Pedro de Alvarado and all his soldiers fought with them with the highest courage, and the Indians wounded twenty-six or twenty-seven soldiers and two horses; nevertheless he [Alvarado] put them to flight, but they had not gone far before they rallied with other squadrons and turned to fight again, thinking to defeat Pedro de Alvarado. It was near a spring that they awaited them so as again to come hand to hand, and many of the Indians would lay in wait by twos and threes near to a horse and try by force to pull it down, and others caught them by the tail. And here Pedro de Alvarado found himself in great straits, for the enemy were so numerous they were not able to bear up against the squadrons who attacked them from so many directions. Then he and all his men, as soon as they saw that they had either to conquer or die, fearing that they might not defeat the enemy on account of the cramped position in which they found themselves, made a bold attack with the muskets and crossbows and with sturdy sword cuts, and obliged them to draw back somewhat. Then the horsemen were not slow in spearing the enemy and trampling them down and passing through them until they had them routed, so that they did not assemble again for three days. When he [Alvarado] saw that there was no longer any enemy with whom to fight, he remained in the open country foraging and seeking for food, without going to any settlement for two days. Then he went with all his army to the pueblo of Quetzaltenango, and there he learnt that in the past battles they had killed two Captains who were Lords of Utatlan. While he was resting and tending the wounded he received the news that all the forces of those neighbouring pueblos were again marching against him; that a great number had assembled together [blotted out in the original, "more than two Xiquipiles, that is sixteen thousand Indians, for each Xiquipil numbers eight thousand warriors"], and they were coming with the determination to die to the last man or to conquer.

When Pedro de Alvarado knew this he sallied out with his army to a plain, and as the enemy came on with such determination and began to surround the army and to shoot javelins, arrows and stones and [to attack] with lances, and as the ground was level, and the horses were able to gallop in all directions, he charged on the squadrons of the enemy in a way that soon made them turn their backs. Here many soldiers were wounded as well as a horse, and it seems that some Indian Chieftains from that pueblo itself were killed as well as from all that country, so that after the victory those pueblos had a great fear of Alvarado, and the whole of the district agreed to send to him and beg for peace, and they sent him a present of gold of little value to induce him to make peace.

It was fully agreed between all the Caciques of all the pueblos in the province that they should again collect a far greater number of warriors than before, and they ordered their warriors to assemble secretly among the barrancas of that town of Utatlan.

If they sent to ask for peace it was because Pedro de Alvarado and his army were in Quetzaltenango making expeditions and raids and continually bringing in Indian men and women as prisoners, and so as to induce him to go to another pueblo named Utatlan which was stronger and surrounded by barrancas, in order that when they had him inside, in a place where they thought they could get the better of him and his soldiers, they might attack them with their warriors who were already prepared and hidden away for that purpose.

Let us go back to say that when the numerous chieftains came before Pedro de Alvarado with the present, after making obeisance according to their custom, they asked his pardon for the past wars and offered themselves as vassals of His Majesty, and said that as their pueblo was large and in a pleasanter position and was nearer to other townships where they could attend to him better, they begged him to go there with them.

Pedro de Alvarado received it [the present] with great [show of] affection, and did not understand the cunning they were employing, and after alluding again to the evil they had done in making war, he accepted their overture of peace. The next day early he accompanied them with his army to Utatlan ["Vtlatan" in the text] for so the pueblo was called.

When he had made his entry, he saw what a stronghold it was, for it had two gateways, and one of them had twenty-five steps before entering the town, and the other entrance was by a causeway that was very bad and broken in two places, and the houses were close together and the streets narrow, and there were neither women nor children in any part of the town, which was surrounded by barrancas, and no food had been provided except what was bad and [that came] late and the chief-tains were very shifty in their speeches. [Moreover] some Indians from Quetzaltenango warned Pedro de Alvarado that that very night it was intended to burn them all in the town if they remained there and that many squadrons of warriors had been stationed in the barrancas so that as soon as they saw the houses were burning they should join the people of Utatlan and attack them [the Spaniards] some from one side and some from the other and that with the fire and the smoke they would be helpless and would be burned alive.

When Pedro de Alvarado understood the grave danger in which they stood, he quickly ordered his Captains and all his army without delay to get out into the open, and he told them the danger they were in, and when they understood it there was no delay in getting out on to the level part close to some barrancas, for just then they had not time to get [right] out into the open plain from the midst of such dangerous passes.

Throughout this Pedro de Alvarado displayed goodwill towards the Caciques and chieftains of that town and of the other towns in the neigh-bourhood and told them that as the horses were accustomed to go about grazing in the fields for a part of the day, that was the cause of his having come out of the town, as the houses and streets were so crowded. The Caciques were very sorrowful at seeing them depart in this way, and Pedro de Alvarado could no longer tolerate the treason which they had planned in concert with the squadrons that they had assembled, so he ordered the Cacique of the town to be seized and as justly ordered him to be burned, and he gave the lordship to his son. Then he promptly got out on to the level land away from the barrancas and fought the squadrons which had been got ready for the purpose I have mentioned, and after having thus provoked his strength and ill will, they were defeated.

Let us cease talking about this and say how at that time news had reached a large pueblo called Guatemala ["Guatimala" in the text; this is Tecpan-Guatemala, or Iximché, about twenty-three miles northeast of the Lake of Atitlan] of the battles that Pedro de Alvarado had fought since he entered the Province, in all of which he had been victorious, and that at present he was in the land of Utatlan whence he was making expeditions and attacking many pueblos. As the people of Utatlan and their dependent pueblos were enemies of the people of Guatemala [Utatlan was the capital of the Quichés, Guatemala the capital of the Cachiquels], the latter determined to send messengers with a present of gold to Pedro de Alvarado and offer themselves as Vassals to His Majesty and they sent word that if he had any need of their personal services for that war they would come.

Pedro de Alvarado received them with goodwill and gave them many thanks for their offer, and in order to see if what they had told him was true, and because he knew nothing of the country, he sent to ask for two thousand warriors to show him the way, and he did so on account of the many barrancas and bad passes that had been intentionally made in order to impede their passage, so that if it were necessary they [the native warriors] should put them in order, and they could carry the baggage. The people of Guatemala sent them (the warriors) to him with their captains.

Pedro de Alvarado remained in the province of Utatlan seven or eight days, making raids against the rebel pueblos which had given their fealty to His Majesty and after giving it had risen in revolt. They branded many slaves and Indian women, and after the royal fifth was paid the rest were divided among the soldiers. Then he went to the City of Guatemala and was received and entertained by the Caciques of that city, who told him that nearby there were some pueblos on the borders of a lake who were their enemies and made war on them and they held possession of a very strong rocky hill, and that the people of that pueblo although they knew well that they [the Spaniards] were not far off, and that Pedro de Alvarado was with them, did not come to tender their fealty as the other pueblos had done, and they were bad people and of worse habits. The said pueblo was called Atitlan ["Atitan" in the text] and Pedro de Alvarado sent to summon them to come and make peace, and told them that he would treat them well and sent them other smooth messages.

The reply they made was to ill-treat his messengers. Seeing that this availed nothing, he sent other messengers to induce them to make peace, and because he sent three times to ask for peace, and each time they used abusive words [to his messengers], Pedro de Alvarado went in person to them, and he took with him over one hundred and forty soldiers and among them twenty musketeers and crossbowmen and forty horsemen and two thousand Guatemalans. When he arrived near the pueblo he again requested them to make peace, and they only replied to him with bows and arrows and began to shoot.

When he saw this and that not far off there was a rocky hill in the water crowded with warriors, he went to the margin of the lake and two fine squadrons of Indian warriors came out to meet him with great lances and good bows and arrows and many other arms and corselets, sounding their drums, and with ensigns and plumes, and he fought with them for a good while and many of the soldiers were wounded, but the enemy did not remain long on the field but went fleeing for protection to the rocky hill, with Pedro de Alvarado and his soldiers after them.

They soon gained possession of the Peñol and many [of the enemy] were killed and wounded, and there would have been more if they had not all thrown themselves into the water and crossed to an island.

Then they [the Spaniards] looted the houses which were near the lake and went to a plain where there were many maize fields and they slept there that night. The next day early in the morning they went to the pueblo of Atitlan, for so I have already said it was called, and found it deserted. Then he ordered his men to scour the country and the orchards of Cacao trees [Alvarado, in his letter to Cortés describing this expedition, says nothing about cacao plantations, certainly there are no cacao plantations at the level of the lake, five thousand feet above the sea—the Spaniards must have gone over the pass and down the Pacific slope to find them] of which there were many, and they brought in two chieftains of that pueblo as prisoners.

Pedro de Alvarado promptly sent these two chieftains, together with those who had been captured the day before, to beg the other Caciques to make peace, saying that he would give up all the prisoners to them and would receive them and pay them honour, but if they did not come he would wage war on them as he had on the people of Quetzaltenango and Utatlan and would cut down the trees in their Cacao plantations and do all the damage he could.

At the end of more arguments with these promises and threats they soon came to make peace and brought a present of gold and offered themselves as vassals to His Majesty.

Then Pedro de Alvarado and his army returned to Guatemala and were there some days without doing anything worthy of record, but all the pueblos of the neighbourhood made peace as well as others on the south coast named the Pipiles. Many of these pueblos which came to make peace complained that on the road by which they came there was a town called Escuintepeque [Escuintla or Mataquescuintla?] where there were bad people who would not allow them to pass through their country, but came to rob their pueblos and they made many other complaints against them, and they were not true, for persons whose words are worthy of credit say that they [the complaints] were made up, and he [Alvarado] went there to rob them of very beautiful Indian women and did not summon them to make peace.

Pedro de Alvarado determined to go to them with his entire force of horsemen, musketeers and crossbowmen and many allies from Guatemala, and he fell upon them one morning by surprise and did them great damage and made many captures, and it would have been better had he not done so, for, as in justice must be admitted it was an ill deed and not in accordance with His Majesty's commands.

Now we have told the story of the Conquest and pacification of Guatemala and its provinces and it is told more completely in a history which has been compiled of it by a settler in Guatemala a relation of the Alvarados, named Gonzalo de Alvarado, where it can be seen more fully, in case I have here made any mistakes.

I say this because I was not present at these conquests [and did not enter this country] until the time that we passed through these provinces when they were all at war in the year 1524, and that was when we came from Higueras and Honduras with Captain Luis Marin, and we found ourselves there at the time that we were returning to Mexico, and moreover I state that we had at that time some warlike encounters with the natives of Guatemala and they had made many pits and impediments in bad passes among the mountains so that we should not pass on account of the great barrancas, and even between a town named Cuajiniquilapa ["Juanagaçapa" in the text] and Petapa in some deep ravines we were detained fighting with the natives of that land for two days for we could not cross a bad pass, and then they wounded me with an arrow shot, but it was a small matter, and we got through with great difficulty although many warriors from Guatemala and other towns, were stationed in the pass.

As there is much to tell about this and I am obliged to recall to mind some things which should come in their proper time and place, (and all this happened at the time when there was a report that Cortés and all of us who had gone with him to Higueras were dead) I will leave it now and tell about the expedition that Cortés sent to Higueras and Honduras; I will also state that in this province of Guatemala the Indians were not fighters for they only lay in wait for us in the barrancas, and with their arrows they did nothing.

TURMOIL IN CHIAPAS

When Captain Luis Marin saw that we could not pacify those provinces I have named, but, on the contrary, they killed many of our Spaniards, he decided to go to Mexico to ask Cortés for more soldiers and assistance and military stores, and he ordered that while he was away none of the settlers should leave the town to go to pueblos far away but should only go to those within four or five leagues and then only to procure food. When he reached Mexico he reported to Cortés all that had happened and he (Cortés) ordered him to return to Coatzacoalcos and sent with him about thirty soldiers and among them Alonzo de Grado, whom I have often mentioned, and he gave orders for us to go with all the settlers in the town and the soldiers that he (Luis Marin) was bringing with him to the province of Chiapas which was hostile, to pacify it and establish a town.

When the Captain arrived with those despatches we all of us got ready, both those who were settled there as well as those he had just now brought, and we began to clear a road through some very bad forest and swamps, and we threw into them logs and branches so that the horses could pass, and after great difficulty we managed to come out at a pueblo named Tepuzuntlan [on the Río Mescalapa or Grijalva], for up to that time we were accustomed to go up the river in canoes, for there was no other road opened. From that pueblo we went to another pueblo up in the hills called Quechula ["Quechula," "Cachula" in the text, on the right bank of the R. Mescalapa, or Grijalva, District of Tuxtla], and that it may be clearly understood, this Quechula is in the mountains in the province of Chiapas, and I say this because there is another town of the same name near Puebla de los Angeles. From Quechula we went to some other small towns subject to this same Quechula and we went on opening new roads up the river which comes from the town of Chiapas for there was no road whatever.

All the people in this neighbourhood stood in great fear of the Chiapanecs [the people of Chiapas ("Chiapa" in the text)] for certainly at that time they were the greatest warriors that I had seen in all New Spain, although that includes Tlascalans, Mexicans, Zapotecs and Mijes ["Minxes" in the text], and this I say because the Mexicans had never been able to master them. At that time the province was thickly peopled and the natives of it were extremely warlike and waged war on their neighbours the people of Zinacantan [near San Cristóbal] and all the pueblos of the Quilena language, also against those called the Zoques and continually robbed and took prisoners in other small pueblos where they were able to seize booty, and with those whom they killed they made sacrifices and glutted themselves.

In addition to this on the roads to Tehuantepec ["Teguantepeque" in the text] they had many warriors stationed at bad passes to rob the Indian merchants who traded between one province and the other, and because of the fear of them trade between one province and another was sometimes stopped. They had even brought other pueblos by force and made them settle and remain near to Chiapas, and held them as slaves and made them cultivate their fields.

Let us return to our road, we proceeded up the river towards their city, and it was during Lent in the year fifteen hundred and twenty-three, but this matter of the year I do not remember well, and before reaching the town of Chiapas a review was held of all the horsemen, musketeers, crossbowmen and soldiers who went on that expedition, and it could not be done before this time, because some of the settlers of our town and others from outside had not joined, for they were busy in the pueblos of the allotments of Quechula demanding the tribute that these were obliged to pay, for now that they came under the protection of a Captain and soldiers they dared to go among those who before had neither paid tribute nor cared a snap of the fingers for us.

Let us go back to our story, there proved to be twenty-seven horsemen fit for fighting and another five who were not fit, fifteen crossbowmen and eight musketeers and one cannon and plenty of powder and a soldier for gunner and this same soldier said that he had been in Italy, and I say this here because he was no good at all and a great coward, and we mustered seventy soldiers with sword and shield, and about eighty Mexicans and the Cacique of Quechula with some of his chieftains, and these people of Quechula that I have mentioned went trembling with fear, and by flattering them we got them along so that they might help us to clear the roads and carry the baggage.

As we went along in good order, and were already near to their townships, four of the most active soldiers, of whom I was one, always went ahead as spies and scouts. I left my horse for others to bring along, for it was not [the sort of] country where horses could gallop. We always kept half a league ahead of the Army, and as the Chiapanecs are hunters, they were then out hunting the deer. As soon as they perceived us they were all called together by great smoke signals, and as we arrived at their townships we observed they had very broad roads and large plantations of maize and other vegetables, and the first pueblo we came upon which is called Ixtapa ["Estapa" in the text, about fifteen miles northeast of Chiapas], which is about four leagues distant from the Capital, had just then been deserted, and there was much maize and other supplies there and we had plenty to eat for our supper. While we were resting at this spot, and had stationed our sentinels, spies and scouts, two horsemen who had been acting as scouts came in to report, shouting: Alarm! Alarm! they are coming, all the fields and roads are crowded with Chiapanec warriors! We who were always fully on the alert went out to meet them before they reached the pueblo and fought a great battle with them, for they had many fire-hardened javelins and their throwing sticks and bows and arrows, and lances much longer than ours, and good cotton armour and plumes, and others had clubs like macanas and where the battle took place stones were plentiful and they did us much damage with their slings, and they began to surround us so cleverly that with the first shower of arrows they killed two of our soldiers and four horses, and wounded over thirteen soldiers and many of our allies, and they gave Captain Luis Marin two wounds. We were fighting that battle from the afternoon until after nightfall, and as it grew dark and they had felt the edge of our swords, and the muskets, crossbows and lance thrusts, they retreated at which we rejoiced. We found fifteen of them dead and many others wounded and unable to get away, and with two of those whom we captured there, who appeared to us to be chieftains, we held conversation and obtained news, and they said that the whole country was prepared to attack us on the following day. That night we buried the dead and looked after the wounded and the Captain who was ill with his wounds for he had lost much blood because he would not leave the fighting to attend to them or bind them up and they had become chilled.

As soon as this was done we stationed good sentinels, spies and scouts and we kept the horses saddled and bridled and all of us soldiers were on the alert, for we felt sure that they would attack us during the night, and as we had seen their tenacity in the past battle, and that neither with crossbows, lances nor muskets and not even with swordplay could we make them retreat or give way a single step, we took them to be very stout fighters and high-spirited in battle.

That night orders were given as to how we horsemen were to attack in parties of five each, with the lances held short, and that we were not to stop to give lance thrusts until they were put to flight, but to hold the lances high, aimed at their faces, and to trample them down and go on ahead. This method I have already said before, Luis Marin and even some of us old Conquistadores, had given as advice to the newcomers from Castile, and some of them did not trouble to obey the command, thinking that in giving a lance thrust to the enemy they were doing some good, but it turned out badly for four of them, for the Indians seized their lances and with these they wounded them and the horses. I wish to say that six or seven of the enemy got together and threw their arms round the horses thinking to capture them by hand and they even dragged one soldier off of his horse, and if we had not come to his rescue they would have carried him off to be sacrificed,—he died within two days.

To return to our story, the next morning we decided to continue our march to the city of Chiapas for truly one can call it a city and it was thickly peopled and the houses and streets well arranged, and there were more than four thousand citizens, not counting many other subject pueblos around it. We went on our way in good order, with the cannon loaded and the gunner wide awake to what he had to do, and we had not marched four leagues when we met all the forces of Chiapas, plains and hills were crowded with them, they came on with their great plumes and good armour, long lances, arrows and javelin throwing sticks, slings and stones, and with loud shouts, yells and whistles, it was appalling to see how they attacked us hand to hand and began to fight like raging lions. Our negro gunner whom we had brought with us—and well one may call him black— restrained by fear and trembling, neither knew how to aim nor to fire the cannon, and when at last through the shouts we hurled at him he did fire it, he wounded three of our own soldiers and did no good whatever.

When the Captain saw how things were going, all of us horsemen charged, formed in groups as we had arranged, and the musketeers, cross-bowmen and soldiers with sword and shield forming in a body helped us very much, but the enemy who fell upon us were so numerous that it was fortunate that we who were present in those battles were men who were inured to even greater dangers by which others would have been scared, and even we were astonished ourselves, and when Captain Luis Marin said to us "Señores, Santiago and at them, let us repeat our charge once more," with brave spirit we struck them such a blow that they soon turned their backs. Where this battle was fought there was some rocky ground very bad for galloping horses, so we were not able to pursue them. As we went along after them not very far from where the fight began, and we were going rather carelessly thinking that they would not get together again that day, there were other squadrons of warriors, larger than the last, all fully armed, behind some hills, and many of them carried ropes with which to cast lassos over the horses and tie them so as to pull them over, and on all sides they had stretched many nets such as they use for catching deer, for the horses and for us. All the squadrons that I have mentioned were coming to clash with our army and being very strong and vigorous warriors they gave us such a drubbing with arrows, javelins and stones that they wounded nearly all of us, and they captured four lances from the horsemen and killed two soldiers and five horses. Then they brought in the middle of their squadrons a rather aged and very fat Indian woman, and they were said to look on that woman as a goddess and prophetess, and she had told them that as soon as she arrived where we were fighting we should at once be vanquished, and she brought some incense in a brazier and some stone Idols, and all her body was painted and cotton was stuck on to the painting, and without the slightest fear she went among our Indian allies who came on in a body with their captains, and the cursed goddess was promptly cut to pieces.

To go back to our battle, as soon as Luis Marin and all of us saw such a multitude of warriors coming against us and fighting so boldly, we commended ourselves to God and charged upon them in the same order as before, and little by little we broke them up and put them to flight. They hid themselves among some great rocks and most of them threw themselves into the river which was close by and was deep, and went off swimming, for they are especially good swimmers.

As soon as we had defeated them we gave thanks to God, and we found many of them dead where the battle had been fought, and others wounded, and we decided to go to a village on the river (near to the ford [leading] to the city) [the site of the city appears to have been on the left bank of the river], where there were very good cherries, for as it was Lent it was the time when they were ripe, and in that village they were very good.

There we halted all the rest of the day, burying the dead in places where the natives of the village could not get at them or find them and we attended to the wounded and ten [wounded] horses and there we decided to sleep with every precaution of sentinels and spies. A little after midnight ten Indians crossed over from two villages which were situated near the capital City of Chiapas, and they came in five canoes across the river which is here large and deep and they came rowing in silence, and the rowers were ten Indians, persons of importance, natives of the villages which were near the Rio de los Pueblos, and they disembarked near our camp, and as they jumped on shore they were promptly captured by our sentinels, and they were content to be captured and taken before the Captain and said "Sir, we are not Chiapanecs but belong to other provinces called Xaltepeque, and these evil Chiapanecs in the great wars they have made on us have killed many people and the greater part of our townspeople with their women and children they brought here to settle, and they have taken all the property we possessed and have already held us as slaves for more than twelve years and we work their plantations and maize fields, and they make us go fishing and do other service and they take our daughters and wives from us, and we come to give you notice that tonight we will bring you many canoes in which you may cross the river, and we will also show you a ford although it is not very shallow, and what we beg Señor Captain, if we do this good deed, is that when you have conquered and routed these Chiapanecs you will give us leave to get out of their power and return to our own lands. To incline you the more to believe our statements to be true we are bringing you in the canoes, which have now crossed over and been hidden away in the river with some of our companions and brothers, presents of three jewels shaped like diadems, and we also bring poultry and cherries." Then they asked leave to fetch them and said that it had to be done very silently so that the Chiapanecs who were watching and guarding the passes of the river should not perceive them.

When the Captain understood what these Indians told him and the great assistance they would be in crossing that strong and rapid river, he gave thanks to God, and showed goodwill to the messengers, and promised to do what they asked him and even to give them clothes and the spoil we might gain in that city. He learned from them that in the two last battles we had killed and wounded more than one hundred and twenty Chiapanecs, and that they had many other warriors ready for the next day and they had made the villages where these messengers lived come out to fight against us, but that we should have no fear of them, on the contrary they would assist us, and that they [the Chiapanecs] would be waiting for us when we crossed the river although they thought it impossible that we should have the daring to cross it, and that when we were crossing it they would there defeat us.

When they [the Xaltepecs] had given this information, two of these Indians stayed with us and the rest went to their pueblo to give orders that very early in the morning twenty canoes should be brought, and they kept their word very well.

After they had departed we rested a little during what remained of the night, but not without caution and patrols, sentinels and spies for we heard the great murmur of the warriors who were assembling on the bank of the river and the sound of their trumpets, drums and horns.

As soon as it was dawn we saw the canoes which were being openly brought, in spite of the Chiapas forces, for it seems that they [the latter] had already found out that the natives of those small pueblos had risen in revolt and had gained courage, and were on our side, and some of them had been captured, and the rest had entrenched themselves in a great Cue, and for this reason there were skirmishes and fights between the Chiapanecs and the small pueblos I have mentioned. They promptly went to show us the ford, and these allies made us hurry on so as to cross the river quickly for fear lest their companions who had been captured that night should be sacrificed. Then when we came to the ford which they showed us, it was running very deep, all of us formed up in good order, both crossbowmen, musketeers and horsemen, and the friendly Indians from the two small pueblos with their canoes, and although the water reached nearly to our chests we all huddled together so as to resist the force and impetus of the water, and it pleased Our Lord that we crossed nearly to the other side of the river, but before we finished crossing many warriors came against us and poured on us a rain of javelins from throwing sticks, and arrows and stones, and others came with great lances and wounded almost all of us some with two or three wounds, and they killed two horses, and one horse soldier named something Guerrero or Guerra was drowned while crossing the river by falling with his horse into a strong rapid, he was a native of Toledo, and his horse got to land without his master.

To return to our fight, for some time they were attacking us as we crossed the river and we could neither make them retreat nor were we able to reach the land, but just then the people of the small pueblos who had grown valiant against the Chiapanecs came to our aid and fell on the rear of these who were fighting with us in the river, and they killed and wounded many of them, for they were very hostile to them for having kept them captive so many years. As soon as we saw this the horsemen quickly got to land and next the crossbowmen, musketeers, the sword and shield men and the friendly Mexicans, and we gave them a good drubbing and they went fleeing to their pueblo, and no Indian waited for another. Then without further delay we formed up in good array with our banners unfurled, and with many Indians from the two small pueblos in our company, we entered the city and when we reached the densest part of it where their great Cues and Oratories stood, the houses were so close together that we did not dare to make our camp there but [went out] into the open and a site where even if they did set fire to it, they could do us no damage.

Our Captain at once sent to summon the Cacique and Captains of that town to make peace, and three Indians from the small friendly pueblos went as messengers, one of them was called Xaltepec, and six Chiapanec Captains whom we had taken prisoners in the late battles were sent with them. And he [Luis Mario] sent to tell them to come promptly to make peace and he would pardon them for what was past, but if they did not come, we would go and look for them and make worse war on them than before, and would burn their city. Owing to those hectoring words they came at once and even brought a present of gold and excused themselves for having made war and gave their fealty to His Majesty, and prayed Luis Marin not to allow our allies to burn any houses, for before entering Chiapa they had already burned many houses in a small pueblo situated a short distance before reaching the river, and Luis Marin gave them his promise and he kept it, and ordered our Mexican allies and those we had brought from Quechula not to do any harm or damage. I wish to say that this Quechula that I mentioned here is not the one that is near Mexico but a pueblo of the same name in the mountains on the road to

Chiapas over which we passed. Let us leave this and say that in that city we found three prisons of wooden gratings, full of prisoners fastened by collars round their necks, and these were those whom they had captured on the roads, some of them were from Tehuantepec and others Zapotecs and others Quilines and others from Soconusco; these prisoners we took out of the prisons, and each one went to his own home, and we broke up the gratings.

We also found in the Cues very evil figures of the Idols they worshipped, and many Indians and boys sacrificed two days ago, and many evil things of the sodomy they practise.

The Captain ordered them at once to go and summon the neighbouring towns to come in peaceably and give their fealty to His Majesty.

The first to come were from a township named Zinacantan and Copanahuastla [not marked on the map] and Pinola, Gueyguistlan [modern Huistan near San Cristóbal? spelled in the text "Gueguistlan," "Quiaguyztlan," "Guequyztlan," and "Gueyguyztlan"] and Chamula [near San Cristóbal] and other towns whose names I do not remember of the Quilines, and other pueblos of the Zoque tongue, and all gave their fealty to His Majesty, and they were still astounded that, few as we were, we had been able to defeat the Chiapanecs, and they certainly showed great satisfaction for they were ill disposed towards them.

We stayed in that city for five days, and just then one of the soldiers whom we had brought in our army strayed from our camp and went without leave from the Captain, to a pueblo which had made peace, which I have already mentioned, named Chamula, and he took with him eight of our Mexican Indians and he ordered the people of Chamula to give him gold, and said that the Captain commanded it. The people of that pueblo gave him golden jewels and because they did not give him more he took the Cacique prisoner, and when the people of the pueblo saw him commit that excess they wished to kill this daring and inconsiderate soldier and they at once revolted, and not only they, but their neighbours the people of another pueblo, named Gueyguistlan were also inclined to revolt.

When Captain Luis Marin heard of this, he seized the soldier and ordered him to be taken posthaste to Mexico for Cortés to punish him. Luis Marin did this because this soldier thought himself a man of importance and for his honour's sake I will not mention his name, until occasion arises at a time when he did a thing that was worse, and because he was wicked and cruel to the Indians; about a year later he died in the affair of Xicalango in the hands of the Indians as I will tell later on.

When this was done the Captain sent to summon the pueblo of Chamula to come and make peace and sent to tell them that he had already punished and sent to Mexico the Spaniard who demanded gold and did them those injuries, and the reply they gave him was bad, and we thought it all the worse because of the neighbouring pueblos which had made peace, lest they should revolt. So it was decided to fall upon them at once and not to leave them until they were brought to peace. After this the Chiapanec Caciques were spoken to very gently and they were told through good interpreters things concerning our holy faith, and that they must abandon their Idols and sacrifices and sodomies and robberies, and crosses were set up and an image of Our Lady on an altar that we ordered them to make. They were made to understand that we were the Vassals of His Majesty and many other things that were fitting, and we still left more than half their city inhabited.

The two friendly pueblos that had brought us the canoes to cross the river and had helped us in the war were freed from their power, and with all their property and women and children went to settle lower down the river about ten leagues from Chiapas, where the town of Xaltepec is now established. The other small pueblo called Ystatan [Ishatan (?), near the Laguna Inferior, in the District of Juchitan] went to its own home for they belonged to Tehuantepec.

Let us return to our expedition to Chamula, we at once sent to summon the people of Zinacantan who were sensible people and many of them traders, and he [Luis Marin] told them to bring us two hundred Indians to carry our baggage and that we would go to their pueblo for it was on the road to Chamula. At the same time he demanded from the people of Chiapas another two hundred Indian warriors with their arms to go in his company, and they gave them at once and we set out from Chiapas one morning and went to sleep at some salt pits where they had made us very good ranchos, and the next day at midday we arrived at Zinacantan and there we kept the Holy feast of the Resurrection [5 April 1523]. Then we again sent to summon the people of Chamula to make peace and they would not come, and we had to go to them and it was a matter of three leagues from where Zinacantan then stood, and the houses and town of Chamula were at that time situated in a fortification very difficult to capture with a very deep fosse on the side where we had to attack, and on other sides it was worse and stronger. Thus as we approached with our army they shot from above so many stones, javelins and arrows that they covered the ground. Then [they had] very long lances with more than two fathoms of flint cutting edge ["dos braças de cuchilla de pedernales" in the text] which, as I have said before, cut better than our swords, and shields made like *pavesinas* which cover the whole body when fighting, and when they are not needed they roll and double them up so that they are no inconvenience to them. They had slings and plenty of stones and they shot arrows and stones so fast that they wounded five of our soldiers and two horsemen and with so many shouts and loud yells, whistles, howls, and trumpets, drums and shell trumpets it was enough to frighten anyone who did not know them.

When Luis Marin saw this and understood that the horses could be of no use there as it was mountainous, he ordered them to turn and descend to the plain, for where we stood was a steep hill and fortification. He ordered them to do this because we feared that the warriors from other pueblos that were in revolt called Gueyguistlan would come to attack us there, so that the horsemen might oppose them.

THE ARRIVAL OF THE TWELVE FRANCISCANS

I have already stated in former chapters which treat of the subject how we had written to His Majesty asking him to send us Franciscan Friars of good and holy lives to help us in the conversion and in teaching the natives of this land the holy doctrines so as to make them Christians, and to preach our holy faith, as we had explained it to them ever since we entered New Spain. Cortés together with us conquistadores who had won New Spain had written about it to Don Fray Francisco de los Angeles, who was general of the Franciscan Order and was afterwards Cardinal, [begging him] to do us the favour to send us friars of holy life so that our holy faith might always be exalted and the natives of these lands might understand what we told them at the time when we were fighting against them, namely that His Majesty would send friars of much better mode of living than ours to teach them the arguments and sermons which we had told them were true; and the General Don Fray Francisco de los Angeles did us the favour promptly to send twelve friars as I have related. Among them came Fray Toribio Motolinia, and the Caciques and lords of Mexico gave him this name of Motolinia which, in their language, means "the poor friar" because whatever was given to him in the name of God he gave to the Indians, so that he sometimes went without food, and wore a ragged habit and walked barefoot, and always preached to the Indians who loved him greatly for he was a holy man.

To go back to our story, when Cortés knew that they were at the Port of Vera Cruz he ordered all the Indian pueblos as well as the Spanish settlements that, whichever way they came, the roads should be swept, and wherever they halted, even in the open country, ranchos should be built for them, and that when they reached the towns or pueblos of the Indians they should go out to meet them and should ring the bells, (which at that time they had in each pueblo) and that all without exception after they had received them should pay them great reverence and that the natives should carry lighted wax candles and the crosses they possessed—and he ordered the Spaniards with all humility, to fall on their knees and kiss their hands and garments, (so that the Indians might observe it and follow their example) and moreover Cortés sent off plentiful supplies along the road and wrote to the Friars very affectionately. As they came on their way, when they arrived near to Mexico Cortés himself accompanied by us courageous and valiant soldiers went out to receive them, and together with us went Guatemoc the lord of Mexico with all the principal Mexicans there were, and many other Caciques from other cities. When Cortés knew that the Friars were approaching he dismounted from his horse, as did all of us, and when we met the reverend friars the first to fall on his knees before Fray Martin de Valencia and to kiss his hands was Cortés himself, and the Friar would not permit it, so he kissed his garments and those of all the other ecclesiastics and so did nearly all the captains and soldiers who were present and Guatemoc and the Mexican chieftains. When Guatemoc and the other caciques saw Cortés go down on his knees to kiss hands they were greatly astonished, and when they saw that the friars were barefoot and thin and their garments ragged, and that they had no horses but came on foot and were very jaundiced looking, and [then] turned to Cortés, whom they looked on as an Idol or one of their Gods, on his knees before the friars, all the Indians from that time forward followed his example, and now when friars arrive they give them a reception and pay them reverence in the way I have described; moreover I say that when Cortés conversed with those ecclesiastics he always doffed his cap and held it in his hand and in all ways paid them great respect, and certainly those good Franciscan Friars did much to the advantage of all New Spain. Three years and a half afterwards or a little earlier, twelve Dominican Friars arrived, and there came as their Provincial or Prior a friar named Fray Tomas Ortiz who was a Biscayan, and they said he had been Prior or Provincial in a country called Las Puntas and it pleased God that when they arrived they fell ill of sleeping sickness [Mal de Modorra] and most of them died. I will relate later on, when and with whom they came and the rank which they say the Prior held and other things that happened and how many other good priests came here belonging to the same order of St. Dominic, men of holy life, who impressed by this grand example, are very holy and have successfully instructed the natives of this province of Guatemala in our holy faith and have been very helpful to all.

I wish to leave this holy matter of the friars and state that as Cortés was always in fear that in Castile the proctors of Diego Velásquez governor of Cuba, instigated by the Bishop of Burgos, would again come together and speak evil of him before our Lord the Emperor, and as he had trust-worthy news by letters which his father Martin Cortés and Diego de Ordás sent to him, that they were arranging a marriage [for him] with the Señora Doña Juana de Zuñiga the niece of Dan Alvaro de Zuñiga, Duque de Bejar, he endeavoured to send all the pesos [he could collect] from the whole country, on the one hand in order that the Duque de Bejar might know of his great riches as well as his heroic deeds and great exploits, but more especially in order that His Majesty might befriend him and grant him favours, so then he sent His Majesty thirty thousand pesos and wrote to him what I shall go on to state.

To return to my story, we started with Mazariegos, a company of eighty soldiers in canoes which the Caciques gave us, and when we arrived at the villages, all with the utmost willingness gave us of what they possessed, and we brought back over one hundred canoes with maize and supplies, and fowls, honey and salt, and ten Indian women whom they held as slaves, and the Caciques came to see Cortés. So the whole camp had plenty to eat, and within four days nearly all the Caciques took to flight and only three of the guides remained with whom we set out on the road.

We crossed two rivers, one on bridges which promptly broke down on our crossing them, and the other on rafts, and we went to another pueblo subject to Acalá, which was already abandoned, and there we searched for food which had been hidden away in the forest.

Let us cease talking about our hardships and journey and I will relate how Guatemoc the great Cacique of Mexico, and other Mexican chieftains who accompanied us, had been deliberating or had arranged to kill us all and return to Mexico, and when they had reached their city to unite all their great forces and attack those [Spaniards] who remained in Mexico.

Those who made this known to Cortés were two great Caciques named Tapia and Juan Velásquez: this Juan Velásquez was Guatemoc's Captain-General when they were fighting us in Mexico. When this came to the knowledge of Cortés he had the evidence taken down [in writing] not only of the two who revealed the plot, but of other Caciques who were involved in it. What they confessed was, that as they saw us travelling over the roads carelessly and discontentedly, and many soldiers suffering from illness, and that food was always wanting, and that the four players on the oboe, and the acrobat, and eleven or twelve soldiers, had already died of hunger; and three other soldiers had fled back on the way to Mexico and had taken their chance of a state of war along the road by which we had come, and preferred to die rather than continue the advance; it would be a favourable opportunity to attack us when we were crossing some river or swamp, for the Mexicans numbered three thousand, bearing arms and lances, and some of them had swords. Guatemoc confessed that it was as the others had said, but the plot was not hatched by him, and he did not know if they were all privy to it or would bring it to pass, that he never thought to carry it out but only [joined in] the talk there was about it. The Cacique of Tacuba stated that he and Guatemoc had said that it were better to die once for all than die every day on the journey, considering how their followers and kinsmen were suffering famine.

Without awaiting further proofs Cortés ordered Guatemoc and his cousin the Lord of Tacuba to be hanged; and before they were hanged the Franciscan Friars aided them and commended them to God through the interpreter Doña Marina.

When they were about to hang him, Guatemoc said "Oh! Malinche I have long known that you meant to kill me and I have understood your false speeches for you kill me unjustly, and God will call you to account for it, for I did not do myself justice when you delivered yourself to me [into my hands] in my city of Mexico." The Lord of Tacuba said that death was welcome, dying as he did with his Lord Guatemoc. Before they were hanged the Franciscan Friars confessed them through the interpreter Doña Marina.

In truth I grieved keenly for Guatemoc and his cousin, having known them as such great lords, and they had even done me honour during the journey when occasion offered, especially in giving me Indians to bring forage for my horse, and this death which they suffered very unjustly was considered wrong by all those who were with us.

Let us turn to continue our march, which we did with the greatest caution from fear lest the Mexicans seeing their chieftains hanged, should rise in revolt; however, they were bearing such sufferings through hunger and sickness that they could give no thought to it. After the chieftains had been hanged as I have related, we at once continued our march towards another small pueblo, and before entering it we passed a deep river on rafts and found the town uninhabited, for the people had fled that day. We searched for food among the farms and we found eight Indians who were priests of Idols, and they willingly returned to their pueblo with us. Cortés told them through Doña Marina to summon the inhabitants and to have no fear, but to bring us food. They replied to Cortés begging him to give orders that no one should go near some Idols, which were close to a house where Cortés was lodged, and they would bring food and do all they were able. Cortés told them he would do what they requested and nothing should happen to the Idols, but "why did they care for such Idols which were made of clay and old wood for they were evil things which deceived them?" and he preached such [convincing] things through the Friars and Doña Marina, that they replied favourably to what he said, and [declared] they would abandon them, and they brought twenty loads of maize and some fowls.

Cortés then asked them how many days' journey from there were there men with beards like us, and they replied seven days' journey, and that the pueblo where the men with horses lived was called Nito, and that they would go as guides as far as the next pueblo, but we should have to sleep one night in an uninhabited country before reaching it.

Cortés ordered them to make a cross on a very large tree called a Ceiba which stood near the houses where they had their Idols.

I also wish to say that Cortés was in a bad humour, and even very regretful and discontented at the hardships of the journey we had undertaken, and because of having ordered Guatemoc and his cousin the Lord of Tacuba to be hanged, and at the daily hunger, and the sickness and death of so many Mexicans, and it appears that he did not rest at night through thinking about it, but got up from his bed where he slept to walk about in a room where the Idols stood, which was the principal apartment of that small pueblo where they kept other Idols, and he was careless and fell. It was a fall of more than twice the height of a man and he injured his head, but he kept quiet and said nothing about it only tended the wound and endured and suffered it all. The next day very early in the morning we began to march with our guides without anything happening worth recording, and slept by a lagoon near some forests, and the next day we continued our march and about the time of high Mass arrived at a new pueblo, and its inhabitants had deserted it that same day and taken refuge in some swamps. The houses had been newly built only a few days before, and in the town were many barricades of thick beams and all surrounded by other beams of great strength, and there were deep ditches in front of the entrance, and inside two fences, one like a barbican with towers and loopholes, and in one part in place of a fence were some very lofty rocks full of stones fashioned by hand, with great breastworks, and on the other side was a great swamp which was [as good as] a fortress.

At that time one Diego de Ordás, often named by me, had returned from Castile, he was the man whom Cortés had sent as Solicitor from New Spain, and what he solicited was for himself a commandery [of the order] of Señor Santiago, which he brought by decree from His Majesty, besides Indians and a coat of arms representing the volcano which is near Huexotzingo. When he arrived in Mexico, Diego de Ordás wished to go and search for Cortés, and this was because he saw the revolts and discords, and because he became a great friend of the Factor. He went by sea in a large ship and a launch to find out whether Cortés were alive or dead, and coasted along until he reached a port called Xicalango, where Simon de Cuenca and Captain Francisco de Medina and the Spaniards who were with him had been killed, as I have related at length in the chapter which treats of it. When Ordás heard this news he returned to New Spain without disembarking, and on landing he wrote to the Factor by some passengers, that he was certain that Cortés was dead. As soon as Ordás had published this news, he promptly crossed over to the Island of Cuba to purchase calves and mares, in the same vessel in which he had gone in search of Cortés.

As soon as the Factor saw the letter from Ordás, he went about showing it to people in Mexico, and the next day he put on mourning and had a tomb and monument placed in the principal church of Mexico, and paid honour to Cortés. Then he had himself proclaimed with trumpets and drums as Governor and Captain General of New Spain, and ordered all the women whose husbands had died [in the company of Cortés] to pray for their souls and to marry again. He even sent this message to Coatzacoalcos and to other towns, and because the wife of one Alonzo Valiente, named Juana de Mansilla, did not wish to marry and said that her husband and Cortés and all of us were alive; and that we old Conquistadores were not of such poor courage as those who were at the Rock of Coatlan with the Veedor Chirinos, where the Indians attacked them, and not they the Indians; and that she had trust in God that she would soon see her husband Alonzo Valiente and Cortés and all the rest of the Conquistadores returning to Mexico; and that she did not want to marry; because she spoke these words the Factor ordered her to be whipped through the public streets of Mexico as a witch.

There are always traitors and flatterers in this world, and it was one of these (one whom we held to be an honourable man, and out of respect for his honour I will not name him here) who said to the Factor, in presence of many other persons, that he had been badly scared, for as he was walking one night lately near Tlatelolco, which is the place where the great Idol called Huichilobos used to stand, and where now stands the church of Señor Santiago, he saw in the courtyard the souls of Cortés and

Dona Marina and that of Captain Sandoval burning in live flames, and that he was very ill through the fright from it. There also came another man whom I will not name, who was also held in good repute, and told the Factor that some evil things were moving about in the courtyards at Texcoco, and that the Indians said they were the spirits of Doña Marina and Cortés, and these were either all lies and falsehoods only reported to ingratiate themselves with the Factor, or the Factor ordered them to be told.

MEXICO CITY BECOMES A ROMAN CIRCUS

*The Roman Circus was a building for exhibitions of horse races, staged bat-
tles, displays featuring trained animals, and theatrical events. Bernal Díaz's
description of the transformation of the main plaza shows that traditions of
the Roman Circus were revived, if only momentarily, in Mexico City in 1538.
We witness an almost magical transformation of the city's center into a mythi-
cal forest where animals, "savages," Turks, knights, ships, and horses appear
in tours and tableaus of embroidered dramas, followed by a detailed list of
dishes at various feasts.*

In the year thirty-eight [1538] news reached Mexico that the most
Christian Emperor, our Lord of Glorious Memory, went to France, and
Don Francisco, the King of France, gave him a great reception at a port
called Aguas Muertas, where peace was made, and the Kings embraced
one another with great affection in the presence of Madam Leonor, the
Queen of France, wife of this same king Don Francisco and sister of the
Emperor, our Lord of Glorious Memory, and great solemnization and
festivals took place on account of that peace.

In its honour, and by way of rejoicing over it, the Viceroy Don Antonio
de Mendoza and the Marques del Valle* and the Royal Audiencia and certain gentlemen of the Conquistadores held great festivals, and at that time
the Marques del Valle and the Viceroy Don Antonio de Mendoza had
become friends, for they had been somewhat embittered over the counting
of the vassals of the Marquisate, and because the Viceroy greatly favoured
Nuño de Guzman in his refusal to pay the number of pesos de oro which
he owed to Cortés from the time when Nuño de Guzman was President
in Mexico. They decided to hold great festivals and rejoicings, and they

---

*The Marques del Valle is Hernán Cortés.

were such that it seems to me I have not seen others of the same quality [even] in Castile, both as regards jousts and reed games, and bullfights, and the encounters of one party of horsemen with others, and other great representations which were [provided]. All this that I have mentioned is as nothing compared to the many other devices of other displays which were customary in Rome when the Consuls and Captains who had won battles entered in triumph, and the competitions and challenges connected with every event. The inventor who prepared these things was a Roman gentleman named Luis de Leon, a man said to be of the lineage of the Patricians who were natives of Rome. To return to our festival, it began with a wood made in the great Plaza of Mexico with a great variety of trees as natural as though they had grown there, and in the middle some trees as though they had fallen down from old age and decay, and others covered with mould and little plants which seemed to grow out of them while from others hung a sort of down [either barbas di viejo, a lichen, or a bromeliad], again others in various ways so perfectly arranged that they were worth observing. Inside the wood were many deer, rabbits and hares, foxes and jackals, and many sorts of small animals native to the country, and two young lions and four small tigers, and they were confined within fences made within the wood itself, so that they could not escape until it was time to drive them out for the chase, for the native Mexican Indians are so ingenious in arranging those things that in the whole universe, according to what many say who have travelled all over the world, there have not been seen their like. On the trees there was a great diversity of small birds of all sorts, native to New Spain, which are so numerous and of so many breeds that it would make a long story had I to count them. There were other very dense groves somewhat apart from the wood, and in each of them a party of savages with their knotted and twisted cudgels, and other savages with bows and arrows, and they set off for the chase, for at that moment [the animals] were let out of the enclosures, and they ran after them through the wood and came out onto the great Plaza, and the killing of them led to a violent row between one lot of savages and the other, and it was worth seeing how they fought on foot with one another, and after they had fought for a short time they returned to their grove. Let us leave this, which was as nothing in comparison with the display made by cavaliers and negroes and negresses with their king and queen all on horseback, more than fifty [blotted out in the original: "one hundred and fifty"] in number, and with the great riches which they carried on their persons of gold and precious stones, small pearls and silverwork, and they promptly attacked the savages and there was another dispute about the hunting.

It was wonderful to see the diversity of faces in the masks which they wore, and how the negresses suckled their negro children, and how they paid court to the queen.

After this, on the following morning, half this same Plaza had been turned into the City of Rhodes with its towers and battlements, loopholes and turrets, all fenced round, as natural as Rhodes itself, and one hundred knights commanders with their rich embroidered insignia of gold and pearls, many of them on horseback with short stirrups and lances and shields, and others with long stirrups, in order to break lances and pierce shields, and others on foot with their arquebuses, and the Marquis Cortés was their commander and the Grand Master of Rhodes. They brought in four ships with their main and foremasts and mizzens and sails so natural that many persons were astonished at seeing them go under sail across the Plaza and make three circuits of it, and let off so many cannon which they fired from the ships; and there were some Indians on board dressed to look like Dominican Friars when they came from Castile, some engaged in plucking chickens and others fishing.

Let us leave the Friars with their guns and trumpets, and I will go on to relate how two companies of Turks were placed in an ambuscade, most Turklike with rich silk robes all purple and scarlet and gold, and splendid hoods such as they wear in their country. All of them were on horseback, and they were in ambush ready to make a dash and carry off some shepherds and their flocks which were grazing near a fountain, and one of the shepherds who were guarding them took to flight and warned the Grand Master of Rhodes that the Turks were carrying off the flocks and their shepherds. Then the Knights sallied forth and a battle was fought between them and the Turks, and they recaptured the flocks.

Then other squadrons of Turks came in from other directions and fell upon the Rhodians and fought other battles with the Knights, and many of the Turks were taken prisoners, and then a lot of fierce bulls were let loose so as to separate them.

Now I wish to tell about the many ladies, wives of the Conquistadores and other settlers in Mexico, who were at the windows of the Great Plaza, and the riches they wore of crimson and silk and damask and gold and silver and jewels, which was a splendid sight, and in other corridors were more ladies very richly adorned, whom gentlemen served with a splendid repast, which was provided for all those ladies both those at the windows and those in the corridors; and they served them marzipan, sweetmeats of citron, almonds and comfits, and others of marzipan with the arms of the Marquis, and others with the arms of the Viceroy, all gilded and silvered, and among them some containing a lot of gold without any other kind of sweets were distributed. About the fruits of the country I will not write here, for it is too lengthy a matter to relate. Besides all this there were the best wines obtainable, *aloza* [*aloja*, a beverage made of water, honey and spice (mead)], *chuca* [*chicha*, a beverage made from fermented fruits], and cacao all frothed up, and *suplicaciones* [a kind of thin, light pastry], all served on a rich table service of gold and silver. This repast commenced an hour after vespers and continued for two hours, when everyone went home.

Let us stop telling these stories about entertainments and past festivals, and I will tell about the other banquets which were given. One was arranged by the Marquis in his palace, and the other by the Viceroy in his palace and royal house, and these were suppers. The first was given by the Marquis, and the Viceroy and all the gentlemen and Conquistadores who could be counted upon supplied him with all the ladies, who were the wives of the gentlemen and Conquistadores, and other ladies, and it was a most ceremonious affair, and I will not try to remember all the courses for it would be a long story, sufficient to say that they were very abundant. The other supper was given by the Viceroy [blotted out in the original: "the entertainment was greatly varied"], and this feast took place in the corridors of the Royal Palace, which were transferred into bowers and gardens, interwoven overhead with many trees with their fruits which appeared to grow on them, and above the trees as many [kinds of] birds as can be found in the country; and they had copied the spring at Chapultepec, just like the original, with some tiny springs of water which burst forth from some parts of this same fountain, and there close to it was a great tiger tied with chains, and on the other side of the fountain was the figure of a man of great bulk dressed like a muleteer, with two skins of wine on his back, who had gone to sleep through weariness; and there were figures of four Indians who had untied one of the skins and had got drunk, and it appeared as though they were drinking and were making grimaces, and it was all done so true to life that many persons of all classes with their wives came to see it.

When the tables were set they were very long and each one had its seat of honour, in one was the Marquis and in the other the Viceroy, and for each seat of honour there were stewards and pages and a full and well-arranged service.

I should like to recite what was served, although it is not all written down here. I will state what I remember, for I was one of those who supped at these great feasts:—

To begin with there were salads made in two or three ways, and then kids and cured hog hams dressed *à la ginovisca*, after this pies of quails and pigeons, and then turkeys and stuffed fowls, then *manjar blanco* [a dish made of the breast of fowl mixed with sugar, milk and rice flour], after this a fricassee, then *torta-real*, then chickens, partridges of the country and pickled quails, and then after this they took off the tablecloths twice and there were clean ones beneath with napkins. Then pasties of every sort of birds and wild fowl, these were not eaten and many things of the earlier courses were not eaten.

Then they served other pasties of fish, none of this too was eaten, then they brought baked mutton and beef and pork, turnips, cabbage and garbanzos [chickpeas], but none of these were eaten, and in between these courses they placed on the table various fruits to incite the appetite, and then they brought the fowls of the country baked whole with their beaks and feet silvered, and after that mallards and geese whole, with gilded beaks, and then heads of pigs, deer and calves whole, by way of pretentiousness. Together with this much music of singers at each seat of honour, and trumpetry and all sorts of instruments, harps, guitars, violas, flutes, dulcimers and oboes, especially when the stewards served the cups which they brought to the ladies who were supping there, who were more numerous than they were at the supper of the Marquis, and many gilt goblets, some with aloja [a beverage made with honey and spice], others with wine, others with water, others with cacao, others with mulled wine. After this they served, to the ladies of greater distinction, some very large pasties, and in some of them were two live rabbits and in others small live rabbits, and others were full of quails and doves and other small birds all alive, and when they placed them on the tables it was at one and the same time, and as soon as they took off the top crusts the rabbits went fleeing over the tables and the quails and birds flew off.

I have not yet told about the service of olives and radishes and cheese and artichokes [blotted out in the original: "and then marzipan and almonds and comfits and citron and other sorts of sugar plums"], and fruits of the country—no more can be said than that all the tables were full of such courses.

Among other things were jesters and versifiers who in praise of Cortés and the Viceroy recited things that were very laughable [blotted out in the original: "and some of them were drunk and spoke on their own account and indecently, until they were taken by force and carried out, so as to silence them"]. I have not yet spoken of the fountains of white wine, Indian sherry and red wine [blotted out in the original: "and there were many drunkards"], and other store of bottles, or of another service there was in the courtyards, for the people and equerries and servants of all the gentlemen who were supping above at that banquet, more than three hundred of them with over two hundred ladies. I have forgotten the young oxen roasted whole, stuffed with chickens and fowls, quails and pigeons and bacon, these were in the courtyards below among the equerries and mulattos and Indians. I must state that this banquet lasted from nightfall until two hours after midnight, when the ladies cried out that they could stay no longer at table, and others were indisposed, and the tablecloths were changed by force because other things had [still] to be served, and everything was served on gold and silver and great and rich table service.

One thing I saw was that each room was full of Spaniards who were not invited guests, who came to see the supper and banquet, and they were so numerous that the corridors would not hold them. Not a single piece of plate belonging to the Viceroy was missing throughout the supper, but at that of the Marquis more than one hundred marks of silver were missing; the reason why nothing was missing belonging to the Viceroy was because the chief Mayordomo, who was named Augustin Guerrero, ordered the Mexican Caciques to place an Indian on guard over each piece, and although many plates and porringers with manjar blanco and pastry and pasties and other things of the sort were sent to every house in Mexico, an Indian went with each piece of plate and brought it back; what was missing was some silver salt cellars, [a good] many tablecloths and napkins and knives, and this was told me by Augustin Guerrero himself the next day. The Marques took it [as a sign of] grandeur that he lost over a hundred marks of silver plate.

Let us leave the suppers and banquets and I will relate how the next day there were bull [fights] and reed games, and the Marquis received a blow from a reed on the instep from which he suffered and went lame. The next day there were horse races from the plaza called Tlatelolco to the great Plaza, and certain yards of velvet and satin were given [as prizes] for the horse which galloped best and arrived first at the plaza. Then too some women raced from under the colonnade of the Treasurer Alonzo de Estrada to the royal palace, and some golden jewels were given to her who arrived first at the post.

Then many farces were acted, and they were so many that I cannot now call them to mind, and by night they had masks and ballads and jokes. There were two chroniclers of these great festivals, who recorded them just as they happened, and [noted] who were the Captains and the Grand Master of Rhodes, and they [the descriptions] were even sent to Castile that they might be seen by the Royal Council of the Indies (for His Majesty was then in Flanders).

I want to add an amusing story concerning a settler in Mexico called the Master of Rhodes, already an old man, who had a great wen on his neck. He had the name of Master of Rhodes because they called him purposely Master of Rhodes, and it was he for whom the Marquis had sent to Castile to heal his right arm, which he had broken in a fall from a horse after his return from Honduras, and he paid him very well for coming to cure his arm and gave him some pueblos of Indians.

There will already have been understood from the past chapters all that has been reported by me about the benefits and advantages which have been conferred by our renowned and holy exploits and conquests. I will now speak of the gold and silver and precious stones and other riches, from cochineal to sarsaparilla and cowhides, which have gone from New Spain and are going every year to Castile to our King and Lord, both on account of his Royal Fifths, as well as through many other presents which we sent him as soon as we took possession of these lands for him, not counting the great quantity which merchants and passengers took. Since the wise King Solomon built and ordered to be constructed the Holy Temple of Jerusalem with the gold and silver which they brought him from the Islands of Tarsis, Ophir and Saba, there has never been reported in any ancient writings more gold and silver and riches than what has gone daily to Castile from these lands. I assert this, although already from Peru, as is notorious, innumerable thousands of pesos of gold and silver have been sent. At the time we conquered New Spain the name of Peru was not known, nor was it discovered or subdued until ten years [blotted out in the original: "two three four"] later. Always from the very beginning we sent very rich presents to His Majesty, and for this reason and for others which I will state I place New Spain first, for we well know that in the events which have taken place in Peru the Captains, Governors, and soldiers joined in civil war, and all has been upset in blood and in the deaths of many soldier bandits, because they have not had the respect and obedience which was due to our Lord and King, and there has been a great decrease [in numbers] of the natives. In this New Spain we all bow down, and will forever bend our breasts to the ground, as we are bound to do, to our King and Lord, and place our lives and fortunes, whatever may happen, at the service of His Majesty. Besides, let the interested readers take note that the cities, towns and villages which are peopled by Spaniards in these parts (and they are so numerous that I do not know their names) keep quiet and pay attention to the bishops, who number ten, not counting the Archbishop of the very distinguished City of Mexico. There are three Royal Audiencias, all of which I will speak about further on, and also of those who have governed us, and of the Archbishops and bishops that there have been. Let them observe the holy cathedral churches and the monasteries where there are Dominican Friars, as well as Franciscans, and those of the order of Mercy, and Augustinians, and let them observe the Hospitals and the great indulgence they receive, and the Holy Church of our Lady of Guadalupe which is at Tepeaquilla, where the camp of Gonzalo de Sandoval used to be stationed when we captured Mexico, and let them observe the holy miracles which she has performed and is still doing every day, and let us give many thanks and praise to God and to His Blessed Mother Our Lady, for granting us favour and help so that we could win these lands where there is [now] so much Christianity.

Moreover, let them take note that there is in Mexico a university where grammar and theology, rhetoric, logic and philosophy, with other arts and branches of science, are studied and learned. They have type and craftsmen to print books both in Latin and in the Spanish, and they graduate as licentiates and doctors.

There are many other grandeurs and riches which one might mention, thus the rich silver mines which have been discovered here and are continually being discovered, by which our Castile is made prosperous and favoured and respected. As enough has been said about the advantages which have followed over and over again out of our heroical conquests, I wish to add that wise and learned persons may read this my story from beginning to end and they will see that in no writings which have been written in the world, nor in the records of human exploits, have there been seen men who have conquered more kingdoms or principalities than we the true conquistadores have done for our Lord and King, and among the brave conquistadores my comrades, (and there were very valiant ones among them) they included me [blotted out in the original: "as having the reputation of a good soldier"] as being the eldest of them all.

I once more assert, and I repeat it so many times, that I am the oldest of them, and have served as a very good soldier of His Majesty, and I say it with sorrow in my heart, for I find myself poor and very old, with a marriageable daughter and my sons young men already grown up with beards, and others to be educated, and I am not able to go to Castile to His Majesty to put before him things which are necessary for his Royal Service, and also that he should grant me favours, for they owe me many debts.

MAPS

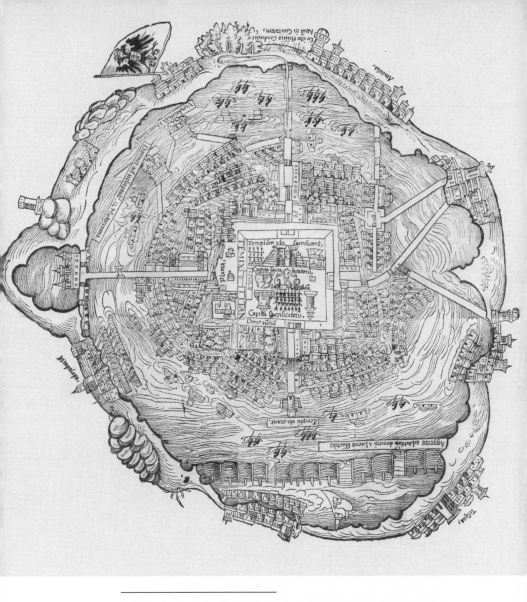

1. This 1524 woodcut shows a Spanish map of the Aztec island capital of Tenochtitlan (today Mexico City). Produced by order of Hernán Cortés, it shows that the city was organized around a huge ceremonial center, the Templo Mayor or Great Temple compound, where a ritual sacrifice is depicted. The map also shows aqueducts, dikes made of reeds, palaces, Moctezuma's royal aviary. Note that four major causeways emerge from the ceremonial center and divide the city into four great quarters. (Detail, map of Mexico City from the Latin translation of Cortés's Letters by Pietro Savorgnana, 1524, Maudslay, Vol. III.)

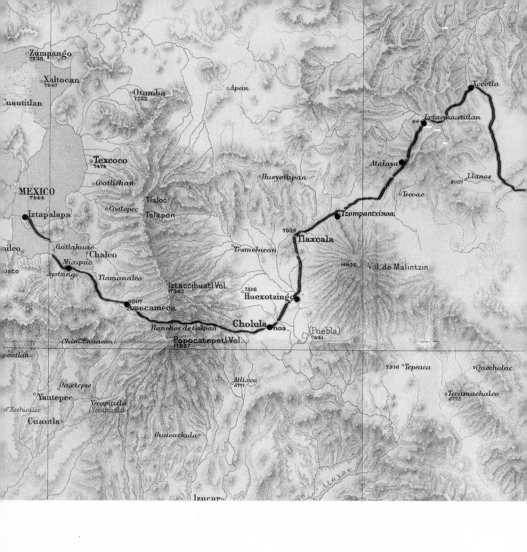

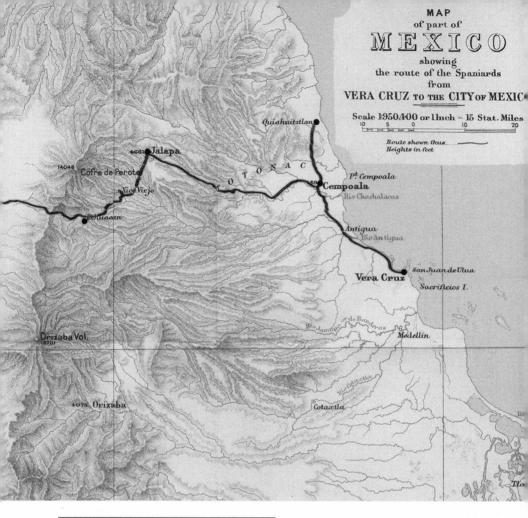

2. This map shows the route the Spaniards took under Cortés's command from Vera Cruz to Tenochtitlan. They set out from Vera Cruz in August 1519 and arrived in Tlaxcala on September 23. They left for Cholula on October 12 and soon after carried out a massacre in the city. They first saw the splendor of Tenochtitlan on November 8. The written narrative reveals the different ethnic groups and city states the Spaniards interacted with along the way. Note the numbers on the map indicating the mountainous regions the Spaniards had to traverse. (Detail, map of part of Mexico showing the route of the Spaniards from Vera Cruz to the City of Mexico by H. F. Milne, Royal Geographic Society, Britain, Maudslay, Vol. I.)

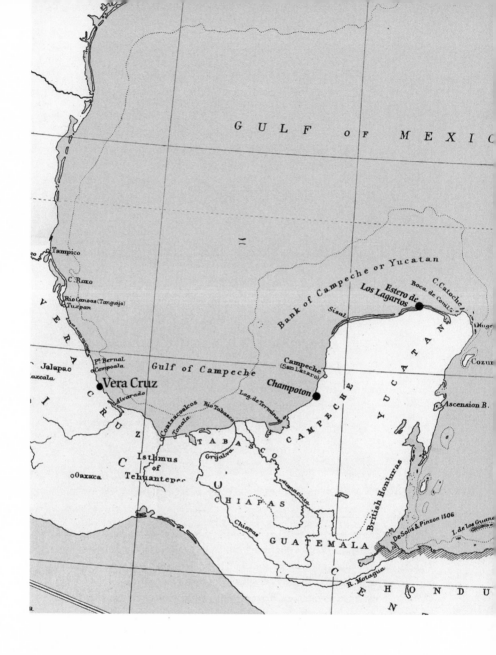

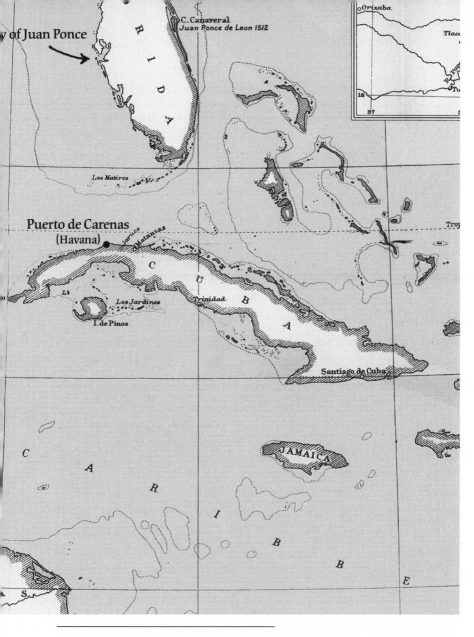

3. This map indicates the long, indirect journey that the Córdova expedition took on its return from Mexico to Cuba. Díaz del Castillo tells us that after leaving Champoton in search of fresh water along the coast, the Spaniards landed briefly at a place they named Estero de los Lagartos. Soon after, instead of returning directly to Cuba, the exhausted expedition decided to "cross over" to Florida, which it reached in four days, landing at the "very spot" where Ponce de Leon landed fifteen years earlier. "Ill and wounded," they soon returned to Havana. (Detail, Spanish sailing routes circa 1516 in the West Indies and Spanish Main by H. F. Milne, Royal Geographic Society, Britain, Maudslay, Vol. I.)

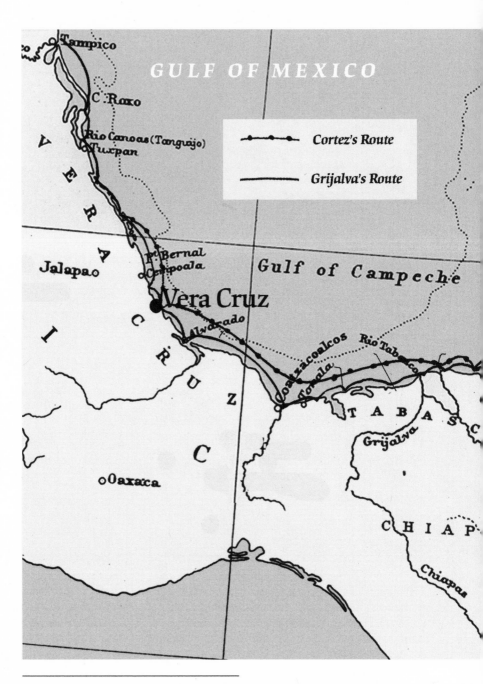

4. This map shows the itinerary of Juan de Grijalva's and Hernán Cortés's expeditions along the coast of Mexico in 1518 and 1519.

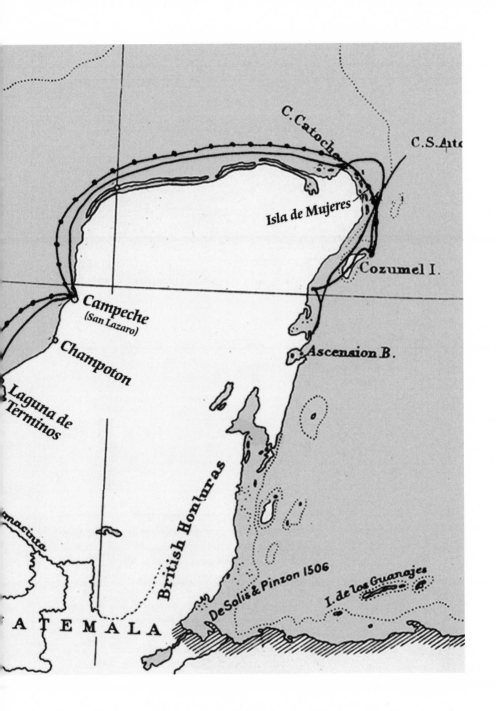

C. Catoche

C.S. An...

Isla de Mujeres

Cozumel I.

Campeche
(San Lazaro)

Champoton

Ascension B.

Laguna de
Terminos

...macinta

British Honduras

...ATEMALA

De Solis & Pinzon 1506

I. de los Guanajes

Facing page: 5. This map shows the position of the Aztec capital of Tenochtitlan in the lake and how it was linked to the mainland by three great causeways. Díaz del Castillo describes in fascinating detail the Spanish march into the capital along the Iztapalapa causeway coming from the south. Note that the causeways intrude into the island city and meet at the great ceremonial center of the Templo Mayor. Tepeyac, where the apparitions of La Virgen de Guadalupe subsequently took place, is located at the end of the northern causeway. Note also the Cerro de la Estrella on the southern mainland where the Aztec New Fire Ceremony took place once every fifty-two years. (Plan of Mexico City's causeways by A. P. Maudslay, Maudslay, Vol. II.)

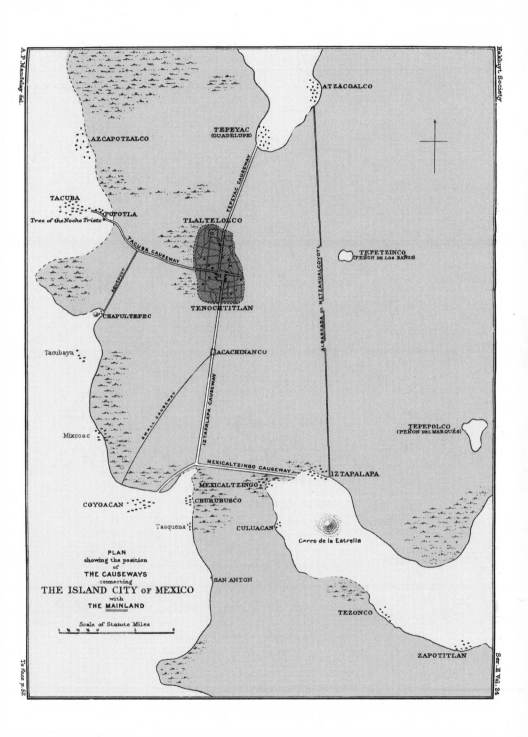

ATZACQALCO

TEPEYAC
(GUADELUPE)

AZCAPOTZALCO

TACUBA

POPOTLA

Tree of the Noche Triste

TACUBA CAUSEWAY

TLALTELOLCO

TENOCHTITLAN

AQUEDUCT

CHAPULTEPEC

Tacubaya

ACACHINANCO

TEPETZINCO
(PENON DE LOS BAÑOS)

ALBARRADA DE NETZAHUALCOYOTL

IZTAPALAPA CAUSEWAY

SMALL CAUSEWAY

Mixcoac

TEPEPOLCO
(PENON DEL MARQUÉS)

MEXICALTZINGO CAUSEWAY

IZTAPALAPA

MEXICALTZINGO

COYOACAN

CHURUBUSCO

Tasquena

CULUACAN

Cerro de la Estrella

PLAN
showing the position
of
THE CAUSEWAYS
connecting
THE ISLAND CITY OF MEXICO
with
THE MAINLAND

Scale of Statute Miles

SAN ANTON

TEZONCO

ZAPOTITLAN

383

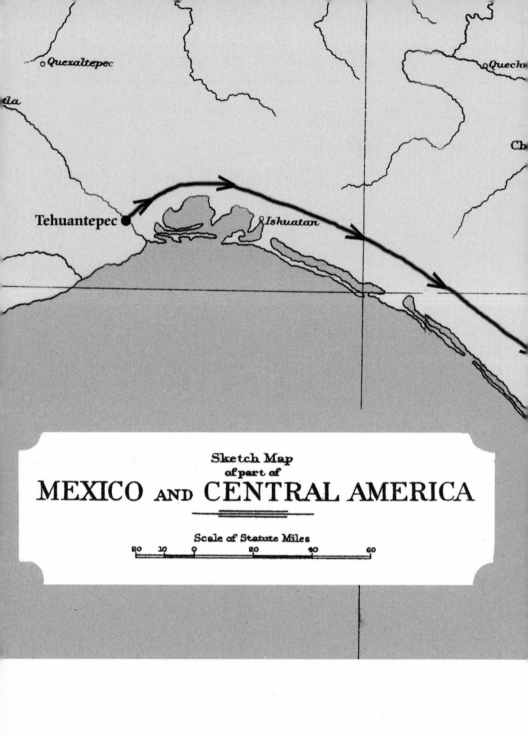

Sketch Map
of part of
MEXICO AND CENTRAL AMERICA

Scale of Statute Miles

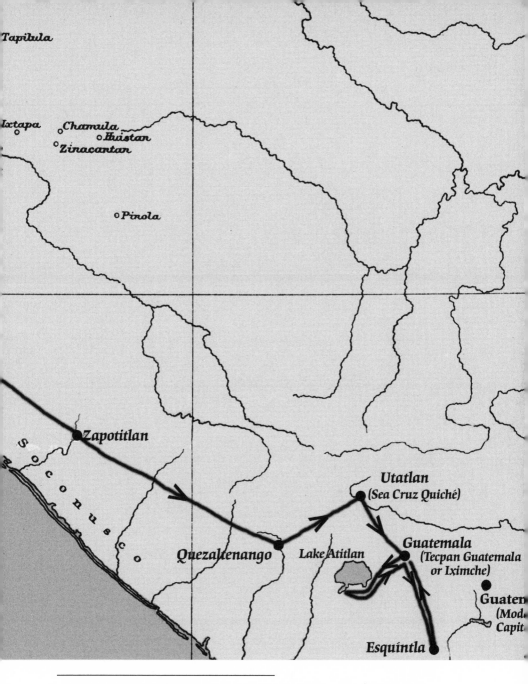

6. This map traces the Spanish expedition to Guatemala led by Pedro de Alvarado according to Díaz del Castillo from 1523–1527. Note that the Spaniards visited Lake Atitlan, where they fought a major battle with Maya warriors. (Detail, sketch map of Mexico and Central America, Maudslay, Vol. IV.)

Essays

Bernal Díaz del Castillo
Soldier, Eyewitness, Polemicist

Rolena Adorno

Bernal Díaz del Castillo (c. 1495–1584) is acclaimed today as the author of the most popular and comprehensive eyewitness account of the conquest of Mexico. Despite the extravagance of many of his claims and the seemingly interminable length of his work (hence the value of an abridgment), his *Historia verdadera de la conquista de la Nueva España* (*True History of the Conquest of New Spain*) remains the most rich and compelling version available, eclipsing even Hernán Cortés's *Cartas de relación*, his famous letters to the emperor Charles V.

Born in Medina del Campo in Old Castile, Bernal Díaz declared that he arrived in the New World in 1514 on Pedrarias Dávila's voyage to Tierra Firme (Nombre de Dios in Panama) and that he participated in the first three expeditions to Mexico, which were those of Francisco Hernández de Córdoba (1517), Juan de Grijalva (1518), and Hernán Cortés (1519). Although it is doubtful that he took part in the Grijalva expedition, he participated as a foot soldier (some published editions of his work elevated him to the rank of captain) in Cortés's initial overland march to the Aztec capital of México-Tenochtitlan in 1519. Bernal Díaz also participated in the second major offensive that resulted in the fall of that island city (the site of today's Mexico City) in August 1521. He accompanied Cortés on the disastrous expedition to Hibueras (Honduras) in 1524–26 and spent the remainder of his life in New Spain, sustained by the labor and goods produced by the native inhabitants of the lands over which he held titles of trusteeship (*encomienda*) that had been granted to him by the Spanish king, Charles V. After receiving in the 1520s encomienda grants near Coatzacoalcos in Tabasco and Chiapas and losing them in the 1530s,

Bernal Díaz settled permanently in Guatemala in the 1540s after the first (1539–41) of his two trips to Spain to secure greater reward for his conquest efforts. The second trip, which either awakened or confirmed his worst forebodings about the future prospects of the *encomendero* class, occurred in 1550–51. He died an octogenarian in Santiago de Guatemala on February 3, 1584.

Bernal Díaz began to write his *Historia* after his second trip back to Spain, some thirty years after the fall of the Aztec capital; in 1568 he finished a version of the work that he sent to Spain in 1575 for publication. In the meantime, he continued to work on the manuscript in his possession, augmenting it until nearly the time of his death in 1584. In addition to the recollection of his own experiences, Bernal Díaz used as his sources the published letters of Cortés (1522–26), Francisco López de Gómara's history of the conquest of Mexico (1552), and Juan Ginés de Sepúlveda's 1540s arguments favoring war against the Indians, justifying such actions on the basis of the Indians' perceived violation of natural law through human sacrifice, cannibalism, and sodomy. Bernal Díaz also appreciated the Mexican pictorial record. He observed that native paintings provided warfare intelligence to allies or enemies (chapters 38, 78, 110), gave historical accounts of significant battles (chapters 89, 128), mapped the coast of the Gulf of Mexico (chapter 102), and preserved native history and culture in ancient books and paintings (chapter 92). As Benjamin Keen pointed out in *The Aztec Image in Western Thought* (1971), Bernal Díaz and Cortés are unsurpassed among members of the conquest generation in their acknowledgment and recording of Mesoamerican cultural achievements. Bernal Díaz's work provides a still partially untapped resource for insight into Mesoamerican culture at the time of the conquest.

Why did Bernal Díaz write his history of the conquest of Mexico? There is no doubt that he sought to herald the deeds of the common soldier (especially singling out and highlighting his own efforts) to counteract the impression created in the published accounts of Cortés and Gómara that focused exclusively on Hernán Cortés. Bernal Díaz's creation of a dialogue with the allegorical figure of Fame (chapter 210) provides the most vivid and entertaining account of his concerns. Yet events in Bernal Díaz's life after the conquest also influenced his decision to write his work. When in Spain in 1550–51, he had made at least two appearances at the royal court, as advocate (*procurador*) and representative of the encomenderos of the city of Santiago de Guatemala. In the last chapters of his work, he refers indirectly to one of those experiences, and he narrates in detail the events of the second of those occasions (his appearance at court in Valladolid in 1550, in chapter 211). The latter meeting was a junta convened by the Royal Council of the Indies in order to deliberate about the right of Spanish settlers to hold encomiendas in perpetuity.

Bernal Díaz had made his case favoring grants in perpetuity in formal petitions of 1549 and 1550, but the interests of himself and his encomendero peers were bested and defeated by the arguments made by the Dominican friar Bartolomé de Las Casas (1484–1566) and like-minded colonial officials and members of the royal court. After these experiences, Bernal Díaz undertook the writing of his book. His appearances at court had shown him that his heirs would not likely receive rights in perpetuity to his encomienda grants, or he learned, at least, that such long-term rewards for his long-ago efforts in the conquest of Mexico were far from being assured.

Although Bernal Díaz's *Historia* concentrates on the events of the Mexican conquest from 1519 to 1521 (chapters 19–156), his narration covers events in Mexico from 1517 through 1568 (chapters 1–18, 157–212) and includes accounts of affairs pertinent to the viceroyalty of New Spain that occurred at court in Spain as well as in the seats of governance on the islands of Hispaniola and Cuba. Broader in scope than the 1519–21 conquest of Mexico that is the heart and soul of his narrative account, Bernal Díaz's objective was to place New Spain in the context of Spain's imperial possessions at the time and to assure that the importance of Mexico was not eclipsed in the eyes of his countrymen by the newly discovered Inca Peru and its spectacular mineral wealth in the South American Andes.

Equally if not more pressing was his desire to claim for the common conquistador (himself and his remaining peers and their heirs) the privileges and prestige that he understood to be their due and to ensure that those rewards would endure through future generations. His two trips back to Spain taught him that the interests of the ex-conquistador encomenderos were being eroded by a series of royal decrees that included legislation that sought to abolish the encomienda system and Indian slavery (the New Laws of 1542). He also became aware of competing claims for royal recognition by other constituencies, not the least of which was the developing royal bureaucracy dedicated to managing the Crown's resources at home and abroad. Politically, the conquests in America had come under increasingly severe pressure from Las Casas and his colleagues who persuaded Charles V, in the name of Christian evangelization and justice, to curtail the prerogatives of private citizens and their virtually unfettered access to the labor and resources of the native populations of the Indies.

Even the writing of history had dealt the conquistadores a severe blow. Cortés's published letters effectively attributed the Spanish victory over the Aztecs to his own brilliance as a military strategist and his faith in Divine Providence, and Gómara and other historians likewise emphasized Cortés's role to the detriment of that of his Castilian soldiers. These authors also inadvertently but effectively undermined the conquistadores' interests by complacently assuming (rather than forcefully arguing) that the conquests had been legitimate and just. Bernal Díaz wrote his book at the very time those military campaigns were coming under political and legislative attack, being characterized as brutal and unjustified in their execution and devastating to native peoples and natural resources in their consequences. This attack was most vividly carried out in Las Casas's well-known *Brevíssima relación de la destruyción de las Indias* (Brief Account of the Destruction of the Indies), which appeared in print in Seville in 1552 and which would be rebutted by Bernal Díaz in his *Historia* (chapters 83, 125) with the same or greater vehemence and scorn than he heaped on López de Gómara's history of the conquest.

Bernal Díaz thus understood that, regarding the conquest of Mexico, there was a second war to be fought and won: it would take place at court, and it had to be engaged on the battlefield of the documentary record and especially in historical accounts of those events. The challenge was to bring alive those forever absent deeds and to do so not only in relation to conquest events themselves, but more importantly in hand-to-hand combat with those works that constituted the "library" of published works on the subject. Thus he remarked,

> I wish to return to my story, pen in hand as a good pilot carries his lead in hand at sea, looking out for shoals ahead, when he knows that they will be met with, so will I do in speaking of the errors of the historians, but I shall not mention them all, for if one had to follow them item by item, the trouble of discarding the rubbish would be greater than that of gathering in the harvest. (*True History* 1:68 [chapter 18])

During Bernal Díaz's lifetime, other historians of Mexico, such as Alonso de Zorita (1560s) and Diego Muñoz Camargo (1576), mentioned Bernal Díaz's writings in their own; at least one local resident in Santiago de Guatemala, the municipal official Juan Rodríguez del Cabrillo, stated in 1579 that he had read Bernal Díaz's manuscript chronicle. His work thus had at least a limited circulation in manuscript during his lifetime, but the version sent to Spain was not published until 1632. It was brought out by the royal printing house under the supervision of the learned chronicler of the Order of Mercy, Fray Alonso Remón, who sought to highlight the role of Fray Bartolomé de Olmedo, as well other members of the Mercedarian Order and the Christian mission in general, in the Spanish conquest of Mexico. The manuscript that remained in Guatemala was transcribed and published in Mexico by Genaro García in 1904–5 and is regarded, by the present author, as the authoritative version of the work. (Its translation by Maudslay is the text used in this abridged edition.)

Bernal Díaz's *Historia* is of great interest today not only for its suspenseful and dramatic account of the conquest of Mexico, written several decades after the fact, but also for the way Bernal's work disguises polemical argumentation as neutral historical narration and exemplifies the capacity of prose exposition both to contain and conceal the argumentation that drives it. His claims to write using "plain speech" and to convey the "unvarnished truth" belie a highly mediated and nuanced account that blurs the boundaries between history, jurisprudence, and eyewitness testimony.

Bernal Díaz's ruminations on the writing of history reveal the dilemma he had faced as a soldier-cum-encomendero who entered a field of activity customarily occupied only by the learned. Two types of authority—one of humanist learning, the other of Castilian law—were called up; Bernal Díaz acknowledged that he could not meet the demands of the former, but he strove mightily to master those of the latter. To express his views in the debate on authority in history he cast his argument in the form of a conversation he presumably had with two learned gentlemen (chapter 212).

As Bernal Díaz told the tale, two gentlemen with university degrees asked to read his just-finished account of the conquest of Mexico in order to determine if and how his version differed from the *Historia de la conquista de México* (History of the Conquest of Mexico) of Francisco López de Gómara. Bernal Díaz loaned his interlocutors his manuscript and warned that they were not to change anything in it because its contents were all true: "And I told them not to alter a single thing, for all that I write is quite true" (*True History* 5:286 [chapter 212]). After having read Bernal Díaz's account, one of these readers rebuked him for having written about his own deeds: the old conquistador should have relied on the historians who had written about those events, because a man could not serve as a witness on his own behalf (*True History* 5:287). Thus, in a single stroke, Bernal Díaz's sole claim to authority—that of the eyewitness—was dismissed and his monumental efforts brushed aside. He reports that he replied, "But if I tell the truth (and His Majesty and his Viceroy, the Marquis, witnesses, and evidence attest it, and moreover the story gives evidence of it), why should I not say so? For it ought to be written in letters of gold. Would they wish the clouds or the birds which passed above at the time to report it?" (*True History* 5:288).

Bernal Díaz thus responded to the challenge placed before him from within his own frame of reference by proclaiming the authority of the mundane documents that certified his achievements. He remarked that the Marqués del Valle, Hernán Cortés, had made a report to the emperor in 1540 commending his deeds and services; he pointed out that the viceroy Antonio de Mendoza had done the same. Alongside these witnesses, Bernal Díaz declared, stood the *probanzas* (the certified testimony of witnesses to his deeds) that had been presented on his behalf at the Council of the Indies in Spain in 1540. Readers in Bernal Díaz's day would have known that the probanza was a written document consisting of the plaintiff's statement of his case, along with the testimony of friendly witnesses who corroborated his petition. As a form of legal testimony taken of witnesses under oath, a probanza or *información* represented the plaintiff's side of the case only. Witnesses were called and presented with an interrogatory, on which basis they affirmed the points the party sought to prove. Designed to clarify facts or assertions that the plaintiff wished to set forth in perpetuity, the probanza was the means by which lawyers or advocates informed the judges about the claims of the parties they represented.

If the marqués and the viceroy and the captains (the latter as witnesses in his probanzas) and the probanzas themselves were not enough, Bernal Díaz insisted, he would call as his witness the emperor, whose "royal letter, sealed with his royal seal" ("sus cartas selladas") had been sent to the viceroy and other officials on Bernal Díaz's behalf. Thus, for Bernal Díaz, historical authority rested on sworn testimony of the type taken in a legal proceeding and that relied on eyewitness validation so as to serve as the legitimate basis for the resultant actions of the emperor in favoring his petitions. The sworn probanza and the grants and decrees that resulted from their royal acceptance were the very basis—and the highest possible legal ground—on which Bernal Díaz could stake his claim to write the history of the events in which he had participated. When he declared he would introduce as a witness on his behalf the emperor himself, he meant that Charles V's royal seal was the ultimate proof of his services and his truthfulness in reporting them.

The great lesson that the reading of Bernal Díaz's chronicle teaches us today is that he did not derive his literary authority from the truth of historical events nor even solely from having been an eyewitness to many of them. He sought the source of his credibility instead in the juridical tradition that, on the basis of medieval legal principles and the legacy of the reconquest of Castile from the Muslims (completed in 1492), took shape in his day with regard to the Spanish conquests in the Indies. Bernal Díaz did not defer to the writings of Cortés or Gómara on certain points because he was polemicizing against them on many others (and sometimes he polemicized against Gómara and others when, in fact, his and their accounts agreed). He openly opposed the accounts of Las Casas. The model that Bernal Díaz's work provides invites consideration of other ways, outside the events of history, in which writers of his day and afterward staked their claims to historical and literary authority.

The portrait of Bernal Díaz as historical protagonist and narrator that emerges responds to the final transformation of the old chivalric formula of the valorous vassal in ever loyal service to his lord: this vassal's most dreaded enemies were not barbarous princes and savage warriors but rather royal bureaucrats and court councilors. Royal vacillation and bureaucratic chaos, Bernal Díaz claimed, brought insecurity and hardship to the veteran of the conquest of Mexico who rightfully expected to live out his life being served and supported by the native peoples whose souls, through a just war of conquest, he insisted, he had helped to save.

Considering Bernal Díaz's work in the light of the writings of his literary interlocutors (Las Casas, Gómara) adds an essential, missing dimension to the overall portrait of this "true conqueror"; it expands the objectives of the *Historia verdadera* and takes account of the high-stakes polemics into which they fed. The facets of the literary narrator Bernal Díaz include, as elaborated at various moments in his narration, the adventurous young soldier mesmerized by the fabulous sight of México-Tenochtitlan (chapters 87, 91, 92), the conquistador who recalls with considerable eloquence and sympathy the person and plight of Moctezuma (chapters 91, 95–126), and the disgruntled, unappreciated war veteran and aging colonial settler who wants to ensure that the grants of Indian labor and the fruits of the land will be passed on to his descendants in perpetuity (chapters 211, 212). Like many Castilians of those first decades who journeyed into never-before-seen lands and colonized its peoples, Bernal Díaz can be characterized by what he hoped to achieve (royal recognition of his efforts, a comfortable life) while at the same time a set of attitudes, emerging at the royal court and its councils, confounded and conflicted with those goals and required him to rationalize and justify his right to gain. He did so not only during his visit to court but most enduringly in his "true history," creating the scenes of his hardships and his glory so as to serve his interests in portraying the conquest as just and his rewards as merited.

Bernal Díaz's truest and most far-reaching achievement is his rhetorical persuasiveness. Although he did not persuade the members of the emperor's royal councils of his right to recognition and reward that would ensure the prosperity of his heirs and descendents for all time, his work has succeeded in convincing many generations of readers of the literary if not political merits of his case. As a writer, he did so by setting up a David and Goliath–like narrative and argumentative oppositions: Bernal Díaz the worthy soldier versus the self-serving captain (Cortés), Bernal Díaz the eyewitness participant versus the ill-informed professional historian (Gómara). Another opposition present in his work, also highlighted here, is that of the petitioning advocate and encomendero versus the court councilor (Las Casas) who decried the events and long-term consequences of the conquests.

These oppositions, plus Bernal Díaz's acknowledgment of his role as encomendero and his insistence that it was unappreciated and unrewarded by the authorities, make it possible to overcome the simple, dichotomous distinctions that Bernal Díaz repeatedly emphasized: himself as foot soldier versus Cortés as captain, himself as eyewitness versus Gómara as armchair historian. Yet the consideration of Bernal Díaz's polemical response to the vigorous and influential writings of Las Casas brings up not only the problem of the relationship of the Castilian conquistador and enco-mendero to the elite circles of Spanish royal and colonial administration, but also, and more significantly, to the conquered peoples of Mexico. The attentive reading of Bernal Díaz's work demonstrates that he never forgot the stakes of this contest; they account, at least in part, for the passions that stimulated him to write his equally passionate "true history."

For further reading on Bernal Díaz and the historians whose work he engaged, see Rolena Adorno, *The Polemics of Possession in Spanish American Narrative* (New Haven, CT: Yale University Press, 2007).

CORTÉS AND THE SACRED CEIBA
A Maya Axis Mundi

DAVÍD CARRASCO

During the Spanish march to the Aztec capital of Tenochtitlan, Díaz del Castillo describes Cortés's quick study of indigenous ways of thinking and acting. In both Cortés's *Letters to the King of Spain* and in the *True History*, Cortés communicates with and intimidates caciques (chiefs), deciphers local customs, forms effective alliances, and exploits geopolitical conflicts among the natives. No doubt he was greatly aided during the journey in his decipherments of Maya thought and religion by the bilingual (a Spanish and Maya speaker) Francisco Aguilar who had been shipwrecked ten years earlier and had survived in a Maya community before rejoining the Spaniards soon after Cortés came ashore. Later in the march to Tenochtitlan, Cortés depended on Malintzin (known as Malinche or Doña Marina by the Spaniards) for understanding native speech and customs. Malintzin was born into a Nahuatl-speaking family and learned a Maya language after later being adopted into a Maya community. She knew the world of nature, religious symbols, and cultural practices of both communities.

One of the most interesting examples of Cortés's knowledge of native cosmovision* (worldview) and his manipulation of native beliefs (even before Malinche comes into the story) is found in two events associated with the ceiba tree that was sacred to the Maya. Early in the military campaign the Spaniards come to a town where Cortés "took possession of that land for His Majesty, performing the act in His Majesty's name." We expect from our reading of other parts of the narrative that he planted

---

Cosmovision means the religious worldview of a people that contains their local codes about how space and time are integrated into a meaningful picture of the universe.

a flag, spoke a sermon, or uttered a prayer in the traditional Spanish Catholic style of taking possession of a territory. Instead he carries out a public performance of cutting marks in a tree that, in the worldview of the local people, represented the central, dynamic power of the Maya universe. We are told, "It was done in this way; he drew his sword and as a sign of possession he made three cuts in a huge tree called a Ceiba, which stood in the court of that great square, and cried that if any person should raise objection, that he would defend the right with the sword and shield which he held in his hands."

By looking *through* Díaz del Castillo's account of this tree cutting and *into* Maya religion we can come to understand what the ceiba tree meant to the Maya and what Cortés was trying to accomplish in this symbolic action. Cortés has come to the central courtyard of the town with his entourage of soldiers and priests. Native priests, warriors, traders, farmers, women, and children are watching from public and private locations. Displaying himself as a warrior with weapons in his hands, Cortés attacks a tree standing in the center of the community, a "huge tree called a Ceiba" by making three cuts in its trunk. He then yells defiantly to the onlookers. He must have learned from Aguilar and other informants that the ceiba tree had special power and significance. But what was his specific intention and what did his actions mean to the Maya?

The Cosmic Ceiba in Mesoamerican Nature and Art

In Mesoamerica, ceiba trees grow to great heights, and their gargantuan size includes expansive limbs and rugged roots that appear above the ground and then burrow beneath the earth, spreading out to grip the land around it. Its height, breadth, and root system literally invade the branches and root systems of other trees, that is, it dominates space both above- and belowground. It is also the tree most often hit by lightning from the sky. And it rejuvenates itself every year.

Native speakers, Catholic priests, and anthropologists have since taught us that in Maya cosmovision or worldview, then and now, the ceiba was *the* World Tree, that is, it was believed to embody the most essential powers of fertility, stability, and the renewal of life on earth. It stood at the "center" of the cosmos and connected, in the native mind, the three levels of the universe: the sky, the earth, and the underworld. Its roots were believed to reach into the underworld and connect the earthly Maya to the ancestors and gods below. Its height had a religious meaning as it was said to touch the sky and connect the Maya with the powers of rains, storms, the lights of the atmosphere, and the sky gods. Imagine what it must have meant for the Maya to have the invader Cortés suddenly cutting at the community's sacred ceiba while yelling and threatening the local people.

The *cosmological* significance of the ceiba tree was depicted in many examples of Mesoamerican symbolism, and one of the most spectacular images was found on the sarcophagus lid of a great Maya king buried deep within a pyramid in the city of Palenque. Here is the image of that funerary lid showing the ceiba tree, depicted as a four-part jeweled structure with a bird on top and dragons for branches growing out of the underworld. The dead ruler Pakal is falling backward into the underworld (symbolized by the huge jaws rising up around his neck and knees) immediately in front of the sacred ceiba.

As this famous image shows, the ceiba tree was depicted not literally as a tree but as a stylized cross, emphasizing that it had four connected parts (a two-part vertical trunk and a two-part horizontal branch system all connected in the center of the tree) and stood at the *center* of the world or cosmos. Among its many other significances, it was also the spot marking the entrance to where the ancestors lived on beneath the surface of the earth! As revealed in Díaz del Castillo's account, some Maya towns were built around or near a ceiba tree, thus putting them close to the "center" of the world, the place of connection between heaven, earth, and the underworld.

To catch a glimpse of how widespread and profound the connection between sacred trees and cosmic order was for Mesoamerican peoples (and thereby get more understanding of what Cortés's actions meant to the Maya), look at this image from another pre-Columbian codex, the

1. Drawing of Pakal's sarcophagus by Merle Greene Robertson.
Reproduced with permission.

2. Xiuhtecuhtli. Unknown artist, fifteenth century. From the *Codex Fejérváry-Meyer.*
© Foundation for the Advancement of Mesoamerican Studies, Inc., www.famsi.org.

colorful *Codex Fejérváry-Mayer.* We are presented with a cosmogram—a symbolic map of the entire cosmos. Here we see, organizing a complex series of colors, objects, body parts, and calendar signs, four trapezoidal shapes symbolizing the four quarters of the universe, each with a blooming tree in the center. On each side of the tree, paying homage to it, are two ancestral deities in ritual poses. Each of the four sacred blooming trees has a bird on top representing the heavens. In the center of the four quarters stands a warrior who is bleeding into the four quarters of the cosmos (this theme of human sacrifice will be addressed in another short essay in this book).

Sacred trees, like the ceiba, symbolize much more than fertile nature to the Maya. They symbolize cosmic order and its regeneration, even at the moment of death.

Given this discussion linking Díaz del Castillo's references to wider research on Maya cosmology, *what do you make* of the political and religious significance of Cortés's actions with the ceiba tree? His intentions become clearer only ten pages later in the narrative when, on Palm Sunday, he elaborates his symbolic attack on the ceiba. Cortes "ordered the Caciques to come with their women and children" to pay homage to the Virgin Mary and the Cross. What he does next is audacious: "Cortes ordered them to send six Indian carpenters to accompany our carpenters to the town of Cintla, there to cut a cross on a great tree called a Ceiba, which grew there, and they did it so that it might last a long time, for as the bark is renewed and the cross will show there forever."

Was he humiliating the Maya? Or was he communicating to them that he understood the importance of the tree and wanted to be identified with it? To turn it into a Christian symbol? And what is the meaning of his three cuts?

Your thoughts?

For further reading on the topic of sacred trees in Mesoamerican cultures, see Phil Arnold, "Cosmic Trees," in *The Oxford Encyclopedia of Mesoamerican Cultures*, ed. Davíd Carrasco (New York: Oxford University Press, 2001), 1:236–37; and Alfredo López Austin, *Tamoanchan y Tlalocan: Places of Mist* (Niwot: University Press of Colorado, 1997), especially chapter 2, "Tamoanchan."

COLONIAL SEXUALITY
Of Women, Men, and Mestizaje*

KAREN VIEIRA POWERS

The Spanish invasion of the Americas was the occasion of rampant interracial sexual unions, usually between Spanish men and indigenous women. These unions could be the result of marauding soldiers taking the booty of war or relationships of mutual consent. Suffice it to say that in the early stages, most of them were forced. Whether rapes or consensual, these unions gave rise to a new race of people called mestizos, whose racial and cultural heritage was now mixed, part European and part indigenous. The process by which this mixture took place is called mestizaje.

In the Plaza of the Three Cultures in Mexico City hangs a plaque that states, "In 1521, Cuauhtemoc surrendered to Hernán Cortés; it was neither a victory nor a defeat, but the birth of the mestizo people who are the Mexico of today." While the overt message is about the result of a military battle between two male protagonists, the implicit and more important message is about the racial and cultural product of relationships between men and women. Once again, women's role is obfuscated, even in a historical setting in which it was so obviously essential.

The role of indigenous women in mestizaje, perhaps the most formative sociocultural process of Latin America's history, is also curiously the theme that the region's scholars have most ignored or about which they have produced the most constricted histories. When women's place

---

*This chapter is an excerpt from "Colonial Sexuality: Of Women, Men, and Mestizaje," originally published in *Women in the Crucible of Conquest: The Gendered Genesis of Spanish American Society, 1500–1600*, by Karen Vieira Powers (Albuquerque: University of New Mexico Press, 2005). Reproduced with permission. While it focuses more on Peru than Mexico, the patterns of colonial sexuality were very similar in both places.

in their sexual unions with Spanish men has been discussed, it has usually been within the frame of the victim/whore paradigm. Here is where the Spanish male discourse of sexual conquest and the indigenous male discourse of female betrayal, [. . .] have had the most influence. Since most histories have taken one or both of these discourses as their points of departure, woman's historical experience has been explained as either rape by or complicity with the Spanish invader. Here is what two male chroniclers of the time, one Spanish and one Indian, had to say about the subject of women and mestizaje.

In 1598 a Franciscan friar testified about his experiences in northern Mexico: "While accompanying Oñate on an expedition to the Pueblos, I overheard the Spanish soldiers shouting: 'Let us go to the pueblos to fornicate with Indian women. . . . Only with lascivious treatment are Indian women conquered.'"[1] In 1615 the indigenous chronicler Guaman Poma reported in a letter to the Spanish king: "All Indian women are deceitful, lustful, thieving, disobedient, and above all, great whores. . . . They prefer to live as concubines of the Spaniards, and on occasion with black and mulatto men, than marry an Indian commoner."[2]

The portrayal of Indian women's role in mestizaje as either rape victims or traitors still echoes in the national literatures of Latin America today. Perhaps no Native American woman has been as implicated in this particular discourse as the much maligned "La Malinche," Cortés's famous interpreter and lover. From nationalist Mexican rhetoric to twentieth-century Chicana feminist works, La Malinche, or Doña Marina, has consistently been dragged through the mud of rape, sexual promiscuity, treachery, treason, and dupery.[3] In popular Mexican history, she and Cortés are figured as the parents of the first mestizo and hence the mother and father of today's Mexico—a highly conflicted national heritage, to say the least. Referring back to Malinche's sexual union with Hernán Cortés, Octavio Paz in *Labyrinth of Solitude* describes Mexico's mestizo nation as "hijos de la chingada" (the sons and daughters of rape and seduction). More misogynist contemporary interpretations of Malinche are exemplified by the Mexican cartoonist Rius, who portrays her as a prostitute who speaks three languages and knows how to kiss in three more.[4] Finally, Richard Rodríguez provides us with a somewhat more dignified, though equally restrictive, interpretation of women's agency in the making of mestizo Mexico: "I count my life to be the result not simply of the European man's will on my ancestral Indian mother, but of her interest in the European too."[5] As important as it may be for a nation to come to terms with its painful origins, Mexico's historical record still invests too much in the varied yet recurring paradigm of Spanish man as always already sexual conqueror. Similarly, totalizing women's historical experience as either rape, betrayal, or sexual interest may be too high a price to pay in the search for a fuller record of women's history. Surely, indigenous women experienced all of these and more.

Because of the "sexual conqueror" and "Indian/*casta* woman as always already mistress/concubine" images, we are often left with a stilted Hollywood rendering of colonial interracial unions that continues to cast both men and women in restricted, unidimensional roles. This has had an especially negative effect on interpretations of colonized female partners, because it leaves them as "tainted, loose, or lost women" whom we are still forcing to shoulder the shaming onus of extramarital, interracial relationships.

What we are about to embark upon is a careful exploration of the range of women's lived experiences in their relationships with Spanish men. How and why these interracial unions began is as varied a story as the myriad racial categories into which the Spanish regime would slot their progeny. Though rape and betrayal probably represented opposite poles of the spectrum, in its interstices we are likely to find mutual consent, economic opportunism, physical attraction, political alliances, social mobility, genuine love, and other scenarios among the events and motives that catapulted indigenous women into sexual relationships with Spanish men. Once in those relationships, their experiences ranged from domestic bliss and material reward all the way to violent abuse and abandonment. Since the racial and cultural heritage of present-day Latin America harkens back to these sexual unions between Spanish men and Amerindian women, we must examine gendered roles and experiences during this pivotal historical moment.

The catalytic nature of interracial sexual unions and women's part in their proliferation is illuminated if examined in the broader context of Spanish imperial organization, as it has been constructed by Latin Americanist historians until now. In the New World, the colonizers attempted to reconstruct an accentuated version of the corporate society of their homeland and superimposed it on a multiracial, colonial situation. Spaniards, Amerindians, and Africans were incorporated into a race-based social hierarchy—a legal caste system conceived in Iberian traditions, informed by its intersection with preexisting, indigenous sociopolitical organization, and exacerbated by the relations of European colonialism. The conquest of one race by another placed the conquerors' race on top and that of the conquered on the bottom, giving the former the "natural" right to collect tribute and labor services from the latter. This division was further manifested by the spatial and political segregation of the two main groups (Spaniards and Amerindians) into two separate republics based on race: the Republic of the Spaniards and the Republic of the Indians. It was a construct intended to facilitate colonial exploitation and to preserve cultural and racial "purity." Interracial sexual unions, however, led to accelerated mestizaje, eventually turning the dual republics concept on its head and throwing the original three-tiered caste system into disarray. In addition, as the myriad interracial progeny of these unions grew in number, they represented a growing challenge to the colonial order. As we shall see, women's role in this process was not insignificant. By examining the gamut of women's experiences regarding the origins and inner workings of interracial sexual unions, we will also uncover women's agency in both the formation and subversion of the race-based social hierarchy, both of which were the result of sexual choices made by women and men.

Let us begin with the experiences of the women of the Mexica and Inca nobility, who were among the first to form unions with Spanish men and who gave birth to some of Latin America's first interracial children— mestizos. The imperial rulers of the Aztecs and Incas presented women, usually their female relatives, to the Spaniards, both upon the latter's arrival and after their decisive military success. Through these unions between Mexica or Inca women and their Spanish partners, the imperial ruling class hoped to form marital alliances with the powerful newcomers, as was their custom. The offspring of these unions would represent the mingling of indigenous royal blood with Spanish conquering blood, thereby creating kinship bonds and stronger royal lineages. Little did these unsuspecting women know that the Spaniards would have very different intentions toward them and that the mechanism of polygynous marriage alliances would have results far distant from those intended by indigenous rulers. The latter saw this practice as a political strategy like that which they had always practiced with surrounding groups and subjugated peoples. The Spaniards, on the other hand, considered it an opportunity to receive sexual services without a marital commitment or to accumulate, with or without marriage, enough material resources to move up the social ladder.

Sometimes marriage took place between these men and women and sometimes it did not, the choice to make a formal commitment usually depending on the sociopolitical background of the Spanish man and the economic position of the indigenous woman. High-ranking Mexica daughters of the royal lineages of Tenochtitlan and Texcoco, for example, were formally married to Spanish conquistadores from the outset; many of these indigenous noblewomen brought large dowries, rich tracts of land, and sometimes even *encomiendas* to their marriages.[6] Two of Montezuma's daughters, Doña Isabel and Doña Leonor, for example, were married several times to notable Spanish men as one husband after the other died and the women remarried. During her lifetime, Doña Isabel was married to six different Aztec and Spanish leaders. Before the Aztec defeat at Tenochtitlan, she was first married to her father's presumed successor, Atlixcatl, and then to the next two imperial leaders, Cuitlahuac and Cuauhtemoc. Upon Cuauhtemoc's execution by Cortés and the military success of the Spanish regime, Doña Isabel spent a short period of time with Hernán Cortés, the man who appeared, at least momentarily, to be the new ruler, and bore a child with him. Afterward, she married the Spanish conquistadores Alonso de Grado, Pedro Gallego, and Juan Cano successively.

Spaniards of lesser rank often married noblewomen of lesser kingdoms in an effort to accumulate wealth and make their fortunes in the New World. Marrying an Indian heiress became a familiar path to success as the women's dowries often provided enough resources for such a Spaniard to set himself up in mining, textile production, or some other lucrative trade. Indeed, the caciques of one Mexica kingdom, Tlaxcala, complained in 1585

> that in that province many Spaniards have married [indigenous] women who were the widows of caciques and other rich natives who have left property, houses and other estates which [although] belonging to the children of the first husbands the said Spaniards whom they, the widows, marry, spend, take and diminish it and sue to have it left to their children, in which there is great disorder and much harm to their republic, entreating me to order that as soon as the said widows marry the said Spaniards or any other person, since the property of the first husband is entailed they should be put under guardianship, with which will be restored much property of orphans who are now dispossessed and poor because their estates have been usurped in this way.[7]

Sometimes Spanish men also derived access to labor from their marriages to Indian women, since their wives and in-laws would be sure to have influence in the indigenous villages under their jurisdictions. Clearly, there were vast differences between what the indigenous nobility intended by marrying its daughters to the Spanish newcomers and what the Spanish grooms' expectations actually were. Mexica and Inca hopes of forming politically advantageous kinship bonds with the new colonial rulers were frustrated, more often than not, by the Spaniards' hopes of using their indigenous wives' wealth to further their social positions. For the Mexica and the Inca, such marriages were good politics; for the Spaniards, they were good business.

When a Spaniard had promised to marry an indigenous noblewoman and then did not, the kin members who had made the arrangement some-times expressed bewilderment. Indeed, the parents of such women (or other of their kin) often complained that at the time they had turned their daughters over to an individual Spaniard, it was with marriage in mind. Some noblewomen cohabited with Spanish partners, providing them with support and bearing children with them, only to be cast aside after a few years for a younger or richer indigenous woman or, more often than not, for a Spanish wife. Apparently, these men were able to gain access to the important economic resources and political alliances of indigenous noble families through temporary relationships of concubinage with their daughters and saw no reason to marry these women.

Indeed, some Spanish conquistadores established sexual relationships with several indigenous women at the same time, recalling the polygy-nous practices of the pre-Hispanic Indian nobility as well as the Islamic "harem," both of which the Catholic Church railed against in its indoc-trination efforts with both Iberian Muslims and New World peoples. One Spanish expeditionary to Peru, Alonso de Mesa, lived with six different indigenous women simultaneously in his house in Cuzco and had a child with each of them by 1544. Finally, in 1552, he married Doña Catalina Huaco Ocllo, an Inca noblewoman. I would like to point out that he was the only conqueror of Peru to marry an indigenous woman.[8]

Occasionally Mexica or Inca noblewomen who were partnered with Spanish men were abandoned altogether; more often they were later married to Spaniards of lesser social status than themselves and than the "conquerors" to whom they had been betrothed. Such was the case with Doña Inés Huaylas Yupanqui, the sister of Atahualpa. Atahualpa was, of course, the contender to the Inca throne, who had just triumphed over his half brother, Huascar, upon the Spanish arrival. Doña Inés, or Quispe Sisa, as she had been called in pre-Christian times, was Huayna Capac's (the previous Inca king and also Atahualpa's father) daughter by one of his secondary wives, Contarhuacho. As such, under Inca rule she would have customarily entered into marriage with an important military leader as a way of consolidating a political alliance.

After the Spanish invasion of Peru and his abduction, Atahualpa undoubtedly saw Francisco Pizarro as a powerful chief who needed to be co-opted, so he arranged for his sister to marry Pizarro, although a formal marriage never took place. Doña Inés Huaylas Yupanqui was a beautiful fifteen-year-old in the full blossom of her youth, while Pizarro, at fifty-six, was already considered an old man by the standards of the time. Even so, she and Pizarro lived together for a few years and she had two children with him: Francisca, who was born in 1534, and Gonzalo, in 1535, both of whom Pizarro legitimized. Sometime thereafter, she married Francisco de Ampuero, Pizarro's page. The old conquistador probably arranged the marriage himself, since he also granted Ampuero an encomienda, presumably to support the couple.[9]

Pizarro then went on to the company of another Inca noblewoman, Doña Angelina Yupanqui, Atahualpa's principal wife, on whom he had probably long had his eye. Doña Angelina bore two additional children with the aging leader: another son, Francisco, in 1537, and Juan, who died in childhood. Neither did he marry Doña Angelina, nor did he legitimate the children of that union as he had Doña Inés's son and daughter. After Pizarro's death by assassination in 1541, Doña Angelina Yupanqui married Juan de Betanzos, a Spanish interpreter, making him a very wealthy man, since as a member of the Inca nobility, she owned extensive lands and other properties.

One cannot escape wondering what the psychic costs must have been for these women, and others like them, who found themselves in intimate relationships, at times against their will, with the very men who had brutally killed their fathers, husbands, brothers, and uncles. These were strange times, and they lived with strange men whose presence and actions were transforming every aspect of indigenous life, from the deities who inhabited their supernatural world to the diseases from which their children would die. Even more incomprehensible, what must it have been like to bear children with these men, mestizo children, progeny of Spaniard and Indian, sons and daughters of the conquering power and simultaneously of those who had been defeated?

Indeed, indigenous women who participated in interracial sexual unions with Spanish men led highly conflicted lives. For decades now, there has been much to-do about male caciques' struggles to straddle the colonial divide, how they were forced to live in two worlds and to appease both the Spanish colonial regime and their own people. Yet until recently, we have not heard much about the equally or even more tenuous position of indigenous women who were partnered with Spanish men. Whether they were forced into or chose these unions, these women also lived their lives between two worlds—though more intimate worlds than that of the cacical dilemma. They straddled, painfully, the indigenous world of their family, ethnic, and cultural loyalties on the one hand and the Spanish world of their male partners, colonial oppressors, and mestizo children on the other.

"World straddling" most likely occurred more often among indigenous women in urban settings and probably with more frequency among elite women who were married or partnered with Spanish notables. These women were caught between two worlds and experienced a number of painful predicaments, one of which we will refer to as "living with the enemy." Indeed, for indigenous women partnered with Spanish men, "living with the enemy" must have brought with it agonizing dilemmas. What feelings must have surged in the Inca and Mexica noblewomen who became lovers to Pizarro and Cortés upon the respective defeats of the Inca and Aztec empires? Both Inés Huaylas Yupanqui and Angelina Yupanqui, the sister and intended wife of Atahualpa, were expected to fulfill the sexual needs of Francisco Pizarro, the very man who had so ignominiously murdered their beloved Inca king. Doña Isabel Montezuma, the daughter of the Aztec ruler, was forced to spend time as Hernán Cortés's sexual partner and had a daughter with him, Doña Leonor, before being married to another Spaniard of lesser standing. Cortés was responsible not only for the circumstances of her father's death but also had executed her Mexica husband, Cuauhtemoc, the last Aztec ruler.

Using indigenous noblewomen as war trophies would not end with the Spaniards' initial military successes. After the Spanish takeover of Peru, Francisco Pizarro appointed the Inca Manco as native ruler and attempted to rule through his mediation. The "puppet" Inca became a target for extortion and taunting on the parts of Pizarro's partisans to the extent that his brother, Gonzalo, decided that he must "have" Manco Inca's wife, the Coya Cura Ocllo. Although the humiliated Inca tried to dissuade him with treasures and even to fool him by sending another woman in Cura Ocllo's place, the scornful interloper would not be appeased. Gonzalo took the Inca's beloved wife, along with the treasure, and kept her for a protracted time.[10] In a similar vein, in 1572 the Spanish annihilated Vilcabamba, a much reduced Inca kingdom that postdated the failed rebellion of Manco Inca. Tupac Amaru, its last Inca ruler, was executed, and the latter's sister, Cusi Carhuay Coya, and his niece, Doña Beatriz Clara Coya, were forced to marry Spaniards. When her Inca husband died, the viceroy Toledo obliged Cusi Carhuay to marry a poor Spanish soldier of low status. Worse, he then arranged to marry Doña Beatriz, Tupac Amaru's niece, to Martín García de Loyola, her uncle's captor.

Dissimilarly, however, Inca women sometimes took rather surprising positions regarding their loyalties in the many wars that plagued the viceroyalty of Peru in the first half century of Spanish rule. A poignant example is the siege of Lima in 1536 during the uprising of the Inca Manco II. Contarhuacho, the female ruler of Huaylas and Doña Inés Yupanqui's mother, came to Pizarro's aid with one thousand troops from her jurisdiction to help defeat the rebel Incas. Having been one of Atahualpa's secondary wives, she had supported the very man who both killed her husband and fathered her grandchildren. On the other hand, at the Inca retreat from Cuzco, one of Manco II's lovers was burned to death by Spanish troops without making a sound rather than divulge the Incas' whereabouts.[11]

Perhaps the most heart-wrenching dilemma experienced by indigenous women in interracial unions, however, was their frequent, and sometimes permanent, separation from their mestizo children. In colonial Lima and Cuzco, Indian women, even noblewomen, were brutally separated from their mestizo children, often at tender ages, by Spanish partners who perceived them as being incapable of providing their progeny with a "proper" Spanish upbringing.[12] Mestizos who were raised by their Indian mothers were not accorded legitimate status in elite Lima society. A mestizo child's future would, thus, depend on the dispossession of the Indian mother and the rejection of her culture. Sometimes the children of such unions would be shipped off to Spain to be educated there, with the result that mother and child might never see each other again.

The case of Francisco Pizarro and Doña Inés Huaylas Yupanqui is instructive. Pizarro carried on a relationship of concubinage with Inés, who was the daughter of the Inca, Huayna Capac, for a few years and then abandoned her for another Inca noblewoman. He did not leave his children in her care, however. Instead, he entrusted their upbringing to his half brother, Martín de Alcántara, and his wife, Doña Inés Muñoz. Another daughter of Huayna Capac experienced the same wrenching dispossession of her children. Tocto Chimbo engaged in a relationship of concubinage with Hernando de Soto, one of the primary conquistadores. De Soto entrusted his *mestiza* daughter to the care of a tutor rather than leave her in the keeping of her Indian mother.[13]

The separation of Indian mothers and mestizo children undoubtedly derived from the Iberian practice of dispossessing "wayward" women of their children. Spanish mothers whose sexual conduct was thought to be questionable and hence did not live up to the social ideals prescribed by Iberian society for women were deemed to be incapable of raising children. When this practice found its way to the New World and was applied to indigenous mothers who had borne children with Spanish men, their prescribed racial "inferiority" was combined with the "natural" inferiority of their gender to produce a generalized negative attitude toward their ability to socialize their children properly. This is a perfect example of the "double jeopardy" suffered by indigenous women in Spanish colonial society.

Doubts about native women's capacity to raise their mestiza daughters were especially acute. As discussed earlier, the Spanish emphasis on sexual purity—premarital virginity, for example—was not as valued in Mexica and Inca societies, leading to fears that mestiza daughters who had been raised by their indigenous mothers might bring dishonor to the families of their Spanish fathers. Hence, Spanish men often insisted on removing these girls from the care of their indigenous partners. One Spanish colonial jurist, Polo de Ondegardo, was even reported to have said that Indian mothers were "an impediment to instilling anything good" in their racially mixed daughters.[14] Often, Spanish women, either relatives or nuns, would instead be placed in charge of socializing mestizo children born of interracial unions.

Notes

1. Ramón A. Gutiérrez, *When Jesus Came, the Corn Mothers Went Away* (Stanford, CA: Stanford University Press, 1991), 51.

2. Felipe Guamán Poma de Ayala, *Nueva corónica y buen gobierno*, ed. John Murra and Rolena Adorno, trans. and textually analyzed from Quechua by Jorge Urioste (México: Siglo (XX)I, 1980), 869. Cited in Alejandra Osorio, "Seducción y conquista: Una lectura de Guaman Poma," *Allpanchis* 35/36 (1990): 310.

3. Works on the historiographical treatment of La Malinche include Sandra Messinger Cypess, *La Malinche in Mexican Literature: From History to Myth* (Austin: University of Texas Press, 1991); Jean Franco, *Plotting Women: Gender and Representation in Mexico* (New York: Columbia University Press, 1989); Tzvetan Todorov, *The Conquest of America: The Question of the Other* (New York: Harper & Row, 1984); Frances Kartunnen, "To the Valley of Mexico, Doña Marina (La Malinche)," in *Between Worlds: Interpreters, Guides, and Survivors* (New Brunswick, NJ: Rutgers University Press, 1994), 1–23; Cherrie Moraga, "From a Long Line of Vendidas," in *Race, Class, Gender and Sexuality: Philosophy, the Big Questions*, ed. Naomi Zack (Malden, MA: Blackwell, 1998), chap. 33.

4. Frances Kartunnen, "Rethinking Malinche," in *Indian Women of Early Mexico*, ed. Susan Schroeder, Stephanie Wood, and Robert Haskett (Norman: University of Oklahoma Press, 1997), 297–98.

5. Richard Rodríguez, "The Indian Doesn't Need Our Pity," *Los Angeles Times*, October 9, 1992. Cited in Matthew Restall, "He Wished It in Vain: Subordination and Resistance among Maya Women in Post-Conquest Yucatan," *Ethnohistory* 42 (Fall 1995): 578.

6. It was unusual for marriages to take place between high-ranking indigenous noblemen and Spanish women; this is said to be owing to the fact that a woman's status in society was determined by her husband's status. In a colonial race-based society, it would not have been advantageous for a white woman to marry an Indian man even if he were from the nobility, especially when there was a shortage of Spanish women and ample opportunities for the latter to form more beneficial marriages with Spanish men. Even so, a few cases did occur. A Spanish woman, María de Esquivel, for example, married Carlos Inca.

7. AGI México 1091, Libro C2, f.129v–130r, as cited in Pedro Carrasco, "Indian-Spanish Marriages in the First Century of the Colony," in *Indian Women of Early Mexico*, ed. Susan Schroeder, Stephanie Wood, and Robert Haskett (Norman: University of Oklahoma Press, 1997), 97.

8. James Lockhart, *The Men of Cajamarca: A Social and Biographical Study of the First Conquerors of Peru* (Austin: Published for the Institute of Latin American Studies by the University of Texas Press, 1972), 229.

9. There were, however, some elite Inca women who refused to participate in unions with the Spanish invaders. Atahualpa's sister, Azarpay, for example, fled to Cajamarca rather than be handed over to the royal paymaster, Navarro. She was hunted down and brought back to Francisco Pizarro, however, who then "took" her for himself.

10. John Hemming, *The Conquest of the Incas* (New York: Harcourt, Brace, Jovanovich, 1970), 182–83.

11. María Rostworowski de Diez Canseco, *Doña Francisca Pizarro: Una ilustre mestiza 1534–1598* (Lima: Instituto de Estudios Peruanos, 2004), 25–27.

12. María Emma Mannarelli, "Sexualidad y desigualdades genéricas en el Perú del siglo XVI," *Allpanchis* 35/36 (1990): 231–35; Nancy van Deusen, "Los primeros recogimientos para doncellas mestizas en Lima y Cuzco, 1550–1580," *Allpanchis* 35/36 (1990): 261; Kathryn Burns, *Colonial Habits: Convents and the Spiritual Economy of Cuzco, Peru* (Durham, NC: Duke University Press, 1999), 16.

13. Mannarelli, "Sexualidad y desigualdad," 234–35.

14. Domingo de Angulo, ed., "Libro original que contiene la fundación de monesterio de monxas de señora Sta. Clara desta ciudad del Cuzco, por el qual consta ser su patrono el insigne Cabildo, Justica y Reximiento desta dicha ciudad: Año de 1560," *Revista del Archivo Nacional del Peru* 11 (1939): 83. Cited in Burns, *Colonial Habits*, 16.

La Malinche as Palimpsest II*

Sandra Messinger Cypess

The conquest of Mexico begun in 1519 by the Spanish conquistadores is a pervasive subtext for Mexican culture. The invasion constituted a clash of cultures involving archetypal patterns that have formed a myth more consequential than the historical reality. The historical event has been described, interpreted, and converted into a symbolic construct that is reinterpreted by each successive generation. The conquest remains a reverberating presence in the Mexican and Latin American psyche, and the characters of the dramatic spectacle sustain both Mexican and world literature. The participants themselves differed in their views of the circumstances, as a comparison of the existing documents reveals. Hernán Cortés, leader of the Spanish expedition that conquered the Aztec empire and brought the several Indian nations of Mexico under Spanish control, wrote ongoing reports to his king, Charles V, and his *Cartas de relación* (*Letters from Mexico*) offers his point of view. His secretary and biographer, López de Gómara, also published a version of the conquest, which was considered sufficiently controversial that one of Cortés's foot soldiers, Bernal Díaz del Castillo, was motivated to "set the record straight." Accounts of indigenous reactions to the conflict can be found in the collection compiled by Miguel León-Portilla, *La visión de los vencidos*,

*This essay is a new version of Sandra Messinger Cypess's groundbreaking, original essay by the same title that opened her book *La Malinche in Mexican Literature: From History to Myth* (Austin: University of Texas Press, 1991). She has kindly reshaped and shortened the essay for the readers of this book to aid in their understanding of how Bernal Díaz's presentation of La Malinche served as part of the foundation for the later layering of this indigenous woman's significances in history and myth. Readers stimulated to know more about the palimpsest character of her influences are encouraged to return to the original essay.

3. Malinche/Malintzin/Doña Marina. Unknown artist, sixteenth century. From the *Lienzo de Tlaxcala*. © Foundation for the Advancement of Mesoamerican Studies, Inc., www.famsi.org.

translated in 1962 as *The Broken Spears*. Moreover, key literary texts in subsequent historical periods have provided alternatives to the traditional telling of the conquest. Each narrator focuses on different elements of the event, reflecting the distinct historical and political needs of that period. The opinions of all participating groups have been represented in the formation of the tradition, except for the voice of one major figure whose role IS considered crucial and consequential but whose discourse does not appear in a firsthand account: La Malinche, the Indian woman who became the interpreter, guide, mistress, and confidante of Cortés during the time of the conquest. Although her voice may have been silenced, her presence and functions are documented in the chronicles. For that reason she may be considered the first woman of Mexican literature, just as she is considered the first mother of the Mexican nation and the Mexican Eve, symbol of national betrayal.

She is also known by different names, a characteristic she shares with another prominent historico-literary woman, Queen Boadicea. La Malinche is called Malinal, Malintzin, Malinche, or Doña Marina. Malintzin is formed from her Nahuatl birth name, Malinal, and Marina was given to her at her Christian baptism. La Malinche is the syncretic, mestizo form by which I shall call her, employing the others according to their use in the literary texts.

La Malinche has been transformed from a historical figure to a major Mexican and Latin American feminine archetype, a polysemous sign whose signifieds, for all their ambiguity, are generally negative. Like Don Quixote or Don Juan, La Malinche has become an international figure whose story has enriched the literature of other cultures and a variety of artistic forms. Despite the many controversies concerning other participants in the conquest, no figure is as ambiguous and abstract as La Malinche.

Disputes abound concerning the formation of her very name, her birthplace, her early life before her encounter with Cortés and recorded history. The events of her life after the military phase of the conquest are also shrouded in mystery, and the date and causes of her death remain unknown. Very few Mexicans before the modern period were willing to accept her as anything other than a prostitute or traitor. I must agree with the Mexican psychologist Juana Armanda Alegría that "La Malinche was the only important woman during the conquest of Mexico, and in that role, she deserves to be reconsidered. History has not been just to Doña Marina."[1]

The surviving image of La Malinche in a variety of literary and artistic traditions, including Mexican, European, Chicano, and US cultures, is a product of interpretations by both popular culture and the writers who have reworked the literary tradition that first formed in Mexico. Since the conquest, La Malinche has been the subject of biographical, fictional, pictorial, and symbolic interpretation, but this study, first published in a longer form in 1991, is the first to delineate the transformation of the historical figure into a literary sign with multiple manifestations. It is also the first study to identify the formation of a Malinche paradigm, characterize its features, and show the changes that have occurred in the use of the sign through the impact of sociopolitical events on the literary expression. My study uses the notion of intertextuality as a guiding principle in my reading of "La Malinche." I discovered that texts about her were continually being incorporated into other, newer texts about her, suggesting that no single La Malinche text is a self-contained unit. This discovery obliges one to be as fully aware as possible of the ways a historical event and historical figure, such as this indigenous woman, enter into the discursive space of a culture where the texts of the past coexist within the present, while the present image becomes intelligible only in terms of prior discourse. My study reveals that "La Malinche" functions as a continually enlarging palimpsest of Mexican cultural identity whose layers of meaning have accrued through the years. With each generation the sign "La Malinche" has added diverse interpretations of her identity, role, and significance for individuals and for Mexico.

The palimpsest is an important archaeological image in Mexico and describes the way the Aztecs, Mayans, and other tribes built one pyramid atop another, or how the Catholic Church constructed its religious sites on pre-Hispanic foundations. As a way to understand more fully the way the Malinche myth is an example of a palimpsest, it is important to review the Aztec environment in which La Malinche was reared as Malinal and the attitudes toward women in that society as well as the sociopolitical alliances of the indigenous groups in the region and the conventions at work that affected the behavior of the protagonists of the conquest. Readers of this abridgment can get access to some elements of indigenous and Spanish attitudes toward women in Karen Powers's essay "Colonial Sexuality: Of Women, Men, and *Mestizaje*" elsewhere in this volume.

The foundational layers of La Malinche come to us from the historical accounts of her life among the Spaniards found in *La historia verdadera de la conquista de la Nueva España* and in Hernán Cortés's *Cartas*. As a way of helping the reader engage more directly with this early deposit of La Malinche into literary history, I will explore Bernal Díaz's many references before turning to Cortés's shorter portrayal. I will close with a concise view of my own semiotic analysis of their historical inventions and her fate in the hands of a selection of Mexican and Chicana writers. Readers interested in a fuller exposition of La Malinche as palimpsest can turn to the longer, original essay by that title.

La Malinche in Bernal Díaz's *True History*

Although there is no way to prove Bernal Díaz's version right or wrong, it has been accepted in the historical tradition of Spain and Mexico. In the past his text was considered basically factual, while it has also been acknowledged that he "carefully selected portions of her life that enhance her stature as a participant in the Conquest. His elaboration of these episodes makes her into a true heroine."[2] The contemporary reader may well wonder which aspects of his narrative were invented and which actually occurred, but whatever the answer, we can evaluate the elements he chose to include. In contrast to the paucity of textual information regarding the Indian woman on the part of his leader, Bernal Díaz provides a detailed and vivid portrait of this "most excellent" woman, the first descriptive phrase he applies to La Malinche. In the words of Julie

Greer Johnson, "Bernal Diaz is the only early colonial writer to make a woman a major figure in the historical events unfolding in Spain's American possessions."[3] Throughout his text, Bernal Díaz describes the intelligence, beauty, and amazing acts of heroism of La Malinche, as well as her unusual strength, spirit, courage, and resourcefulness. He also praises the abilities she displayed during the various military incursions she was forced to endure, commenting, "Doña Marina, although a native woman, possessed such manly valor that . . . she betrayed no weakness but courage greater than that of a woman." Bernal Díaz emphasizes the sufferings and tribulations of the Spaniards, which La Malinche shared without complaint (he considered this atypical for females). He compares her to models from the Bible and the Spanish literary tradition that were well-known to his readers.

Bernal Díaz's second reference to La Malinche is also positive in the way he substantiates Cortés's comment that she was one of the twenty young women given to the Spaniards as a present by the Tabascan chief; he singles her out: "One of the Indian ladies was christened Doña Marina. She was a truly great princess, the daughter of Caciques and the mistress of vassals, as was very evident in her appearance." Because of her beauty and other excellent attributes, she was first given to a prominent conquistador, Alonzo Hernández Puertocarrero; when he left for Castile, she was transferred to Cortés, "to whom she bore a son named Don Martin Cortés." This concise phrase referring to the birth of a child in 1522—after the major events of the military enterprise—may lead a reader to bypass its significance. By providing that information immediately after referring to her noble status and before elaborating on the other contributions of Doña Marina as translator and guide, Bernal Díaz reveals his own implicit attitude toward the significance of her role. He affirms her noble Indian lineage first, as proof of her appropriateness for her subsequent function in the formation of another family line, the mestizos, for all of whom Cortés and La Malinche serve as symbolic parents.

After providing the context within which to locate La Malinche, Bernal Díaz then adds background information on the birth and youth of

La Malinche in the following chapter. The Spanish reader of Bernal Díaz's text would readily notice that events in the early life of this young Indian woman corresponded to events during the childhood and adolescence of Amadís de Gaula, the exemplary Christian knight of a fictional work of the same name. As Johnson points out, "Both Doña Marina and Amadís are of noble lineage and as children, they became victims of efforts to deny them their birthright. After the departure of their fathers—one dies and the other undertakes a journey—their mothers, with the aid of family servants or slaves, abandon them in secret. Amadís and Marina are then reared at some distance from their homes and by people whose culture is different from their own."[4] When Doña Marina and Amadís are each reunited with their families as adults, their Christian religious beliefs lead them to forgive the ills done to them. Johnson points out that in their reconciliation scenes, "both young people serve as defenders of the faith, Amadís by exemplifying good in his performance of noble deeds and Marina by symbolizing the conversion of an entire race of pagans. They accepted without question God's will in determining their destiny."[5]

In addition to the implicit presence of the Spanish subtext of Amadís, Bernal Díaz strengthens his case for the nobility and righteousness of Doña Marina by explicitly comparing her forgiving attitude toward her mother and half brother with that of the biblical Joseph. Like Joseph confronting his brothers in Egypt, the Marina of Bernal Díaz's narrative has also grown in political power and wisdom because of the train of events begun as a malign act to rid the family of an unwanted sibling. La Malinche's discourse at the encounter with her family, as reported by Bernal Díaz using the form of indirect monologue, also stresses cultural values the Spaniards considered as their important gifts to the Indians:

They were afraid of her, for they believed that she sent for them in order to kill them, and they cried. And when she saw them crying, she comforted them and told them not to be afraid, that God had been very gracious to her in freeing her from the worship of

idols and making her a Christian, and allowing her to bear a son
to her lord and master Cortés, and in marrying her to a gentleman such as Juan Jaramillo, who was now her husband; that she
would rather serve her husband and Cortés than anyone else in
the world, and would not exchange her lot to become leader of all
the provinces of New Spain . . . and this seems to me to imitate
what happened to Joseph and his brothers in Egypt, when they
fell into his power in the episode with the wheat (51).

As William Prescott observes in his *History of the Conquest of Mexico*,
Bernal Díaz ends this important account with an additional solemn comment regarding its veracity, "And all this I say, I heard most assuredly, and
I swear it, amen," a variant of his usual claim that his version is the accurate one, not Gómara's.[6] As informed modern readers, however, we should
make note of the textual location of the speech that he reproduces as an
eyewitness: he inserts the reunion of Doña Marina with her family as part
of his introduction of her to his audience, at the narrative moment that
corresponds to her first encounter with the Spaniards. The irony of this
textual juxtaposition should not go unnoticed. Doña Marina's encounter
with the Spaniards in Tabasco was the result of her having been disinher-
ited by her family. She is reunited with them only after she has fulfilled her
functions for the conquerors, encountering her mother and stepbrother
in 1524, as she accompanied Cortés during his expedition to Honduras, to
quell a rebellion among the Spaniards sent there earlier. After that episode
she disappears from the historical record, if not from literary texts.

Other readers—most notably Chicana writers such as Adelaida Del
Castillo and Cordelia Candelaria—wonder about how much suffering it
must have caused her to have been sold into slavery after being a princess.
For Bernal Díaz and Bernal Díaz's Marina, however, the end result is the
important thing, that is, the assimilation by Marina of Spanish culture.
Bernal Díaz presents her initiation into Spanish culture and its results
all in one chapter as the appropriate context within which his readers
may then place the succeeding deeds of Doña Marina as related in his

subsequent chapters. Bernal Díaz configures the sign "Doña Marina" as filled culturally with the attributes of a worthy *Spanish* mother.

After establishing Doña Marina's credentials in terms of lineage and nobility of deeds, Bernal Díaz then briefly asserts that it was her talent for languages that "was the great beginning of our conquests. . . . I have made a point of telling this story because without Doña Marina, we could not have understood the language of New Spain and Mexico." Indeed, he gives credit to Dona Marina as the translator of record during the many interviews that took place between Moctezuma and Cortés once the Spaniards successfully reached the Aztec capital on November 9, 1519. He also reaffirms the enmity of the Tlaxcalans toward the Aztecs and their willing support of the Spaniards' attempt to overthrow their enemies.

La Malinche in Cortés's Letters

Although Cortés was responsible for the significant part that La Malinche played in the conquest as Doña Marina, his own writings about her are remarkably reserved, as sparing of words as possible despite her numerous roles. He briefly refers to her in *Letter Two* as his translator: "my interpreter, who is an Indian woman from Putunchan [Tabasco]." In *Letter Five*, after having described so many important events without bothering to refer to the Indian woman who had played such a significant—but obviously to him subservient—position, Cortés is only a bit more expansive in his narrative to the king:

> If he [the Amerindian Cancec] wished to learn the truth he had only to ask the interpreter with whom he was speaking, Marina, who traveled always in my company after she had been given me as a present with twenty other women. She then told him that what I had said was true and spoke to him of how I had conquered Mexico and of all the lands which I held subject and had placed beneath Your Majesty's command.[7]

Cortés used Marina's role as translator to verify his own deeds and loyalty to the king; her indirect discourse served as a reflection of himself. Such self-serving practices would be incorporated into characterizations of him by subsequent writers, most notably Carlos Fuentes in *Todos los gatos son pardos*. Because Cortés himself provided so little information on the full ramifications of the activities of La Malinche, we must read the subtext as well as the surface signs in order to determine the context within which to understand her role and their relationship. Both letters in which the references to La Malinche occur also contain Cortés's version of two especially controversial events of the conquest. In *Letter Two* Cortés mentions her in relation to the discovery of the conspiracy in Cholula and the events leading up to the massacre of the Cholulans, an exploit of great significance for the success of the conquest and for contributing to the so-called Black Legend of Spain's role in the New World. It is also of great significance with regard to the "black legend" of La Malinche's role; according to the accounts of Cortés, Gómara, and Bernal Díaz del Castillo, she was the key source of information regarding the planned ambush of the Spaniards. Similarly, *Letter Five* refers to the 1524–25 voyage to Hibueras, today's Honduras, during which time Cortés ordered the torture and assassination of Cuauhtemoc; for La Malinche it was also the time of her marriage to Juan Jaramillo and the subsequent diminution of her role in the life of New Spain. The significance of these juxtapositions needs to be considered.

Cortés refers to the Indian woman as "Marina," without the title "Doña" usually used by Bernal Díaz. Cortés himself is referred to by a form of her name, "El Malinche," when he is addressed by the Indians. As Bernal Díaz tells us, "He was given this name because Doña Marina, our interpreter, was always in his company, especially when ambassadors arrived and during talks with chiefs, so they called Cortés 'the captain of Marina' in their language, or 'Malinche' for short." This observation regarding La Malinche's accompaniment of Cortés at all the major meetings with chiefs and other important officials emphasizes the significance of her intervention in the negotiations despite the reticence of Cortés.

Although he did not give official recognition to her presence in the *Letters*, the Indians who witnessed the transactions acknowledged her role by calling him "Malinche." Tzvetan Todorov's wry remark, that "for once, it is not the woman who takes the man's name,"[8] reminds us that the situation remains unusual to this day.

The Semiotics of La Malinche

The subsequent image we have of La Malinche has been produced largely through fiction and therefore can be studied as a literary construct. Based on the idea that literature is a social institution that has provided role models and set patterns of acceptable and unacceptable behavior, the following section chronicles the presentation of La Malinche in selected Mexican and Chicana literary texts: her historical significance, her evolving literary representations, and the changing interpretations of her role from the historians of the conquest to contemporary Mexican American/Chicana and Mexican women writers who consider La Malinche a symbol of the tensions, contradictions, and oppression inherent in their own sexual, racial, and ethnic identity.[9]

I follow the semiotic definition of the linguistic sign as an arbitrary combination of a signifier and a signified. As the science dedicated to the study of the production of meaning, semiotics recognizes that each element we call a word is a sign, composed of two aspects, the expression plane, or the signifier, and the content plane, or the signified. Within this semiotic framework, the construction of meaning is seen as an active process rather than something intrinsic in the sign. The following pages explore how literary texts configure the sign "La Malinche." Similarly, for each reader "La Malinche" is a textual sign loaded with presuppositions that influence the reader's relationship with the sign and its text. When La Malinche was transformed into a sign, she became part of her culture's myth system. From an anthropological perspective, the dramatic stories that become myths authorize the continuance of ancient institutions, customs, rites, and beliefs. Myths provide examples to be emulated, precedents to be repeated, and in light of that function their study enables us to decode a culture's attitudes toward its members. Because La Malinche, as an archetypal female figure in Latin America, plays such a vital role in Mexican and Latin American myths, the role she is traditionally assigned must be evaluated and reevaluated. Such a study may contribute to cultural revisionism in Mexico, a society deeply involved in the process of change.

The Mythic Mexican La Malinche

For too long, false myths have distorted the images of women; and especially in Mexico, the myth of La Malinche has been one of the most restrictive. It is not, however, the only myth to generate images of women. As Luis Leal points out, La Malinche constitutes one of the two major female archetypes in Mexico, along with the Virgin of Guadalupe.[10] The Virgin of Guadalupe embodies the most virtuous feminine attributes: forgiveness, succor, piety, virginity, saintly submissiveness. La Malinche is the Mexican Eve, the tainted sex "who is selfish and rejecting, while Guadalupe is giving and nurturing. . . . A polarized perspective of women emerges whereby only La Malinche as supreme evil and La Virgen as supreme good are possible."[11]

Rosario Castellanos adds the seventeenth-century nun Sor Juana Inés de la Cruz to this list in "Once Again Sor Juana," her 1961 essay on the archetypes of Mexican culture: "There are three figures in Mexican history that embody the most extreme and diverse possibilities of femininity. Each one of them represents a symbol, exercises a vast and profound influence on very wide sectors of the nation, and arouses passionate reactions. These figures are the Virgin of Guadalupe, La Malinche and Sor Juana."[12] As a feminist, Castellanos sees the figure of Sor Juana as an enigma because of her dual configuration as genius and female. The lonely, oxymoronic stance of female genius, implied by the appellation "the Tenth Muse," as Sor Juana was called, has symbolized for Mexican culture not what women in their plurality were capable of achieving, but what only an idealized Women, the rara avis, could attain. For Castellanos, the Virgin of Guadalupe and La Malinche are less ambiguous figures. She agrees that only positive elements are associated with the figure of the Virgin, an observation supported by specialized studies by literary critics, historians, and sociologists. Veneration of the Virgin transcends pure religiosity and has become equated with a sense of unselfish motherhood and positive national identity. La Malinche, at the opposite pole, embodies both negative national identity and sexuality in its most irrational form, sexuality without regard to moral laws or cultural values. Although Castellanos is more intent on focusing on the controversial views relating to Sor Juana, she tacitly acknowledges that La Malinche is fundamentally a polemical figure who influences contemporary behavior patterns: "Some call her a traitor, others consider her the founding mother of our nationality, according to whatever perspective they choose to judge her from."[13] La Malinche comes to signify the traitor to national goals; the one who conforms to her paradigm is labeled *malinchista*, the individual who sells out to the foreigner, who devalues national identity in favor of imported benefits. Castellanos compares the power of La Malinche to that of the Greek mythological figure Antaeus, who was always revived when he came into contact with the earth. Similarly, La Malinche has not departed but remains in contact with Mexico, and her power to influence behavior has not diminished with time.

In the same way that the lexical term *malinchista* was derived from her experiences, so have the figures of La Chingada and La Llorona become involved with her paradigm. La Malinche's sexual involvement with Cortés led to her designation as the first "*chingada*," a term charged with severe negative connotations for Mexicans, conjuring up personal violation and submission to rape. The image of La Llorona, or "weeping woman," at one point became conflated with the image of La Malinche because they share a sadness relating to lost children. In popular mythology La Malinche serves as a synecdoche for all Indian women who lament the fate of their progeny born to the Spanish conquistadores.

Textual analyses of the figure of La Malinche demonstrate how the cultural myth has evolved through time and how it continues to serve as a paradigm for female images in Mexico, for the ways men and women

relate to each other. Paradigms serve as guidelines for eth
or conventional actions. I consider La Malinche to be a ro
in the way Victor Turner uses the term. According to Turne,
root paradigm goes beyond the cognitive and the moral to the
domain; in so doing, it becomes "clothed with allusiveness, implications,
and metaphor."[14] A root paradigm is a cultural model that is continually
reinvested with vitality within the social drama.[15] The time of the conquest,
from 1519 to 1521, was a complex and dramatic liminal period that generated new myths, symbols, paradigms, and social structures. This was the
period during which the political and cultural consequences of European
dominance in the Americas were set. The conquest was the crucial event
in the formation of male-female relations. Succinctly described by Elu
de Leñero, the traditional image influencing male-female relationships is
derived from Cortés being served by La Malinche. In the way a Mexican
man enjoys dominating a woman, wants service from her, and expects to
impose his will and body on her and then dispose of her, he repeats the
pattern Cortés established with La Malinche.[16]

In the literary texts that employ the Malinche image, the popularly
known characteristics of the paradigm have been added to the legendary
character because of past literary interpretations rather than the actual
deeds of the historic figure. Although folkloric narratives and popular
poetry make use of the conquest theme and La Malinche, I analyze in
this work only those elements of the popular expression that have been
successfully incorporated into literary texts. Future studies will attempt to
cover the many variations of the paradigm that are found in expressions
of popular culture as well as in the texts of other cultures.

Other Layers of La Malinche

During the colonial period, Doña Marina was largely ignored in the literary texts of the colony, including those by the major writer of the period,
Sor Juana Inés de la Cruz. After the War of Independence, the identity
of Doña Marina was subsequently transformed from its Spanish cultural
form to a version circumscribed by the patriarchal culture developing in

a newly independent Mexico. The Spanish conquistadores had read La Malinche as Doña Marina, an object of desire—of male dominance of the female, of desire for the land newly conquered. The newly independent Mexicans, in contrast, as a way of declaring their political autonomy, invented new interpretations for the signs of the colonizers; they required a construction of the signs that would serve as a signal of the new socio-political agenda.

From the feminine version of the biblical Joseph, then, La Malinche becomes in the works of the postindependence period both the snake and the Mexican Eve, the traitor and temptress, the rationalization for the Amerindian failure to overcome the Europeans. From Great Lady to Terrible Mother, La Malinche serves the particular historical needs of a complex society in change. The transformation can be found in *Jicoténcal* (1826?), also known as *Xicoténcatl*, one of the first known novels to deal with the events of the conquest. Published anonymously in Philadelphia, it is one of the first texts to present a negative view of La Malinche, according to Luis Leal. Calling her Doña Marina, the unknown author paints a literary portrait of her as the evil temptress and betrayer of *la patria*. This text made an impact in Mexico. By 1870, the phrase "seller of her nation" had become integrally associated with Marina in the portrait developed by Eligio Ancona in *Los mártires del Anahuac* (The Martyrs of Anahuac).

Ireneo Paz, the grandfather of the well-known Mexican Nobelist Octavio Paz, contributed a more tempered picture to the formation of the legend of La Malinche in his romantic novels *Amor y suplicio* (Love and Torment; 1873) and *Doña Marina* (1883). His work is representative of the postreform period of Mexican history, and his texts attribute to the literary Malinche and to other Amerindian women the characteristics associated with the historical Malinche: willingness to consort with the newcomers, betrayal of her people in favor of the Spaniards, rejection of Amerindian culture, and acceptance of the Catholic religion. Paz uses the Cortés-Malinche paradigm as the emblematic encounter between Europeans and Amerindians.

By rewriting the military and political exploits of the conquest in terms of a sexual encounter, he follows the patriarchal view of women as objects of exchange; but instead of considering the woman an inferior social being, he romanticizes her as a noble individual whose actions were dictated by destiny and the gods. He offers a positive interpretation of Mexican mestizaje, providing his readers with an affirmative conception of themselves and their history. He rewrites history in a way that fits the social and political ideologies of his time: a nationalism that strives to incorporate the Indian within the paradigm of Mexican identity.

From the time of the novelist Ireneo Paz to that of his grandson, Octavio Paz, Mexico underwent a major liminal experience: the Mexican Revolution. The literary explosion of works dealing with Mexican national themes concentrated on the revolution, while the Conquest of Mexico as a literary motif was slighted by most writers. Aesthetic expressions of the theme of the conquest were created within the context of the indigenism of the great muralists of the twenties and thirties, José Clemente Orozco and Diego Rivera. In *The Aztec Image in Western Thought*, Benjamin Keen describes the presentation of both Cortés and La Malinche in these murals.

Mexican and Chicana Reinterpretations of La Malinche

The written text that synthesizes the most representative aspects of the modern attitude toward the Malinche legend is *El laberinto de la soledad* (*The Labyrinth of Solitude*; 1950) by Octavio Paz. The section "Los hijos de la Malinche" defines La Malinche for the mid-twentieth century. Paz shows La Malinche's relationships with the biblical Eve and with Mexican figures such as La Chingada and La Llorona. He sees La Malinche as representative of the "cruel incarnation of the feminine condition."[17] For Paz, the conquest of Mexico was a violation, and Doña Marina represents the violated mother, the passive figure in the events—La Chingada. This study emphasizes the intense negativity with which La Malinche is regarded and shows the polarized perspective with regard to women in Mexican society. The successful dissemination of Paz's portrayal in the modern period can be gauged by its use in popular books destined for foreign consumption, such as Irene Nicholson's *The X in Mexico: Growth within Tradition.*

Nicholson uses Paz's essay to substantiate her view that modern Mexicans consider themselves the sons of Malinche and, therefore, "they are traitors in their own minds."[18] Although Paz did not invent the negative role for La Malinche, the synthesis found in his essay serves as a norm for most of the texts written during this period. In the interest of being instructive rather than exhaustive, I have selected for analysis some representative texts that portray the traditional negative image of La Malinche in their presentation of female figures. While during the nineteenth century, narrative form was popular for addressing the theme of the conquest and its role in the building of the Mexican nation, in the aftermath of the Mexican Revolution the theme of the conquest was displayed on the Mexican stage; narrative was employed instead to record the experiences of the more recent bloody and violent conflict that was the Mexican Revolution. *Corona de fuego* (Crown of Fire; 1960) by Rodolfo Usigli and *Cuauhtémoc* (1962) by Salvador Novo provide examples of attempts to offer enthusiastic support of the Amerindian contribution to modern mestizo Mexico, to the detriment of the reputation of La Malinche.

La Malinche o La leña está verde (Malinche or The Firewood Is Green; 1958) by Celestino Gorostiza re-creates an image of La Malinche that is meant to be more positive and supportive of her role as First Mother. Nevertheless, Gorostiza betrays his heroine on the sacrificial stone of patriarchal patterns of behavior. *Todos los gatos son pardos* (All Cats Are Gray; 1970) by Carlos Fuentes also attempts a positive portrayal, or at least one that breaks the traditional configuration, yet this Marina, too, is restricted by the paradigms of patriarchy. While Gorostiza was writing at a time in which positive Mexican nationalism was strong, Fuentes's play reads the events of the conquest within the context of the Tlatelolco Massacre of 1968. His recall of the contemporary political scene is similar to the double readings offered by the authors of *Xicoténcatl* and *Los mártires del Anahuac*, who were writing during earlier complex and dramatic liminal periods. The deadly clash between the Mexican armed forces and university students on the same site that witnessed the conflict between Amerindians and Spaniards during the conquest leads Fuentes to conclude that the repetitive patterns in the social drama of Mexico remain intact. Although he calls his character Malintzin/Marina/Malinche in an effort to reflect his all-inclusive agenda, the character fails in the attempt to organize a new social structure.

One positive response to the dramatic nature of interactions occurring during the liminal period of the Mexican social scene after the Tlatelolco Massacre is that the theater has become a site where cultural change is not simply reflected but also enacted. Theatrical representations not only make use of the iconic value of La Malinche as a sign but also change the signified elements. The project of creating new readings of Mexico's past indicates a rejection of the belief that the past is predictor of the future. This new perspective is reflected in the plays of Rosario Castellanos, Willebaldo López, and Sabina Berman. They accept the idea that the past is not a closed system but "a dialectical field of forces whose artifacts can be actively engaged through theory, interpretation, transformation parody, subversion, whatever."[19]

The traditional image of La Malinche continues to be transformed by writers who question past interpretations of the sign and judge them as no longer appropriate for today's perspective on female–male relations. Rosario Castellanos's poem "La Malinche" re/views the paradigm from a point in the history of the figure itself, initiating an approach developed by Chicana women. La Malinche is a part of the cultural heritage of today's Chicanas, who see the need to place her contributions to history within a sociopolitical context corrected for distortions. Many are feminist writers, whose representations of La Malinche have radically altered the configuration of the image. The revisionist works of these Chicana writers are significant because they react to the negative presentations of La Malinche as a direct defamation of themselves.

Representative of this attitude is the comment by Adelaida Del Castillo: "Any denigrations made against her indirectly defame the character of the Mexicana/Chicana female. If there is shame for her, there is

shame for us; we suffer the effects of these implications."[20] For many of
the Chicanas, La Malinche stands at the base of *la mexicanidad* and *el
mestizaje*—the origin of the mestizo nation. Her body becomes the locus
of origin of the contemporary Chicana and her offspring are symbolic
daughters and sons. The Mexicana/Chicana writers point out that the
use of La Malinche as a scapegoat figure can be interpreted as an effort
to sustain male power by treating women as sexual objects and inferior
moral entities. Her participation in the conquest as an active and vital
figure needs to be re/viewed as a way to reject the destructive implications
of previous interpretations and to recover the positive attributes brought
forth by feminist and nationalist perspectives.

Several writers who challenge the accepted conventions offer in their
texts a different reading of the historical record. They begin with the old
presuppositions but critique the traditional assumptions of the patriarchal
culture. Two texts by Elena Garro, *Los recuerdos del porvenir* (Recollections
of Things to Come) and "La culpa es de los tlaxcaltecas" (The Tlaxcalans
Are to Blame), fit into this new agenda, as do two recent plays by Emilio
Carballido: *Ceremonia en el templo del tigre* (Ceremony in the Temple of
the Tiger; 1986) and *Tiempo de ladrones: La historia de Chucho el Roto* (Time
for Thieves: The History of Poor Chucho; 1983). Although these texts do
not deal ostensibly with the conquest, the figure of Marina and the events
of that historical period serve as a subtext, thereby inserting aspects of the
paradigm into a consideration of male–female relations and into the theme
of nationalism. These works that use the Malinche paradigm as a subtext
prove the continuing impact of the image in Mexican culture and point to
the need for a revision of the paradigm. The traditional image presented
a script that determined male–female behavior patterns according to a
patriarchal model. Yet the tightly bound image of a patriarchal Malinche,
rooted, in part, in Bernal Díaz's memories and retellings, that once crystal-
lized the thoughts and emotions of a nation has been refashioned as an icon
with new signification that reflects a new cultural agenda. Re/formations
and re/visions of the meaning inherent in the sign of La Malinche signal
the development of real structural changes in social relationships.

Notes

1. Juana Armanda Alegría, *Psicología de las Mexicanas*, 69.

2. Julie Greer Johnson, *Women in Colonial Spanish American Literature* (Westport, CT: Greenwood Press, 1983), 15.

3. Ibid., 20.

4. Ibid., 16.

5. Ibid., 17.

6. William H. Prescott, *History of the Conquest of Mexico and the History of the Conquest of Peru, 1843–1847* (New York: Modern Library, 1936), 651n23.

7. Hernán Cortés, *Letters from Mexico*, ed. and trans. A. R. Pagden (New York: Grossman, 1971), 376.

8. Tzvetan Todorov, *The Conquest of America: The Question of the Other*, trans. Richard Howard (New York: Harper & Row, 1985), 101.

9. Although I have just mentioned *Mexican American* and *Chicana* as apparently equivalent terms, their use may involve misconceptions and requires further explanation. Both may refer to the same individual, that is, one who lives in the United States but whose cultural roots are Mexican, yet the political and social implications differ depending on the context of use, the speaker, and the audience to whom the terms are addressed. In the 1970s, more conservative people considered themselves "Mexican Americans" and identified the term *Chicano* with politically radical attitudes or with social position rather than ethnic origin. Some writers still use the terms interchangeably, focusing on the common ethnic elements and overlooking the possibly different political perspectives. I use *Chicana* henceforth to refer to the women writers working in the United States whose cultural roots are Mexican in recognition of their acceptance of the term to describe themselves.

10. Luis Leal, "Female Archetypes in Mexican Literature," in *Women in Hispanic Literature: Icons and Fallen Idols*, ed. Beth Miller (Berkeley: University of California Press, 1983), 227–42.

11. Alfredo Mirandé and Evangelina Enríquez, *La Chicana: The Mexican American Woman* (Chicago: University of Chicago Press, 1979), 28.

12. Rosario Castellanos, "Once Again Sor Juana," in *A Rosario Castellanos Reader*, ed. and trans. Maureen Ahern (Austin: University of Texas Press, 1988), 222.

13. Ibid., 223.

14. Victor Turner, *Dramas, Fields, and Metaphors: Symbolic Action in Human Society* (Ithaca, NY: University of Cornell Press, 1974), 154.

15. Turner defines social drama as a period in which conflicting groups and personages attempt to assert their own paradigms; he includes the Mexican Revolution of Independence in 1810 as an illustration of "a root paradigm at work in a series of social dramas" (*Dramas, Fields, and Metaphors: Symbolic Action in Human Society* [Ithaca, NY: Cornell University Press, 1975], 98). For Turner, the years between 1810

and 1821 comprise a complex and dramatic liminal period in which those being moved in accordance with a cultural script were liberated from normative demands. The period of transition from colonial rule to Mexican nationhood generated "new myths, symbols, paradigms, and political structures" (99).

16. María del Carmen Elu de Leñero, *¿Hacia dónde va la mujer mexicana?* (México: Instituto Mexicano de Estudios Sociales, 1969), 22–23.

17. Octavio Paz, *El laberinto de la soledad* [The Labyrinth of Solitude] (México: Cuadernos Americanos, 1950), 86.

18. Irene Nicholson, *The X in Mexico: Growth within Tradition* (Garden City, NY: Doubleday, 1966), 103.

19. Kevin Brownlee and Stephen G. Nichols, "Images of Power: Medieval History/Discourse/Literature," *Yale French Studies* 70 (1986): 1.

20. Adelaida Del Castillo, "Malintzin Tenépal: A Preliminary Look into a New Perspective," in *Essays on La Mujer*, ed. Rosaura Sánchez and Rosa Martínez Cruz (Los Angeles: Chicano Studies Center, 1977), 141.

The Exaggerations of Human Sacrifice

Davíd Carrasco

*When Pedro de Alvarado reached these towns he found that they
had all been deserted that same day, and he found in the cues bodies
of men and boys who had been sacrificed, and the walls and altars
stained with blood and the hearts placed as offerings before the Idols.
He also found the stones on which the sacrifices were made and the
stone knives with which to open the chest so as to take out the heart.*

—Bernal Díaz del Castillo

*I remember that in the plaza where some of their oratories stood, there
were piles of human skulls so regularly arranged that one could count
them and I estimated them at more than a hundred thousand. I repeat
again that there were more than one hundred thousand of them.*

—Bernal Díaz del Castillo

*We slept near a stream, and with the grease from a fat Indian
woman whom we had killed and cut open, we dressed our wounds,
for we had no oil, and we supped very well on some dogs which the
Indians breed.*

—Bernal Díaz del Castillo

No topics have inflamed more argument and confusion about Aztec and Maya cultures than "human sacrifice" and "cannibalism." Chroniclers, Spanish priests, anthropologists, and writers have repeatedly returned to these two topics, some to condemn them, some to refute them, and some to try and understand the indigenous purposes and cultural meanings of ritual killing and the ritual ingestion of human flesh. As the readers of this book know, Díaz del Castillo makes references to human sacrifice ad infinitum as part of his strategy to paint a picture of Mesoamerican brutality and civilizational inferiority to Spanish Christians. In Hernán Cortés's many "sermons," as recounted by Díaz del Castillo, the Spanish captain tells the natives that human sacrifice, "idol" worship, and sodomy are the very practices that the King of Spain sent the conquistadores to stop. Of course the Spanish sovereigns knew nothing of Mesoamerican ritual or sexual practices when the Spaniards set out for Mesoamerica. The reader of the *True History* is confronted with bloody temples, skull racks with "more than a hundred thousand skulls," dismembered human remains, and eventually descriptions of Spaniards and their horses being sacrificed and dismembered.

As a way of helping the reader evaluate these Spanish descriptions and understand something of the indigenous purposes of these troubling ritual practices, we will present two short essays on the "exaggerations" of ritual killing. By using *exaggerations* I mean to raise the issues of both the distortions in Díaz del Castillo's accounts *and* the actual scale of ritual human violence in Aztec society. Responding to the previous quotes, this first essay discusses the exaggerated and prejudiced descriptions of ritual violence in the *True History*. Later in this abridgment we will find a more direct analysis of how the Aztecs constructed their religious rationale for their prodigious ritual killings of human beings. In what follows I will use the question and answer format by asking some direct questions followed by direct answers about human sacrifice and its exaggerations by the invaders.

(1) Did the Aztecs really "sacrifice" and eat parts of human beings?

There is strong evidence that they did, but the word sacrifice *is a poor match for the indigenous terms referring to the ritual killing of humans in ceremonial settings. The indigenous texts repeatedly refer to ritual ceremonies in which humans, animals, and plants were killed as* nextlaoalli *or "debt payments." The idea behind the term* nextlaoalli *is that (a) the gods suffered and died (often killing each other) during mythic times in order that human, plant, and animal life could be created, and (b) humans must now pay the debt back to the gods in ritual killings designed to regenerate the energy that resides in the object (person, animal, plant, or thing) being killed and transmit that energy to the gods. The evidence for the ritual eating of flesh is also strong, though it, too, is very hard to understand when reading Díaz del Castillo and other Spanish accounts. I discuss cannibalism later.*

(2) Was it a common practice carried out every day of the year as the Spanish accounts tell it?

No. These rituals were carried out according to a strict calendar schedule marking sacred days and in sacred places. It was not a random or casual act triggered, for the most part, by bursts of outrage or madness. A ritual calendar, as in the Christian ritual year, was the guide. Still, specific days in each of the eighteen months of the ritual calendar included human sacrifices, sometimes of children, sometimes women, but mainly males.

(3) Were there more than a hundred thousand skulls in the ceremonial precinct in Cempoala as Díaz del Castillo insists twice?

No way! An "arrangement" of skulls was called a tzompantli, *or "skull rack," which was set up in some ceremonial centers for the public display of human skulls. The Aztecs were so committed to this practice of display that they even sculpted stone racks to memorialize sacred skulls. In Aztec cosmovision, the human skull was the site of one of the three "souls" or animistic entities that had been deposited within the human body by the gods. Scenes of Aztec conquest sometimes show the victorious warrior grasping the hair over the fontanel area of the human skull as a symbol of capturing the "soul" of the enemy warrior located in the skull. Cutting off the heads and displaying them in the ceremonial precinct was a political/religious sign of gaining control over the souls, the divine energy of enemy warriors and their communities.*

All the Spanish chroniclers of the conquest of Tenochtitlan, in attempting to justify their own extreme violence and acquisitions of land and laborers, exaggerated, to some degree, the aggressions of Aztec ritual life and its periodic violence. These overstatements and gross depictions of ritual violence were also used to inflame further Spanish aggression toward the natives. The Dominican priest Diego Durán insisted in one of his books that eighty thousand people were sacrificed at one ceremony! But no archaeological dig has found human remains approaching even one-half of 1 percent of these numbers.

(4) Did the Spaniards ever actually see sacrifices or cannibalism taking place?

Yes. They saw their own soldiers being killed, skinned, and eaten during the battles in Tenochtitlan. It was a terrifying and heartbreaking scene. See page (287) for a vivid example. We know that even prior to the Spanish invasion, Aztec sacrifices were used in public rituals to strike terror in the hearts and minds of their enemies as well as to feed the gods. The second essay on ritual violence will speak more about the indigenous meanings of these sacrifices on pyramids.

(5) Did the Spaniards give an accurate account of their own aggressions, killings, murders, and body mutilations?

No, but Díaz del Castillo describes Spanish killings, executions (of both natives and Spaniards), exemplary punishments, and dismemberments throughout his book. Spanish violence is depicted as defensive or provoked, skillful, and clever while Mesoamerican warriors are both admired and defamed. Bernal appears to exaggerate how many natives are killed, and he underestimates how many Spaniards are vanquished. We know for certain that he sometimes claims victories for the Spaniards when they were defeated and sent running in retreat. When Cortés writes that two hundred enemies were killed in a certain battle, the number rises to twice or more times that in

4. Tzompantli (skull rack). Unknown artist, 1587. From the *Codex Tovar*.
Courtesy Wikimedia Commons.

5. Depiction of Mexica human sacrifice. Unknown artist, sixteenth century.
From the *Codex Magliabecchiano*.

Díaz's account. Díaz del Castillo and Cortés are careful to justify their own murderous actions, that is, when "we" were killers, the victims fully deserved it (even when they were Spaniards) due to their own moral evil or threats to us. Many political and psychological forces drive Díaz's narrative of good violence (ours) versus bad violence (theirs), including the desire to build a case for gaining perpetual access to Indian labor and lands from the Spanish Crown. See elsewhere in these essays (389–96) for a discussion of the "just war" rationale that drove much of Díaz del Castillo's narrative.

(6) Did the Spaniards carry out any horrendous group killings or massacres?

The Spaniards carried out at least two large-scale massacres of native peoples—one in the city of Cholula and the other during a festival in the capital of Tenochtitlan. Díaz del Castillo writes carefully about both of these mass killings in part because by the time he was writing they had become widely known in New Spain and Spain and resulted in withering criticism by other Spaniards who sought to show that the war against the Mesoamerican peoples was "unjust" and un-Christian. Both of these slaughters became shameful stories that Spaniards, and especially those seeking encomiendas *(lands and laborers), were forced to face and justify in Spanish courts. Because of many eyewitnesses who spoke widely about Spanish cruelty, Díaz del Castillo was forced to address these massacres but did so in the spirit of "we were justified" but "they were beasts when they killed people." See especially Díaz del Castillo's twisted rationale for the "preemptive strike" led by the Spanish soldier Pedro de Alvarado who slaughtered scores of Aztec dancers during a religious ceremony on pages (211–14). To give you an impression of how this slaughter was remembered by the other side, the indigenous people, here is an account that differs significantly from Díaz del Castillo's.*

At this moment in the fiesta, when the dance was loveliest and when song was linked to song, the Spaniards were seized with an urge to kill the celebrants. They all ran forward, armed as if for battle. They closed the entrances and passageways, all the gates of

6a–b. Representations of Spanish violence, top (a): Lámina Numero 48. bottom (b): Lámina Numero 04. Unknown artist, sixteenth century, *Lienzo de Tlaxcala*, BANC xff F1219.L58. Courtesy of the Bancroft Library, University of California, Berkeley.

the patio. . . . They posted guards so that no one could escape, and then rushed into the Sacred Patio to slaughter the celebrants.

They ran in among the dancers, forcing their way to the place where the drums were played. They attacked the man who was drumming and cut off his arms. Then they cut off his head, and it rolled across the floor.

They attacked all the celebrants, stabbing them, spearing them, striking them with their swords. They attacked some of them from behind, and these fell instantly to the ground with their entrails hanging out. Others they beheaded; they cut off their head, or split their heads to pieces. . . . Some attempted to run away but their intestines dragged as they ran; they seemed to tangle their feet in their own entrails. . . . The Spaniards saw them and killed them. . . . The blood of the warriors flowed like water and gathered into pools.[1]

And Spanish murder and mutilation of bodies is recited several times in non-chalant tones as in this passage.

We slept near a stream, and with the grease from a fat Indian woman whom we had killed and cut open, we dressed our wounds, for we had no oil, and we supped very well on some dogs which the Indians breed.(93)

In other words, there was more than enough physical violence to go around during the wars of encounter and conquest in Mexico. I find Tzvetan Todorov's distinction appropriate here: the Aztecs had a sacrifice society, and the Spaniards brought in massacre or mass sacrifice practices. Later in our book we will revisit the practice of debt payment/human sacrifice from the Aztec point of view.

For further reading on debt-payment rituals and ritual human sacrifice, see Alfredo López Austin, *Human Body and Ideology: Concepts of the Ancient Nahuas* (Salt Lake City: University of Utah Press, 1988); Davíd Carrasco, *City of Sacrifice: The Aztec Empire and the Role of Violence in Civilization* (Boston: Beacon Press, 2000); and Leonardo López Luján, *The Offerings of the Templo Mayor of Tenochtitlan* (Albuquerque: University of New Mexico Press, 2005).

Note

1. Miguel León Portilla, ed., *Broken Spears: The Aztec Account of the Conquest of Mexico* (Boston: Beacon Press, 1990), 76.

Tenochtitlan as a Political Capital and World Symbol

David Carrasco

The centerpiece of Bernal Díaz del Castillo's narrative is his description of Tenochtitlan during the Spanish arrival, occupation, flight, and siege of the Aztec capital. We get an initial sense of the "great city of Mexico" on page (156) where he writes,

> During the morning, we arrived at a broad Causeway and continued our march towards Iztapalapa, and when we saw so many cities and villages built in the water and other great towns on dry land and that straight and level causeway going towards Mexico, we were amazed and said that it was like the enchantments they tell of in the legend of Amadis on account of the great towers and *cues* and buildings rising from the water and all built of masonry. And some of our soldiers even asked whether the things that we saw were not a dream? . . . the appearances of the palaces in which they lodged us! How spacious and well built they were, of beautiful stonework and cedar wood, and the wood of other sweet scented trees, with great rooms and courts, wonderful to behold, covered with awnings of cotton cloth.

In reality, Tenochtitlan was the supreme settlement of a political and cultural empire made up of over four hundred towns and city-states spread through many regions of central Mesoamerica. It was the leader of a Triple Alliance of cities made up of Texcoco, Tlacopan, and Tenochtitlan itself. After a troubled early history, the Mexicas—the ethnic group we know as the Aztec—married into the royal Culhua-Toltec noble line and gained political legitimacy to rule in central Mexico. They eventually overthrew the dominant Tepanec kingdom through political skill and military force and unified around fifty other city-states in the Valley of Mexico as well as numerous petty kingdoms in nearby and distant parts of Mesoamerica. According to demographers, the central city of Tenochtitlan contained nearly two hundred thousand people and directly influenced, through the combined powers of the Triple Alliance, over three million people in thirty-eight provinces through its political decisions, religious ceremonies, marketplaces, and military elites residing in the ceremonial city located in Lake Texcoco. It was this city and its political order that became the primary goal of the Spanish conquest.

Early in Díaz del Castillo's story, during the expedition of Francisco Hernández, the Spaniards learn of a great city in the highlands where the "Culhua" live. Each time the invaders press local chiefs for more gold and trade goods, they are pointed in the direction of this great city and its wealth. Once Cortés's expedition begins to penetrate the edges of the Aztec empire, he becomes obsessed with finding his way to the rich, distant city. While other towns and cities attracted and repulsed the Spaniards with their architecture, marketplaces, and ritual killings, no other settlement compared in size, riches, religious intensity, or political prestige with the "great City of Mexico" that the Spaniards first saw in 1520. Continuing with Díaz del Castillo's passage of this pivotal moment that has fascinated readers for centuries, we read on pages (156–57),

> It is not to be wondered at that I here write it down in this man-
> ner, for there is so much to think over that I do not know how to
> describe it, seeing things as we did that had never been heard of or
> seen before, not even dreamed about . . . we went in the orchard
> and garden, which was such a wonderful thing to walk in . . .
> great canoes were able to pass into the garden from the lake . . .
> and all was cemented and very splendid with many kinds of stone
> monuments with pictures on them. . . . I say again that I stood
> looking at it and thought that never in the world would there be

discovered other lands such as these, for at that time there was no Peru, nor any thought of it.

The Aztec Capital as World Pivot

In this eyewitness account the capital appears as a splendid monumental settlement with sophisticated architecture, grand sculptures, and fertile gardens, crowned in sweet fragrances, and all in the midst of an effective transportation system working so smoothly it must be in the higher realm of legend. But what did the Aztecs think and say about their capital city? Did they put the same emphasis in their poetry and songs on the surfaces of buildings and lakes? By moving *through* Díaz del Castillo's enthusiastic description of towers, cues (pyramids), fragrant gardens, and the splendid costumes of gold and jade worn by the nobles *into* indigenous appreciations of their capital, we learn more about the political prestige and cosmic symbolism of the city. One term that aids in understanding the tie between the political and the religious dimensions of Aztec life is *cosmovision*. *Cosmovision* simply means the *religious worldview of a people that contains its local codes about how space and time are integrated into a meaningful whole or picture of the universe.* When we turn to an Aztec song about the city in order to *gain some access* to what the city meant for the Aztecs themselves, we see the link between the social settlement and the cosmovision that it represented.

> Proud of itself,
> Is the City of Mexico, Tenochtitlan
> Here no one fears to die in war
> This is our glory
> This is Your Command
> O Giver of Life
> Have this in mind, oh princes
> Who could conquer Tenochtitlan
> Who could shake the foundation of heaven?[1]

In this passage the city is more than just an economic, sculptural, or even military wonder. The city is a proud, fearless, and glorious place. It is an invincible center that linked the world of fearless warriors with their greatest god referred to here as the "Giver of Life" (Ometeotl). This High God appears in many primary sources as a primordial creative force, the generator of all life and power in the universe who presided over scores of other deities related to all aspects of nature and social life. In Aztec cosmology, Ometeotl dwelled eternally in the thirteenth level of heaven above the earth. These heavens were conceived of as a powerful, fertilizing vertical shaft reaching from the surface of the earth upward to the highest heaven where this Ometeotl, a single deity consisting of male and female dimensions, dwelled.

The city's crucial location in the cosmological scheme and its link with this deity is evident in the statement that the city is "the foundation of heaven." For the Aztecs, Tenochtitlan was not just a very important and beautiful city, it was the foundation, the basis, that is, the bottom level of the celestial shaft that linked people to their gods. It was *the crucial point of union* between the celestial powers above the earth and life on earth—a kind of linchpin holding the city close to the cosmic forces of the gods. In Aztec thought, the city that Díaz del Castillo described as akin to the legend of Amadís had to be unshakable, for if it was disturbed and conquered, the cosmos would collapse.

On the horizontal plane of the cosmos, the Aztecs called the land containing their city and empire Cemanahuac or "Land Surrounded by Water." This terrestrial world, like the universe above and around it, was divided into four major cosmic zones, referred to in at least one text as *nauchampa* or "four directions of the wind" or merely "four quarters of the world." We saw this kind of division in our essay on the ceiba tree when we examined the shape and ordering of the universe as depicted in the *Codex Fejérváry-Mayer*. When we follow this four-quartered design into the scholarship done on Mesoamerican cosmovision and human settlements, we learn that each quadrant of the universe was associated with specific names, colors, influences, and calendar signs. Although the pattern varied from culture to culture, a typical Mesoamerican version was as follows: east, Tlalocan (place of dawn), yellow, fertile, and good; north, Mictlampa (region of underworld), red, barren, and dangerous; west, Cihuatlampa (region of women), blue, green, unfavorable, and humid; south, Huitzlampa (region of thorns), white; and center, Tlalxico (navel), black. In the typical cosmogram of the universe, there were waters surrounding the inhabited land in the middle. These waters were called *inhuica atl* (the celestial water), which extended upward, from the edges of the land, in the vertical direction merging with the sky and supporting the lower levels of heaven. At the edge of the four quarters stood four mighty ceiba trees that held up the heavens and participated in the rejuvenation of the cosmos.

These are all elements of the worldview that informed the lives, politics, and ritual practices of the indigenous inhabitants of Tenochtitlan who knew and defended it as the "foundation of heaven." It was the pivot of the four quarters and a religious symbol all in one.

The City of Wonders and the Four Quarters

Fortunately we have both the vivid descriptions of Bernal Díaz and a Spanish map made during the war of conquest of this "land surrounded by water." Bernal Díaz describes in detail the architectural wonders of the city, signaling to the reader that it had great centripetal power and drew what was most valued in the world beyond the city into the city itself for the benefit of its inhabitants and especially its elites. Bernal Díaz describes Moctezuma's two armories,. "shields great and small . . . lances longer than ours . . . with a fathom of blade with many knives set in it"; the royal aviary, "birds of great size, down to tiny birds of many-coloured plumage, also the birds from which they take the rich plumage which they use in their green feather work . . . birds with long stilted legs, with body, wings and tail all red"; a zoo filled with "infernal noise when the lions and tigers roared and the jackals and foxes howled and the serpents hissed"; plus houses where craftsmen who made "such an immense quantity of fine fabrics with wonderful feather work designs"; and scenes of the nunnery and dance halls and gardens of flowers, and we can read a vivid, detailed description of Montezuma's elaborate dinners. These dinners showed that the ruler was lord and center of the wider world for he had "three hundred plates of the food that Montezuma was going to eat and more than a thousand for the guard."

This abundance alone led the Spaniards to realize that the city was a great capital. We have evidence that they learned that the overall design of the capital had special significance. In a stunning piece of coincidence, a Spanish mapmaker working with Cortés composed a map that appeared in Cortés's 1520 letter to the emperor, Charles V, and which imitates Aztec cosmovision. It was published as early as 1522 in Seville, Spain, but had been used in 1521 to help plan the siege of Tenochtitlan (described in real detail in Díaz del Castillo). Known as the Cortés map, it shows a huge lake surrounding a landmass of houses, palaces (the aviary), and neighborhoods linked by bridges and canals all centered by an immense ceremonial precinct where the great Aztec temple and symbolic skull racks dominate the space. Remarkably there are four main causeways emerging from this ceremonial center, which divide the entire city into four major precincts. The city, even in Spanish eyes, was divided into five major sections suggesting that, even though the Spaniards did not know it, the city was a material expression of cosmovision.

In fact, archaeologists digging in and around Mexico City have discovered that the capital of Tenochtitlan enjoyed an enormous prestige of being the center of the horizontal world. In actual fact, four major highways did meet at four entranceways to the sacred center of the city. These pathways crossed at the base of the Templo Mayor, the great Aztec temple that was the axis mundi of the capital and empire. (Díaz del Castillo describes climbing this temple as well as a ferocious battle that takes place on its steps.)

According to one primary source, this spatial order of the city into four parts and a center was dictated by the deity who founded the city, Huitzilopochtli (referred to repeatedly by Díaz del Castillo as "Huichilobos"). The text reads that the god ordered the priest to "divide the men, each with his relatives, friends and relations in four principal

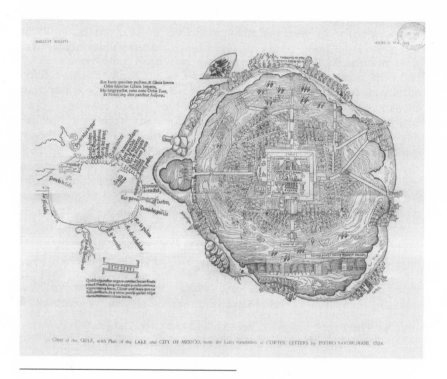

7. Map of Mexico City and Gulf of Mexico from the Latin translation of Cortés's Letters by Pietro Savorgnana, 1524, Maudslay, Vol. III.

barrios, placing at the center the house you have built for my rest."[2] The divine command is to lay out the new settlement on the model of the horizontal cosmos of the four directions, assimilating the city to the form of the four quadrants that constituted the cosmos.

Nobles Imitate the Cosmos

In our attempts to "see through" Díaz del Castillo's narrative into aspects of the Aztec understandings of their city and society, we have discovered that his amazement at the architectural and natural landscape leads us into the *cosmovision* of the spatial order of the Aztec world. There is at least one other moment in his description of the Spanish arrival in the city where he, unknowingly, reveals to us the indigenous notion of the four quarters and the center, only this time in terms of *the social arrangements of the nobles*. As

8. This is the frontispiece of the *Codex Mendoza* depicting the foundation of Tenochtitlan. Note that the island city is divided into four quarters with the Giant Eagle landing on a blooming cactus in the middle. The scene below shows the Aztec warriors conquering Culhuacan and Tenayucan. Unknown artist, sixteenth century. Courtesy Wikimedia Commons.

the Spaniards approach the heart of the capital on that first morning long ago, they pass groups of chiefs and lords who gracefully glide by them. The visitors are amazed at the "very rich mantles, the brilliant liveries of one chieftain different from those of another and the causeway was crowded with them." Here, I quote at some length the relevant passage (158), asking the reader to decipher how Aztec cosmovision is encoded in this royal welcome in ways that the Spanish chronicler did not recognize.

> When we arrived near to Mexico, where there were some other small towers, the Great Moctezuma got down from his litter, and those great Caciques supported him with their arms beneath a marvelously rich canopy of green-coloured feathers with much gold and silver embroidery and with pearls and chalchihuites suspended from a sort of bordering, which was wonderful to look at. The Great Moctezuma was richly attired according to his usage and he was shod with sandals, (*cotoras*) for so they call what they wear on their feet, the soles were of gold and the upper part adorned with precious stones. The four Chieftains who supported his arms were also richly clothed according to their usage, in garments which were apparently held ready for them on the road to enable them to accompany their prince, for they did not appear in such attire when they came to receive us. Besides these four Chieftains, there were four other great Caciques, who supported the canopy over their heads, and many other Lords who walked before the Great Moctezuma, sweeping the ground where he would tread and spreading cloths on it, so that he should not tread on the earth. Not one of these chieftains dared even to think of looking him in the face, but kept their eyes lowered with great reverence, except those four relations, his nephews, who supported him with their arms.

Fortunately, we can look squarely into Díaz del Castillo's account and see through it into some of the ways the Mexicas imagined and constructed their capital city. We can also empathize with how both Spaniards and Mexicas remembered the destruction of their city. Consider first Díaz del Castillo's mild lament, "But today all that I then saw is overthrown and destroyed: nothing left standing." A Mexica song found in the *Cantares mexicanos*, probably composed in 1523 long before Bernal sat down to write his memories, takes the lament about the collapse of the pivot of the four quarters much deeper. The Mexica poets cried and sang to their High God, Ometeotl, the Giver of Life who, in their view, brought about their downfall.

> Nothing but flowers and songs of sorrow
> Are left in Mexico and Tlatelolco
> Where once we saw warriors and wise men
>
> We know it is true
> That we must perish,
> For we are mortal men
> You, the Giver of Life
> You have ordained it . . .
>
> There is nothing but grief and suffering
> In Mexico and Tlatelolco
> Where once we saw beauty and valor.[3]

For further reading on Tenochtitlan, see Inga Clendinnen, *Aztecs: An Interpretation* (Cambridge: Cambridge University Press, 1991); Michael Smith, *The Aztecs* (Oxford: Wiley-Blackwell, 2002).

Notes

1. Miguel León Portilla, *Pre-Columbian Literatures of Mexico* (Norman: University of Oklahoma Press, 1969), 87.

2. Diego Durán, *History of the Indies of New Spain* (Norman: University of Oklahoma Press, 1994), 46.

3. Miguel León Portilla, ed., *Broken Spears: The Aztec Account of the Conquest of Mexico* (Boston: Beacon Press, 1990), 149.

HUMAN SACRIFICE/DEBT PAYMENTS FROM THE AZTEC POINT OF VIEW

DAVÍD CARRASCO

We address the question, "How did the Aztecs act and think about ritual killing?" Another way of asking this question is "What did they think they were up to?" Let us begin with an astonishing passage from Díaz del Castillo and use it for its clues that can lead us into indigenous attitudes toward ritual sacrifice. During the ferocious Spanish siege of Tenochtitlan, the Aztecs carry out a *nextlaoalli* or "debt payment" with Spanish soldiers in front of their sun and war god Huitzilopochtli's shrine, which sat at the top of the Templo Mayor in the heart of the ceremonial center. Driven back from the battle to their camp and out of reach of the javelins, arrows, and spears, the Spaniards huddle together to share news. Suddenly they hear

> the dismal drum of Huichilobos and many other shells and horns and things like trumpets and the sound of them all was terrifying, and we all looked toward the lofty *Cue* where they were being sounded, and saw that our comrades whom they had captured when they defeated Cortes were being carried by force up the steps and they were taking them to be sacrificed. When they got them up to a small square in front of the oratory, where their accursed idols are kept, we saw them place plumes on the heads of many of them and with things like fans in their hands they forced them to dance before Huichilobos and after they had danced they immediately placed them on their backs on some rather narrow stones which had been prepared as places for sacrifice, and with some knives they sawed open their chest and

drew out their palpitating hearts and offered them to the idols
that were there, and kicked the bodies down the steps, and the
Indian butchers who were waiting below cut off their arms and
feet and flayed the skin off the faces, and prepared it afterwards
like glove leather with the beards on, and kept those for the
festivals when they celebrated drunken orgies and the flesh they
ate in *chilimole* (287).

To begin to understand the ritual actions in this passage, from an
Aztec point of view, we will define and discuss the following Nahuatl
terms: *nextlaoalli* (debt payment), *altepetl* (hill of water), *teotl ixiptla*
(deity image). We will see that these dramatic and gruesome actions had
both mythic and military significance for the people carrying them out
expressive of Mesoamerican religious traditions of cosmic protection and
rejuvenation through ritual killing.

(1) Nextlaoalli or "Debt Payment"

In the most detailed and reliable account of Aztec ritual sacrifice ever compiled (Book 2 of the *Florentine Codex*), the Aztec informants repeatedly
called their actions "nextlaoalli" or "debt payments." What we erroneously
refer to as "human sacrifices" were rather ritual acts of paying back to the
gods the life force that the gods had given to humans, animals, and nature
during acts of creation—in order to aid in the regenerative powers of the
gods. The purpose, power, and details of these primordial, divine acts were
recorded in Aztec stories, myths, architecture, and art. Typically, they tell
us that before human life was created, a god, or pairs of gods or groups
of gods, took each other's lives or bled themselves *in order* to create the
sun, water, all life forms on earth and in the heavens, and the cycle of the
seasons. In this worldview, creation emerged out of bleeding and death.
Creation and the creative acts of the gods, in all stages and levels, could
be repeated, rejuvenated, and continued only if humans entered into the
destruction/creation pattern by paying the gods back in ritual actions
for giving life to the cosmos. A heavy burden was placed on humans to

perform the nextlaoalli or debt payment. Here is an example. The English translation of the Nahuatl statement in the section of the *Florentine Codex* called "The Ceremonies" reads, "Twenty-second chapter, in which are described the feast day and the debt-paying which they celebrated in the second month, known as Tlacaxipeualiztli" (the final word means the "feast of the flaying of men"). And in the over 172 pages of descriptions of these debt payments/sacrifices, very few lines actually refer to or describe the moment of killing. Rather, as reflected in Díaz del Castillo's outsider description, there was enormous emphasis in the descriptions on dressing, dancing, music, and public display of the objects to be sacrificed. When the Aztecs ritually kill the Spaniards at the top of the Great Temple they are, in their own eyes, attempting to give new cosmo-magical strength and life nourishment to the two gods who reside there and who are under attack by the Spaniards. Remember that at this point in Díaz del Castillo's narrative the Aztecs have heard countless sermons from Cortés insulting their gods, religious practices, and shrines and have their backs literally against the walls of their temples. In this case the Aztecs are filled with rage and act in a ritual pattern to protect themselves and give more power to their patron gods in a "debt payment."

(2) Teotl Ixiptla

The second term we must understand in order to get beyond the Spanish attitude of human sacrifice is *teotl ixiptla* or "god-image." As the elaborate descriptions of "debt payments" in Sahagún's *Florentine Codex* show us, every person, animal, or object that is used in the debt payment has its identity *cosmo-magically transformed* from human or animal or vegetable to a god. This ontological change happens through ritual dressing, painting, hair cutting, exhaustion, or inebriation. The end result is a teotl ixiptla or a living representative of the god who is going to be killed in order to be reborn.

This is crucial to understand because in Aztec eyes it is the god-image and not the human image that is killed and transformed into creative energy. In the vivid passage by Díaz del Castillo we see that the

9. Representation of an Ixiptla. Unknown artist, sixteenth century. From the *Codex Magliabecchiano*.

Spaniards are stripped (in a ritual way and in a sacred space) of their clothes and dressed and decorated in Aztec fashions, thus signifying the transformation of the men into images of Aztec gods who, when killed, are reborn *as gods* with their full energy. In typical Aztec ceremonies this transformation from human to god-image usually took days, sometimes weeks, sometimes months depending on the god being re-created and the political circumstances. Díaz del Castillo had no understanding that he was watching the preparatory rituals that, in effect, empty the Spaniards of their human identity and fill them with what the Aztecs thought of as "divine fire" or a cosmic being.

For instance, in a ceremony typical of the ritual work done to transform a human into a god-image, Sahagún describes how a young woman, on the way to being killed as a debt payment, is put into a sacred location and ritually dressed with power symbols that in effect erase her humanity and change her into a female deity and cosmic force. She was first dressed from head to foot with an organized array of objects representing the sea, sky, felines, plants, birds, and flowers. Yellow ocher the "color of maize blossoms" was painted on her face below a vivid green paper cap with many outspread quetzal feathers in the form of maize tassels. Golden ear plugs flashed on the sides of her face like squash blossoms, and she wore a shift designed with waves of water and an image of green stones and billowing clouds. This image of water and sky was repeated in the skirt, which partially covered the calves with bound jaguar skins covered with bells. Her ankles were golden bells so that when she walked she rustled, clattered, and tinkled. All this color, design, and symbol were the bright backdrop for the shield with water lily flowers and leaves painted on it. She went dancing for ten days with women wearing artemisia flowers and linked together by the xochimecatl, a flower rope. Then there was dancing, sometimes for days and nights. Here are just a few passages from surviving indigenous priests describing a few elements of the ritual dances and signing typical of a debt payment ceremony: "And they went singing; they cried out loudly; they sang in a very high treble. As the mockingbird takes it, so was their song. Like bells were their voices. . . . And the likeness of Uixtociuatl (the goddess) went erect in the midst of them. A brilliant feather ornament preceded her . . . they daily sang the women's song until the ten days had passed" (Florentine Codex, Book 2, 92).

What Díaz del Castillo sees (or claims he saw from quite a distance) of the ritual changing of the Spaniards at the Great Temple he describes, "We saw them place plumes on the heads of many of them and with things like fans in their hands they forced them to dance before Huichilobos."

Under normal circumstances, the teotl ixiptla were isolated from society, placed in ritual buildings where specialists changed them through cutting their hair, painting their bodies, teaching them songs, sometimes giving them members of the opposite sex for sex, teaching them dances, and elaborately costuming them in the dress of the deity they were becoming. They were then put into processions (in some cases the ritual actions lasted a month, sometimes a year) in order to elevate sacred energies that collected in their heads, hearts, or livers, which is where the Aztecs believed the most potent sacralizations in the universe were gathered during the ritual. When these teotl ixiptlas had been ritually transformed, they were given over to the priests for the ritual of debt payment.

(3) Altepetl

The third term relevant to human sacrifice/debt payment is *altepetl* or "water-hill." What is the significance of the place where these sacrifices of Spaniards happen in Díaz del Castillo's account? He describes it as that "lofty pyramid" dedicated to Huichilobos in the heart of the city. But the Aztecs did not call it a pyramid but rather Coatepec or "Serpent Mountain." Serpent Mountain was a place told about in myth where the Aztec sun god in the form of a great warrior was born out of the womb of the earth resulting in a ferocious battle for domination between the newborn sun named Huitzilopochtli and the moon and the stars, also in the forms of warriors. Just before the sun god is born the enemy warriors rush up to the side of Serpent Mountain in an attempt to stop his birth in the heart of the city. Huitzilopochtli as the sun triumphs in the mythic and daily battle, but in order to maintain his repetitious rising and falling he needs regular debt payments in the forms of ritual offerings at the architectural replica of the mythic Serpent Mountain, which is the Great Temple described by Díaz del Castillo.

Serpent Mountain in the myth is an example of the archetypal altepetl or "water mountain." Water Mountain and its variation of Xochitepetl or "Flower Mountain" were mythic *and* geographic hills *inside of which* the divine ancestors dwelled guarding the potencies, energies, and powers that fertilized plants, gave life to stars and time, and gave animals as gifts to humans. These ancestors, dwelling within the mountain and guarding the gifts, sometimes referred to as "seeds" or "hearts," also needed to receive

10. Frontal view of the Templo Mayor, Tenochtitlan. It was a symbolic altepetl where debt payments to rain and war gods were carried out. Unknown artist, seventeenth century. From the *Codex Ixtlilxochitl.* © Foundation for the Advancement of Mesoamerican Studies, Inc., www.famsi.org.

debt payments in order to rejuvenate their powers. This is one reason why the Aztecs were dragging the Spaniards up the steps of Serpent Mountain. They were repeating both the charge of the enemy warriors up the mythic mountains and the ancient requirement of paying the debt or making sacrifices to the ancestral gods who live in the replica of the sacred mountain in order to regenerate the gods who will give to humans new supplies of "hearts" and "seeds."

The purpose of this essay is not to justify Aztec ritual killing or condemn the Spaniards for their violence or lack of understanding. Rather, by beginning with Díaz del Castillo's point of view as an outsider and harsh critic of Aztec rituals, we move to indigenous words, practices, and perspectives to see through the Spanish account into some dimensions of what the Aztecs and Maya believed they were doing.

For further reading, see Eduardo Matos Moctezuma, *Life and Death in the Templo Mayor* (Niwot: University Press of Colorado, 1995).

Spaniards as Gods
The Return of Quetzalcoatl

Davíd Carrasco

One of the most puzzling statements, often repeated in Díaz del Castillo's *True History*, is that the indigenous people, in the words of Cortés, "take us for gods or beings like their idols" (66). The notion that Maya and Aztec peoples, from the ruler Moctezuma down to regional governors, lords, and local farmers, considered the Spaniards gods or divine beings at first boggles the mind. Especially so when we also read that Spaniards were early on defeated in battles, captured and carefully examined, negotiated with and sometimes sacrificed. Indigenous people had ample evidence that the Spaniards were mortal beings, just like themselves. In order to understand this enigma we will have to look more closely at the written evidence in Díaz del Castillo and elsewhere and also address the question, "How did Mesoamerican peoples experience, define, and identify divine beings and sacred realities?" We will learn that the Mesoamericans believed that extraordinary humans shared and were possessed by the powers of divinities, thereby becoming god-men on earth.

There are many references to the amazement among native peoples caused by the appearances and actions of Spaniards. They were greatly impressed by the white skins, beards, armor, weapons, horses, boldness, crosses, images of Mary, and greed for gold of the Spaniards. A convincing example that we can use as a clue to what and "how" the natives thought about foreigners appears when Cortés is confronting the "Fat Cacique" about the fortified Aztec town of "Cingapacinga." Cortés decides to play on the indigenous notion that the Europeans are superhuman or even gods by sending one of his oldest musketeers, Heredia, out to fight Aztec warriors. How much Cortés had learned through Malinche about the character and nature of indigenous gods is hard to tell, but his choice of Heredia was either a lucky coincidence or an illustration that he had learned something important about Aztec deities. Heredia had very unusual physical features including a "bad twitch in his face, a big beard, a face covered with scars, and was blind in one eye and lame in one leg." Cortés gathered the local caciques who were enemies of the Aztecs and boasted that he was sending out this one soldier who could vanquish the Aztec garrison located nearby. A veteran of wars in Italy, Heredia went along with the ruse and "shouldered his musket . . . fired shots into the air as he went through the forest so that the Indians might see and hear him. And the Caciques sent word to the other towns that they were bringing along a Teule to kill all the Mexicans who were in Cingapacinga" (75). Heredia's weird appearance and boldness greatly impressed the local (non-Aztec) caciques who were amazed at both Cortés's audacity and that Heredia was left unharmed by the Aztecs.

This single, laughable incident, the sending of an elderly warrior with a great beard and twisted body out to confront indigenous warriors, can be used as a pointer toward how the Aztecs thought about gods and the appearance of divine forces in their earthly, everyday world. Indigenous Mesoamericans, as in the case of many cultures, were fascinated by human bodies and animals and plants with strange features, especially if they were grotesque (or unusually beautiful), dismembered, or dressed in lavish or bizarre clothes. Later in the story, the people of Tlaxcala, on seeing the very white skin color of the Europeans and the black skin color of the several Africans who were with them, wondered whether they were gods of water and wind or closely related to these gods. Each of the many Aztec gods was depicted in pictures and costumes with a rich array of physical traits, each representing a specific power, capacity for gift giving or punishment, or event in a myth. In a real sense, the Maya and Aztecs knew their gods *through* the details of their physical features and costumes. In the case of Heredia's physical features, he fit the description, in a detailed way, of two of the most powerful gods in the Aztec world, the rain god Tlaloc and the priestly god Tezcatlipoca. One of the rain god Tlaloc's characteristics/

powers/punishments was a twisted face representing diseases caused by the shock of cold water and frigid weather. And one of the most powerful Aztec gods, Tezcatlipoca, Lord of the Smoking Mirror, had a lame or dismembered foot and was represented in this way in numerous codices. In general, Mesoamericans believed their gods regularly occupied the bodies of other earthly (and divine beings). For example, these gods could show themselves to human beings in distinct forms. Tezcatlipoca is a special case in point because the Aztecs believed his prodigious power was capable of passing into human bodies that had strange or monstrous features, or the bodies of certain animals. Thus, lameness or one-footedness was not seen by Mesoamericans as a weakness but rather as a special form of sacred power, supernatural mobility, or strangeness of being that at least temporarily passed into the lame human or animal. So, what appears to be a kind of boastful joke by Cortés could easily have resonated in the Aztec or Maya ways of thinking with their painted and poetic descriptions of two powerful deities.

There are two other key beliefs in Mesoamerican thought that will enable us to understand how they could have identified Heredia, Cortés, the horses, and canons as divine. The first is the notion of "co-essences" and the second is the notion of the "*hombre-dios.*"

(1) Co-essences

In Spanish and Mesoamerican worldviews there is no strict division between what is human and what is divine. Among the Spaniards, for instance, Jesus is a divine man and Mary is a divine woman. Human flesh and divine powers coexist in them and in very extraordinary people who are designated as saints. For instance, one of the leading religious orders to participate in the conquest was the Franciscans who revered Saint Francis as their founder and spiritual guide who was filled with divine power. In the Spain of the conquistadores' time, divinity appeared in trees, storms, epidemics, and attacks by locusts.[1] Apparitions were both spectacular and common, and they continued to mix the forces of heaven with the material world in which humans dwelled. According to

Díaz del Castillo and other chroniclers, apparitions of Santiago and the Virgin Mary took place many times during the conquest, and Spaniards believed they saw the presence and influence of the diabolical divine in Mesoamerican people, temples, idols, and sexual practices.

Mesoamerican people had an even stronger sense than the Spaniards of the co-essence of deities and humans, the penetration of the divine essence into material nature, the closeness of the sacred and the physical world.[2] Indigenous people did not so much believe in a "supernatural" world or level, but rather that *dwelling within* nature, appearing in every aspect of the environment, were deities, divine signs, omens, and sacred forces. Mesoamerican peoples at the time of Cortés (and to some extent today) believed that (1) there was a hidden essence to human existence, (2) this essence was divine, created by the gods at the primordial dawn of creation, and (3) this divine essence took the forms of deities and was capable of dividing into and uniting with other deities and humans, animals, and plants. Also, (4) divine essence, often imagined as an invisible fire, united with other gods, humans, animals, or forms of nature, including insects and plants, by becoming enclosed in mortal and heavy coverings. Once within these earthly bodies this divine essence or invisible fire continued to exist as a spiritual or animistic power.

These are some of the ways in which Maya and Aztec warriors, priests, rulers, and farmers looked at their everyday world before and during the Spanish presence in their lands (and even today). This is the framework through which they interpreted the appearance and actions of ships, horses, horses with humans on top, white skin, Heredia, Cortés, and much more.

An example of natives "looking for" a divine co-essence is when they ask the Spaniards for one of their helmets so they can take it back to the capital to see if it is like the one worn by their gods. And later, native peoples refer to the extraordinarily violent Pedro de Alvarado as "*tonatiuh*" because his red beard and aggressive actions remind them of their sun god warrior who was often painted red and possessed extraordinarily powerful weapons.

(2) Hombre-Dios

In Díaz del Castillo's *True History* and other accounts, native lords give lavish gifts of costumes to Cortés. Reportedly, Moctezuma sent gifts that were the costumes of the gods Quetzalcoatl and Tezcatlipoca, including their masks and adornments. One mask is described as "a serpent mask inlaid with turquoise," which may today reside in the Museum für Völkerkunde in Vienna. What we see here is the Aztec ruler's attempt to embroider the Spanish arrival with his own symbols and signs as a way of exploring whether there is a co-essence between his gods and the Spaniards. There are several possible meanings of Moctezuma's efforts to identify Cortés with one or more of his deities. On the one hand this action has usually been interpreted as elevating the extraordinary Cortés (who arrived in the year associated with Quetzalcoatl's name) to the level of Quetzalcoatl, the patron god of cities and rulers. On the other hand, from our knowledge of how the Aztecs carried out their sacrifices, he is having Cortés dressed as a *teotl ixiptla* or "god-image" (see essay "Human Sacrifice/Debt Payments from the Aztec Point of View" on ritual sacrifice), which was a typical step in the process toward becoming a debt payment or sacrificial victim. Is Moctezuma playing a sacred game, a divine joke on Cortés by preparing him, at least in the eyes of the understanding Aztecs, for the sacrificial stone? Or is he simply following the implications of reports he had received about the extraordinary Spanish cannons, animals, skin color, and fighting capacity and identifying them as having potent levels of divine "co-essence"? Either way, what we are seeing here is a specific application of the notion of co-essence, only now in the form of what the Spaniards called, referring to Aztec sacred people, "hombre-dioses." An "hombre-dios" or "*mujer-diosa*" was an individual who had received intense amounts or qualities of the divine essence that came (and continues to come) into the world during the mythic period of creation. These individuals sometimes had enormous quantities of divine essence, allowing them to become great shamans, artists, warriors, dancers, diviners, farmers, etc. They had special capacities for periodic transformation and had the capacity to communicate directly with a major deity who was referred to in some sources as the "Corazon del pueblo" or the "Heart of the people." This meant that the human, whether Moctezuma, Cortés, Malinche, or many others, had the capacity to "be possessed, to have inside" their bodies the god, thereby becoming a "man-god."[3] The Aztec ruler was believed to receive portions of the divine essence of Tezcatlipoca, Huitzilopochtli, or Quetzalcoatl at different times and places, giving him incredible powers reflected, for instance, in Díaz del Castillo's descriptions (page 158) of how Moctezuma was treated with extreme reverence by his noble entourage.

There is ample evidence that Maya, Tlaxcaltecas, Mexicas, and other indigenous peoples saw and treated the Spaniards through the lenses of "co-essences" and "hombre-dios." The most significant identification of the Spaniards as gods is found in the ample evidence that Cortés, due to the direction he came from (east), the year of his arrival, and the extraordinary leadership qualities he displayed, was identified, for a time, with the Toltec hombre-dios Quetzalcoatl, the Feathered Serpent ruler of the ancient kingdom of Tollan. Quetzalcoatl was revered as having ruled Tollan during its most creative political and cultural era, only to betray his reign and flee on a raft of serpents toward the eastern shore promising to return one day. His calendar date and name was the year 1-Reed, which coincided with the Christian year 1519 when the Spaniards arrived on the periphery of the Aztec empire. Throughout Bernal Díaz's account there are a number of moments when the Spaniards learn that they are identified as related to ancestors like the Toltecs, though the latter are not mentioned, in the Spanish sources, by name. In fact, according to Bernal Díaz, Moctezuma, while imprisoned, gives a speech that is very similar to other speeches recounted in Cortés's letters and in Sahagún's account, which show the identification, by the Aztecs, of Spaniards with indigenous ancestors and gods. The text reads,

> I must . . . state how, in the discussion that Montezuma held with
> the Caciques of all the territory whom he had called together . . .
> it was reported that he had told them to consider how for many

years past they had known for certain, through the traditions of their ancestors, which they had noted down in their books of records, that men would come from the direction of the sunrise to rule these lands, and that then the lordship and kingdom of the Mexicans would come to an end. Now, he believed, from what his Gods had told him, that we were these men, and the priests had consulted Huichilobos about it and offered up sacrifices. (198)

In my view, after looking at the evidence from many different sixteenth-century texts, the Aztecs did indeed, for a period of time, believe in the possibility that the great powers of the Spaniards as well as the timing and direction of their arrival were signs that an ancient prophecy of returning lords or *new* lords coming to take over the empire was being fulfilled.

Either as relatives through an ancient lineage, as hombre-dioses who manifested the co-essences of the Aztec cosmos, or as mortal enemies who needed to be vanquished, the Spaniards were seen as intimately related in powerful ways to the native peoples. There is also evidence that when some of these interpretive lenses fell away from their eyes and the Spaniards became humans without the divine essences of the Mesoamerican cosmos, the sense of kinship remained important to the rulers of Tenochtitlan. One of Moctezuma's speeches, reported by López de Gómara, Cortés's biographer, tells us graphically of this change of perception as well as of a persistence of a belief in sacred connectedness. Moctezuma is reported as saying to the Spaniards after they arrived in the capital city that previously his people felt

very great fear to face you because of your fierce beards and because you brought horses to which humans were attached, because you came from the sky bringing flashes of lighting and thunder which made the earth tremble, you hurt those who anger you or whomever you choose, but now that I know you are mortal men, who do good and don't cause injury and I've seen that the horses are like deer and that your shots which appear like blowguns I consider it a joke and a lie what they have told me and I even take you now as my relatives.[4]

In the long years of interaction between indigenous and European peoples that followed, these diverse peoples did indeed become relatives through sexual liaisons and intermarriage, trade and imitation, oppression and resistance, religion and politics. Today some people believe or hope that Quetzalcoatl will someday return and restore the ancient world he ruled over.

For further reading on the history and mythology of Quetzalcoatl, see H. B. Nicholson, *Topiltzin Quetzalcoatl: The Once and Future Lord of the Toltecs* (Boulder: University Press of Colorado, 2001).

Notes

1. See William A. Christian, *Local Religion in Sixteenth-Century Spain* (Princeton, NJ: Princeton University Press, 1981) for a detailed picture of the closeness of the divine and the earthly world in Spain at the time of the "conquest" of Mesoamerica.

2. See Alfredo López Austin, *Tamoanchan y Tlalocan: Places of Mist* (Niwot: University Press of Colorado, 1997) for a clear description of this Mesoamerican understanding of "co-essences," especially pages 189–95.

3. Alfredo López Austin, *Hombre-Dios; Religión y política en el mundo náhuatl* (Mexico City: Universidad Autónoma Nacional de México, Instituto de Investigaciones Históricas, 1973) contains an excellent discussion of these types of extraordinary beings.

4. Francisco López de Gómora, *Historia general de las Indias* (Lima: Comisión Nacional del V Centenario del Descubrimiento de America, Encuentro de Dos Mundos, 1993).